福建省社科规划基础研究后期资助项目

商务英语笔译

English-Chinese Business Translation
A Practical Coursebook

主　编　桑龙扬　李孝英
副主编　闵　翠　肖　薇
编　委　顾维忱　张顺生　王华树　吴小兰　洪如月
　　　　叶雅颖　朱亚光　曾水波　周欣瑞　舒　程
　　　　卢东阳

图书在版编目(CIP)数据

商务英语笔译 / 桑龙扬, 李孝英主编. -- 北京：北京大学出版社, 2025.3. -- (职场翻译教材系列).
ISBN 978-7-301-35143-7
Ⅰ.H315.9
中国国家版本馆 CIP 数据核字第 2024ZQ8415 号

书　　名	商务英语笔译 SHANGWU YINGYU BIYI
著作责任者	桑龙扬　李孝英　主编
责任编辑	初艳红
标准书号	ISBN 978-7-301-35143-7
出版发行	北京大学出版社
地　　址	北京市海淀区成府路 205 号　100871
网　　址	http：//www.pup.cn　新浪微博：@北京大学出版社
电子邮箱	编辑部 pupwaiwen@pup.cn　总编室 zpup@pup.cn
电　　话	邮购部 010-62752015　发行部 010-62750672　编辑部 010-62759634
印刷者	北京溢漾印刷有限公司
经销者	新华书店 720 毫米 ×1020 毫米　16 开本　23.25 印张　520 千字 2025 年 3 月第 1 版　2025 年 3 月第 1 次印刷
定　　价	88.00 元

未经许可，不得以任何方式复制或抄袭本书之部分或全部内容。
版权所有，侵权必究
举报电话：010-62752024　电子邮箱：fd@pup.cn
图书如有印装质量问题，请与出版部联系，电话：010-62756370

前　言

随着经济全球化迅猛发展，我国与世界其他各国在经济、文化、教育以及其他领域内的交流与合作更加密切和频繁，对商务英语翻译这一复合型专业人才的需求正在不断上升，要求也越来越高。就国际商务英语专业或其他相近专业的商务翻译课教学来说，需要解决三个问题。一是英语基本功，二是相关商务知识，三是翻译技巧和技能。也就是说，要学好和做好商务英语笔译，首先是打好语言基本功，其次是掌握相关商务知识，最后是通过大量实践和训练，培养翻译能力。这一认识决定了商务英语笔译教学的内容体系和功能，也决定了教材的编写理念和体例。也就是要把语言知识、专业知识的传授和技能培养有机结合起来，帮助学生在实践中运用所学到的语言知识，使知识与技能融会贯通，从而更好地完成商务翻译工作。

有鉴于此，《商务英语笔译》以商务领域各个层面的活动为主线，以商务文本为主要翻译对象，让学生在翻译实践中，了解并熟悉商务英语的基本语言特点、商务领域各个学科的具体的语言特点，并掌握商务知识，了解和培养翻译技能和翻译方法，突破翻译难点，提高翻译感悟能力，打好翻译基础。

《商务英语笔译》主要取材于英美两国的商务专业各学科的原版教材和著作，部分取材于国内相关的重大经济和商务活动的新闻、讲话或报告，以及相关研究成果和企业实务。内容涵盖应用翻译、国际商务、市场营销、商务广告、知识产权、物流、国际招投标、商务信函、商务合同、企业简介、产品说明书、国际财会、电子商务、金融、国际商事法律、国际旅游、公示语等，题材广泛，内容真实，语言贴切。

本教材的主要特点：

1. 贯穿商务主题和翻译主题两条主线。每章包含三大模块。第一大模块是相关知识和翻译技巧，也就是针对该单元的商务主题和内容，介绍相关专业的语言特点，如词汇特点和句法特点以及翻译策略和方法。第二大模块是课内翻译任务，题材都是相关商务理论和实务篇章以及重要讲话或文件，通过翻译任务及重点解析，让学生在翻译学习中了解商务内容，掌握翻译技能。第三大模块是课后翻译训练，包括英汉、汉英句子和段落的翻译训练。

2. 选材内容丰富，涵盖面广，尽可能多地涉及商务领域的各个方面。体现了实用性、时代性、灵活性和专业性。商务英语笔译属于应用翻译范畴，从广义来说，由于学科的交叉性，商务英语笔译几乎包含了应用翻译的所有专业领域，学习商务英语笔译，需要对应用翻译的基本特点有所了解，而限于篇幅和学制，不可能面面俱到。因此，本教材在第一章"应用翻译"部分，专门介绍了应用翻译的定位和翻译标准等知识。

3. 英汉兼顾，难易适度。每章的教学中心是译例研究。译例研究包括英译汉和汉译英两部分，都与各章的商务内容密切相关，可以拓展相关知识，而且难易适度。

4. 英译汉和汉译英并重。一般来说，多数商务英语笔译或商务英语翻译教材都以英译汉为主，缺少汉译英部分。在中国日益成为经济强国、成为世界第二大经济体的背景下，中国企业走出去已是大势所趋，汉译英同样重要，也是学生翻译能力的重要一环。

5. 翻译练习类型多样。每章都设计了英译汉和汉译英的句子和短文翻译，便于从多方面培养学生的翻译能力和检验学生的学习效果。

6. 编写人员既有来自高校的一线教师，也有翻译公司和相关专业公司的专业人员，既有教学经验，又有实践经验和专业知识。

本教程基于OBE理念和课程思政理念，依据商务英语笔译任务和职业特性进行选材和设计，紧贴当今商务英语翻译考试的热点及实用性，为参加全国商务英语翻译考试的学生提供权威可靠的备考辅导教材，使学生在掌握笔译实战技巧的同时，积累考试经验，切实培养"复合型""应用型"商务英语翻译人才。

本教程共17章，各章体例完全一致。第一主编桑龙扬负责全书的组织、筹划、统稿、审校、修改等工作，第二主编李孝英协助落实编写任务。参加本书编写的有桑龙扬（第一章 应用翻译、第二章 商务英语翻译、第三章 金融翻译、第四章 商务广告翻译、第五章 市场营销翻译）、洪如月（第六章 商务合同翻译）、叶雅颖（第七章 企业宣传翻译、第八章 产品介绍翻译）、吴小兰（第九章 商务信函翻译、第十三章 电子商务翻译）、周欣瑞和桑龙扬（第十一章 国际物流翻译）、肖薇（第十二章 财务会计翻译）、曾水波和桑龙扬（第十章 招投标书翻译）、闵翠（第十四章 知识产权文献翻译）、顾维忱（第十五章 国际商事法律翻译）、朱亚光（第十六章 国际旅游翻译）、张顺生（第十七章 公示语翻译）。吴贵民对知识产权部分做了修改和润色，王华树撰写了《大语言模型时代翻译教育实践模式创新研究》（作为补充资料，将以电子版形式提供给读者），舒程、卢东阳担负了一定的协调工作。课内翻译任务参考译文和课后翻译训练参考译文另作为资料，可以电子版的形式发送给老师和其他使用者。

任课教师可以根据商务英语课时量和课程设置，选用具体章节。

本教材的读者对象包括商务英语专业和英语专业的商务英语方向的本科学生、翻译专业本科学生、国际商务或国际贸易等相关专业的本科学生，国际贸易和国际商务的从业人员或翻译人员，准备参加商务英语翻译考试和翻译硕士专业研究生考试的本科学生，其他有志于提高翻译能力和技能的各类学生、老师和从业人员。

在本书的编写过程中，笔者阅读并参考了大量专著、教材和相关学术文章，其中主要参考文献已列于书后。在此，向各位作者深表感谢。

由于编者学术水平和实践能力有限，加上其他学术工作繁重，时间仓促，书中难免有不妥和纰漏之处，敬请各位专家和读者批评指正。

桑龙扬

2024年8月30日

目 录

第一章　应用翻译 / 1
　　第一节　应用文体与应用翻译 / 1
　　第二节　课内翻译任务 / 12
　　第三节　课后翻译训练 / 18

第二章　商务英语翻译 / 22
　　第一节　商务英语的语言特点 / 22
　　第二节　商务英语翻译原则与译者的基本素质 / 26
　　第三节　课内翻译任务 / 31
　　第四节　课后翻译训练 / 41

第三章　金融翻译 / 45
　　第一节　金融英语语言特征 / 45
　　第二节　金融英语翻译策略 / 49
　　第三节　课内翻译任务 / 56
　　第四节　课后翻译训练 / 61

第四章　商务广告翻译 / 66
　　第一节　广告的分类与构成 / 66
　　第二节　广告的语言特征 / 68
　　第三节　广告翻译的策略和方法 / 73
　　第四节　课内翻译任务 / 80
　　第五节　课后翻译训练 / 83

第五章　市场营销翻译 / 87
　　第一节　营销英语的语言特点与翻译 / 87
　　第二节　课内翻译任务 / 95
　　第三节　课后翻译训练 / 101

第六章　商务合同翻译 / 105
　　第一节　商务合同概述 / 105
　　第二节　商务合同的语言特点与翻译 / 111
　　第三节　课内翻译任务 / 117
　　第四节　课后翻译训练 / 121

第七章　企业宣传翻译 / 126
　　第一节　公司名称与企业商号的翻译 / 126
　　第二节　企业宣传资料翻译 / 131
　　第三节　课内翻译任务 / 140
　　第四节　课后翻译训练 / 146

第八章　产品介绍翻译 / 150
　　第一节　产品介绍文本的语言特色 / 150
　　第二节　产品说明书翻译原则 / 167
　　第三节　课内翻译任务 / 169
　　第四节　课后翻译训练 / 174

第九章　商务信函翻译 / 178
　　第一节　商务信函的语言特点 / 178
　　第二节　商务英语信函翻译原则 / 181
　　第三节　课内翻译任务 / 185
　　第四节　课后翻译训练 / 188

第十章　招投标书翻译 / 192
　　第一节　国际招标基本知识 / 192

第二节　国际标书文本的语言特征与翻译 / 200
　　第三节　课内翻译任务 / 212
　　第四节　课后翻译训练 / 218

第十一章　国际物流翻译 / 223
　　第一节　物流简述 / 223
　　第二节　物流英语的语言特征 / 225
　　第三节　物流英语的翻译策略 / 231
　　第四节　课内翻译任务 / 236
　　第五节　课后翻译训练 / 240

第十二章　财务会计翻译 / 244
　　第一节　会计英语的语言特点 / 244
　　第二节　会计英语的翻译原则 / 248
　　第三节　课内翻译任务 / 254
　　第四节　课后翻译训练 / 258

第十三章　电子商务翻译 / 263
　　第一节　电子商务的语言特点 / 263
　　第二节　电子商务英语翻译技巧 / 267
　　第三节　课内翻译任务 / 272
　　第四节　课后翻译训练 / 276

第十四章　知识产权文献翻译 / 280
　　第一节　专利文献语言特点与翻译 / 280
　　第二节　商标语言特点与翻译 / 284
　　第三节　课内翻译任务 / 287
　　第四节　课后翻译训练 / 292

第十五章　国际商事法律翻译 / 296
　　第一节　国际商事法律英语语言特征 / 296

第二节　国际商事法律翻译 / 305
第三节　课内翻译任务 / 312
第四节　课后翻译训练 / 315

第十六章　国际旅游翻译 / 320

第一节　旅游翻译的概念、功能与原则 / 320
第二节　英汉旅游文体的差异 / 323
第三节　旅游资料英译的主要方法 / 327
第四节　课内翻译任务 / 331
第五节　课后翻译训练 / 336

第十七章　公示语翻译 / 340

第一节　公示语的类别与功能 / 340
第二节　英语公示语的语言特点与翻译 / 342
第三节　公示语错译误译解读 / 345
第四节　汉英公示语言的区别 / 349
第五节　公示语的翻译原则与方法 / 351
第六节　课内翻译任务 / 354
第七节　课后翻译训练 / 357

参考文献 / 359

第一章 应用翻译

应用翻译与文学翻译相对,几乎包括除纯文学及纯理论文本以外人们日常接触和实际应用的各类文字,包括政府文件、告示、科技论文、新闻报道、法律文书、商贸信函、产品说明书、科普读物、旅游指南等各类文本。因此,应用翻译可以分为法律翻译、新闻翻译、旅游翻译、经贸翻译、商务翻译、科技翻译等。商务英语翻译就是典型的应用翻译。

第一节 应用文体与应用翻译

一、应用文体

语言是传递信息和交流感情的手段,是人们实现社会交际的工具。因交际环境、交际方式、交际对象和交际目的等的不同,各交际方会选择具有不同功能的语言"变体"(varieties)或相应的表现手段,这些变体或表现手段就是人们所说的"文体"或"语体"(styles)。20世纪70年代中期,人们将现代语言学及文学研究成果运用于各种文体或语体特征的探讨,便产生了"文体学"(stylistics)这门新兴的学科。**应用文体**是一个包容广泛、实用性强的文体类型,包括除小说、诗歌、散文等纯文学语言形式以外的其他一切日常用的语言文体,如商务文体、法律文体、新闻文体、旅游文体、广告文体、科技文体等。

二、应用翻译的定位

应用翻译或应用文体翻译,又称实用翻译,国外的提法有practical translation, applied translation 或 pragmatic translation。其中,pragmatic translation也可以指一种翻译方法,即语用翻译法(pragmatic approach),指的是译者通过语用分析,把源语文化的内涵,用符合译语语用习惯的译文表达出来。(方梦之,2019:55)应用翻译特别区别于传达有较强情感意义和美学意义的文学文体,它以传递信息和唤起读者感情并采取行动为主要目的，文本的"信息"和"呼唤"功能突出，实用性、规范性强。应用翻译都有现实的目的，要求译文达到预期的功能。"应用翻译范围较广，包括人们日常接触和实际应用的各类文字，涉及对外宣传、社会生活、生产领域、经营活动等方方面面，与文学翻译相对。应用翻译的服务面广，具体来说，应用翻译文本包括政府文件、告示、科技论文、新闻报道、法律文书、商贸信函、产品说明书、使用手册、广告、技术文本、科普读物、旅游指南等各类文本。"（方梦之，2019：57）不同的文体需要采用不同的翻译策略和方法。黄忠廉在《应用翻译学名实探》中谈到，"应用翻译学"最根本的概念是"应用翻译"，即在生活和生产领域进行的翻译，包括经贸、军事、外事、科学、技术、工程、会议等领域的翻译活动。（黄忠廉，2013：93—94）

三、应用翻译的特点

应用文体翻译都有现实的甚至功利的目的，要求译文达到预期的功能。翻译目的论认为，原文和译文是两种独立的具有不同价值的文本，各有不同的目的和功能，作者通过源语文本提供信息，译者则将源语的语言和文化信息有条件地传递给目的语的读者。至于译者对源语文本信息的选择、翻译策略的运用以及译文的表现形式，则取决于翻译委托人和译本接受者的需要和愿望。

应用文体包罗广阔，不同层次的语域具有不同的特点。信息性、劝导性、匿名性和时效性是绝大多数应用语篇具有的主要特点。

（一）信息性

信息性（informativity）是指译本对目的语读者提供所需的原文的信息。语篇中有的信息对源语读者来说很重要，而面对目的语读者来说却不然；有的信息对源语读者来说用处不大，而对目的语读者来说却非常有用。考虑到译文的目的以及读者的需要和接受能力，翻译提供的信息既可删除，也可作调整或补偿。

（二）劝导性

应用翻译的劝导性（persuasiveness）表现在译文内容对读者的启示和劝导。劝导人们做什么或不做什么。新闻报道劝导人们相信什么或不相信什么，说明书指导人们该做什么或不该做什么，广告诱导人们购物，旅游指南吸引人们参观景点，科普读物劝导人们辨别真伪，就连有的科技论文也带有劝导性。

（三）匿名性

匿名性（anonymity）包括两方面的内容。一是大多数应用翻译语篇因业务交往或工作之需，仅在有限的范围内交流，译者对委托人负责，有时委托人可能就是读者本人,没有必要署名。对于公开出版物,译者有署名的,也有不署名的,这由出版单位与译者协商决定。二是大部分应用翻译缺乏译者的个性和风格,文本的互文性强,有的文本,特别是部分技术文本和商务文本,具有固定的格式,有的甚至有刻板的现成句式,语句的复现率大,遵循大致相同的程式(经常与原文的形式相应),译者无须署名。

匿名并非推脱责任。如果译文有严重的质量问题,委托人一般会向受托人(如翻译公司)追究责任。

(四)时效性

时效性(timeliness)指两个方面。一是译文本身的时效。应用翻译的主要功能是传递信息。信息在一定的时空中产生效益。无论新闻、产品推介、可行性报告、招标书,或是广告、商务协议、技术报告等,都有一定的时间性。超过时间,就意味着失效。二是译本的时效性经常转化为"翻译时限"。翻译时限即指委托人对译者完成译文的时间要求。翻译时限是翻译服务质量的重要指标之一,也是翻译报价的依据之一。

世界已进入网络数字化时代。信息量越来越大,传递的速度越来越快。与之相适应的翻译量与日俱增,翻译速度成倍增长,翻译的无纸化程度急速提高。译者要利用网络与委托人沟通,通过网络了解委托人的翻译要求,接收原文,传递译文。电子化和网络化是保证翻译时效性的工具,译者必须努力掌握。(方梦之,2019:57—60)

四、应用翻译的标准、原则与要求

(一)翻译的一般标准

翻译的标准之争由来已久,"文质之争""直译(literal translation)、意译(free translation)之争""归化(domestication)、异化(foreignization)之争",不一而足。

英国著名翻译理论家泰特勒(Alexander F. Tytler)提出了翻译三原则(the Principles of Translation);奈达(Eugene A. Nida)提出了功能对等理论(functional equivalence);严复提出了信(faithfulness)、达(expressiveness)、雅(elegance)的翻译标准;林语堂提出了"忠实(faithfulness)、通顺(smoothness)、美(beautifulness)"三条标准;钱锺书提出了化境论(transmigration of the soul, reaching the acme of perfection);翻译家傅雷提出了神似论(resemblance in spirit);刘重德提出了"信、达、切(faithfulness, expressiveness and closeness)"

的标准；许渊冲提出了诗歌翻译的三原则，即"三美"（意美、音美、形美）和"三化"（等化、浅化、深化）；辜正坤提出了翻译标准多元互补论。国际译联的《翻译工作者章程》（*Translator's Charter*）指出："Every translation shall be faithful and render exactly the idea and form of the original."（译文应忠实于原文，准确表现原作的思想与形式。）

凡此种种，不管是翻译原则还是翻译标准，核心的标准就是：忠实准确、通顺流畅和风格得体。忠实准确指译文必须忠实于原文的内容，把原文内容完整准确地转达出来。译者不能随意歪曲、增删、遗漏、篡改原文的内容。通顺流畅指译文要充分发挥译入语的语言优势，译文语言必须标准规范、通俗易懂、符合译入语的表达习惯，不存在死译、硬译、生搬硬套、文理不通的现象。风格得体指译文应尽量忠实转达原文的文体特征和写作风格。然而，没有任何一种统一的标准能够规范不同情境、不同语言的翻译工作。我们在评价一篇译作的质量时，同时要考虑到其他方面的一些因素，例如：作者的意图、翻译的目的、顾客的需求、译作读者、译作主题、原作的风格、翻译方法（笔译或口译）、所需时间等。我们从事翻译工作，并不是为自己，而是为别人。如果我们的翻译作品不能令客户及文章使用者满意的话，我们的工作将得不到认可，同时，翻译就成了一件费时费力而收效甚微的工作。总而言之，忠实、通顺、得体是最基本的翻译标准和原则。

（二）应用翻译的标准

应用翻译因文体的多样，翻译标准也是多元的。近年来，以传达信息为根本目的的应用翻译发展迅猛，其特性有别于传达有较强情感意义和美学意义的文学翻译，传统的翻译标准已不能解释这一翻译现象，因而需要一套较为系统的专门针对应用翻译的标准对其进行完整客观的描述。如果把奈达的"动态对等"和"功能对等"的"对等"原理运用到应用翻译之中，就是做到"使原文的语义信息与译文的语义信息对等（equivalence of semantic message of source language and target language）；原文的风格信息与译文的风格信息对等（equivalence of stylistic message of source language and target language）；原文的文化信息与译文的文化信息对等（equivalence of cultural message of source language and target language）；原文的读者反应与译文的读者反应对等（equivalence of response of source language readers and target language readers）"。（翁凤翔，2002：46—47）英国翻译理论家纽马克（Newmark）将文本按照语言的功能分为表达型文本（express text）、信息型文本（informative text）和呼唤型文本

（vocative text），并指出译者应针对不同的文本类型采用不同的翻译方法。纽马克还按照体裁将严肃文学作品、官方文告、自传文学、私人书信等归入"表达型文本"；将自然科学、科学技术、工商经济等方面的文本、报告、文件、报刊文章、备忘录、会议记录等归入"信息型文本"；将通告、说明书、公共宣传品、通俗作品等体裁归为"呼唤型文本"。（顾维勇，2010：4）国内专家学者一般从以下三种途径提出应用翻译的标准：基于中国传统译论之上的标准、翻译家本人实践经验总结的标准，以及基于外国翻译理论之上的标准。方梦之提出了应用翻译的微观—中观—宏观策略，李亚舒、黄忠廉提出了"变译"理论，林克难提出了应用翻译的"看""易""写"标准。

西方则先后经历了直译和意译之争、奈达"功能对等"、费米尔"目的论"等翻译标准的讨论，还有将视角转向文化因素的文化学派观点。种种理论都为翻译标准的研究注入活力。但是，应用翻译独特的目的性、实用性和匿名性等特点及其翻译活动范围的广泛性等，必然导致不同的翻译要求，而翻译标准又随着翻译要求的不同而改变。因此，之前的翻译标准不一定适用于应用翻译。

应用翻译标准不可能是单一且绝对的。应用翻译的标准会因文本功能、翻译目的、读者对象和交际情景的不同而呈现出多维且动态的特性。更为重要的是，因翻译活动的广泛性而产生的多样标准无形中构成了一个较为复杂的标准体系，其内部各个标准之间相互联系、相互补充，同时又因具体情况不同而产生可变主标准和可变次标准的辩证运动。因此，应用翻译的标准是一个多维、动态、系统的开放体系，应符合规范性和互文性的特点。

（三）应用翻译的原则

方梦之先生将应用翻译的原则概括为三条：目的性原则、理论原则和实践原则。

应用文体翻译要求译文达到预期的目的和功能。翻译一则广告是为了向受众宣传或推销产品，翻译科技文本是为了传达科技信息，翻译商贸文本是为了业务往来。目的性还表现在译前有明确的读者对象，可能是个人、多人或群体。

应用翻译主要是信息翻译。信息是可以验证的，包括客观世界中的实践、状态、过程、物体、人物、地点等。应用翻译理论首先要符合信息翻译的特点和要求，经得起科学验证和实践检验。应用翻译的理论原则包括实践性、对策性、功能性、系统性和综合性。

应用翻译的研究者不但从各自熟悉的语域提出翻译实践的对策性理论，而且从中观层面提出翻译的原则和标准。为此，方梦之提出应用翻译达旨—循规—

共喻的总原则。达旨——达到目的,传达要旨;循规——遵循译入语规范;共喻——使读者通晓明白。三者各有侧重,互为因果。(方梦之,2019:64—70)

2006年在广州召开的第二届全国应用翻译研讨会上有学者粗略地提出了应用翻译的功能原则和规范原则。功能原则是指译文必须在目的语环境中具有意义和可读性。而规范原则一般是指,译文必须符合目的语的文体规约和接受习惯;个别情况下,受目的制约,规范原则也指保持原文体的表达规范。一方面,要求译文必须有效地与目的语读者沟通,使他们能够按照自己的知识背景和生活环境来理解文本;另一方面,要求正确传达原文或作者的真实用意。为此,必须区分字面意义与功能意义。字面意义,就是文字本身固有的意义。功能意义就是交际意义,就是目的语中可被接受与理解的信息。字面意义有时等同于功能意义,有时不同于功能意义。功能原则就在于,当字面意义与功能意义不一致时,或不利于交际功能实现时,必须根据交际意图确保将功能意义译出。

例1. 我们要继续坚定不移地坚持以经济建设为中心,继续坚定不移地推行改革开放,继续坚定不移地保持社会稳定,继续坚定不移地贯彻执行独立自主的和平外交政策。

译文:We will steadfastly focus on economic development, press ahead with reform and opening-up, maintain social stability and pursue the independent foreign policy of peace.

原文重复使用了四个"继续坚定不移地",取得了意义不断深化的作用。译文则只使用"steadfastly",不仅达意,而且流畅简洁,通俗易懂,达到了很好的功能效果。(黄忠廉、任东升,2014:266)

例2. 我公司经营各类城市绿化专用树苗几十个品种五十余万株,完全达到随来随购、顾客满意的程度。

译文:The company's stocks of dozens of species (a total of 500,000-odd samplings) are sufficient to meet the demand of urban tree planting.

译文中的sufficient to meet the demand足以传达原文中的"完全达到随来随购、顾客满意的程度"。这里的汉语思维方式无法通过英文传达出去,硬译出来,译文会显得臃肿,不堪卒读。

例3. 学校高度重视教学工作和人才培养的质量,坚持把教学工作摆在学校工作的中心地位,把教学质量作为学校办学的生命线,各项工作始终围绕教学工作进行。通过各项制度、机制和政策措施,保障了本科教学的中心地位,形成了领导重视教学、经费优先教学、政策倾斜教学、舆论导向教学、科研促进教学、管理服务教学的良好局面。

译文：Special stress is laid on the teaching and the training of talents in the university. Teaching is the core work and quality of teaching is the lifeline of the university. The central position of undergraduate teaching is ensured because of various systems, mechanism and special measures. A favorable situation is created in which everything is for teaching.

例3为编者翻译的《九江学院画册》的部分文字，是对图片的说明。原句"领导重视教学……服务教学"为"良好局面"的定语，是对学校各方面工作的肯定评价，做到了面面俱到，在国内的语境下，无可非议。但是，对外宣传这些细节毫无必要，有啰唆之嫌；况且，国外的大学管理体制与我国不同，即便翻译了，读者也很难明白，不如不译。

例4. 碧水清清 却亦无情 河湍势险 请勿戏水

译文：Dangerous Currents No Swimming

汉语讲究辞藻华丽，诗情画意，英语讲究直观、明快。如果依据汉语原文"直译"，有时会显得累赘。例4如果按照汉语原句的字面意思，英文应该译为：So blue water, but also no goodwill, so rushing current, please don't play the water.（引自吕和发、蒋璐、王同军等，2011）

例5. 前进一小步 文明一大步

国内很多公共厕所内都有这样的公示语，而且大都配有英文译文：A small step forward A great leap towards civilization. 原文很符合汉语的表达习惯，两句字数相等，结构对称，读起来非常上口。如果从结构看，英文译文似乎与原文相对应，表层意思也很清楚，但从交际目的与交际功能上来看，外国读者未必十分明白这条公示语的意图，而且civilization在此处属于滥用，并不合适。此公示语的目的是让厕所使用者挨近便池，保持清洁卫生。因此，不必按照原文逐词对应硬译，而应该根据语境和交际意图，按照规约性要求，直截了当地译为"Keep close to the urinal"即可。

（四）应用翻译的要求

方梦之与毛忠明合编的《英汉—汉英应用翻译综合教程》中对实用文体（本章中的应用文体）翻译提出了四点要求。应用文体涉及不同专业、不同行业，翻译应用文体不仅要符合翻译的一般要求，而且要体现不同文体的专业特征，不能望文生义，而且还要有时间性。因此，应用翻译要把握以下五点要求：

1. 准确

应用文体的翻译不论全译、选译或综述,以正确传达原意为第一要义,特别是在表达空间、时间、位置、价值等概念时更需精确,切忌主观臆断。为此在理解原文的前提下,需用反映相关概念的术语或专业(行业)常用语来表达。

例6. "Collusive practice" is an arrangement between two or more parties designed to achieve an improper purpose, including to influence improperly the actions of another party.

原译:"串通活动"意指由双方或多方设计的一种为达到不当目的的安排,包括不适当地影响另一方的行为。

改译:"串通行为"是指两个或两个以上当事人之间为达到不正当目的而进行的安排,包括不正当地影响另一方当事人的行为。

这是国际招标书中的一个例子。国际招标书属于法律文件,必须措辞严谨,用语规范、专业。"collusive practice"不能按照我们通常的理解翻译成"串通活动"或"串通实践",而应翻译为"串通行为"。"designed"译为"设计"也不贴切。

例7. A credit card thief may be sitting on a potential gold mine, particularly if there is a delay in reporting the loss of the card.

译文:信用卡窃贼可能会大发横财——尤其是在失主未能及时挂失的情况下。

"report the loss of"在银行业中意思是"挂失"或"损失"。

英语有些普通词汇用于医学专业时产生了词义变迁,汉译时必须从词的本义出发根据上下文和逻辑关系进一步引申。

例8. The outlook of mumps is almost invariably favorable.

译文:腮腺炎的愈后几乎都是良好的。

例9. The clinical behavior of these diseases varies in ages and sexes.

译文:这两种疾病的临床表现随着年龄和性别的不同而不同。

(黄忠廉、余承法,2012:41)

例8中的outlook本义为"前景,展望",例9中的behaviour本义为"行为,举止"。

2. 适切

根据应用语篇特定的功能和目的,译文需适合译入语国家的政治语境、文化氛围、方针政策和技术规范。为此,译文有时必须加以调整。

例10. 21世纪幼儿园走过了13年的发展历程,他们连续7年被评为区级教育工作和全面工作管理优秀单位;1997—1999年获市卫生先进单位……

译文:The 21st Kindergarten has been a success since it was set up 13 years ago. For 7 consecutive years, it has been given various honorary titles by the District Education Bureau. From 1997 to 1999 it was commended by the municipal government for its hygienic conditions...

原文套话多,"优秀单位""先进单位"之类很难定义。这类话语国内习以为常,但如果直译出去,难免臃肿累赘,且容易引起读者不解。

例11. 庐山,春如梦,夏如滴,秋如醉,冬如玉,是中国的避暑胜地。

译文:With changing beautiful scenery in the four different seasons, Mount Lushan is a well-known summer resort in China, where you can enjoy dream-like spring, refreshing summer, invigorating autumn and snowy winter.

这是从编者翻译的《庐山旅游手册》中选取的例子。在英语世界中,读者很难体会到汉语文化和庐山地域环境中的"梦""滴""醉""玉"的意境,所以翻译时要做处理,才能切合英语世界读者的认知和期待。

3. 得体

源语的一个词、一个词组、一个句子,甚至一个段落,在译入语里可能有几个同义而结构不尽相同的语言形式。这样,在翻译思维中,就有一个选择的层次。选择除了涉及语言结构因素(如词性、词语搭配、上下文)之外,还与文体有关。选择的目的是使译文得体——得相应的文体之体。应用翻译的得体体现在词的得体、词组的得体和句子的得体。

以科技文体而论,词的得体意味着要选择词义严谨的词、符合专业特征的词、与上下文能匹配的词。

例12. This kind of material has been made of great value.

原译:这种材料已被搞得具有很大价值了。

"搞"是个日常用词,词义范围很宽。科技文章应词义明确。

改译:这种材料经过加工具有很大价值。

在英译汉中,英语的一些语法词组可译成汉语习语,特别是四字词组,而汉语采用的惯用的和非惯用的四字词组,汉译英时却需要转化。

例13. The youngest of Rocky Mountains, the Teton Range is a spectacular sight. Enhanced by glaciers, deep canyons, snowfields, and lakes, the range shoots up suddenly, with no foothills around it.

译文：虽为落基山脉的小字辈，特顿山却器宇不凡，它拔地而起，绝壁凌空，冰川映雪地，高峡出平湖，景色蔚为壮观。

译者使用了"器宇不凡""拔地而起""绝壁凌空""蔚为壮观"这四个四字结构以及"冰川映雪地，高峡出平湖"这个对偶句，译文朗朗上口，文采斐然，诗情画意盎然。

例14. 本工艺具有造型速度快、生产效率高、工艺性能优良等特点，引起世界铸造工作者的关注。

译文：This technology has the advantages of great moulding speed, high production efficiency and fine technological performances. Therefore, it has been taken notice of the foundry businesses all over the world.

原句中，"造型速度快""生产效率高""工艺性能优良"均为主谓词组，而英译则采用偏正结构。

例15. Television is the transmission and reception of images of moving objects by radio waves.

译文：电视通过无线电波发射和接收活动物体的图像。

名词化结构the transmission and reception of images of moving objects by radio waves 强调客观事实，而译文的谓语动词则着重其发射和接收的能力。

在英语中，相对比较正式的文体中被动语态的使用率要比普通文体高。应用文体中的科技活动是相当严肃的事情，所以用于描述和记录科技活动的科技文章在语气上就比较正式。再加上为了体现科学研究的客观性，就更离不开被动语态。在英译汉的时候，为表现科技文章的上述特点，在翻译时最好使用无主语结构或被动意义的句子。（穆雷，2008：177—178）

例16. Attention must be paid to the working temperature of the machine.

译文：应当注意机器的工作温度。

实际生活中很少说：You must pay attention to the working temperature of the machine.

例17. The victim of shock will die quickly unless something is done to restore circulation immediately.

译文：如果不立即采取措施恢复血液循环，休克患者就会很快死亡。

英语被动语态"is done"在译文里转换成主动语态，而且隐含的意思也明晰具体化了。

例18. The purpose of establishing the punitive damages of the law is to realize the complete compensation principle better on the basis of protecting the weak's legitimate rights and interests, it does not contradict with the establishment aim of the system of unjust benefit.

译文：法律设定惩罚性赔偿金的目的是在保护弱者合法权益的基础上更好地实现完全补偿原则，与不当得利制度的设立宗旨并不矛盾。

"unjust benefit"字面意思是"不正当利益"，这样的表述不是地道的专业用语，法律或商务用语中地道的表述是"不当得利"。

4. 规范

为了保持术语的规范性，除了平时多看、多记以外，在翻译过程中，还需要查阅报刊和专业词典，不能自行其是。在应用翻译中，会经常碰到具有中国特色的词汇，这时，我们可以参考*China Daily*或*Beijing Review*等英文报刊上的译名，或《中国翻译》登载的中国热门词汇的译名或表述。例如，president对应的中文有很多意思，如总统、主席、校长等。我们在翻译的时候，一定要注意个人特定的身份。比如指中国国家元首的时候，就是国家主席，而不是总统。如果指美国等总统制国家的元首，那就译为"总统"。

例19. China is expected to use the 11th BRICS Summit in Brasilia, Brazil, to strengthen the partnership of emerging markets and send out a clear call for multilateralism to improve global governance as President Xi Jinping attends the two-day event starting Wednesday.

译文：中国将利用在巴西巴西利亚举行的第11届金砖国家峰会，加强新兴市场的伙伴关系，并明确发出呼吁，坚持多边主义，以改善全球治理。中国国家主席习近平将出席周三开始的为期两天的会议。

目前，出现了大量的具有中国特色的术语和短语，翻译时要与官方翻译保持一致，确保译文的规范性和权威性。

例20. 不忘初心，牢记使命，高举中国特色社会主义伟大旗帜，决胜全面建成小康社会，夺取新时代中国特色社会主义伟大胜利，为实现中华民族伟大复兴的中国梦不懈奋斗。

译文：Remain true to our original aspiration and keep our mission firmly in mind, hold high the banner of socialism with Chinese characteristics, secure a decisive victory in building a moderately prosperous society in all respects, strive for the great success of socialism with Chinese characteristics for a new era, and work tirelessly to realize the Chinese Dream of national rejuvenation.

例21. 这个新时代，是承前启后、继往开来、在新的历史条件下继续夺取中国特色社会主义伟大胜利的时代，是决胜全面建成小康社会、进而全面建设社会主义现代化强国的时代。

译文：This new era will be an era of building on past successes to further advance our cause, and of continuing in a new historical context to strive for the success of socialism with Chinese characteristics. It will be an era of securing a decisive victory in building a moderately prosperous society in all respects, and of moving on to all-out efforts to build a great modern socialist country.

（例20、例21原文和译文均引自新华网：http://www.xinhuanet.com/politics/19cpcnc/2017-10/27/c_1121867529.htm，http://www.xinhuanet.com/english/download/Xi_Jinping's_report_at_19th_CPC_National_Congress.pdf，访问日期：2024年8月30日。）

5. 快捷

翻译速度是委托人或客户的要求之一。由于市场经济的运转速度加快，各行各业都重视时效，时间即是金钱已成商场信条。没有速度就没有翻译任务。有的委托人要求朝发夕收——早晨上班通过网络发文，下班之前收到译稿。这些都只能在电脑上进行。过去"慢工出细活"的做法已不可行。现在的要求是既要质量好，又要译得快。（方梦之、毛忠明：2018：27—28）

第二节 课内翻译任务

一、英译汉 English-Chinese Translation

What, How, and For Whom?

Goods and services are the objects that people value and produce to satisfy wants. Goods are physical objects such as cellphones and automobiles. Services are tasks performed for people such as cellphone service and auto-repair service.

What?　What we produce varies across countries and changes over time. In the United States today, agriculture accounts for 1 percent of total production, manufactured goods for 20 percent, and services (retail and wholesale trade, healthcare, and education are the biggest ones) for 79 percent. In contrast, in China today, agriculture accounts for 10 percent of total production, manufactured goods for 45 percent, and services for 45 percent.

How? How we produce is described by the technologies and resources that we use. The resources used to produce goods and services are called factors of production, which are grouped into four categories: Land, Labor, Capital and Entrepreneurship.

● Land The "gifts of nature" that we use to produce goods and services are called land. In economics, land is what in everyday language we call natural resources. It includes land in the everyday sense together with minerals, oil, gas, coal, water, air, forests, and fish. Our land surface and water resources are renewable and some of our mineral resources can be recycled. But the resources that we use to create energy are nonrenewable—they can be used only once.

● Labor The work time and work effort that people devote to producing goods and services is called labor.

Labor includes the physical and mental efforts of all the people who work on farms and construction sites and in factories, shops, and offices. The quality of labor depends on human capital, which is the knowledge and skill that people obtain from education, on-the-job training, and work experience. You are building your own human capital right now as you work on your economics course, and your human capital will continue to grow as you gain work experience.

● Capital The tools, instruments, machines, buildings, and other constructions that businesses use to produce goods and services are called capital. In everyday language, we talk about money, stocks, and bonds as being "capital." These items are financial capital. Financial capital plays an important role in enabling businesses to borrow the funds that they use to buy physical capital. But financial capital is not used to produce goods and services and it is not a factor of production.

● Entrepreneurship The human resource that organizes labor, land, and capital is called entrepreneurship. Entrepreneurs are the drivers of economic progress. They develop new ideas about what and how to produce, make business decisions, and bear the risks that arise from these decisions.

For Whom? Who consumes the goods and services that are produced depends on the incomes that people earn. People with large incomes can buy a wide range of goods and services. People with small incomes have fewer options and can afford a smaller range of goods and services. People earn their incomes by selling the services of the factors of production they own.

（Michael Parkin, *Economics, Global Edition*,
Pearson Education Limited, 2016, 有删减）

重点解析 Notes and Comments

1. What, How, and For Whom? 生产什么？如何生产？为谁生产？

该短文题目翻译要采用增词法，即增加原文中省略但逻辑上隐含的词语"produce"。中文如果不增加"生产"这个动词，则语义不清。文中其他几处也采取同样译法。

2. Goods and services are the objects that people value and produce to satisfy wants. 商品和服务是人们为满足需要而生产或提供的具有价值的产品。

该句"that"引导的定语从句中，value and produce是并列谓语，"value"有"有价值，重视"的意思，但此句按照经济学定义的表述，应理解为"给……定价；赋予……价值"。翻译的时候，应调整顺序，将"produce"（生产）置于"value"之前。"objects"在此处的意思为"产品"或"东西"而不是"对象，目标"等。services在中文里与动词"提供"搭配，翻译时，增加"提供"一词。

3. Goods are physical objects such as cellphones and automobiles. 手机和汽车等产品是有形商品。

"such as cellphones and automobiles" 作定语修饰"objects"，"physical"意思是"有形的，物质的"。

4. In the United States today, agriculture accounts for 1 percent of total production, manufactured goods for 20 percent, and services (retail and wholesale trade, healthcare, and education are the biggest ones) for 79 percent. 在当今美国，农业占总产量的1%，制成品占20%，服务业（零售和批发贸易、医疗保健和教育所占比例最大）占79%。

accounts for 是经济类文体中表达数字、百分比的常见短语，表示"占……比例"。在句子当中，如果for后面有一系列并列宾语，除了第一个宾语完整使用该短语外，其后的宾语省略"account"。

5. factors of production 生产要素，是经济学中的一个基本范畴，包括人的要素、物的要素及其结合因素。生产要素指进行社会生产经营活动时所需要的各种社会资源,是维系国民经济运行及市场主体生产经营过程中所必须具备的基本因素。生产要素包括劳动力、土地、资本、企业家才能四种,随着科技的发展和知识产权制度的建立,技术、信息也作为相对独立的要素投入生产。这些生产要素进行市场交换,形成各种各样的生产要素价格及其体系。

6. The work time and work effort that people devote to producing goods and services is called labor. 此处effort指的是something done by exertion or hard work, or an achievement,是"成就"之意,不宜译为"努力"。labor指的是ability to work,劳动力。

7. capital资本。例如:human capital人力资本,financial capital金融资本。

8. Entrepreneurs are the drivers of economic progress.企业家是经济发展的动力。

driver指的是one that provides impulse or motivation,推动者、驱动者。例如:a driver in economics,经济发展的驱动力。此句也可以翻译成"企业家是推动经济发展的驱动力",具体名词抽象化。

二、汉译英 Chinese-English Translation

推动共建丝绸之路经济带和21世纪海上丝绸之路的愿景与行动(节选)

一、时代背景

当今世界正发生复杂深刻的变化,国际金融危机深层次影响继续显现,世界经济缓慢复苏、发展分化,国际投资贸易格局和多边投资贸易规则酝酿深刻调整,各国面临的发展问题依然严峻。共建"一带一路"顺应世界多极化、经济全球化、文化多样化、社会信息化的潮流,秉持开放的区域合作精神,致力于维护全球自由贸易体系和开放型世界经济。

共建"一带一路"旨在促进经济要素有序自由流动、资源高效配置和市场深度融合,推动沿线各国实现经济政策协调,开展更大范围、更高水平、更深层次的区域合作,共同打造开放、包容、均衡、普惠的区域经济合作架构。共建"一带一路"符合国际社会的根本利益,彰显人类社会共同理想和美好追求,是国际合作以及全球治理新模式的积极探索,将为世界和平发展增添新的正能量。

共建"一带一路"致力于亚欧非大陆及附近海洋的互联互通,建立和加强沿线各国互联互通伙伴关系,构建全方位、多层次、复合型的互联互通网络,实现沿线各国多元、自主、平衡、可持续的发展。"一带一路"的互联互通项目将推动沿线各国发展战略的对接与耦合,发掘区域内市场的潜力,促进投资和消费,创造需求和就业,增进沿线各国人民的人文交流与文明互鉴,让各国人民相逢相知、互信互敬，共享和谐、安宁、富裕的生活。

当前，中国经济和世界经济高度关联。中国将一以贯之地坚持对外开放的基本国策，构建全方位开放新格局，深度融入世界经济体系。推进"一带一路"建设既是中国扩大和深化对外开放的需要，也是加强和亚欧非及世界各国互利合作的需要，中国愿意在力所能及的范围内承担更多责任义务，为人类和平发展作出更大的贡献。

（引自人民网：http://politics.people.com.cn/n/2015/0328/c1001-26764639.html，访问日期：2024年8月11日。）

重点解析 Notes and Comments

1. 《推动共建丝绸之路经济带和21世纪海上丝绸之路的愿景与行动》由国家发展改革委、外交部、商务部经国务院授权于2015年3月28日发布。该文件着眼于共建原则、框架思路等八个方面，为"一带一路"建设指明了方向。

2. "一带一路"：Belt and Road Initiative。在有的场合，比如作定语时，只译为Belt and Road，不需要Initiative。

3. 该文件第一部分"时代背景"共有四个自然段。每一段落的翻译都需要从全局考虑，必要时需根据上下文语义和逻辑关系对句子结构进行调整。

4. 第一自然段翻译成英语时，可分为四个长句，但要注意每个英语句子的语法结构和句子成分。"当今世界正发生复杂深刻的变化"作为全段的首句独立成句，其他各句子之间用分号隔开。

5. "国际投资贸易格局和多边投资贸易规则酝酿深刻调整"中的"酝酿"一词不要拘泥于字面意思，否则会造成搭配不合理、不符合逻辑。此处"酝酿"一词可用"undergo"来表达。

6. 各国面临的发展问题依然严峻 countries still face big challenges to their development

该句的中心词是"发展问题"，作主语，但在英译时以"countries"作主语，句子结构做了调整。注意：英语中表达不确定的多个、各个时，名词用复数即可，如此句中的"各国"译为"countries"。

7. 在第二段中，动宾结构短语"共建'一带一路'"出现三次，在原句中均用作主语。第一个"共建'一带一路'"译成不定式短语；第二个"共建'一带一路'"不重复翻译，以代词"It"替代；第三个"共建'一带一路'"直接翻译成动名词短语"Jointly building the Belt and Road"。英语表达形式灵活多样，尤其是在同一段落、同一篇章中，一种表达形式尽量不要重复。

8. 共同打造开放、包容、均衡、普惠的区域经济合作架构 jointly creating an open, inclusive and balanced regional economic cooperation architecture that benefits all

原句"开放、包容、均衡、普惠的"是"区域经济合作架构"的定语，在译文中，前三个词译成形容词，仍作前置定语，但"普惠"译成定语从句"that benefits all"，作后置定语。

9. 共建"一带一路"符合国际社会的根本利益，彰显人类社会共同理想和美好追求，是国际合作以及全球治理新模式的积极探索，将为世界和平发展增添新的正能量。Jointly building the Belt and Road is in the interests of the world community. Reflecting the common ideals and pursuit of human societies, it is a positive endeavor to seek new models of international cooperation and global governance, and will inject new positive energy into world peace and development.

原句由四个并列句构成，主语是"共建'一带一路'"。如按照原句结构翻译成英语，则英语句子会很冗长。因此，第一句独立成句，主语是"共建'一带一路'"（Jointly building the Belt and Road）；后三句译成一个并列句，"彰显人类社会共同理想和美好追求"翻译成分词短语，代词"it"做主句的主语。

10. 第三段第一句中的"共建'一带一路'"是全句的主语，此处译为名词短语"The Belt and Road Initiative"。

11. 互联互通原为电信领域术语，指的是电信运营商的网络与不在该网络中的设备或设施之间的物理链接，现引申指涉及两个及以上国家包括基础设施、规则制度、人员交流等在内的相互链接与沟通，是一个涉及政治、经济、文化、社会等多领域的交互机制。"互联互通"译为英语connectivity即可。

12. 让各国人民相逢相知、互信互敬，共享和谐、安宁、富裕的生活 enable them to understand, trust and respect each other and live in harmony, peace and prosperity

该句为"让"字句，不要译为"let"句，"相逢相知、互信互敬"两个叠声词翻译成三个具体的英文单词，"相""互"译为"each other"作三个动词的宾语。

13. 第四段中的"推进'一带一路'"是动宾结构，但此处只译为一个单词"Initiative"。

14. 中国愿意在力所能及的范围内承担更多责任义务，为人类和平发展作出更大的贡献。China is committed to shouldering more responsibilities and

obligations within its capabilities, and making greater contributions to the peace and development of mankind.

该句中的"愿意"译为"is committed to",作谓语,"在力所能及的范围内"译为"within its capabilities"。

第三节 课后翻译训练

一、将下列句子翻译成汉语 Translate the following sentences into Chinese

1. The law of demand states that, all else being equal, the quantity demanded of an item decreases as the price increases and vise versa.

2. Because a lower real income generally leads to lower consumption, the income effect will normally reinforce the substitution effect in making the demand curve downward-sloping.

3. Under some circumstances the resulting demand curve is very price-elastic, as where the consumer has been spending a good deal on the commodity and ready substitutes are available.

4. We now complete the link between production and cost by using the marginal product concept to illustrate how firms select the least-cost combinations of inputs.

5. Hard news consists of basic facts: who, when, where and how. It is news of important public events, such as government actions, international happenings, social conditions, the economy, crime, environment, and science.

6. Ecosystems such as wetlands, forests and lakes are an important part of the natural regime of a river. They are a buffer(缓冲)between river and terrestrial (地球的,陆地的)ecosystems and play an important role in storing or attenuating (衰减,减弱)floodwaters.

7. The move will help raise consumers' awareness for safety and energy conservation, and put more new models on the market as well.

8. This unwanted effects(副作用)usually disappear spontaneously after 7—14 days or following reduction in the dosage.

9. The standard life span of air conditioners starts from date of production, and that of other home appliances from date of sale.

10. An electron tube is generally used for amplification, and vacuum tube is another name for this device.

二、将下列句子翻译成英语 Translate the following sentences into English

1. 股票进一步震荡下跌，直到找到某个新的平衡点。
2. 部分投资者认为，如果政府觉得有必要进行更大规模的干预，那就说明问题可能比表面上所显现的更严重。
3. 随着互联网的普及（accessible）和电子商务的兴起，许多人的购物习惯正悄悄发生着变化。
4. "一带一路"主要涵盖东亚、东南亚、南亚、中亚、中东和欧洲等区域。
5. 在经济学中，经济效益指的是充分利用资源，从而使商品和服务的生产达到最大化。
6. 在社会主义市场经济条件下，政府职能主要包括经济调节、市场监管、社会管理和公共服务。
7. "一带一路"合作倡议符合有关各方共同利益，顺应了地区和全球合作潮流，得到了国际社会广泛响应和支持。
8. 由于市场的需求是来自个人的需求，因此它取决于决定个体买家需求的所有因素。
9. 没有外力的作用，运动的物体就会连续做匀速直线运动。
10. 中国医药学有着数千年的历史，是中国人民长期同疾病做斗争的经验总结，是我国优秀文化的一个重要组成部分。

三、将下列短文翻译成汉语 Translate the following passage into Chinese

Markets and Prices

When you need a new pair of running shoes, plan to upgrade your cellphone, or need to fly home for Spring Festival, you must find a place where people sell those items or offer those services. The place in which you find them is a market. A market is any arrangement that enables buyers and sellers to get information and to do business with each other. A market has two sides: buyers and sellers.

There are markets for goods such as apples and hiking boots, for services such as haircuts and tennis lessons, for factors of production such as computer programmers and earthmovers, and for other manufactured inputs such as memory chips and auto parts. There are also markets for money such as Japanese yen and for financial securities such as Yahoo! stock. Only our imagination limits what can be traded in markets. Some markets are physical places where buyers and sellers meet and where an auctioneer or a broker helps to determine the prices. Examples of this type of market are the New York Stock Exchange and the wholesale fish, meat, and produce markets.

Some markets are groups of people spread around the world who never meet and know little about each other but are connected through the Internet or by telephone and fax. Examples are the e-commerce markets and the currency markets. Each buyer can visit several different stores, and each seller knows that the buyer has a choice of stores. A competitive market has many buyers and many sellers, so no single buyer or seller can influence the price.

Producers offer items for sale only if the price is high enough to cover their opportunity cost. And consumers respond to changing opportunity cost by seeking cheaper alternatives to expensive items. In everyday life, the price of an object is the number of dollars that must be given up in exchange for it. Economists refer to this price as the money price. The opportunity cost of an action is the highest valued alternative forgone. If, when you buy a cup of coffee, the highest-valued thing you forgo is some gum, then the opportunity cost of the coffee is the quantity of gum forgone. We can calculate the quantity of gum forgone from the money prices of the coffee and the gum.

(Michael Parkin, *Economics, Global Edition*,

Pearson Education Limited, 2016.)

四、将下列短文翻译成英语 Translate the following passage into English

中 医

中医，一般指以中国汉族劳动人民创造的传统医学为主的医学，是研究人体生理和病理、对疾病做出诊断和防治的一门学科。中医对亚洲国家影响十分深远，日本的汉方医学、韩国的韩医学等都是以中医为基础发展起来的。

中医诞生于原始社会，春秋战国时期（前770—前221）中医理论已基本形成。两宋时期（960—1279），中医医学取得全面发展，医学理论也越来越规范化和系统化。明清时期（1368—1911），中医学趋向科学化，中医学界冲破当时社会的重重阻碍，实现了对中医学的革新。

中医学讲究阴阳五行（five elements），将人体视为气、形、神的统一体。中医大夫通过"望闻问切"（observation, auscultation, inquiry, and pulse-feeling）四种诊病方法查看病性、探求病位、研究病因、分析病机及人体内各器官和经络关节等的变化，以判断邪正，进而得出病名，制定治疗方法；随后结合中药、针灸（acupuncture）、推拿（massage）、拔罐（cupping）、食疗（diet therapy）等多种治疗手段，以使人体达到阴阳调和的状态，进而康复。

近代以来，"西学东渐"的风气曾一度使中医失去大众的信赖。今天，现代中医一方面保持和发扬了中医传统，另一方面注重利用现代技术，重视汲取他国医学的精华，加之国家对中医文化的大力宣传，中医重获国人青睐，更被外国人视为神秘的医术，正在焕发生机与活力。

（注：部分中医术语可以用通行的音译，中国朝代年份在英语译文中要明晰化。）

本章译例研究及部分练习材料主要引自：Laszlo Tihanyi et al., *Institutional Theory in International Business and Management*, Emerald Publishing Limited, 2012.

第二章 商务英语翻译

商务翻译（Business Translation）包括商务口译和商务笔译。作为翻译的一个分支，商务翻译属于翻译学的范畴，或者更准确地说，属于应用翻译的范畴。商务翻译就是指与商务活动有关的翻译。一般说来，这些活动都是国际性的，涉及两个或两个以上国家的企业或代理商，内容涉及技术引进、对外商业宣传、对外贸易、招商引资、对外劳务承包、国际金融、国际投资、国际运输等各个方面。商务翻译就是指与商务活动有关的翻译。

"商务英语"包含商务与英语两个方面。"商务"既可指市场营销、广告文案策划、商务谈判、进出口业务、证券交易，也可指商业公司、银行等金融机构的一系列内部管理活动和对外事务。从广义上说，"商务"的概念亦可涵盖金融、贸易、运输、投资、财务、经济和贸易相关法律、国际合作与惯例、商务理论与原则等各个方面。"商务"是传播的内容，"英语"则为传播的媒介，但"商务英语"并非二者的简单叠加，而是有机的融合，是商务领域内经常大量使用的反映这一领域专业活动内容的英语词汇、句型、文体等的有机总和，在技术引进、对外贸易、招商引资、涉外保险、国际金融、国际运输、对外劳务承包等商务活动中所使用的英语均属于商务英语的范畴。此外，商务英语是世界范围大市场发展形成的产物，因此其概念是动态的，在全球化大背景下，其含义与手段仍在不断延伸。（岳峰、刘茵，2014：1）简而言之，商务英语是一种社会功能的变体，属于专门用途英语，是英语在商务场合中的应用，或者说是一种包含了各种商务活动内容、适合商业需要的英文。

第一节　商务英语的语言特点

随着国家之间经济贸易的互相渗透、国际商贸活动的日益频繁，其应用性与普及性愈发广泛。正是因为商务英语属于专门用途英语的范畴，涉及经济、金融、营销、会计和管理学等许多边缘学科,内容还包括商务报刊、商标专利、商务广告、企业宣传资料、产品说明书、商务信函、商务合同或协议等,也包括商务备忘录、商务会议纪要、商务通知以及各种相关的商务票据、表格等。所以其翻译要求有别于普通翻译,译者不仅需要精通中英两种语言与文化,熟悉翻译技巧,还需了解商务英语独特的语言现象和表现内容,以及语言之外的商务、法律等方面的相关知识,以达到翻译精确规范的效果,实现功能对等。(岳峰、刘茵,2014:1—2)

一、词汇特点

（一）专业术语丰富

作为专门用途英语,商务英语与商务活动密切相关,承载着对外贸易和国际商务等方面的信息交流,涉及范围广,包含金融、贸易、会计、营销、保险、法律等多个领域,而每个领域都有特定的专业术语,其意义单一固定,所以,商务英语的突出特点就体现在专业术语的大量运用上。

例1. The distributor agrees to accept, on presentation, and to pay with exchange, sight draft against bill of lading attached.

译文:经销商同意在提示时予以承兑,凭所附提单以即期汇票的方式支付。

上面短短的一句话中,包含了多个专业术语,如:distributor经销商、accept承兑、on presentation提示、sight draft即期汇票、bill of lading提单等。不难看出,没有对商务知识的深入了解和专业术语的熟练掌握,要进行商务英语的翻译必然举步维艰。

此外,商务英语中出现的普通词语亦可具有专业词汇的意义,因此必须首先从专业角度去分析。比如"negotiation",通常意思为"谈判",而在"negotiation of the relative draft"(议付有关汇票)中则意为"议付",与普通英语中的含义相去甚远。又如:

futures　期货　　　　　securities　有价证券　　　　average　海损

（二）缩略语多

在商务语境中,缩略语以简单的形式指代复杂的含义,具有言简意赅、快速便捷的特点。使用缩略语能够避免使用烦琐的语言,尤其是在文书文体中,以适应当代快节奏的商务活动。正因为如此,国际商务领域中广泛使用缩略语。其形式主要有四种:首字母缩略、截短词、拼缀词与首字母拼音词等。

这些缩略语经过长期使用,已被广泛接受,但若需要准确翻译,则必须理解其全称，例如：

D.P.：Documents against payment　付款交单

D.A.：Documents against acceptance　承兑交单

F/N：fixture note　订舱（租船）确认书

T-bond：treasury bond　长期国库券

ENCL：enclosure　随附

I.R.O.：in respect of　关于

中国人民银行即中国央行发行的数字货币属于央行负债，具有国家信用，与法定货币等值。数字货币是digital currency，英文简称DC。要注意中国央行数字货币与电子支付electronic payment（缩写为EP）的区别。

（三）用词正式、严谨

商务活动大多具有正式、庄重的特点，与之相适应，商务英语用词一般也较为正式、严谨，以书面语为主，尤其是商务信函、法律文书、协议或合同等公文文体，多使用一些正式，有时候甚至是冷僻的词汇。

例2. The Buyer shall, 10 days prior to the time of shipment/after this Contract comes into effect, open an irrevocable Letter of Credit in favor of the Seller. The Letter of Credit shall expire 10 days after the completion of loading of the shipment as stipulated.

译文：买方应在装运期前/合同生效后10日内，开出以卖方为受益人的不可撤销信用证。信用证在按照合同装船完毕后10日内到期。

例句中使用了prior to而非before，用expire而非end。

在动词使用方面，多用正式的单个单词，而非由动词+介词+名词或副词构成的短语。比如常常使用appoint而非make an appointment of，使用continue而不使用keep on或go on，使用supplement而不使用add to等。在介词和连词使用方面，用in the nature of 代替like，用along the lines of 替代like；用in the case of 或in the event of/that 替代if，用 with regard to 和with reference to替代about等。另一方面，为了保证普通大众能理解，保证所有词语具有国际通用性，也要选取明白易懂的词汇，尽量多用常用的词语；但与此同时还要注意又不能过于口语化，一般不用俚语，更不能使用粗俗用词。除此之外，古体字亦常见于商务文体中，如合同及法律文本中常使用由where, there与in, by, with, after等构成的复合词汇。这类词汇的特点是明晰古朴。尽管thereinafter的意义与in that part which follows相等，但前者简洁明了，而后者累赘冗长。（邹力，2013：21—22）

二、句法特点

（一）结构严谨、逻辑严密

商务英语要求表达效果的准确性、时效性和逻辑性，句子往往要求结构严谨、逻辑严密，因商务活动涉及双方利益，在思维调理上要求清晰，在语言表达上更注重精炼缜密，做到准确无误，此类文体以涉外合同最为典型，还涉及国际公约、信用证、提单等单证类文本。

例3. The sellers shall, immediately upon the completion of the loading of the goods, advice by fax the buyers of the Contract No., commodity, quantity, invoiced value, gross weight, name of vessel and date of delivery etc. In case due to the sellers not having faxed in time, all losses caused shall be borne by the sellers.

译文：卖方应于装货后，立即用传真将有关合同号、品名、数量、发票价值、毛重、运输工具名称、交货日期等资料通知买方。由于卖方未能通知买方而造成的所有损失，均由卖方承担。

第一句虽长，但其主干结构为：The sellers shall... advice...of, 后接一连串名词作介词宾语，immediately upon the completion of the loading of the goods是介词短语作状语，表示时间，翻译时对词序作必要调整，以符合汉语表达规范。

例4. The availability of venture capital financing to young, high technology companies has been a primary contributor to the dramatic revenue growth enjoyed by, and the increased competitiveness of, America's high technology industry and to the economic expansion and increased employment levels experienced in California's Silicon Valley and other areas of high technology company concentration.

译文：新兴的高科技公司可以获得风险资本融资，这使得美国高科技产业的收入大幅度增长，竞争力不断提高，同时还促使加州硅谷和其他高科技公司集中地的经济蓬勃发展，就业人数大大增加。

这个句子虽然很长，但仔细分析，全句的结构为系表结构。句子的主语是the availability，表语是has been a primary contributor。句子之所以显得非常复杂，主要是句中对主要成分的修饰过多："the availability"后面的"of venture capital financing to young, high technology companies"，"primary contributor"后的"to...to..."，第一个介词短语中的过去分词短语"enjoyed by"和"the increased competitiveness of"，以及第二个介词短语中的"experienced in"。译文几乎将所有的英语名词转译成动词，并将英语的长句译成汉语的并列短句，读起来更加符合汉语的表达习惯。

（二）常用程式化的套语，语气委婉礼貌

国际商务英语应用文，特别是国际商务信函中，礼貌用语是非常重要的，这是国际商务交往的一大特点。此外，信息型文本既要简明直接，又要礼貌得体，同时又要避免过于亲密，因此形成了一套国际上通用并认可的公式化套语句型。

例5. We thank you for your letter of contents of which have been noted/have had our careful attention.

译文：谢谢贵方……月……日来信，内容已悉。

例6. We are sorry for the inconvenience that may have caused you.

译文：对给贵方造成的不便我方深表歉意。

例7. We shall appreciate your prompt attention to the adjustment of these errors.

译文：望即修正这些差错，不胜感激。

例8. This contract is made by and between the buyers and the sellers, whereby the buyers agree to buy and the sellers agree to sell the undermentioned commodity subject to the terms and conditions stipulated below.

译文：买卖双方同意按以下条款购买、出售下列商品并签订本合同。

以上例句中，thank, be sorry, appreciate都是固定的客套语，whereby, undermentioned, subject to, stipulated below等都是程式化的套语。

（三）具体、明确

商务英语在陈述事物时往往应具体、明确，避免笼统、抽象。

例9. This offer remains effective/valid/open for ten days from 18th October.

译文：本报盘自10月18日起，有效期10天。

如该句改为"This offer remains effective/valid/open for ten days."（本报盘有效期10天），因没有具体起止时间，则显得含糊、笼统。再比如：This draft is payable on the 19th of November.该句时间具体明确，毫不含糊，而不是笼统说11月份。

第二节　商务英语翻译原则与译者的基本素质

随着全球经济一体化的进一步发展，我国整体实力逐步加强，与世界各国在经济、文化、教育以及其他领域的交流与合作变得更加密切，国内外贸易公司的交往也大大增加。在国际经济交往和商务活动中，翻译起到了交流中介的桥梁作用。商务英语翻译是商家获取商业信息，促成对外贸易和商务活动成功的有力工具。然而，商务英语翻译与普通英语翻译或文学翻译有很大不同，译者除了要有扎实的双语基本功和熟练的翻译技巧之外，还需要具备商务专业知识，了解其他行业的语言特征和特殊的表达方式，强调语义的对等和等效，追求"地道、准确"，"适合、对应"。

一、文体适合性原则

文体适合性原则是指译语与源语从文体角度上来说是相应的，不同的文体译成另一种语言后读者会感到所用的语言与原文是符合的，商务信函翻译后还是商务信函，合同语言翻译后读起来还是合同语言。

在商务英语翻译中，文体适合性原则还体现在译语语篇对源语语篇的忠实方面，也就是要求译者能准确地将原文语言的信息用译文语言表达出来，相比起形式，意义更为重要，因此，无须刻意苛求语法与句子结构的一致，而应追求信息对等。如涉及贸易、合同、保险、金融等领域的商务类的文章，译文应该从措辞、结构及行文上忠实于源语的语言与行文规范，以再现严谨和正式的语篇。（岳峰、刘茵，2014：5—6）

文体适合性原则也意味着译文表达的地道性，也就是译文的术语、表达都应符合商务文体的要求，商务术语翻译成另一种语言时，仍使用对应的术语，即行话，而不是普通的语言。如果英语的术语经翻译不能以另一种语言中表示相同意义的术语来表达的话，那么这种译文不能算是地道的译文，甚至会因不能准确地表达出源语的意思而产生误解或者误读，从而出现术语空缺甚至阅读障碍，不能达到交流的目的。（方梦之、毛忠明，2018：106—107）

例10. We are delighted to receive your letter of November 29 asking whether we can supply you with Art. No. 3609.

译文：我方很高兴收到贵方11月29日来函询问可否提供3609号货品。

该例句为外贸函电常用的表达方式，措辞正式、客套，译文也必须保持正式、客套的风格。

例11. We thank you for your letter of November 20, contents of which have been noted/have had our careful attention.

译文：谢谢贵方11月20日来信，内容已悉。

该译文用"贵方"表示"your"，用"内容已悉"翻译which从句。which从句如果译成"内容已经注意到了"就不够正式得体。

例12. The credit which evidences shipment of 2,000 tons of steels may be used against presentation of the shipping documents.

译文：本信用证证明2000吨钢材已装船，凭装运单据议付。

在商务语境下，这里应将use理解为"议付"，而不是"被用于"，shipping documents应译成"装运单据"。

例13. It should be noted that a quota system is always protectionist and provides no revenue to the country.

译文：应该注意到，配额制度是一种贸易保护主义，并且不会给国家带来税收收入。

"quota"在此句中是"配额"，而不能译为"限额，定额"。

例14. Kindly tell us what steps you are going to take in the way of compensations for the damage.

译文：用什么方式来弥补这次损失，敬请告知。

商务函电常用语"Kindly tell us..."得说话的语气显得十分客气，翻译成中文为"敬请告知"。

例15. A note receivable usually includes the maturity date and rate of interest.

译文：应收票据的内容通常包括到期日和利率。

"note receivable"是会计英语专有词汇。"maturity"在日常英语中是"成熟"的意思，而在会计英语中则是"到期"的意思。

例16. We have examined the Conditions of Contract, Specification, Drawings, Bill of Quantities, the attached Appendix and Addenda Nos for the execution of the above-named Works. We offer to execute and complete the Works and remedy any defects therein in conformity with this Tender which includes all these documents, for the sum of Kshs....................(In words) ...

译文：我方认真审核了与实施上述工程相关的合同条件、技术规范、图纸、工程量清单及（标号为……）附件和附录。我方同意按照本标书及其所有相关文件条款，实施并完成该项工程，并对其中的任何缺陷进行纠正。该工程总金额为……………（大写）肯尼亚先令。

这是肯尼亚工程招标文件的合同条款。Works首字母大写，在招投标中特指"工程"；in words不是"用词语"的意思，而是"大写"之意。比如我们在财务上先用阿拉伯数字表示金额，但为了表达正式，避免有涂改机会，一般都要求同时用汉字壹、贰、叁、肆等表达，这就是大写。execution在此应译为"履行"而非"执行"。

例17. If the safekeeping duration expires or the depositor claims and retrieves the article before the expiry date, the safekeeping party shall return to the depositor the original article and the interest generated therefrom.

译文：保管期满或者寄存人提前领取保管物的，保管人应当将原物及其孳息归还寄存人。

the interest generated therefrom 不能翻译为"由此产生的利息"，在商务合同或法规中，应译为"孳息"。

二、准确原则

准确就是指译文所传达的信息与原文传达的信息保持一致，准确无误，也就是概念表达确切，数据与单位要精确，尤其是商务英语中的大量专业词汇、缩略语等，以实现译文在规范性、礼貌性与功能等方面的对等。近年来，随着经济发展的全球化趋势，新的词语层出不穷，在一般的词典中不一定都能查到。在翻译中必须根据上下文和具体语境理解其真正含义，或者利用专业词典，辨清词义，选择恰当的词语翻译。

例18. This contract is made in two originals in both English and Chinese, each party holding one. In case of any discrepancy between the two versions, the Chinese version shall prevail.

译文：本合同以中英文同时书就，一式两份，双方各执一份。两种文本如有冲突，以中文为准。

"prevail"为动词，意思是"胜过；流行；成功；占优势"。但在此句中，"prevail"不能按照词典的普通意思来译，所以，"the Chinese version shall prevail"应该译为"以中文为准"。

例19. Few managers seriously question the benefits of delegation, but many are still reluctant to delegate.

译文：公司经理大都对授权的好处深信不疑，但其中大多数仍不愿意授权他人。

这句话中的"delegation"和"delegate"是"to commit or entrust to another"（委托他人）的意思，译成"代表"就不合适。

例20. Amendments to this Contract may be made only by a written instrument signed by a duly authorized representative of each of the parties.

译文：对本合同的修改，只能通过各方正式授权的代表签署协议进行。

此处"instrument"是指"a legal document"（文书，契约，合同），而不是指"仪器"。

例21. He was disappointed by his failure to secure the top job with the bank.

译文：他因没能得到银行的高层工作而失望。

"secure"在此不是"担保，保护"的意思，而是"获得，设法得到"之意。

例22. Credit is offered only when creditors believe that they have a good chance of obtaining legal tender when they present such instruments at a bank or other authorized institution.

译文：只有当债权人相信，一旦他们向银行或其他授权机构递交此类信用票据就有把握获得法定货币时，他们才会提供信贷。

这里的"instrument"是指"票据"，如a credit instrument（信用票据）、a negotiable instrument"可转让票据"。

三、统一性原则

统一是指在商务英语翻译过程中所采用的译名、概念、术语等在任何时候都应该保持一致。比如世界知名品牌名称Microsoft（微软），Coca-cola（可口可乐），McDonald's（麦当劳）。Microsoft不能随心所欲译为"麦克罗索芙特"，Coca-cola不能译为"蝌蝌啃蜡"，McDonald's不能译为"麦克唐纳德"。

四、商务翻译者的基本素质

从上面的例子可以看出，要准确进行商务翻译，译者不仅要有扎实的语言功底、熟练的翻译技巧、丰富的商务知识，还要熟悉不同文本的文体格式和术语，行文用字力求符合行业规范。不仅要通晓两种语言，还要通晓两种文化，需要有两种文化背景才能"读懂言外之意"。遇到不懂或者陌生的专业术语时，切不可望文生义，要多查阅参考资料，勤查词典。只有这样，才能保证译文规范、地道、措辞准确、专业。

翻译人员是知识传播和文化交流的桥梁，从事商务翻译的人员除了需要熟练掌握所从事翻译文体的专业知识外，还需要具有一些基本素质，不仅要了解、学习一些翻译理论，能够灵活运用各种翻译技巧，而且还要不断总结自己的实践经验，提升为理论，供他人学习借鉴。此外，具有良好信息技术技能的译者可以在较短的时间内完成更多的翻译工作，从而提高翻译水平，减少时间、精力和成本，用最少的付出可以得到最多的收获。

翻译的种类不同，对译者的要求也不尽相同。然而，不管是专业译员，还是临时从事翻译工作或接受翻译任务，不管是口译工作还是笔译工作，都需要具备良好的心理素质，需要有严谨、认真的工作态度和高度的责任感，还要有足够的耐心和敏锐的政治意识。2009年，笔者受托翻译《九江学院画册》。画册翻译完成后由校宣传部送至深圳的一家彩印公司付印。恰逢时任国家副主席习近平参加柬埔寨首家孔子学院揭牌仪式。该孔子学院为九江学院、柬埔寨王家研究院合作建立。因此，画册需立即补充相关信息：习近平副主席为九江学院在柬埔寨设立的孔子学院揭牌。原译文是：Vice President Xi Jinping attended the opening ceremony of the Confucius Institute established by Jiujiang University in Cambodia. 译文交付后，是夜，思考当日所做之事，猛然想起译文不足之处。因为Vice President既可以是副主席，也可以理解为副校长，对于不太熟悉中国政治文化的外籍人士可能并不太明确，可能会误解为九江学院副校长。因此，笔者立即修改译文为：Xi Jinping, Vice President of the People's Republic of China, attended the opening ceremony of the Confucius Institute established by Jiujiang University in Cambodia.

第三节　课内翻译任务

一、英译汉 English-Chinese Translation

Impact of Globalization on International Business

Globalization is not a new concept. It has been around throughout history with mankind exchanging goods and services. The difference today is the development of new technologies, primarily tools of communication like the internet, which have played a major role in accelerating exchanges. Globalization is a process which cannot be stopped or slowed. What we can do is to ensure that globalization is shaped by common and deliberate efforts so that all involved, people and countries, are benefited by it.

Economists have proven that those countries experiencing the most accelerated growth have also been those with greatest increase in exports. For countries with small population, export-led growth is the principal source of jobs and government revenue. However, increasing exports is just part of the development challenge that both governments and private sector face. They have to prepare people to take advantage of globalization and one of the best ways to promote globalization is to promote well-paying, high-skilled jobs through investment in education which is essential for the development of any business. International business community should play a role in helping to reduce the downsides of globalization while availing the benefits.

Reducing the disadvantages in the long run help to create wealth in a country and thus playing an important role in reducing global poverty through economic development. Most international businesses try to gain a foothold in a foreign country by formulating sustainable development. International business community sees globalization as a way of reaching out to the masses and this has definitely altered the way global business is conducted, the way existing technologies are utilized and the way products are produced and consumed.

(N. Venkateswaran, *International Business Management*,

New Age International Ltd., 2011.)

重点解析 Notes and Comments

1. It has been around throughout history with mankind exchanging goods and services. 全球化一直伴随着人类交换商品和服务的历史。

该句"it"指"globalization"。

2. What we can do is to ensure that globalization is shaped by common and deliberate efforts so that all involved, people and countries, are benefited by it. 我们所能做的是确保所有有关各方、人民和国家，深思熟虑、共同努力，推动全球化的进程，都能从全球化中受益。

"that"引导的宾语从句是被动语态，这是商务英语惯用的语法结构。但在英译汉时，要将被动语态转换成主动语态，"common and deliberate efforts"翻译成两个短语——"深思熟虑、共同努力"，"are benefited by it"也应翻译成主动语态，而不能译成"被它给予利益"。尤其要注意的是，英语句子重形态，惯用复合句型，句与句之间常用关联性词语连接；汉语重意合，少用关联词语，句与句之间常常采用并列结构。所以，该句中"so that"引导的目的状语从句不要译成

"以至于……"这样的表目的的从句结构，而应依从汉语的习惯表达形式，翻译成几个并列的短语。

二、汉译英 Chinese-English Translation

坚守初心 团结合作
携手共促亚太高质量增长
——在亚太经合组织第三十次领导人非正式会议上的讲话
（2023年11月17日，旧金山）
中华人民共和国主席 习近平

尊敬的拜登总统，

各位同事：

很高兴同大家相聚在美丽的旧金山。这是亚太经合组织领导人第三十次聚首，具有特殊重要意义。感谢拜登总统和美国政府为这次会议作出的周到安排。

亚太经合组织建立领导人定期会议机制以来，始终走在全球开放发展的前沿，有力促进了区域贸易和投资自由化便利化、经济技术发展、物资人员流动，创造了举世瞩目的"亚太奇迹"。

当前，世界百年变局加速演进，世界经济面临多种风险挑战，作为全球增长引擎，亚太肩负更大的时代责任。作为亚太地区领导人，我们都要深入思考，要把一个什么样的亚太带到本世纪中叶？如何打造亚太发展的下一个"黄金三十年"？在这一进程中如何更好发挥亚太经合组织作用？

中国古人说："道之所在，虽千万人吾往矣。"我们应该秉持亚太合作初心，负责任地回应时代呼唤，携手应对全球性挑战，全面落实布特拉加亚愿景，建设开放、活力、强韧、和平的亚太共同体，实现亚太人民和子孙后代的共同繁荣。在此，我愿提出几点建议。

第一，坚持创新驱动。创新是发展的强大动力。我们要顺应科技发展趋势，以更加积极姿态推动科技交流合作，携手打造开放、公平、公正、非歧视的科技发展环境。要加速数字化转型，缩小数字鸿沟，加快落实《亚太经合组织互联网和数字经济路线图》，支持大数据、云计算、人工智能、量子计算等新技术应用，不断塑造亚太发展新动能新优势。

中国坚持创新驱动发展战略，协同推进数字产业化、产业数字化，提出了亚太经合组织数字乡村建设、企业数字身份、利用数字技术促进绿色低碳转型等

倡议，更好为亚太发展赋能。

第二，坚持开放导向。亚太发展的经验告诉我们，开放则兴，封闭则衰。我们要维护自由开放的贸易投资，支持并加强以世界贸易组织为核心的多边贸易体制，维护全球产业链供应链稳定畅通，反对将经贸问题政治化、武器化、泛安全化。要坚定不移推进区域经济一体化，加快推进亚太自由贸易区进程，全面落实《亚太经合组织互联互通蓝图》，共享区域开放发展机遇。

近期，中国成功举办第三届"一带一路"国际合作高峰论坛，为促进全球互联互通、构建开放型世界经济注入新动力。中国坚持高水平实施《区域全面经济伙伴关系协定》，主动对接《全面与进步跨太平洋伙伴关系协定》和《数字经济伙伴关系协定》高标准经贸规则，积极推动加入两个协定进程，同各方共绘开放发展新图景。

第三，坚持绿色发展。面对气候变化、自然灾害等日益严峻的挑战，我们要坚持人与自然和谐共生，加快推动发展方式绿色低碳转型，协同推进降碳、减污、扩绿、增长，落实好《生物循环绿色经济曼谷目标》，厚植亚太增长的绿色底色。

中国坚持走生态优先、绿色发展之路，积极稳妥推进碳达峰碳中和，加快发展方式绿色转型。我们提出亚太经合组织绿色农业、可持续城市、能源低碳转型、海洋污染防治等合作倡议，推动共建清洁美丽的亚太。

第四，坚持普惠共享。当前，全球发展事业面临严峻挑战，发展鸿沟加剧。我多次讲，大家一起发展才是真发展。我们要全面落实联合国2030年可持续发展议程，推动发展问题重回国际议程中心位置，深化发展战略对接，共同解决全球发展赤字。欢迎各方积极参与全球发展倡议，深化减贫、粮食安全、工业化、发展筹资等领域合作，构建全球发展共同体，让各国人民共享现代化建设成果。中国将继续支持亚太经合组织开展经济技术合作，共同做大亚太发展蛋糕。

各位同事！

中国正在以中国式现代化全面推进强国建设、民族复兴伟业。中国坚持走和平发展道路，发展的根本目的是让中国人民过上好日子，不是要取代谁。今年是中国改革开放45周年，我们将坚持高质量发展，推进高水平对外开放，以中国式现代化为推动实现世界各国的现代化提供新机遇。我愿同各位同事一道努力，推动亚太合作取得更多丰硕成果，共同打造亚太下一个"黄金三十年"！

谢谢大家。

（http://cpc.people.com.cn/n1/2023/1118/c64094-40121117.html，访问时间：2024年6月30日。）

重点解析 Notes and Comments

1. 坚守初心 Staying True to APEC Founding Mission

"初心"在不同语境下有不同的表达，意思是：one's original intention/desire/aspiration。

2. APEC 是 Asia-Pacific Economic Cooperation（亚太经济合作组织，简称亚太经合组织）的缩略词，是亚太地区层级最高、领域最广、最具影响力的经济合作机制。1989年11月5日至7日，澳大利亚、美国、日本、韩国、新西兰、加拿大及当时的东盟六国在澳大利亚首都堪培拉举行APEC首届部长级会议，标志着APEC正式成立。APEC现有21个成员。

3. "在亚太经合组织第三十次领导人非正式会议上的讲话"和"中华人民共和国主席习近平"两句，在实际翻译中，需要在语序上做一定的调整，译为："Remarks by H.E. Xi Jinping, President of the People's Republic of China at the 30th APEC Economic Leaders' Meeting"。此外，"Xi Jinping"译成"H.E. Xi Jinping"，这是从外方的角度进行的翻译，以示对习近平主席的尊重。H.E.（或HE）在英式、美式英语里面是通用的，是"Her/His Excellency"的缩写，意为"尊敬的某某阁下"，是对身份尊贵人士的尊称。因为 Her 和 His 都是以 H 开头，所以 H.E. 在男性或女性的名字前都可用。如果参加国际会议的人士是某个国家的国王（女王），或者是皇室成员，用 H.E. 就不合适了，要用 Majesty 或者 Highness。比如英国伊丽莎白女王，她的尊称是 Her Majesty，表示"女王陛下"。有一点要注意，Her 是第三人称，如果当面称呼她，要用第二人称，即 Your Majesty。王子、公主、亲王或王储等，就不能用 Majesty，而要用 Highness，表示"殿下"。

4. 亚太经合组织建立领导人定期会议机制以来，始终走在全球开放发展的前沿，有力促进了区域贸易和投资自由化便利化、经济技术发展、物资人员流动，创造了举世瞩目的"亚太奇迹"。Since the establishment of the economic leaders' regular meeting mechanism, APEC has always stood at the global forefront of openness and development. It has played a robust role in promoting Asia-Pacific trade and investment liberalization and facilitation, economic growth and technological progress, and the flow of goods and people. It has helped create the "Asia-Pacific miracle" that has staggered the world.

该句由四个短句构成，逻辑主语是"亚太经合组织"，翻译成英语时可以拆分成三个英语句子，后两个句子的主语仍然是"亚太经合组织"。当多个英语句子并列时，习惯上不重复出现同一主语，因此，用代词"It"替代"亚太经合组织"。

5. 当前，世界百年变局加速演进，世界经济面临多种风险挑战，作为全球增长引擎，亚太肩负更大的时代责任。In the world today, changes on a scale unseen in a century are unfolding at an accelerating pace. The world economy faces multiple risks and challenges. The Asia-Pacific region, which is an engine of global growth, thus has greater responsibility in these times.

原句"当前，世界百年变局加速演进"在其他正式场合常常表述为"当今世界正处于百年未有之大变局"。此处原文虽没有"未有"一词，但包含了这层意思，因此，"百年变局"翻译成英语"changes on a scale unseen in a century"最为准确。

6. 中国古人说："道之所在，虽千万人吾往矣。"An ancient Chinese sage said, "For a righteous cause, I shall press forward, undaunted by thousands standing in my way."

"道之所在，虽千万人吾往矣"的意思是："真理所在之处，即使面对千万人的阻拦，我也义无反顾地前往。""虽千万人吾往矣"出自《孟子·公孙丑上》，表达了孟子对真理的执着追求。

习近平总书记在文章、讲话、著作中常常引用古代典籍中的经典名句，用中国经典讲"中国经验"，以中国道理说"中国道路"，以体现中国文化的博大精深，增强语言效果和说服力。翻译这类经典名句，首先要理解原文意思，了解原文出处；其次译文要准确、精练。

7. 我们应该秉持亚太合作初心，……共同繁荣。In the same spirit, we must remain steadfast in our commitment to APEC's founding mission...

该句是一个由六个短句组成的长句。汉译英时采用拆句法，即把由六个短句组成的长句，根据逻辑关系拆分成三个独立的英语句子，由"we"分别担任三个句子的主语，以使句子逻辑清晰。此外，在译文前面加上"In the same spirit"，以便与"道之所在，虽千万人吾往矣"一句在语义上更好地衔接，这在翻译方法中称作增译。

8. 第一，坚持创新驱动。First, staying committed to innovation-driven development.

"坚持创新驱动"是动宾结构，"坚持"是动词，但没有主语，而英语句子需要主语，构成主谓宾结构。为与汉语原句在结构和语气上保持一致，英语译文也用无主语的短语。在该讲话中，习近平主席提出了四点建议，均包含"坚持"一词，译文都用"staying committed to"，后接名词短语。

9. 要加速数字化转型，缩小数字鸿沟，加快落实《亚太经合组织互联网和数字经济路线图》，支持大数据、云计算、人工智能、量子计算等新技术应用，不断塑造亚太发展新动能新优势。We should accelerate digital transformation, narrow the digital divide, redouble our efforts to implement the APEC Internet and Digital Economy Roadmap, support the application of big data, cloud computing, artificial intelligence, quantum computing and other new technologies, and create new momentum and new drivers of growth in the Asia-Pacific region.

"要……"是无主语结构，是中文官方文件和领导人讲话的常用结构，这类结构简洁、有力。汉语属于意合语言，时常会出现主语缺失的现象；英语属形合语言，需要有明确的主语。因此，翻译此类句子时应根据上下文和逻辑关系，补充缺失的主语，可以使用"人"，也可以使用"物"。本文译成英语时大都用"we"作主语。

10. 中国坚持创新驱动发展战略，协同推进数字产业化、产业数字化，提出了亚太经合组织数字乡村建设、企业数字身份、利用数字技术促进绿色低碳转型等倡议，更好为亚太发展赋能。China remains committed to its strategy for driving growth and development through innovation. China is advancing both its digital industry and the digital transformation of traditional industries. China has put forward a number of initiatives for promoting growth and development in the region through digital empowerment, such as digital technology-driven rural development, corporate digital identity, and transition to a green and low-carbon economy through the application of digital technologies.

原句是由几个句子构成的长句，因逻辑主语都是"中国"，汉英翻译采用拆句法，分译成三个独立的英语句子，每个句子的主语均为"China"。

本句中"创新驱动发展战略"，翻译成英语时以"战略"作为核心词汇，整个词组译为"its strategy for driving growth and development through innovation"，意思是"通过创新来驱动增长与发展的战略"。

"产业数字化"译为"the digital transformation of traditional industries"，意思是"传统产业数字化转型"，也就是说，相对于数字化产业，现有的产业是传统产业模式。

"倡议"一词是热点词汇，官方正式文件中"倡议"大多翻译成"initiative"

或"initiatives"。

"利用数字技术促进绿色低碳转型等倡议"中有三个动词"利用""促进""转型"，这体现了汉语多用动词的特点，而英语往往少用动词，多以抽象名词或介词短语代替。

11. 亚太发展的经验告诉我们，开放则兴，封闭则衰。As manifested by the Asia-Pacific experience, an economy thrives in openness and withers in seclusion.

该句如果按照原句结构顺序，应翻译成"The Asia-Pacific experience tells us that an economy thrives in openness and withers in seclusion."这样的表达显得生硬，不符合英语表达习惯，且未能分清主次。使用"as"短语，则分清了主次，突出了主句。

12. 反对将经贸问题政治化、武器化、泛安全化 We must say no to any attempt to politicize, weaponize, or impose security implications on economic and trade issues.

此处用"say no"表示"拒绝""反对"之义，较之"be opposed to"更加干脆、有力。

泛安全化是指对传统安全概念边界的过度扩大，将多种议题安全化，导致国际关系趋于复杂和敏感。泛安全化使得安全的内涵无限扩大，包括经济、文化、科技、环境等非传统领域。众多原本不属于安全范畴的问题被赋予安全意义，使得各国在应对时往往采取非常手段。这一概念在当今国际政治与国际关系领域中日益显著。泛安全化不仅影响国家间的合作与竞争，还可能导致资源错配和浪费，以及国内外政策的保守化和封闭倾向，最终反而不利于实现安全目标。当前全球非传统安全挑战频发，西方一些国家过度扩展"安全"概念，追求单方面安全，不但对他国利益造成损害，还迫使他国采取措施维护非传统安全，导致国家间竞争的升级和扩散。本句中的"泛安全化"的英译，与"政治化、武器化"的英译不同，应根据其丰富的含义来表达。此处用"impose security implications on economic and trade issues"来表达"泛安全化"，意指某些国家主要是西方国家故意扩大"安全"概念内涵，将正常的国家间经贸问题都纳入国家安全范畴。

13. 《亚太经合组织互联互通蓝图》（APEC Connectivity Blueprint）是由亚太经合组织于2014年在北京通过的一份重要文件。这份蓝图旨在加强亚太地区硬件、软件和人员交往的互联互通，推动区域一体化进程。

14. 近期，中国成功举办第三届"一带一路"国际合作高峰论坛，为促进全球互联互通、构建开放型世界经济注入新动力。The recent third Belt and Road

Forum for International Cooperation that China hosted was a success, injecting fresh impetus into global connectivity and the building of an open world economy.

原句的主语是"中国",但译文按照英文行文习惯,将短语"中国成功举办"译为定语,以"高峰论坛"作主语,将两个短句合并成一个英语长句,将"为……"句译作伴随状态的分词短语,从而突出了"高峰论坛"的成功举办。

15.《区域全面经济伙伴关系协定》(Regional Comprehensive Economic Partnership,简称RCEP)是以发展中经济体为中心的区域自贸协定,也是全球规模最大的自贸协定,由东盟十国于2012年发起,成员包括东盟十国、中国、日本、韩国、澳大利亚、新西兰,于2020年11月15日正式签署。

16.《全面与进步跨太平洋伙伴关系协定》(Comprehensive and Progressive Agreement for Trans-Pacific Partnership,简称CPTPP),是亚太国家组成的自由贸易区,是美国退出跨太平洋伙伴关系协定(TPP)后该协定的新名字。2021年9月,我国正式提出申请加入CPTPP。

17. 面对气候变化、自然灾害等日益严峻的挑战,我们要坚持人与自然和谐共生,加快推动发展方式绿色低碳转型,协同推进降碳、减污、扩绿、增长,落实好《生物循环绿色经济曼谷目标》,厚植亚太增长的绿色底色。Given the increasingly grave challenges such as climate change and natural disasters, we must continue to promote harmony between man and nature, accelerate the transition to green and low-carbon development, and see to it that reducing carbon emissions and mitigating pollution operate in parallel with expanding green transition and promoting economic growth. We must deliver on the Bangkok Goals on Bio-Circular-Green (BCG) Economy, making "green" a defining feature of Asia-Pacific growth.

"面对"句的逻辑主语是"我们",译为"Given"引导的分词短语。主语"我们"后面带有五个动宾结构的短句,分别由"坚持""推动""推进""落实""厚植"作谓语。如果这五个短句都翻译成并列的英语句子,则句式结构显得松散,没有重心,不符合英语的表达习惯。英译则将后两个句子提出来,另组成一个独立的句子。

"协同推进降碳、减污、扩绿、增长"一句中,协同推进后接四个动词,如按照原句式结构翻译,则显得生硬。英译时依据语义,对句子进行了重组,"降碳、减污"和"扩绿、增长"译成动名词短语,增加"operate"作谓语,以介词短语"in parallel with"(协同)连接,使得句子更为地道。

18. 我们提出亚太经合组织绿色农业、可持续城市、能源低碳转型、海洋污染防治等合作倡议，推动共建清洁美丽的亚太。China has put forward initiatives for cooperation between APEC member economies in green agriculture, sustainable city development, green and low-carbon energy transition, and marine pollution control and prevention. All such initiatives aim to build a clean and beautiful Asia-Pacific region.

该句主语"我们"不是指所有与会者，而是专指"中国"。"推动共建清洁美丽的亚太"独立成句，作为全句的总括句，表达目标之意。该句采用增译法，根据语义，补充"All such initiatives"作主语，"aim to"作谓语，将目的之意表达出来。

19. 普惠共享

汉英翻译，尤其是政治文献中的专业词汇，需要对词义准确理解。应通过相关资料和网络资源，查找释义，不能只按照字面意思进行翻译。

普惠共享是经济全球化背景下的一种发展理念，旨在推动各国经济共同发展，实现利益共享。因此，"普惠共享"可译为"inclusive development that delivers benefits to all"。

20. 欢迎各方积极参与全球发展倡议，深化减贫、粮食安全、工业化、发展筹资等领域合作，构建全球发展共同体，让各国人民共享现代化建设成果。China welcomes participation by all parties in the Global Development Initiative (GDI) to deepen cooperation in poverty reduction, food security, industrialization and development financing and build a global community of development so that the fruits of modernization are shared by people across the world.

整句话是一个复合句，由一个主句和两个并列的从句组成，表达的是欢迎并鼓励各方面加强合作与共同发展的意愿。该句无施事主语，但逻辑上或隐含的主语是"中国"或"我们"，因此译文要增补"China"作主语。"欢迎"是动词，"各方积极参与全球发展倡议"为宾语，后接并列句"深化……""构建……""让……"，"让……"句可以看作是目的状语。

按照英语形合语言的特点，该句采用合句法，将全句译成主从结构，将"深化……"和"构建……"两个短句译成不定式句，表示目的，"让……"句译成由"so that"引导的目的状语从句。英语译文结构紧凑，语义明晰，符合英语的结构特点。

第四节　课后翻译训练

一、将下列句子翻译成汉语 Translate the following sentences into Chinese

1. The vendors had been banned to keep the cities clean, and their return is expected to help increase people's incomes and revive local economies hit hard by the novel coronavirus outbreak.

2. Since imports subtract from gross domestic product and exports add to it, a smaller trade gap—fewer imports and more exports—is generally good for the economy.

3. Both being ancient civilizations, China and Greece have a long tradition of friendship and the two nations have supported each other on issues related to core interests and major concerns.

4. Buyer should pay total amount to the seller by T/T within 30 days after shipment.

5. The country will only get better once markets, enterprises and individual traders get back on their feet and develop. We will give you our support.

6. The business cycle is a swing in total national output, income, and employment, usually lasting for a period of 2 to 10 years, marked by widespread expansion or construction in most of the economy.

7. So far, the auto industry in China is at a critical point of transforming from high-speed growth to high-quality growth. We should be confident in its development, seize strategic opportunities, and make endeavors in the four respects of structural adjustment, quality improvement, brand-building and expansion into international markets.

8. A portfolio can encompass a whole array of different investment vehicles, ranging from cash to commodities and including binds, equities and alternatives investments.

9. Observers see the trade agreement as an indication that the two countries are capable of steadying their relationship and are willing to solve problems through negotiation in the face of multiple headwinds.

10. Vast cultural gaps, differing work ethics and expectations exist between the Chinese and the Zambians.

二、将下列句子翻译成英语 Translate the following sentences into English

1. 文化包括行为、信仰、价值观和物质成果。文化为群体所共享。

2. 集体主义文化强调共同利益、互相合作、相互依赖程度强。个人主义则更注重"自我"而不是"我们"。

3. 希望各国坚持开放合作，拒绝保护主义；争取共赢，避免"多输"。

4. 我们都有充分的理由支持这一发展方向，世界是中国未来发展的利益攸关方。

5. 中国愿与世界各国深化新能源产供链合作，促进技术创新和产业发展。

6. 习近平主席将在金砖国家工商论坛闭幕式上发表演讲，这是金砖国家——巴西、俄罗斯、印度、中国和南非——商界领袖的一次重要聚会。

7. 公司有必要成为一种企业社区，在本企业的员工中，在相关外部网络组织和社区中，开发、利用、释放员工的企业潜力。

8. 通过识别他们的个人人生意义、信念和价值观，并且把这些与他们的兴趣、力量和才能相结合，我们就可以开始把个人的目标与领导者具有强制性的看法统一起来。

9. 我国的低税收、大市场、稳定的政治社会环境，吸引了越来越多的海外投资者来华。

10. 坚持安危共担，提升协作水平，以全球安全倡议为指引，为维护世界和平作出不懈努力。

三、将下列短文翻译成汉语 Translate the following passage into Chinese

Managing International Negotiations

Negotiation is the process of bargaining with one or more parties to arrive at a solution that is acceptable to all. Negotiation often follows assessing political risk and can be used as an approach to conflict management. If the risk is worth it, then the MNE must negotiate with the host country to secure the best possible arrangements. The MNE and the host country will discuss the investment the MNE is prepared to make in return for certain guarantees and/or concessions.

The Negotiation Process There are several basic steps that can be used in managing the negotiation process. Regardless of the issues or personalities of the parties involved, this process typically begins with planning.

Planning starts with the negotiators identifying those objectives they would like to attain. Then, they explore the possible options for reaching these objectives. Research shows that the greater the number of options, the greater the chances for successful negotiations. Next, consideration is given to areas of common ground between the parties. Other areas include: (1) the setting of limits on objectives, such as deciding to pay no more than $10 million for the factory and $3 million for the land; (2) dividing issues into short and long-term considerations and deciding how to handle each; and (3) determining the sequence in which to discuss the various issues.

Impersonal Relationship Building The second phase of the negotiation process involves getting to know the people on the other side. This "feeling out" period is characterized by the desire to identify those who are reasonable and those who are not. In contrast to negotiations in many other countries, those in the United States often given little attention to this phase; they want to get down to business immediately, which often is an ineffective approach.

Exchanging Task-Related Information In this part of the negotiation process, each group sets forth its position on the critical issues. These positions often will change later in the negotiations. At this point, the participants are trying to find out what the other party wants to attain and what it is willing to give up.

Persuasion This step of negotiations is considered by many to be the most important. No side wants to give away more than it has to, but each knows that without giving some concessions, it is unlikely to reach a final agreement. The success of the persuasion step often depends on: (1) how well the parties understand each other's position; (2) the ability of each to identify areas of similarity and differences; (3) the ability to create new options; (4) the willingness to work toward a solution that allows all parties to walk away feeling they have achieved their objectives.

Agreement The final phase of negotiations is the granting of concessions and hammering out a final agreement. Sometimes, this phase is carried out piecemeal, and concessions and agreements are made on issues one at a time. This is the way those from the United States like to negotiate. As each issue is resolved, it is removed from the bargaining table and interest focused on the next. Asians and

Russians, on the other hand, tend to negotiate a final agreement on everything, and few concessions are given until the end. Simply put, to negotiate effectively in the international arena, it is necessary to understand how cultural differences between the parties affect the process.

（Alberto F. De Toni, *International Operations Management：Lessons in Global Business*, Taylor & Francis Group, 2011.）

注释：
MNE: multinational enterprise 跨国公司

四、将下列短文翻译成英语 Translate the following passage into English

让5G技术惠及全球

在2019世界5G大会上，如何让5G技术惠及全世界，成为全球信息通信领域科研机构、知名企业代表、专家学者等热议的焦点。

……作为全球范围内广泛使用的新一代移动通信技术，5G的全时空、全现实、全连接技术将深刻改变人类的生产生活，驱动人类社会进入万物互联的时代。

通过与教育、医疗、工业制造、智慧城市等行业的深度融合，5G技术正促进数字经济与实体经济深度融合发展，创造出更多新应用、新业态、新价值。据测算，未来15年，5G将为全球GDP增长贡献超过3万亿美元，2035年，5G将拥有价值高达12万亿美元的市场规模，并为全球带来2200万个就业机会。

……2019年，中国政府发放了5G商用牌照，正式启动了5G商用服务。目前，全国已开通5G的基站达到11.3万个，预计到年底将达到13万个，5G套餐的签约用户已有87万户。

根据全球移动通信系统协会（Global System for Mobile Communications Association）的数据，到2025年，中国将成为全球最大的5G市场，拥有4.6亿5G用户。该协会表示，到那时，中国的5G用户数量预计将超过欧洲（2.05亿）和美国（1.87亿）的总和。

（https://www.sohu.com/a/355221606_123753，访问日期：2020年8月31日。）

第三章 金融翻译

金融（Finance）是以货币本身为经营标的，目的是通过货币融通使货币增值的经济活动，主要指与货币流通和银行信用相关的各种活动。国际金融（International Finance），就是国家和地区之间由于经济、政治、文化等联系而产生的货币资金的周转和运动。国际金融由国际收支、国际汇兑、国际结算、国际信用、国际投资和国际货币体系构成，它们之间相互影响，相互制约。譬如，国际收支必然产生国际汇兑和国际结算，国际汇兑中的货币汇率对国际收支又有重大影响，国际收支的许多重要项目同国际信用和国际投资直接相关等。

国际收支是一国和其他国家之间的商品、债务和收益的交易以及债权债务的变化。国际汇兑是指因办理国际支付而产生的外汇汇率、外汇市场、外汇管制等安排和活动的总和。国际结算是指国家间办理货币收支调拨，以结清不同国家中两个当事人之间的交易活动的行为。它主要包括支付方式、支付条件和结算方法等。国际结算方式主要有信用证、托收和汇付方式。根据进口业务和出口业务，汇款又分为国外汇入汇款和汇出国外汇款，信用证又分为出口信用证和进口信用证，托收又分为出口托收和进口代收。国际信用是国际货币资金的借贷行为。在现代金融业中，中央银行处于主导地位，它是货币发行银行、政府的银行和银行的银行，负责制定和执行国家的金融政策，调节货币流通和信用活动，一般也是金融活动的管理与监督机关。

第一节 金融英语语言特征

金融是现代经济的核心。随着经济全球化和区域经济一体化深入发展以及"一带一路"格局的形成，国际商务活动日益增多，全球许多国家融入世界经济。金融成为国际政治、经济与文化交往和实现国际贸易、引进外资、加强国际经济技术合作的纽带，国际金融在国际商务中占有重要地位。国际金融涉及货币、外汇、汇率、银行业等金融领域，金融英语就是在这些领域中所使用的英语。

一、金融英语的词汇特征

（一）普通词汇专业化

大量的金融业专业词汇是由普通词汇转化或引申而来，是在普通词汇含义的基础上形成的具有专业性的金融词汇，而与本义相去甚远。与通用英语相比，大量金融英语专业词汇还具有词义转换的特性，这就是在普通英语词汇含义基础上经过联想演化为行业特殊词汇。例如，prospect在日常英语中的意思是"预期，将来发生的事"，在金融英语中就引申为"潜在的客户"。weak本义是"脆弱的"，将这一形象特点引申为抽象含义，就出现了金融词汇weak currency，意思是"疲软货币"。trust本来的含义是"相信"，引申为金融含义是"信托"。launder一词的一般含义是"洗涤，洗熨"，在这一意义基础上就引申出money-laundering（洗黑钱）的意思。balance 原义为"平衡，天平"，后来引申出会计中的资产负债表（Balance Sheet）的意思。pool在日常英语中是"池塘"的意思，而在金融英语中是"共享基金，组合基金"的意思。

随着社会各方面的进步与发展，以及日益加速的全球化进程，仅仅运用旧的词汇已经不能满足金融领域中新鲜事物的表达，因此一些具有现代意义、借用自发达国家的金融词汇应运而生，如toxic assets（有毒资产），future transaction（期货交易），cyber-trade（网上交易），easy credit（放松信贷），virtual value（虚拟价值），mega-issue（大盘股）等。这些专业词汇也都是由普通词汇转化而来。（管妮，2015：73—74）

例1. Primary banking functions of the commercial banks include：1. Acceptance of deposits; 2. Advancing loans; 3. Creation of credit; 4. Clearing of cheques; 5. Financing foreign trade; 6. Remittance of funds.

译文：商业银行的主要职能包括：1. 吸收存款；2. 发放贷款；3. 创造信用；4. 支票结算；5. 外贸融资；6. 汇款。

该句中的"Acceptance of deposits"在金融专业里的意思是"吸收存款"而不是"接受存款"。"advance"在普通英语里意思是"发展，推进"，在金融英语里有"预付"的意思。"advance loans"在金融专业里的意思是"发放贷款"。"Clearing of cheques"在金融专业里的意思是"支票结算"，"clear"不是普通英语的"清理，清除，使干净"等意思。

（二）专业唯一性

金融专业术语的重要特征之一是专业唯一性，即词义的单一性，一个术语只表达一个概念或同一个概念只用同一个术语来表达。这主要表现在两个方面，一是每个专业术语所表示的都是一个特定的金融概念，与其他领域的词汇毫无关联，在使用时不能用其他任何词语替代。例如：remittance（汇款），bankable（银行可承兑的），defaced coin（表面磨损的货币），double-entry accounting（复式会计），standby credit（备用信用证），credit standing（资信状况），profit and loss account（损益表），等等。二是某一个专业术语即使在通用英语中属于多义词，在金融英语中也只保留一个"特有义项"。例如：principal在普通英语中作名词时意思是"首长，负责人"，作形容词时意思是"主要的"，但在金融领域，principal作名词意思是"本金"，作形容词时是"本金的"，而无其他词语可以替代。hedge在普通英语中是"树篱，篱笆"，在金融英语中是"套期保值"。（冯长甫、李文中，2011：46—47）

（三）常具有简约性

在全球化大背景下，金融业活动需要高效率，信息传递要快捷、丰富。这就要求金融词汇言简意赅，以有限的篇幅给出最充分的表达。

1. 大量使用缩略语。金融英语术语简约性的突出表现之一就是缩略语的大量运用。例如：SDR（Special Drawing Rights，特别提款权），EPS（Earnings Per Share，每股收益），IPO（Initial Public Offering，首次公开发行），TT（telegraphic transfer，电汇），B/L（bill of lading，提货单），D/B（documentary bill，跟单汇票），等等。

2. 大量使用合成词与派生词。金融英语词汇的显著特征之一就是合成词与派生词的大量涌现，这些合成词大都由连字符连接，例如：interest-rate（利率），T-bill（国库券），short-dated note（短期票据），over-the-counter（场外交易市场），asset-price bubble（资产价格泡沫），mortgage-backed security（抵押担保债券），pass-through security（过手债券），preferred stock（优先股），repurchase agreement（购回协议），domestically-produced goods（国内产品），US-controlled market（美国控制的市场），pre-export financing（出口前资金融通），等等。运用合成词的优点在于使句子结构简洁精悍，避免歧义。（张卉婷、江秀丽，2016：35—36）

3. 大量使用名词性结构。使用名词性结构，即名词连用，就是几个名词在不改变形式的前提下，按一定逻辑顺序排列在一起表示一个完整的新意思，要防止过多使用介词，造成语义不连贯或导致理解困难。例如：housing purchase contract（购房合同），而不用 contract of housing purchase；export credit insurance institutions（出口信保机构），而不用 insurance institutions of export

credit; consumer sale disclosure statement(消费者销售条件披露书),而不用 statement of disclosure of consumer sale;等等。

（四）词义的多样性与固定性

有些金融专业英语词汇来自普通英语,而这些词汇在金融领域中也根据语境的不同包含多层含义,不过在具体语境中的含义又是保持不变的。例如:acquire在普通英语中的含义是"获取",而在金融专业英语中,含义是"收购";box的一般含义是"盒子",而在金融英语中的意思是"保险箱"。

current的普通含义为"当前的;流通的;涌流;趋势",而在金融英语中则根据语境的不同有多重含义,如:current assets（流动资产）,current debt（短期债务）,current audit（日常审计）。

例2. These banks finance mostly for the foreign trade of a country. Their main function is to discount, accept and collect foreign bills of exchange.

译文:这类银行的主要职能是为一个国家的对外贸易提供资金。它们的主要功能是贴现、承兑和托收外国汇票。

"accept"在普通英语中意思是"接受",在国际金融中除了表示商业银行"吸收"存款之外,还有"承兑"之意;collect的意思不是"收集",而是"托收"。

（五）包含专有名词的词语多

专有名词是指人名、地名、机构团体名和其他具有特殊含义的名词或名词词组。在金融英语中,有许多专有名词。例如:Dow Jones Index（道·琼斯指数）,American Exchange（美国证券交易所）,Lloyds Bank（劳埃德银行）,Sherman Antitrust Act（谢尔曼反托拉斯法）,European Monetary System（欧洲货币体系）,International Monetary Fund（国际货币基金组织）等。

二、金融英语句子的语言特征

金融英语句子的主要特征是结构严整,多长句。所谓英语长句,一般是指20个词左右的句子。有些句子除了主、谓、宾或主、系、表以及"there be"的结构主干外,还带有各种修饰成分（如从句、短语或独立主格等）,其定语或状语可以一环套一环,修饰中另有修饰或限定,形成了峰回路转、错综复杂的长句结构。（宋天锡,2009:338）从语言形态变化来看,英语重形合,句子结构完整,以形寓意,严密规范,属于主语+谓语结构框架的语法性语言。由于严格受到语法形式的制约,句子中许多相关成分常通过各种表示关系的连接手段直接或间接地粘连在主谓结构的周围,这就使英语句子显得叠床架屋、繁复冗长,但语法将这一繁复的结构联系在一起,使整个句子结构严整,不至流散。(冯长甫、孙小兰,2011: 61—62)

例3. Within 30 days after the signing and coming into effect of this contract, the buyer shall proceed to pay the price for the goods to the seller by opening an irrevocable L/C for the full amount of US $30,000 in favor of the seller through a bank at an import port。

译文:买方须于本合同签字并生效后三十天内,通过进口银行开立以卖方为受益人的不可撤销的信用证,支付全部货款30000美元。

这一句虽然是简单句,但句子较长,整个句子的重心不是句子的动作,而是发生动作的时间;同时还含有一个较为复杂的方式状语"by opening an irrevocable L/C…",其中三个介词短语作定语修饰"an irrevocable L/C"。

例4. Foreign investor's renminbi income in a legally terminated foreign invested enterprise which has completed liquidation procedures and fulfilled tax obligations in accordance with the relevant regulations of the government may be converted into foreign currency through financial institutions duly authorized for foreign exchange sale and purchase operations and remitted out of the People's Republic of China.

译文:依法终止的外商投资企业,按照国家有关规定进行清算、纳税后,属于外方投资者所有的人民币,可以向有权经营结汇、售汇业务的金融机构购汇汇出中华人民共和国。

该句是主从结构,由"which"引导的定语从句修饰"enterprise",另有and引导的并列结构,含有多个介词短语以及过去分词短语"duly authorized for"引导的句子做后置定语。全句重重叠叠,十分复杂,需要仔细分析才能理解和翻译。

第二节　金融英语翻译策略

金融英语文体及翻译主要应用于正式的金融商务场合,所以,用语和格式的规范是其首要特征,往往采用特定的术语体系和表达方式——国际通用的语言,避免口语化,通过规范的用语保证准确地传达金融信息。金融行业文本翻译最大的特点就是具备高度的专业性和保密性。(廖国强,2014: 222)

一、金融英语词汇的翻译

金融文体翻译的专业性主要体现在词汇上。金融英语词汇涉及特定的文体和专业术语。金融英语涉及金融行业的各个领域,专业术语特别多。要做好金融词汇翻译的工作,顺利传达源语信息,就要掌握金融文体和用语的特点,同时还需要相关的行业背景知识,对行业内的表达方式比较精通,避免误解误译,规范地道地使用术语。

（一）准确选择词语使意义专业化

金融英语词汇中有大量词汇是一词多义的,常常借用日常词汇,有时利用特殊事件引出金融词汇,专业术语非常多。不了解金融翻译与普通翻译的区别,就很难做到行业表达的专业性。而某些英语词汇只通过网络搜索或查阅传统词典是不够的。翻译时要加强语境理解,谨慎选择对应词语。对于词义单一固定的词语,应通过查证有关资料,确认译名的准确性、统一性,不得随意另起译名,也不得随意添加或减少字词。比如：listed company意思是上市公司,list在通用英语里释义为"清单；计入名单"等,而在金融英语里是"上市"的意思；stand-by credit（备用信用证）,此处的stand-by不能用spare替代,同理,credit在金融专业中意思是"资信"而不是"诚信",spare是"备用"而不是"零用"。

例5. In general, a nation's balance of payments is affected by the appreciation or depreciation of its currency in the foreign exchange market.

译文：通常,外汇市场上一个国家的货币升值或贬值会影响其国际收支。

此例中,appreciation在普通英语中是"鉴赏,欣赏"的意思,在金融英语中却是"升值"之意。depreciation在金融词汇中,有"折旧""贬值"两个义项,此处对应的是"贬值"。

例6. For example, a central bank may regulate margin lending, whereby individuals or companies may borrow against pledged securities.

译文：比如,中央银行可以对边际借贷进行监管,从而使个人或者企业进行抵押借贷。

这里的margin lending（边际贷款）是指借贷投资,用自己的储蓄和借贷基金来投资,获取的回报会更多。pledged securities（抵押证券）指证券发行人以其财产抵押而发行的保证按期支付本息的证券。这两个术语意义都很固定,必须直译。

（二）根据不同语境选择不同的对应词语

有些词汇并非金融语体所独有,它们也可以出现在其他语体中,但在金融语体中具有确切的含义。由于金融英语词汇具有一词多义性,因而,对词汇的理解一定要结合上下文,从语境中理解词义,正确辨别词义的内涵。

例7. If the forward exchange rate is higher than the spot exchange rate, a currency is said to be at a premium.

译文:当一种货币的远期汇率大于即期汇率时,该货币升水。

例句中的premium在保险业中是"保险费"的意思,但是在上述语境里,它们具有金融专业术语的特殊意义,即"升水"。

例8. This means that IDA charges little or no interest and repayments are stretched over 25 to 40 years , including 5 to 10-year grace period.

译文:这意味着IDA只收取很低的利息或不收利息,还款期限也延长至25年到40年,包括5年到10年的宽限期。

grace period意思是"宽限期",指在贷款协议中商定的,在还款期的头若干年,由于工程效益尚未充分发挥,借方不还本金,只付利息的年数。grace在这里不是"优雅"的意思。

IDA(The International Development Association 国际开发协会)是世界银行的附属机构。

(三)比喻辞格要意译

金融英语大量使用比喻修辞格,比如明喻和暗喻等。有些普通词汇在金融英语中具有比喻意义。除了尽可能保持原文的形象比喻和修辞效果外,还需要忠实地表达原文比喻性词语的意义。在很多情况下,直译会不专业、不通顺,所以在这种情况下,需要采取意译的方法,同时还需要改变比喻词汇的词性和调整句子结构。

例9. So also, a commercial bank deals in credit, i.e., it creates credit by making advances out of the funds received as deposits to needy people. It thus, functions as a mobiliser of saving in the economy.

译文:因此,商业银行是从事货币交易的金融机构。同样,商业银行也涉及信贷,也就是将吸收到的存款预支给有需要的人,从而创造信贷。因此,它在经济中起着动员储蓄的作用。

mobiliser本义是"移动装置,移动器",字面意思是"动员者",过于抽象,翻译时要转译,并改变词性,译成"它……起着动员储蓄的作用"。

例10. A bank is, therefore like a reservoir into which flow the savings, the idle surplus money of households and from which loans are given on interest to businessmen and others who need them.

译文：商业银行就像一个蓄水池，把储蓄即家庭剩余的闲钱吸收进来，再贷给商人和其他需要钱进行投资或生产的人，并收取利息。

like a reservoir是明喻，reservoir既表示"水库"，也可以表示"水池"。这里译为"水池"更形象、更贴切。该句定语从句into which flow the savings, the idle surplus money of households 是倒装结构，因主语较长，谓语flow是不及物动词，被置于主语之前，以避免头重脚轻。翻译时，把作定语从句谓语的flow（流动，流淌）的隐喻意义转译为"吸收"。

二、金融英语短语结构的翻译

金融文本中，会大量使用各种类型的短语结构，如并列短语、名词短语、主谓结构短语。

（一）并列短语的翻译

并列短语的用法在金融文本中相当普遍，翻译时可以采用换序法，对源语顺序进行一些变更。这里的换序是指在小范围内对原文顺序进行小规模调整，一般为两个对象之间的换序。金融英语的并列介词短语、并列定语和并列名词短语的翻译，就可以采用这种方法。

1.介词短语连用。介词短语连用主要是指两个介词短语的连用，这些介词短语主要表示时间、地点、方式、动作的施动者或对象等含义。翻译时经常运用换序法，以确保译文达意、准确和通顺，使译文尽可能符合金融业务操作的实际需要。

例11. A member with a balance of payments deficit can borrow foreign currency from the IMF in exchange for its own currency.

译文：国际货币基金组织中有逆差的成员可以用本币从该组织购借外币。

在此例中，将borrow foreign currency from the IMF in exchange for its own currency翻译成"用本币从该组织购借外币"，是通过将介词短语from the IMF [从该组织（国际货币基金组织）]与in exchange for its own currency（用本币）换序的方法而得到的恰当译文。

2.并列定语连用。修饰性并列定语包括名词、形容词、分词、不定式短语以及介词短语等，在遵循语言规律的基础上运用两个或多个定语修饰同一名词，使语言形式灵活多变。

对于两个并列连用的修饰定语，可以通过前后顺序的变换，使译文更准确、

更灵活地呈现出国际贸易金融市场的复杂意义。(徐珺, 2018: 327)

例12. If reserves are zero and there is an overall deficit, the country has no choice but let the exchange rate fall, or restrict capital flows and risk a black market in foreign exchange.

译文:如果外汇储备已经用尽且依然存在逆差,就不得不选择让本币贬值或者限制资本流动,但同时会面对出现外汇黑市的风险。

a black market in foreign exchange译为"外汇黑市",而不是"黑外汇市场"或"黑市在外汇中"。

（二）名动搭配短语的翻译

名词与动词互相搭配的短语主要包括逻辑主谓结构和逻辑动宾结构两大类。一般情况下,主谓结构和动宾结构的翻译不必变更顺序,但在国际贸易金融文本中,对于逻辑主谓结构和逻辑动宾结构的翻译,变更顺序是一种重要的译法。

例13. The exchanges and transfers also include the movement of interest and dividends, gifts, and short-term and long-term investment.

译文:这些交易和转移也包括利息与股息的调拨、赠金和长、短期投资。

在此例中, the movement of interest and dividends是一个含有逻辑主谓结构的短语。将逻辑主语interest and dividends提到逻辑谓语movement之前,将movement of interest and dividends翻译成"利息与股息的调拨"。

例14. In the United States an independent federal agency, the Overseas Private Investment Corporation, also extends loans and loan guaranties to help finance their projects.

译文:美国的一个独立联邦机构——海外私人投资公司——也发放贷款或担保贷款。

此例中,将原文的finance their projects译成"项目融资",将逻辑宾语提到逻辑谓语前面,但意义保持不变,译文却更符合汉语的表达习惯。(以上译例选自徐珺主编的《国际贸易翻译实务》)

三、金融英语句子的翻译

在句法方面,金融文本为了在表达上明确、严谨、完整,常常使用长句,且句子结构比较复杂。英语是重形合的语言,常常借助语言形式手段实现词语或句子的连接。汉语是重意合的语言,一般不借助语言形式手段,而借助词语或句子所含的意义的逻辑联系来实现他们之间的连接。英语长句译成汉语时,除了意思准确之外，还必须地道通顺，逻辑清晰。因此，对长句的翻译不能拘泥于原句的形式，有时可按照原来句子的顺序翻译，有时需要调整顺序，将原句拆开翻译，或者综合运用各种方法翻译，最后译出意思准确、符合汉语逻辑即意合的汉语句子。此外，金融文本中为了突出受动者和陈述的客观性，常常使用被动语态。

（一）调整句子顺序

一般来说，英语句子多重心前置，汉语句子多重心后置。句中如果有叙事和表态部分，英语常常是表态部分（判断、结论等）在前，叙事部分（事实、描写等）在后，即先总提后分述，或先讲结果后追叙过去，而汉语的顺序往往相反。因此，翻译包含许多修饰成分或从句的英语长句时，应将汉语译文调整为叙事在前，表态在后，即句子重心由前置调整为后置。

例15. The documentary credit offers a unique and universally-used method of achieving a commercially acceptable compromise by providing for payment to be made against documents that represent the goods and make possible the transfer of rights to those goods.

译文：跟单信用证提供了一种独特的、全世界都采用的方法，即凭代表货物的单据付款，从而使货权的转移成为可能。这是一种商业上可以接受的折中方式。

此例中，method of achieving a commercially acceptable compromise 译为"这是一种商业上可以接受的折中方式"，置于全句的句尾。

（二）采用拆句或合句法

拆句法也叫拆译法，就是将英语长句中的各种复杂的成分拆开，翻译成汉语的短句和简单句。有些句子虽在形式上是一个句子，但句子许多成分的意义是独立的，将它们断开分成短句是完全可以的。断开的位置一般可选在有联系性词语处，这些词语通常由关系代词、关系副词、独立副词、非谓语动词等担任。合句法就是将多个短句或分散的句子合并起来，形成一个长句，一般用于汉译英翻译。由于英语重形合、汉语重意合的特点，因此，往往要将两个或多个汉语句子合并成英语的复合句结构。

例16. 国际贸易最普遍采用的货款支付方式是信用证（缩写为L/C），这种支付方式对买卖双方来说，既安全又可靠。

译文：The most generally used method of payment in financing international trade is the Letter of Credit (abbreviated to L/C), which is reliable and safe for both sellers and buyer.

该句采用合译方法。因前后两句都有"支付方法"一词，可以用which 引导的非限制性定语从句将两句合并，以符合英语的表达习惯。

（三）转换句型结构

英汉两种语言句子长短不同，一般英语长于汉语，而且句型也不一样。为了既准确又忠实于原文，可改变句型结构。

例17. It has already been stated that a cheque payable to order must be endorsed by the payee or endorsee before it can be transferred to another person.

译文：已经说过，记名支票必须经付款人或背书人背书后才能转让给第三者。

该例句原文句子结构是形式主语+谓语（被动语态）+"that"从句[从句形式是主谓结构+（被动）谓语+时间状语从句]，译文的结构是主句（省略了形式主语）+主谓结构+时间状语+谓语+宾语。

（四）转换语态

英语中的被动语态比较常见，而汉语不经常使用被动语态。被动语态能加强陈述的客观性，因此，作为专门用途英语，金融英语中被动句的使用很多，汉译时多转译成主动语态。（汪玉兰，2005：75—76）

例18. Transferable credit can be transferred once only.

译文：可转让的信用证只限转让一次。

本句译文如果从句型上看，因未指明行为的主体，属于主动语态；但从它的含义上看却是被动的，因为受益人是行为主体。本句实际意思是：可转让信用证只能被受益人转让一次。但在金融文体中，翻译成汉语时使用被动语态就显得拖沓、拗口、不简洁。

例19. The banks are commercial enterprises and like many other businesses are organized as companies which are owned by shareholders.

译文：银行是商业企业，它的组织结构和其他企业一样，是由股东共同拥有的公司型组织。

该例句中的businesses are organized并没有译成被动语态"被组织"，而是译成"由"字结构，符合汉语的表达习惯。

在进行国际金融翻译时，译者需要正确理解国际金融术语，准确把握翻译所涉及的国家或地区的相关法规条例，同时还需要注意几个方面：第一，金融相关资料中的数字务必准确；第二，国际金融翻译以直译为主；第三，严格把握好金融语境。（徐珺，2018：340）

第三节 课内翻译任务

一、英译汉 English-Chinese Translation

Types of Banks

Broadly speaking, banks can be classified into commercial banks and central bank. Commercial banks are those which provide banking services for profit. The central bank has the function of controlling commercial banks and various other economic activities. There are many types of commercial banks such as deposit banks, industrial banks, savings banks, agricultural banks, exchange banks, and miscellaneous banks.

1. Deposit Banks: The most important type of deposit banks is the commercial banks. They have connection with the commercial class of people. These banks accept deposits from the public and lend them to needy parties. Since their deposits are for short period only, these banks extend loans only for a short period. Ordinarily these banks lend money for a period between 3 to 6 months. They do not like to lend money for long periods or to invest their funds in any way in long term securities.

2. Industrial Banks: Industries require a huge capital for a long period to buy machinery and equipment. Industrial banks help such industrialists. They provide long term loans to industries. Besides, they buy shares and debentures of companies, and enable them to have fixed capital. Sometimes, they even underwrite the debentures and shares of big industrial concerns.

3. Savings Banks: These banks were specially established to encourage thrift among small savers and therefore, they were willing to accept small sums as deposits. They encourage savings of the poor and middle class people.

4. Agricultural Banks: Agriculture has its own problems and hence there are separate banks to finance it. These banks are organized on co-operative lines and therefore do not work on the principle of maximum profit for the shareholders. These banks meet the credit requirements of the farmers through term loans, viz., short, medium and long term loans. There are two types of agricultural banks, (a) Agricultural Co-operative Banks, and (b) Land Mortgage Banks. Co-operative

Banks are mainly for short periods. For long periods there are Land Mortgage Banks. Both these types of banks are performing useful functions in India.

5. Exchange Banks: These banks finance mostly for the foreign trade of a country. Their main function is to discount, accept and collect foreign bills of exchange. They buy and sell foreign currency and thus help businessmen in their transactions. They also carry on the ordinary banking business. The industrial and commercial development of a country depends these days, largely upon the efficiency of these institutions.

6. Miscellaneous Banks: There are certain kinds of banks which have arisen in due course to meet the specialized needs of the people. In England and America, there are investment banks whose object is to control the distribution of capital into several uses. American Trade Unions have got labour banks, where the savings of the labourers are pooled together. In London, there are the London Discount House whose business is "to go about the city seeking for bills to discount." There are numerous types of different banks in the world, carrying on one or the other banking business.

(N. T. Somashekar, *Banking*, New Age International Ltd., 2000.)

重点解析 Notes and Comments

1. deposit bank 英国的存款银行，也称为开户行或普通银行。

2. miscellaneous banks 其他各类银行。

miscellaneous意思是"各种各样的；多方面的"，miscellaneous banks此处应译为"其他各类银行"。

3. these banks extend loans only for a short period 所以它们的贷款期限也很短。

extend loans译为"提供贷款"，不能译为"扩大或延伸贷款"。该句子不能按照表层结构翻译为"这些银行只为短期提供贷款"，而应改变句子结构，同时转换词性，将作介词宾语的"period"转换为主语，原来作谓语的extend loans转换为名词"贷款"作定语修饰"期限"。

4. they even underwrite the debentures 他们甚至承销大型工业企业的债券和股票。

underwrite的词典定义是"给……保险；承诺支付；签在……下"，此处译为

"承销"或"购买"。

5. Industrial Banks 实业银行，也可译为工业银行。

中国工商银行就是"Industrial and Commercial Bank of China"。

6. These banks were specially established to encourage thrift among small savers 这些银行是专门为鼓励小储户储蓄而设立的。

thrift原义为"节俭，节约"，含有把钱省下来存在银行之意，此处应译为"储蓄"。

7. These banks are organized on co-operative lines and therefore do not work on the principle of maximum profit for the shareholders 这些银行是按照合作的方式组织起来的，因此并不以股东利益最大化为原则。

on co-operative lines译为"按照合作的方式"，lines不宜译为"路线"等义。

8. Their main function is to discount, accept and collect foreign bills of exchange 它们的主要功能是贴现、承兑和托收外汇汇票。

accept在国际金融专业中含义不是"接受"，而是"承兑"，collect不是"收集"而是"托收"。

conversion在国际金融中意思是货币的"兑换"，而不是"转换"。

9. There are certain kinds of banks which have arisen in due course to meet the specialized needs of the people 为满足人们的特殊需要，某些类型的银行应运而生。

in due course如译为"在适当的时候"则不够通顺，译文中，把该介词短语转换成四字词组作该短句的谓语。

10. the savings of the laborers are pooled together 劳工银行把工人的储蓄集中起来。

此句不宜译为"工人的储蓄被集中起来"。英语的被动语态在译成汉语时，往往要转换成主动语态，才符合汉语的表达习惯。pool作动词用时意为"积水成池"，此处取其基本意"集中起来"。

11. the London Discount House 伦敦贴现公司，也称为Discount Company。

二、汉译英 Chinese-English Translation

国际货币基金组织

国际货币基金组织（IMF）简称"基金组织"，是由189个国家组成的国际组织，致力于促进全球货币合作，确保金融稳定，促进国际贸易、高就业和经济可持续增长，减少世界各国的贫困。国际货币基金组织成立于1945年，由189个国家共同管理，并对这些国家负责。

国际货币基金组织是根据1944年7月在美国新罕布什尔州布雷顿森林召开的一次联合国会议上的决定成立的。参加此次会议的44个国家试图建立一个经济合作框架，避免再次出现加剧了20世纪30年代大萧条的竞争性货币贬值。因此，与会国家创建了国际货币基金组织，以促进国际货币合作。从那时起，国际货币基金组织在维护全球经济稳定和确保广泛共享繁荣方面发挥了至关重要的作用。

国际货币基金组织的主要目的是确保国际货币体系的稳定。国际货币体系是指使各国（及其公民）能够相互进行交易的汇率和国际支付体系。2012年，国际货币基金组织的使命又增添了新的内容，将影响全球稳定的所有宏观经济和金融领域的问题纳入其中。

国际货币基金组织的任务

国际货币基金组织的根本任务是确保国际货币体系的稳定。这一任务体现在三个方面：跟踪全球经济和成员经济，向国际收支出现困难的成员提供贷款，并给予成员实际的帮助。

国际货币基金组织监督国际货币体系的运行，并监督其189个成员的经济和金融政策。作为这一过程的一部分，国际货币基金组织对可能存在的危及稳定的风险提出警告，并就必要的政策调整提出建议。

贷款

国际货币基金组织向国际收支出现实际或潜在问题的成员提供贷款，帮助它们重建国际储备，稳定货币，继续支付进口款项，恢复经济强劲增长的条件，同时纠正潜在的问题。

能力开发

国际货币基金组织与世界各国政府合作，使它们的经济政策和机构现代化，为各国人民提供培训。这有助于各国加强经济发展，促进增长，创造就业。

组织和财政

国际货币基金组织有一个管理团队和17个部门来执行其有关国家、政策、分析和技术方面的工作。一个部门负责管理国际货币基金组织的资源。

管理

基金组织对成员政府负责。其组织结构的最高层次是理事会，由每个成员的一位理事和一位候补理事组成，通常由中央银行行长或财政部部长担任。

工作人员

国际货币基金组织的雇员来自世界各地,他们对国际货币基金组织负责,而不是对他们所在国家的政府负责。国际货币基金组织工作人员的工作主要按地区、功能、信息和支持等方面的职责进行安排。

(该文根据国际货币基金组织官方网站的英文原文"The IMF at a Glance"删减翻译而成,网址:https://www.imf.org/en/About,访问日期:2020年3月10日。)

重点解析 Notes and Comments

1. 国际货币基金组织:The International Monetary Fund(IMF)。

2. 致力于促进全球货币合作 working to foster global monetary cooperation

原句"致力于"之后有五个并列的动宾结构,英语用working to分词短语表伴随状态,后接to foster, secure, facilitate, promote, and reduce连续五个动词构成的不定式短语,表目的。英文中"促进"一词分别用了foster, facilitate和promote三个不同的动词。

3. 国际货币基金组织是根据1944年7月在美国新罕布什尔州布雷顿森林召开的一次联合国会议上的决定成立的。The IMF was conceived at a UN conference in Bretton Woods, New Hampshire, United States, in July 1944.

"成立"译为was conceived。conceived意为"构思,设想成立"。

布雷顿森林(Bretton Woods)位于美国的新罕布什尔州。1944年7月,美、苏、中、法等44个国家的代表在联合国货币金融会议上签订了《国际货币基金组织协定》,决定成立国际货币基金组织,确立了布雷顿森林体系。

4. 大萧条(Great Depression),是指1929年至1933年之间发源于美国,后来波及整个资本主义世界的经济危机。

5. 2012年,国际货币基金组织的使命又增添了新的内容,将影响全球稳定的所有宏观经济和金融领域的问题纳入其中。The Fund's mandate was updated in 2012 to include all macroeconomic and financial sector issues that bear on global stability.

updated表示"更新"之意,后一句中"将……纳入其中"即包含了纳入、增添新的内容之意。

6. 国际货币基金组织对可能存在的危及稳定的风险提出警告,并就必要的政策调整提出建议。IMF highlights possible risks to stability and advises on needed policy adjustments.

原句是个并列句，主语是"国际货币基金组织"，后接两个动宾结构"对……提出警告""就……提出建议"。译文将两个句子合并成一个并列复合句，以highlights作谓语，后接宾语risks和advises。highlight表示"使引起注意，强调"（to attract attention to or emphasize something important）。

7. 向国际收支出现困难的成员提供贷款 lending to members with balance of payments difficulties

该短句中"成员"前的定语后置，用介词短语with连接。国际收支出现困难即国际收支平衡方面（balance of payments）出现困难。

8. 国际货币基金组织向国际收支出现实际或潜在问题的成员提供贷款。The IMF provides loans to members experiencing actual or potential balance of payments problems.

原句的宾语"成员"前定语较长，译文将定语后置，用experiencing连接后置定语。

9. 国际货币基金组织与世界各国政府合作，使它们的经济政策和机构现代化，为各国人民提供培训。The IMF works with governments around the world to modernize their economic policies and institutions, and train their people.

原句三个分句在译文中合并成一个并列结构，"使它们的经济政策和机构现代化"转换成不定式表目的。这一转换，一方面使句子结构简化，另一方面也体现了汉语重意合、英语重形合的特点。

第四节 课后翻译训练

一、将下列句子翻译成汉语 Translate the following sentences into Chinese

1. During the 1930s, the United States raised trade barriers, refused to act as an international lender of last resort, and declined calls to cancel war debts, all of which further aggravated economic hardship for other countries.

2. 2.China will further bring down its overall tariff level, strive to remove non-tariff trade barriers, and slash institutional costs in imports.

3. It will be no exaggeration to say that a modern central bank is the central arch to the monetary and fiscal framework in almost all the countries developed or developing in the world.

4. This approach reduces credit rating（信用评级） agencies' confidence in

the country as an issuer, and as a result both reduces the attractiveness of the country to lenders and increases the cost of the foreign currency borrowings.

5. The term "World Bank" generally refers to just the IBRD and IDA, whereas the term World Bank Group or WBG is used to refer to all the five institutions collectively, namely, the International Bank for Reconstruction and Development, the International Development Association, the International Finance Corporation, the Multilateral Investment Guarantee Agency and the International Centre for Settlement of Investment Disputes.

6. Any surplus of supply of foreign exchange over demand, whether from a current account or capital account surplus, would tend to push the price of the domestic currency up relative to foreign currencies.

7. In floating exchange rate countries the net change in reserves is zero and the two accounts are brought into balance by changes in the exchange rate.

8. The largest US bank holding companies, which went through the Supervisory Capital Assessment Program exercise, have more and better quality capital, having raised more than $100 billion of common equity over the past year in the capital markets and generated nearly as much common equity via preferred stock conversions and from gains on asset sales.

9. The central bank liaises with and advises the Government on monetary policy and ensures that the necessary steps are taken to carry it through.

10. Holding a company's stock means that you are one of the many owners (shareholders) of a company and, as such, you have a claim (albeit usually very small) to everything the company owns.

二、将下列句子翻译成英语 Translate the following sentences into English

1. 这些银行通过定期贷款，即短期、中期和长期贷款来满足农民的信贷需求。

2. 外汇银行主要为一个国家的对外贸易提供资金。它们的主要功能是贴现、承兑和托收外国汇票。

3. 国际货币基金组织的主要目的是确保国际货币体系的稳定。国际货币体系是指使各国（及其公民）能够相互进行交易的汇率和国际支付体系。

4. 全球金融危机酝酿了一段时间，真正显示其影响是从2007年中期到2008

年开始的。

5. 单据必须完整，做到单单相符，单证相符，符合UCP的条款。

6. 衍生工具就是一种金融工具，其价值取决于基础工具的价格，比如货币、商品或有价证券。

7. 保兑信用证即经过另一家银行保兑的信用证，在受益人提交的单据符合信用证条款时，保兑行有独立和第一性的付款责任。

8. 中国将在货物贸易、服务贸易等领域进一步开放市场，逐步推进商业、外贸、金融、保险、证券、电信、旅游和中介服务等方面的对外开放。

9. 我方要求在签署技术转让协议时，贵方要向我方提供支付所有技术转让费用的银行担保。

10. 尽管银行业的债务股本比（debt/equity ratios）都在100%以上，发行债券只是大多数银行在股本较低的情况下采取的措施。

注释：

debt/equity ratios 债务股本比，也称为负债股权比率、负债对所有权益的比率，是衡量公司财务杠杆的指标，即显示公司建立资产的资金来源中股本与债务的比例。

三、将下列短文翻译成汉语 Translate the following passage into Chinese

Documents vs. Goods/Services/Performance

Goods should (not) be dispatched directly to the address of a bank or consigned to or to the order of a bank without prior agreement on the part of that bank.

Nevertheless, in the event that goods are dispatched directly to the address of a bank or consigned to or to the order of a bank for release to a drawee against payment or acceptance or upon other terms and conditions without prior agreement on the part of that bank, such bank shall have no obligation to take delivery of the goods, which remain at the risk and responsibility of the party dispatching the goods.

Banks have no obligation to take any action in respect of the goods to which a documentary collection relates, including storage and insurance of the goods even when specific instructions are given to do so. Banks will only take such action if, when, and to the extent that they agree to do so in each case. Notwithstanding the provision of Sub-ARTICLE 1 this rule applies even in the absence of any specific advice to this effect by the collecting bank.

Nevertheless, in the case that banks take action for the protection of the goods, whether instructed or not, they assume no liability or responsibility with regard to the fate and/or conditions of the goods and/or for any acts and/or omissions on the part of any third parties entrusted with the custody and/or protection of the goods. However, the collection bank must advise without delay the bank from which the collection instruction was received of any such action taken.

Any charges and/or expenses incurred by banks in connection with any action taken to protect the goods will be for the account of the party from whom they received the collection.

Notwithstanding the provisions of Sub-ARTICLE 10 where the goods are consigned to or to the order of the collecting bank and the drawee has honored the collection by payment, acceptance or other terms and conditions and the collecting bank arranges for the release of the goods, remitting bank shall be deemed to have authorized the collecting bank to do so.

Where a collecting bank on the instructions of the remitting bank or in terms of Sub-ARTICLE 10 (1) above arranges for the release of the goods, the remitting bank shall indemnify such collecting bank for all damages and expenses incurred.

四、将下列短文翻译成英语 Translate the following passage into English

国际业务

近年来，国际金融市场发展迅猛，为各国商业银行扩展国际业务提供了广阔的空间和巨大的商机。我国商业银行也开始利用这一契机扩大国际业务的规模和范围，到国外设立分支机构，提高金融服务的水平和质量，加入跨国银行的行列。

在银行的国际业务中，除了国际结算外，外汇资金业务所占的份额也比较大。银行外汇资金业务的对象主要是银行同业以及有外汇兑换需求的贸易企业、跨国公司、政府及个人。银行外汇资金交易可以分为：外汇买卖业务（个人/对公外汇买卖、即/远期结售汇、人民币外汇掉期等）、代客理财（个人、企业）、代客风险管理业务（期权等）。其中，规模最大的是即期结售汇业务。

跨国银行的快速发展使国际结算业务变得快捷、方便，效率也得到了较大提高。目前，国际结算的方式主要有三种基本形式：汇款、托收、信用证。常用的结算工具包括：汇票、本票、支票（包括旅行支票等）。

国际贸易融资业务是指银行对进出口商提供的与进出口相关的短期融资（不包括短期外汇贷款）或信用便利，主要包括打包放款（package loan, packing finance）、出口押汇/贴现（bill purchase/discount）、福费廷（forfaiting）、国际保理（international factoring）等。

（摘自徐珺，2018：135）

第四章 商务广告翻译

广告（Advertising）语言作为语言中的特殊语体，传达着丰富、生动并含有感情色彩的文化信息。广告英语，作为一种应用语言，已经从普通语言发展成规范的专业语言，形成了一种特殊的文体。成功的广告翻译在目标语的语境中起着同样的作用，即以地道的翻译语言促使跨文化的消费者认可异域产品或服务，以实现即刻或未来的消费行为。要做好广告翻译，译者首先应当熟悉并掌握广告的专业知识和一定的广告心理学知识，以及英语、汉语广告的语言特点，即语体特征、修辞特征、句型特征等。除此之外，还需要掌握足够的跨文化背景知识，熟悉广告语言所反映出的社会文化差异性。（吕和发、蒋璐、王同军等，2011：37）在广告语言翻译中，译者切忌拘泥于原文的字、词、句等表层结构，而应仔细体会原文的主要功能，发挥译者的想象力和创造力，力求在功能上与原文对等，从而使英语广告的汉语翻译本土化，使汉语广告的英语翻译国际化，达到广告的宣传效果，最终对中国经济文化的进一步发展起到促进作用。

第一节 广告的分类与构成

Advertising一词源于拉丁文advertere，含有"注意"和"诱导"的意思，意为引起公众对某事物的注意，广而告之，传之天下，其目的是促进某种观念和信息的传递和交流，向公众推介某种商品或者服务。广告是将各种精练的信息，采用艺术手法，通过各种媒介传播给大众，以加强或改变人们的观念，最终导致人们采取购买等行动的活动。广告是一种多维的宣传方式，可以通过一定的媒体如电视、报纸杂志、条板张贴、网络等形式向公众提供警示、商品推介等。

一则成功的商务广告应当能够实现以下几种基本功能：传播信息功能、劝说功能、美感功能、刺激消费功能，或者可理解为ACCA要求，即认知（Awareness）、理解（Comprehension）、说服（Conviction）、行动（Action）。其中最主要的是劝说功能,它起到最大的诱导说服作用,来影响更大的消费群体,其他功能起辅助作用。

一、广告的分类

按照不同的目的与要求,广告可以按照不同的区分标准进行分类。从其宣传目的来看,可以分为公共形象广告(Institutional Advertisement)和商业广告(Commercial Advertisement)两类。公共形象广告的目的是树立、维护、保护公司或机构的形象,或宣传某种理念。(廖国强,2014:10)广告按其内容可以分为四大类,即商品广告(Product Advertisement)、服务广告(Service Advertisement)、企业形象广告(Corporation Advertisement)和公益广告(Public-Welfare Advertisement)。

传统上将广告定义为"赞助商使用大众媒体来说服受众的付费信息"Thorson & Rodgers, 2012)。随着互联网(如Facebook, Twitter, Instagram,或抖音、快手、头条等社交媒体)和新设备[如移动智能手机(mobile smartphone)、上网本(netbook)、智能手表(smartwatche)]的发展,数字通信系统成为可能,对内容媒体作为广告发布渠道的依赖直线下降,取而代之的是广告商自己控制的自媒体(owned media),比如他们的社交媒体页面(social media page)、网站(website)、博客(blog)和应用程序(app),还有抖音、快手等平台。为此,广告商不得不依靠发展自己的受众来取代被内容媒体所吸引的受众。这些变化的最终结果是,广告不再需要"付费"媒体。此外,"自创"(earned media)媒体也变得很重要。(Powell et al., 2009)

按广告的目的分类,可分为以营利为目的的"商业广告"和不以营利为目的的"非营利广告"(或"公关广告")。

二、广告文案的构成

不同的广告媒体,其构成要素(elements)也不尽相同。一般来说,一则完整的书面广告(杂志、报纸上的广告)由五部分组成:插图、标题、正文、口号和标识,其中,广告的标题和口号传达了核心信息。中英文广告都是把最精彩的语言放在标题或是口号中,因而标题和口号的地位最为重要,它们往往决定着整个广告的成败。(吕和发、任林静,2011:38)

大部分广告都有标题,广告的标题如同新闻标题一样,是广告主题思想的浓缩,其主要作用是引起读者的注意,点出广告的主题,获得立刻打动消费者的效果。广告正文也叫广告主体（Body），是承载和传达广告信息主题的语言文字，占据主体地位，主要介绍产品的特点、性能或者服务特色。广告正文可分为信息型（factual copy）、煽情型（emotional）、叙事型（narrative）、对话／独白型（dialogue/monologue copy）。（廖国强，2014：13—14）

第二节　广告的语言特征

广告翻译者除了要具备广告专业知识外，还应当熟悉并研究英汉两种语言在广告中的语体特征、修辞运用和句型特点，这样才能在翻译中运用恰当的语言形式，使译文准确、地道、自然、贴切，才能提高广告的翻译质量，使英文广告和中文广告都能很好地体现出广告的内涵，达到广告的目的。

一、英语广告的语言特征
（一）英语广告的语体特征

广告语是一种交际性很强的语言，为了达到交际和宣传效果，可以根据不同的对象、不同的场景、不同的产品和不同的载体，采用不同的文体，或交叉使用各种文体。从表达形式上看，可以分为口头语体和书面语体。广告语言的口头语体主要是以有声媒介为载体，包括电视、广播、短视频以及网络中的对话、独白、旁白、解说、叫卖等。书面语体多见于报纸、杂志等平面媒体。在广告翻译过程中，语体的对应不是机械的对应，而是根据受众的社会文化背景，即消费者的心理、受教育水平、购买力等，来确定使用的语体。雀巢咖啡广告语"The taste is great."（味道好极了）无论是英文原文还是汉语译文，语言都极为简单和口语化，却最为人们熟悉与喜欢，这句话成功的原因在于它是人们发自内心脱口而出的感受，简单而又意义深远，朗朗上口。后来雀巢虽重金在全球征集新广告语，却发现没有一句比这句更经典，也就保留了这句广告语至今。2010年刊载于某周刊上的飞利浦手机的广告语"Sense and Simplicity"（精于心　简于形），其英文只是押头韵的两个单词，语体属于不完整的书面语体，用词典雅。飞利浦公司选择了工整对仗的汉语书面语体作为其在中国的广告语，汉语对偶句与其英文广告词在形象、音韵和内涵上都达到了对应效果。实际上，对应的汉语译文在音韵美层面上有过之而无不及，具有浓郁的中国古典美，是广告翻译本土化的一则佳例。（吕和发、任林静，2011：39）

（二）英语广告的词汇特征

1. 用词简洁

一般来说，广告都较为简短，用词也要简单易懂，应尽量选用大众耳熟能详的简单词汇，而不是不常出现的生僻词、难词和怪词，应做到简明、易记、通俗，富有感情色彩和感染力。这样就可以不知不觉扩大广告的受众面，最大限度地发挥广告的宣传效果。

例1. Mosquito Bye, Bye, Bye.

译文：蚊虫杀、杀、杀！

例2. Start ahead.（Rejoice）

译文：成功之路，从头开始。（飘柔洗发露）

此外，广告需在有限的时间和空间内达到利益最大化，简洁的语言可以让人一目了然，达到立竿见影的效果，既突出主题，又引起读者的关注和兴趣。所以，广告英语常用单音节动词。常见的有：get, feel, taste, make, do, ask等。

2. 创造新词

商务广告文字要具有创造性，要使文字富有个性和新意，可以故意把人们熟悉的字词拼错或加上前缀、后缀，以达到生动有趣、引人注意的目的。创造新词可以有效地传播商品信息。

例3. Give a Timex to all, and to all a good time.

译文：拥有一块天美时表，拥有一段美好时光。

Timex（天美时）始创于1854年，是美国畅销的运动休闲表品牌。该款表直接用"Time+x"作为品牌名，手表的主要功能——计时功能一目了然。

3. 巧用修辞

广告是一种交际行为，必须具有强烈的感染力，能打动消费者，激发消费者的购买欲望和购买行为。因此，不仅要大量使用修饰性形容词进行渲染，而且要运用各种修辞手段，以其独特的艺术美感，极大地增强广告的表现力，给人留下深刻印象。

广告中的修辞格有：比喻、对仗、重复、拟人、夸张、对比、双关、押韵（头韵、尾韵）等。

对仗：对仗（antithesis）是由结构平行的词语、从句或句子排列而成，语义上相互对立或对照的一种修辞格。由于其结构工整匀称，前后两个相反的意思引人注目，并互为衬托，因而使要表现的意思鲜明突出。

例4. No problem too large. No business too small.

译文：没有解决不了的大问题，没有不做的小生意。

这是IBM公司的广告。该广告对仗工整，又运用了重复和押头韵的修辞格，朗朗上口，而且汉译中的"生意"与"问题"恰好押尾韵，易读、易记，既说明了公司的实力，又表明了公司事无巨细、想顾客之所想的实干精神。

重复：重复也称反复（repetition），其基本用法是连续或间隔重复使用同样的词、短语、语音。

例5. Extra taste. Not extra calories.

译文：滋味无穷，热量正好。

押韵：押韵（rhyme）一般是指诗歌中将韵母互相谐音的文字放在诗文固定的地方（一般在句尾）以使诗文读起来顺口、悦耳的一种修辞手法。

例6. Go for the sun and the fun.

译文：追求阳光与欢乐吧！

此广告sun与fun谐音押韵，使人很容易联想到享受明媚的阳光、游玩时候的快乐。

拟人：拟人（personification）是把物当作人来描写的一种修辞手法。在广告中使用拟人手法，可以让产品生动形象。物与人的结合可以赋予商品人的特点，使消费者倍感亲切。

例7. Unlike me, my Rolex never needs a rest.

译文：劳力士表从不休息。

这是一则劳力士手表广告。"劳力士表从不休息"暗示此表绝不会停止，走时准确，质量值得信赖。

夸张：夸张（hyperbole）意为对事物的形象、特征、特性等着意夸大的修辞方式。

例8. Making the world smaller.

译文：让世界变得更小。

该广告为德国汉莎航空公司的宣传广告，该广告采用夸张的修辞手法，表明乘坐汉莎航空公司的飞机可以让世界变小，强化了汉莎航空公司便利迅捷的特性，从而起到突出主题的效果。

例9. We have hidden a garden full of vegetables where you never expect in a pie.

译文：在你意想不到的地方，我们珍藏了满园的蔬菜，就在一块小小的馅饼里。

小小的馅饼里珍藏了满园的蔬菜，表明馅饼里有丰富的蔬菜，味道鲜美。夸张运用得巧妙，叫人不得不拍案叫绝。

双关：双关（pun）即俗语说的一语双关。一个词在句子里有双重或更多的含义，可做不同的解释，以造成一种滑稽、幽默的效果。

例10. Less bread, no jam.（伦敦地铁广告）。

这则广告字面意思是"少些面包，不要果酱"，似乎是一则介绍早餐的广告口号。实际上这则地铁广告口号巧妙地运用了语义双关的修辞手法。bread常用的意思是"面包"，但在非正式英语里，可以表示"钱"的意思；jam不仅有"果酱"的意思，也有"交通堵塞"的意思。所以，这则广告的实际含义是：乘坐伦敦地铁，省时省钱，绝不堵车。

（三）商务英语广告的句法特征

广告语要吸引读者，必须可读性强、一目了然。因此，英文广告语多用疑问句、祈使句、省略句和并列句。

1. 疑问句和祈使句的运用

商务广告的目的是向潜在的消费者推介产品及服务，激发消费者的兴趣和购买欲望，从而完成购买行为，属于呼唤型文本，旨在号召受众去行动，实现广告的劝说功能（persuasive function）。据语言学家统计，广告中四分之一以上的独立句是祈使句。另据某些学者抽样调查发现，广告英语中疑问句占14%。这两种句式在英语中被人们频繁使用，主要是因为祈使句具有直接劝说、直接鼓动的作用；而疑问句不仅具有劝说、鼓动的功能，还要求读者作出积极的反应，就像在和读者直接对话一样。（方梦之、毛忠明，2018：204）

例11. Pierre sport quilted jacket—well, who should know better than a duck how to keep warm?

译文：Pierre牌羽绒运动夹克——有谁能比鸭子更知道如何保暖呢？

例12. Buy one pair, get one free.

译文：买一送一。

2. 省略句和并列句的运用

广告需要在有限的时间、空间、费用内达到最佳的宣传效果，因此，广告英语中便大量运用省略句，以使句子一目了然，难以忘怀。省略句是广告英语中最引人注目、最具代表性的句型，大量使用省略句更成为广告极为突出的特点之一。

例13. Finest food, most attractive surroundings and a friendly disposition.

译文：饭菜上乘，环境幽雅，服务一流。

本例原文中出现了三个"形容词+名词"结构，可视为省略了主语（We）、谓语（serve）及某些介词（in, with），仅保留了宾语及其修饰语的句子。整个句子读下来感觉语言高度简练及概括，三个并列结构朗朗上口，形成了排比的气势，将餐馆幽雅舒适的环境以及一流的饭菜和服务质量惟妙惟肖、简单明了地表达出来。汉译时，将英文的三个并列结构译成四字结构，文字对仗，言简意赅。（方梦之、毛忠明，2018：204—205）

二、汉语广告的语言特征

广告语言绝不是简单的商业语言，而是运用各种语言技巧并富有艺术魅力的鼓动性语言；它要求用词优美独到，句法洗练而内涵丰富，修辞变化多端，耐人寻味，从而激发消费者的购买欲望。

（一）使用四字结构

中文广告用词十分讲究，广告用词最明显的特点是四字结构的运用，也有八字广告语以及十二字广告语等。特别是介绍产品性能或服务时，大量使用四字结构，如造型美观（beautiful appearance, style, shape）、用料上乘（selected materials）、做工精细（fine workmanship）、服务周到（courteous service）、手续简便（easy and convenient order）、价廉物美（cheap and fine）、美观耐用（attractive and durable）等。

还有一种四字结构不是单独的汉语成语，而是把四字结构嵌入整个译文中。

例14. To me, the past is black and white, but the future is always color.

译文：对我而言，过去平淡无奇；而未来，却是绚烂缤纷。（轩尼诗广告）

该汉语译例中包含了"平淡无奇""绚烂缤纷"四字结构。

（二）引用成语与典故

中国是历史悠久的文明古国，从历史的经典中引用成语与典故作为现代广告语，能够在很大程度上引起消费者的共鸣，最终促进消费行为的产生。（岳峰、刘茵，2014：74）例如，Swatch（斯沃琪手表）的广告语"Time is what you make of it"被译为"天长地久"，该成语出自老子："天长地久，天地所以能长久者，以其不自生，故能长久。"一家名为"福满楼"的餐馆，对外宣传用的英文广告语是"It must be 'FuManLou' for quality food"，回译之后在国内的广告就成了"借问珍馐何处有，牧童遥指'福满楼'"。这句译文就是巧借杜牧的诗句"借问酒家何处有,牧童遥指杏花村"。

(三)句子简短紧凑

广告的正文主要是介绍公司、厂家的情况以及产品的性能、规格、工艺、原料或质量的情况,因此在句型上主要以陈述句为主。但广告的目的是劝购、导购,祈使句也必然是广告中常用的句型。另外,广告语句特别是标题句必须简短紧凑,简单句、省略句和并列结构也频频出现。

第三节　广告翻译的策略和方法

广告口号(slogans)、广告语句(catch phrases)等是一种特殊的语言,它们通常都有一些共同的特点,如语言上引人入胜、说服力强,修辞手法的运用也别具一格,如语义双关、文字游戏等,使人感到幽默中见智慧,平淡中显新奇。广告语言在形式上也极具鲜明特色,或行文工整、对仗押韵,或节奏感强、朗朗上口,或一鸣惊人、令人耳目一新,可以收到耐人寻味、经久不衰的效果。(顾维勇,2005:48)在翻译广告时,无论是英译汉,还是汉译英,绝不能满足于字面上的翻译,作"表面文章"。语言必须翻译得既准确又地道,尤其要把原文中的"潜台词"或言外之意传达出来。此外,还需要利用常用的或者特别的翻译技巧和方法,把广告语的个性表现出来。这样,广告的"呼唤型"特征才能显现出来。

一、广告翻译的常用方法

(一)直译法

直译法就是在不与源语言文化冲突的前提下,使译文的内容和形式与原文对等,同时要求语言流畅易懂。其中"对等"二字是关键,当源语言的字词结构所蕴含的意义和风格与目的语对等的时候,就可以采用直译法。(岳峰、刘茵,2014:79)也就是说,基本保持原句的句法和修辞特点。

例15. Reliable solid, solidly reliable.

译文:安如磐石,磐石之安。(汽车广告)

例16. A business in millions, a profit in pennies.

译文:百万生意,毫厘利润。

(二)意译法

所谓意译法就是改变原文的修辞特点,只保持原文内容,不保持原文形式的翻译方法。

例17. 吸取生物精华，焕发生命潜能。

译文：Essence of Living Beings, Energy for Life.

这是广东"太阳神"生物健口服液广告。汉语是两个并列的祈使句，是动宾结构。英译者利用排偶手法，凭借两个并列的名词短语和它们的前后顺序来暗示"生物精华"与"生命潜能"的关系。（刘季春，2007：250）

例18. All for children as well as adults.

译文：老少皆宜。

该句广告如果直译则是"一切为了孩子和大人"，似乎限定了目标用户，又不上口，而用汉语四字成语翻译，则言简意赅，一语中的。

（三）套译法

套译就是套用目的语文化中家喻户晓的名言佳句、成语、谚语、诗句、歌词等来表达原文的意思，或者本身就是广告标题或口号，使目的语读者产生一种似曾相识的感觉，从而引起共鸣。这种套用译入语中某些惯用结构进行翻译的方法也称为借用（structure borrowing）或仿拟。总而言之，这个被借用的结构必须是人们喜闻乐见、家喻户晓的。（刘季春，2007：252—253）

例19. I'll do a lot for love, but I'm not ready to die for it.

译文：情爱诚销魂，生命价更高！

这是一则推销避孕套的广告标题。这类广告标题最令撰稿人头痛，要么太俗太露，受到大众的批评，传播媒介也不易接受；要么过于笼统，不着边际，让人看了莫名其妙。这则广告标题的成功之处在于抓住了人们恐惧艾滋病的心理，含蓄地表达了这一主题，真可谓"雅俗共赏"。译文套用了在我国传诵甚广的匈牙利诗人裴多菲的诗句，译得既情调高雅，又度量适中。

例20. 有了南方，就有了办法。

译文：Where there is South, there is a way.

这是某"南方"科技咨询服务公司的广告。该英语译文显然是套用了英语中最常见的一句谚语："Where there is a will, there is a way."译文只换了一个词，但因与该公司服务特点挂了钩，恰到好处，韵味无穷。给顾客的印象是：这家咨询公司的办法还真不少！

例21. Not all cars are created equal.

译文：车到山前必有路，有路必有丰田车。

这是丰田汽车广告。丰田公司在美国的英文广告仿拟美国《独立宣言》中"All men are created equal"的名言，改头换面，创新广告内容，意思是"并非所有的汽车都有相同的品质"。但在中国文化中,如果直译很难引起共鸣,因此在中国市场上套用中国的俗语"车到山前必有路",与英语广告相比,有异曲同工之妙。

(四)四字结构法

四字结构法主要是指将英文广告翻译成汉语的四字结构。汉语广告大量使用四字结构,使用约定俗成的成语,这是汉语广告语的鲜明特色。四字结构节奏感强,朗朗上口,便于记忆,用汉语四字结构来译英文广告口号会取得较为理想的效果。

例22. Good to the last drop.

译文:滴滴香浓,意犹未尽。

这是麦斯威尔咖啡(Maxwell)的一句广告语。美国前总统罗斯福访问麦斯威尔工厂时,经理请他品尝一杯咖啡。他一口把咖啡喝完,满意地赞美说:"喝到最后一滴都是香的!"还把杯子倒过来给经理看。总统所激发的灵感立即被经理抓住,所以直到今天麦斯威尔工厂的广告语还是:滴滴香浓,意犹未尽。

套译也可用于四字结构的汉语广告的英译,也就是将汉语四字结构翻译成具有类似的意义和修辞色彩的英语短语。汉语四字结构在英译中通常可译为以下几种结构:

1. 形容词+名词

设计新颖 stylish/novel design

款式新颖 fashionable design

2. 形容词+名词+名词

散热迅速 rapid heat dissipation

保温性强 good heat preservation

3. 形容词+名词+介词短语

花色繁多 a wide selection of colors and designs

老少良伴 good companies for children as well as adults

4. 形容词+and+形容词

轻柔松软 soft and light

典雅大方 elegant and graceful

5. 形容词+介词短语

设计华丽 luxurious in design

制作精巧 perfect in workmanship

6. 形容词+不定式

穿着舒适 comfortable to wear

携带方便 convenient to carry

7. 名词+形容词（或过去分词）

价格公道　the price reasonable

欢迎选购　orders welcome

8. 动词+（形容词）+名词+（其他）

誉满中外　enjoy a high reputation at home and abroad

轻身延寿　reduce one's weight and prolong one's life

9. 介词+（形容词）+名词

式样众多　in many styles

（以上译例部分选自方梦之、毛忠明的《英汉—汉英应用翻译综合教程》）

10. 其他

抗热耐磨　strong resistance to heat and hard wearing

功效神奇　as effective as a fair dose

（五）增补译法

增补译法是指对原文某些关键词的词义进行挖掘、引申或扩充，将原文的意思加以发挥，突出其隐含的意义，即根据语用、语义、语形的需要在译文中增加必要的语言单位的全译方法。增译的原则是增形不增意，即语形上增加了语言单位，但语义上未作任何添加。（黄忠廉，余承法，2012：151—152）

例23. Your future is our future.

译文：与您并肩，迈向明天。（汇丰银行广告）

例24. Taking the lead in a digital world.

译文：领先数码，超越永恒。（三星公司广告）

（六）不译

两种不译现象：第一种是新企业、新品牌、新产品系列的名称或老企业的新产品系列的名称，往往不需要翻译；第二种"不译"是指只需照搬文中的外文名称即可。（邹力，2013：30）

例25. Volvos have always forced other cars to be safer. New S800 will force them to be better.

译文：安全可靠，早已闻名天下。崭新S800一登场，再度成为典范。

S800是新产品系列，不用翻译。其他例子比如IBM，BBC，3M等这些品牌和名称,就都保留了原外文字母形式。

（七）转换句型

由于广告语言本身具有灵活、简洁的特点,在广告翻译的过程中,句型和句式的转换有着很大的自由度。通过句型和句式的转换,通过改变词性,既可以把词组转译为句子,也可以把句子转译成词组。

一般情况下,中文广告语大多喜欢用主谓宾或动宾结构,动感非常强烈。而英文喜欢用短语,而不是完整的句子。

例26. No business too small, no problem too big.

译文：没有不做的小生意,没有解决不了的大问题。

英文原句是并列词组,汉语译为排比句,两句均为动宾结构。

二、广告翻译的功能效果

英语和汉语分属于两种不同的文化背景,因此在人们的生活方式、思维习惯、民族心理、对事物的偏爱、推理模式以及语言表达方式等方面都有明显的差别。这就要求翻译英语广告时必须了解两种文化的差异。因此,英语广告翻译应建立在目的论基础上,以功能对等为准则,使译文对汉语读者产生的效果大致与原文对英文读者产生的效果相当。

翻译过程通常伴随着目的论中的三个法则,即目的法则、连贯法则以及忠实法则。其中目的法则是翻译中的首要法则,连贯法则和忠实法则都服从于目的法则。广告翻译的目的通常有以下三种：（1）让消费者了解品牌的基本情况；（2）激发消费者的购买欲望；（3）推广品牌,促进文化交流。（岳峰、刘茵,2014：77）

例27. Bolla Wines：Wine is a little like love; when the right one comes along, you know it.

译文：宝拉有点像爱情,相知唯有意中人！

宝拉酒庄（Bolla Wines）系意大利著名的葡萄酒厂家。此英文广告语,采用明喻手法,便是从葡萄酒的风味和品酒的方法入手,非常细腻。根据广告原意,译为"宝拉有点像爱情,相知唯有意中人！"将Bolla酒与高品位巧妙地结合起来,隐含了感恩赏识、渴望品尝的诚意。

例28. American Express Credit Card：Don't leave home without it.

美国运通公司（American Express）是一个多元化经营的全球性金融服务公司。原文Don't leave home without it直译是"没有带上它,你就别离家"。直译对中国读者和客户而言,就显得过于平淡。为了体现运通公司在中国业务拓展的情况与中国经济蓬勃发展的实际，可改译为"运通卡在手，伴你走九州！""运通在手，好运长久！""君行千里，运通相随！""神游五湖，运通四海！"等，显得颇具动感，符合公众诉求。（邹春荣、杨晓斌，2009：158）

例29. Kentucky Fried Chicken：Buy a bucket of chicken and have a barrel of fun. We do chicken right.

肯德基的英文广告语中有两句特别具有影响力，即Buy a bucket of chicken and have a barrel of fun和We do chicken right。前者采用比拟（parallelism）的修辞手法，意思是"买一桶肯德基，得到一桶乐趣"；后者使用双关（pun）手法，暗示鸡做得恰到好处，又香又脆，欢迎品尝。汉译时既要努力保持肯德基英文广告的原汁原味，又要尽量避免目标文本（target text）可能存在的种种歧义，所以可译为："品（尝、吃）鸡你快乐，烤鸡我在行！"

中国和英语国家的人在理解一些文化意象方面的时候会有所不同，一旦没有处理好文化意象的翻译问题，就很有可能造成文化冲突，进而使自己的商业产品无法赢得人心，惨遭抵制。（岳峰、刘茵，2014：78）

三、广告中的品牌翻译

好的品牌本身就是无形的广告，一个悦耳的品牌是庞大的无形资产。在经济全球化的今天，不少品牌都有译名。宝洁公司（P&G）旗下的产品大多为广大中国消费者所熟悉，Rejoice（飘柔）和Head & Shoulders（海飞丝）就是其中的两个洗发水品牌。作为中国消费者，一定会喜欢能让我们秀发"丝丝柔滑，飘逸如仙"的洗发水。一个商品的品牌，要能吸引消费者，让其识别和联想产品，并发挥良好的广告宣传效应。因此文字的选择显得十分重要。翻译时要采用灵活的方法。

（一）音译

有些进入国内市场的外来商品，由于在汉语中很难找到对应的词语，有的品牌并无实质意义，也很难意译，所以就采用音译（transliteration）的办法。音译是翻译商品品牌一种极为普遍的翻译方法。英文品牌汉译后往往带有美好的意蕴，给读者留下深刻印象。世界知名品牌大都采用音译，例如：Philips（飞利浦），Audi（奥迪），Chanel（香奈儿），Pierre Cardin（皮尔卡丹），Casio（卡西欧），Boeing（波音），Benz（奔驰），Disney（迪士尼），Louvier（路维亚），等等。

中文品牌名称也有很多采取音译的方法，也就是使用汉语拼音。例如中华（Zhonghua）铅笔、万家乐（Wan Jia Le）燃气具等。

（二）意译

有的商品品牌名本身就有一定的含义，如果音译则体现不出蕴含的意义。大众汽车德文原名为"Volkswagen"，"Volks"是人民大众的意思，"Wagen"是汽车的意思，全名的意思是"人民大众的汽车"。

在汉语品牌翻译过程中要注意谐音引起的歧义。比如著名服装品牌雅戈尔，如果采用拼音翻译就是"YaGeEr"，则无法传神达意，令人困惑；而其实际译名"Younger"则充分表达了"青春活力"的意蕴，起到了良好的广告效果。

（三）直译、意译、音译结合

理想的译法是尽量做到音意结合，音存意生，灵活运用，烘托商品的主题，内涵丰富，新颖独特，如能产生"音美、意美、形美"的效果则更佳。

例如，百脑汇（Buynow）是蓝天电脑集团（CLEVO）的投资项目。Buynow字面上的意思是"现在就购买"，但作为品牌名称就显得俗气，不够简练。"百"是"buy"的谐音，"脑"是"now"的谐音，又蕴含电脑之意，符合产品的内涵意义。"百脑汇"合起来的意思就是各种电脑产品应有尽有。

（四）注意文化背景的差异

商标和品牌蕴含着丰富的文化气息，对于同一品牌，不同的文化有着不同的审美情趣和意象联想。曾有人将"白象牌电池"翻译为"White Elephant Battery"。在英语中white elephant通常指"大而无用的东西"，采用这种译法，电池的销路可想而知，这已成为人们的笑谈。

7-Up（七喜）是知名的柠檬汽水品牌。7-Up的中文译名，是由中国香港的一家公司先翻译出来的。7-Up意译为"七起"，但字面意思不好，因此取其粤语同音字"七喜"作为官方中文名称。7个up的含义包括：1. wake up, 2. dress up, 3. shut up, 4. stand up, 5. look up, 6. reach up, 7. lift up。7-Up如果按照字面基本意思翻译成"七上"，则会使人联想到汉语文化里的成语"七上八下"，很不吉利。

（五）选词注意联想效果

Goldlion品牌，如果按照字面直译为"金狮"，易引起人们不好的联想，因为"狮"与"输"或"死"谐音，故译者巧妙地译为"金利来"，象征"财源滚滚来"，产品相当受欢迎。

译名要能引起联想，确定译名时要反复斟酌其含义，做到画龙点睛。宝马（简称BMW）是德国汽车品牌，隶属于BMW集团。宝马车标的BMW是巴伐利亚发动机制造厂的意思，标志的色彩和组合来自宝马所在地巴伐利亚州的州徽。BMW汉译名"宝马"可谓是神来之笔，既突出了宝马汽车高贵豪华的风格气质，又与中国的传统称谓浑然一体,同时发音也与BMW相差不大。宝马这个传神的译名赋予品牌一种令人神往的气质。

其他例子还有:

Benz	奔驰(联想性能与速度)
Rejoice	飘柔(联想使用效果与美感)
Coca-Cola	可口可乐(联想口感与心情)

第四节 课内翻译任务

一、英译汉 English-Chinese Translation

I want to be where the world comes to play.

Incentive Isle Singapore.

Gateway to Asia.

I want the past.

I want the present.

I want to be dazzled.

I want to taste heaven.

I want to be among the stars.

I want to be a party animal.

I want to shop, shop, shop.

I want to be pampered.

I want to explore.

Incentive Isle Singapore.

(引自吕和发、任林静,2011:50—51)

重点解析 Notes and Comments

1. 这是一则新加坡旅游影视广告。该广告经译者采用归化法处理,实现了与目标旅游者的共鸣,达到了较好的营销效果。这印证了广告翻译"本土化"的有效性。该影视广告的长度大约5分钟,在音乐的烘托下,13行富有诗意的文字以字幕形式出现在画面里。如果采用动态对等策略翻译字幕全文,也能实现译文的顺畅、达意,符合信、达、雅的翻译原则,但很难实现在目标群体中希望产生的传播效果。

2. I want to be where the world comes to play. 人们都说新加坡是南洋皇冠上的一颗明珠。

第一句译文没有采用直译，而是突出了新加坡作为南太平洋皇冠上一颗璀璨的明珠的特色，吸引了受众的注意力。

3. Incentive Isle Singapore 新加坡 南洋梦。

译文并未将"Isle"岛屿的意思直接翻译出来，而是把受众的注意力扩展到历史记忆中的南洋地区。

4. I want the past. I want the present. 传统丰富 文化璀璨 现代潮流 摩登时尚。

译文通过增译手法，运用汉语四字词组的丰富表现力，深挖原广告内涵，把广告隐含的意义显性地表达出来，既朗朗上口，又明白易懂。如译为"我喜欢这里的过去，我喜欢这里的现在"，则平淡无味。

5. I want to be dazzled. 醉在今宵 醉在南洋。

如译为"我喜欢头晕目眩的感受"，会令人感觉莫名其妙，不知所云。

6. I want to taste heaven. 山珍海味 美酒佳肴。

"山珍海味 美酒佳肴"把"taste"一词发挥到淋漓尽致。如译为"我喜欢享受天堂的乐趣"或"我喜欢品尝天堂"，则很难让人体会到什么是天堂的乐趣，或要品尝天堂的什么东西。

7. I want to be among the stars. 与星共舞 与月争辉。

译文充分体现了中华特色，深谙中华文化圈受众的认知心理，把游客在新加坡载歌载舞的欢乐情景活灵活现地展示出来，如译为"我喜欢与星辰为伴"或"我想置身于群星之中"，则很难体现欢乐场景，而以为只是夜宿野外，欣赏群星灿烂。

8. I want to be pampered. 帝王风范 贵妃宠遇。

译文通过夸张的手法，把旅游过程中的疯狂和充满奇遇的幻想表现得惟妙惟肖。如果按照字面意思译为"我想受到宠爱"，则非常直白俗气。

二、将下列广告文案翻译成英语 Translate the following Chinese advertisement copies into English

"贵州茅台酒38%（V/V）"是贵州茅台酒的系列产品，是经先进的科学方法精制而成的白酒。它既保持了酱香浓郁、典雅细致、协调丰满、回味悠长等贵州茅台酒的独特风格，又具有加水、加冰后不浑浊、风格不变等特点，深受国内外各界人士的欢迎。

重点解析 Notes and Comments

1. 此例是一则汉语的茅台酒产品广告，强调了制作方法之先进，茅台酒风格之独特，另具有加水、加冰后不浑浊之特点，深受欢迎。这是一则典型的汉语产品广告正文，"先进……方法""深受……的欢迎"是汉语广告中常用的评价性话语。

2. 四字格"酱香浓郁""典雅细致""回味悠长"等读起来抑扬顿挫、铿锵有力，有效增强了广告的语势。当茅台酒卖向海外市场进行广告翻译时，首先要考虑目标语境中的广告特点。

3. 为了更好地在英语语境中传递原文广告的产品信息，更好地在英语市场吸引消费者的注意力，译文应使用意译的方法，舍弃原文的结构形式，专注传递产品的核心信息。（徐珺，2018：9）

4. 按照官方译写规范，中国的白酒可以直接音译。中国白酒（Chinese Baijiu）、伏特加（Vodka）、威士忌（Whisky）、白兰地（Brandy）、金酒（Gin）、朗姆酒（Rum）号称世界六大蒸馏酒系列。茅台酒是世界知名品牌，可以直接音译。

三、将下列广告语翻译成英语 Translate the following Chinese advertising into English

1. 百闻不如一尝。（食品广告语）
2. 药补不如食补。（食品广告语）
3. 要想皮肤好，早晚用大宝。（大宝护肤品广告语）
4. 情系中国结，联通四海心。（中国联通广告语）
5. 我的地盘听我的。（中国移动广告语）

重点解析 Notes and Comments

1. 百闻不如一尝。Tasting is believing.

这是浙江省粮油食品进出口股份有限公司的一个广告。显然，中文广告套用了"百闻不如一见"的谚语，而英语译文也套用了一个英语谚语："Seeing Is Believing"。所不同的是，中文广告改了汉语谚语的最后一个字，而译文则改了英语谚语的头一个词,新鲜活泼,殊途同归。

2. 药补不如食补。Diets care more than the doctors.

这是一则食品广告。该广告语运用明喻手法,既简练,又深刻。英译同样简练含蓄,同时很容易让人想起英语中的一句谚语:An apple a day keeps the doctor away,可谓妙趣横生。

3. 要想皮肤好,早晚用大宝。Applying "Dabao" morning and night makes your skincare a real delight.

大宝这句广告语首先采用了词义双关手法,"早晚"可以理解为"早晨和晚上",也可以解释为"迟早有一天",一语双关,非常巧妙。既强调了"大宝"的重要性——早晚都要用,又显示了品牌自信,相信顾客迟早会用上"大宝"护肤品。其次,"好"和"宝"语音押韵。这句广告语形式简短、读音上口、简单易记,符合广告语言的风格特征。大宝平易近人的文化在这句广告语中深有体现。

4. 情系中国结,联通四海心。Your emotion in a Chinese knot connecting you to the whole world.

这是中国联通的广告语。这则广告语以对联的形式出现,很有创意,对仗工整,上下两句承接顺畅。既把中国联通四个字嵌了进去,又把中国联通遍布全国的情况写了出来,而且融入了联通人的热情服务,令人久久回味。

5. 我的地盘听我的。My place, my rule.

这是中国移动推出的"动感地带"的广告语,这则广告语可以说是已经响彻了大江南北。这句广告语简洁直率,以鲜明的个性赢得了无数年轻人的青睐。其强烈的自我意识和时尚气息,展示出了强大的号召力。

第五节　课后翻译训练

一、将下列英语品牌翻译成汉语 Translate the following English brand names into Chinese

1. Cannon（照相机）
2. Mercedes-Benz（汽车）
3. Pizza Hut（比萨）
4. Apple（电脑）
5. Johnson's（婴儿用品）
6. Dove（巧克力）

7. Nestlé（咖啡）

8. Dumex（奶粉）

9. Ikea（家居超市）

10. Maxwell（咖啡）

二、将下列英语广告语翻译成汉语 Translate the following English advertising slogans into Chinese

1. Apple thinks different.（苹果公司）

2. Your home in the air.（航空公司）

3. Life is a journey. Travel it well.（航空公司）

4. FIYTA Watch, Once Possess, Nothing More Is Expected.（飞亚达表）

5. Feel the new space.（三星电子）

6. Intelligence everywhere.（摩托罗拉手机）

7. East is east and west is west, but Brown's meat is best.（加拿大布朗肉制品公司）

8. Double delicious. Double your pleasure.（食品）

9. Extra Taste. Not Extra Calories.（食品）

10. You are better off under the Umbrella.（"伞"式保险）

三、将下列英文广告文案翻译成汉语 Translate the following English advertising copies into Chinese

Adidas Sports Shoes

Over twenty-eight years ago, Adidas gave birth to a new idea in sports shoes. And the people who wear our shoes have been running and winning ever since. In fact, Adidas has helped them set over 400 world records in track and field alone.

Maybe that's why more and more football, soccer, basketball, baseball and tennis players are turning to Adidas. They know that, whatever their game is, they can rely on Adidas workmanship and quality in every product we make.

So whether you are pounding the roads on a marathon, or just jogging around the block, Adidas should be on your feet.

You were born to run. And we were born to help you do it better. You will find us anywhere smart sports people buy their shoes.

　　Adidas, the all sports people.

四、将下列中文品牌名翻译成英语 Translate the following Chinese brand names into English

　　1. 康佳（电器）
　　2. 金利来（服饰）
　　3. 海尔（电器）
　　4. 格力（电器）
　　5. 吉利（汽车）
　　6. 小米（手机）
　　7. 太极（医药）
　　8. 百度（网络）
　　9. 雅戈尔（服饰）
　　10. 李宁（服装）

五、将下列中文广告语翻译成英语 Translate the following Chinese advertising slogans into English

　　1. 您想身体好，请喝健力宝。（健力宝饮料）
　　2. 一切皆有可能。（李宁品牌）
　　3. 同一个世界，同一个梦想。（2008年北京奥运会口号）
　　4. 随身携带，有备无患；随身携带，有惊无险。（速效救心丸）
　　5. 药材好，药才好。（宛西制药厂中药材）
　　6. 不求最大，但求最好。（中国光大银行）
　　7. 吉列，男士的选择。（吉列剃须刀）
　　8. 非常可乐，非常选择！（非常可乐）
　　9. 使不可能变为可能。（佳能打印机）
　　10. 我们实行"三包"：包修、包退、包换。（商品三包承诺）

六、将下列中文广告段落翻译成英语 Translate the following Chinese advertising copies into English

　　1. CTY型游梁式抽油机结构简单，安全可靠，制造简易，维修方便，广泛应用于世界石油生产。（方梦之、王忠明，2018：205—207）
　　2. 人无我有，人有我优。电话订餐，送货上门。备有快餐，欢迎品尝。（廖国强，2014：23）
　　3. 燕京地毯店举办地毯展销，提供各种精美华丽的手织地毯，欢迎前来参观选购。

4. "航空牌"人造革衣箱,用料上乘,做工精细,款式新颖,价格合理,规格齐全,欢迎选购。

5. 最佳的礼品"丽兰"空气清新器给您带来大自然的芬芳!"丽兰"使您的房间清香怡人,散发出自然纯美的芳香,使您的卧室、卫生间、汽车等保持诱人的芳香!

第五章

市场营销翻译

营销的基本目的就是以恰当有效的方式使目标客户群体了解并接受符合他们需求的产品或服务。随着经济全球化的发展，各种发源于发达经济体的新的营销理念和方法越来越受到企业的重视，这些新的营销理念及方法是中国企业开拓国外市场，应对竞争所必须掌握的，比如以产品为中心的营销组合"4P"，即产品（Product）、价格（Price）、促销（Promotion）和渠道（Place）；以顾客为导向的"4C"理论，包括顾客（Customer）、成本（Cost）、沟通（Communication）和便利（Convenience）。除此之外，还有大量的与营销相关的概念，包括市场细分（segmentation）、目标市场选择（targeting）、定位（positioning）、需要（needs）、欲求（wants）、需求（demand）、市场供给品（offerings）、品牌（brands）、价值和满足（value and satisfaction）、交换（exchange）、交易（transaction）、关系和网络（relationships and networks）、营销渠道（marketing channel）、供应链（supply chain）、竞争（competition）、营销环境（marketing environment）和营销策划/方案（marketing programs）。这些术语构成了营销职业的词汇库。

第一节 营销英语的语言特点与翻译

市场营销英语作为专门用途英语（English for Specific Purposes，简称ESP）的一个分支，既有普通用途英语（English for General Purposes，简称EGP）的特征，又有自己鲜明的语体特点。市场营销学是20世纪初起源于美国的一门学科。这门以大市场为研究对象的学科所涉及的原理、方法和技巧关系到企业经营的成败。随着中国经济日益与世界接轨，营销学的理论和知识引起了中国企业经营者、实业家和学术界的普遍关注。在现代英语逐渐成为国际商业社会的通用语言的今天，营销英语（Marketing English）的重要性不言而喻。因为它是理解营销学最直接的语言,也是国际经济交流必不可少的沟通手段。为了规范市场营销英语翻译,首先应了解其词汇、句子及语篇特点。

一、营销英语的词汇特点与翻译
(一)词汇的专业性

营销英语的词汇具有比较明显的专业特征。营销英语语境决定或者制约着部分词汇具有其特殊的营销语义。例如:普通英语中promotion和distribution的通常含义分别为"提升"和"分发",但在营销语境中,它们分别是"促销"和"分销"的意思。place在营销英语中的意思是"渠道"。

例1. Congratulations for your promotion.(EGP)

译文:恭喜你升职了。

例2. Promotion plays a crucial part in a company's marketing efforts. (ESP)

译文:促销活动在一个公司的市场营销行为中占有相当重要的地位。

例1中的promotion表达的是升职、升迁的意思,而例2中的promotion指的是促销活动,是营销组合(marketing mix)的一种,与产品(product)、价格(price)、渠道(place)并列。

词汇的专业性还体现在市场营销英语拥有大量的、独特的专业词汇,包括概念性词汇、短语等。例如:mass marketing(广泛营销或大众营销,又称大量市场营销),product life cycle(产品生命周期),intangible(无形产品),product mix(产品组合),market skimming pricing(高额定价法),market penetration pricing(渗透定价法),neutral pricing(均匀定价法),exclusive distribution channel(独家分销渠道),personal selling(人员推销),sales promotion(营业推广),等等。

例3. Today, most competition takes place at the product augmentation level.

译文:如今,大多数竞争都发生在延伸产品这一层面。

product augmentation或augmented product,在营销英语中指的是延伸产品,不能译为"增大产品"。延伸产品是指顾客购买形式产品时获得的各种利益的总和,包括产品说明书、送货、安装、维修、技术培训等附加服务和利益。

例4. Consumer products include convenience products, shopping products, specialty products and unsought products. These products differ in the way consumers buy them, so they differ in how they are marketed.

译文：消费产品包括便利品、选购品、特殊品和非渴求品。消费者通过不同的方式购买这些产品，因此，它们的营销方式也各不相同。

便利品一般指经常购买，购买时无须花费太多的时间和精力的产品；选购品相对而言购买频率不那么高，常需要比较不同产品以便作出最后的选择；特殊品购买频率更低，但一般具有独一无二、不可替代的特征；非渴求品一般需要通过产品促销活动才能使消费者对其产生一定的兴趣。convenience products, shopping products, specialty products and unsought products（便利品、选购品、特殊品和非渴求品）都是市场营销中专有的概念词语，翻译时都要在汉语中找到相对应的专业词汇。

例5. Along with playing a role in the development of new marketing approaches, market segmentation can also help a company identify ways to enhance customer loyalty with existing clients.

译文：市场细分不仅有助于公司制定新的营销方法，还有助于公司制定提高现有顾客忠诚度的方法。

市场细分（market segmentation）或称"市场区分"，是市场学的专业术语，是指将消费者依照不同的特征和消费需求分成若干群体，从而形成多个消费群。segmentation在此不能译为"分割"。

例6. Marketing is the activity, set of institutions, and processes for creating, communicating, delivering and exchanging offerings that have value for customers, clients, partners, and society at large.

译文：市场营销是在创造、沟通、传播和交换产品中，为顾客、客户、合作伙伴以及整个社会带来价值的一系列活动、体系和过程。

offerings通常意思是"供品，祭品，礼品"，此处应转译为"产品"。

营销英语中的部分词汇在其他专门用途英语中也经常出现，是各种ESP文体的共享词汇，但词义则差别很大。如share在金融英语中是指"股票"，而在营销英语中则指"市场份额，市场占有率"，是指某一供应商产品的销量与市场上所有同类产品的销量的比率，如market share。（莫莉莉，2006：37）

例7. In a truly marketing-oriented organization, these values are instilled in all employees.

译文：在一个真正以市场营销为导向的企业中，这些价值观会被灌输给所有的员工。

organization在此句中表示"企业"或"商家"，译为"组织"则不专业。

（二）词汇的跨学科性

营销学涉及的面很广，不仅包含生产、定价、促销、分销等内容，同时还涉及人口学、地理学、消费心理学等，因而其词汇具有明显的跨学科性。而由于营销学与经济学有着千丝万缕的关系，在营销英语中最常见的是经济学上的术语，如supply（供应），demand（需求），revenue（收入），public relations（公共关系），Price Index（价格指数），fluctuation（价格浮动），Gross Domestic Product（GDP）（国内生产总值）等。所以各个经济领域的专业术语夹杂在营销英语中是营销英语的一大特点。

（三）词汇的对义性

营销英语中常使用一组表示矛盾、对立的词语来描述各种互相对立的营销活动的性质或进展，这就是营销语言中的对义词，它们所表示的概念在逻辑上是一种矛盾或者关联的关系。例如：revenue/expenditure 收入/支出；supply/demand 供应/需求；increase/decrease 增长/减少；shortage/surplus 短缺/盈余；net weight/gross weight 净重/毛重。另一类对义词是利用构词法，比如加某个前缀表示反义或词义对应，例如：durable goods /nondurable goods耐用品/非耐用品；tangible/intangible 有形的/无形的；differentiated marketing/undifferentiated marketing 差异化营销/无差异营销；profitable organization/non-profitable organization 营利性组织/非营利性组织。

（四）词语的简化

英语具有一种简化趋势。出于语言经济性的考虑，市场营销英语中大量使用缩略词和复合词。

1. 缩略词

市场营销英语缩略词中最常见的是首字母缩略词，即每个单词的首字母组合而成的缩略词，既方便书写，又便于识别和记忆。如STP（segmentation target position）市场细分、目标市场和市场定位，USP（unique selling proposition）独特的销售主张，BDI（brand development index）品牌发展指数，CLV（customer lifetime value）顾客终身价值，IMC（integrated marketing communications）整合营销沟通，PLC（product life cycle）产品生命周期。在市场营销行业中，缩略词已经成为一种专业术语，翻译时采用直译即可。另外还有一种数字加字母的缩略词。当一组词语尤其是表示概念的词语首字母相同时，该字母大写，前面加上阿拉伯数字表示这几个单词的数量，构成一个缩略词，比如"营销组合"的几个单词product, price, promotion, place在一起使用时，为了方便，可以拼写成4P。4P可以翻译为"营销组合的四个变量",包括产品、价格、促销、渠道。同理,4C代表的是customer solution(顾客解决之道)、customer cost(顾客成本)、convenience(便利)、communication(沟通),也是营销组合的四个变量。需要注意的是,对缩略语的翻译不能望文生义。随着时代的变化,传统的营销观念不断得到充盈和扩展。最新的全方位营销中,4P指营销人员(people)、流程(process)、项目(program)和绩效(performance)。

市场营销中的缩略词可以作为词语和概念词使用,可以置于名词前作修饰语,也可以作为名词被其他词语修饰,如SWOT analysis, contractual VMS, corporate VMS等。SWOT指评价公司的优势(strength)、劣势(weakness)、机会(opportunities)和威胁(threat),因此SWOT analysis就是"对公司优势、劣势、机会和威胁的分析"。这些缩略语能起到简洁、明快、醒目、经济的效果。

2. 合成名词

市场营销英语属于商务英语,具有简明、准确和严谨的特点,在表述中往往需要给某些概念或陈述加上修饰语,用于说明适用范围或条件。

在市场营销英语中,合成名词的使用频率比较高。通常是两个或几个名词连用,用一个或几个不改变形态的名词作另一个名词中心语的前置修饰定语。这样不仅可以减少定语从句或介词短语的使用,还可以使语言结构更加简洁。例如,两个名词连用的情况:品牌决策(brand decision)、经济周期(business cycle);三个名词连用的情况:公司销售预测(company sales forecast)、顾客价值分析(customer value analysis)。在翻译合成名词时,除了要正确理解词本身的含义之外,还要注意词的搭配意义,否则无法准确表达原文的意义。

(五)词性的转换

词性转换在国际市场营销翻译中是一种频繁应用的翻译策略。英语多用名词性词汇或短语,汉语则多用动词性词语。在语际转译时,还需对各种词性作必要的转换,某些复杂的词性转换往往需要通过较大的意义转换才能完成。

例8. The requirements for effective marketing segmentation are that (1)the bases for segmentation be measurable with accessible data; (2) the segments themselves be accessible to existing marketing institutions; and (3) the segments be large enough to be potentially profitable.

译文:有效的市场细分需要满足以下条件:(1)市场细分的数据资料具备可衡量性;(2)市场细分对现成的市场具有可进入性;(3)市场细分须具备足够的潜在盈利性。

将名词requirements转译为动词短语"需要满足",将measurable, accessible与potentially profitable前的系动词be均译为"具有",并把这三个形容词分别转译为名词"可衡量性""可进入性"和"盈利性"。

(六)专有名词多

营销英语中含有大量专有名词,其中包含大量的公司名称和机构名称。比如:the American Marketing Association(美国市场营销协会,简称AMA),the Chartered Institute of Marketing(英国特许市场营销协会,简称CIM)。美国市场营销协会于1937年由市场营销企业界及学术界具有远见卓识的人士发起成立。英国特许市场营销协会是全球最大的营销认证机构之一。其他专业名词还有:China Capital Market(中国资本市场), All China Federation of Supply and Marketing Cooperatives(中华全国供销合作总社), Chinese General Chamber of Commerce(中华总商会), Common Market Nations(共同市场国家)。

二、营销英语的句法特征及其翻译

(一)常用复合句式

在国际贸易和市场营销中,人们常常会运用各种复杂的短语和复合句来表达更复杂的语言意义,这时就必须对原文的语序或结构加以科学的调整,或转换单词的词性,或将英语的复合结构拆分为汉语的短句,以期更明了地表达营销理念与内涵。

例9. Marketing occurs any time one social unit strives to exchange something of value with another social unit.

译文:当某个社会团体试图与另一个团体交换有价值的物品时,就产生了营销行为。

此例是一个复合句,复合句是一种意义上的划分。在翻译时应根据汉语习惯和逻辑关系,对原文中各个组成部分的顺序加以调整,通过这种语序的调整与转换,译文方可产生较强的逻辑性,才能清晰地表达市场营销英语的理念与信息,从而有效地促进国际市场营销活动的顺利进行。

例10. In contrast, if international sales are merely an outlet for excess production capacity, then the firm should focus on finding international markets that are receptive to products that have already been developed for the domestic market.

译文:相反,如果国际销售仅仅是过剩生产力的一种出路,那么公司应重点寻求这种国际市场，它能够接受已经为国内市场开发的现存产品。

该句中动词短语focus on（以……为重点），后接动名词短语，翻译时应转换成状语，将其后接的动名词短语转换成动词谓语。原句主从结构拆成两个句子翻译，that从句独立出来，关系代词that代替先行词markets作句子主语，表语receptive转换成动词谓语"接受"，products作宾语，其后的定语从句在汉语句子中前置，作定语。

（二）句子较长

在营销英语的长句子中，为了保持结构上的合理、平衡，往往将句子中的中心词或词组前移，而由于汉语更加注重语言结构的节奏感和逻辑性，往往在翻译时侧重于语言的经济效用和逻辑效用。

例11. Many individuals within an organization have a responsibility for creating value—not just marketing staff—and a marketing orientation requires that the organization draw upon and integrate its human and physical resources effectively and adapt them to meet customers' needs.

译文：企业中不仅仅营销人员有创造价值的责任，许多人都有创造价值的责任。市场导向要求企业有效地利用和整合其人力和物力资源，并对其进行调整以满足客户的需求。

原句是一个并列复合句，除了并列连词，还用破折号连接句子，句中还套有一个较长的宾语从句，使得句子叠床架屋，结构拉得很长，但非常正式规范。汉译时将句子拆开，这样才能形成通顺的汉语句子。

例12. It is not sufficient for an organization simply to appoint a marketing manager or set up a marketing department—viewed as a philosophy, marketing is an attitude that applies to everybody who works for the organization.

译文：仅仅任命一名营销经理或设立一个营销部门是不够的。营销被视为一种理念，是一种适用于每个为企业工作的员工的态度。

原句由两个长句组成，后一个句子用破折号与前句连接，作补充说明，译成汉语时可以拆分成两个独立的句子，破折号可以不用。

（三）多用被动语态

在专门用途英语文体中，被动语态的使用较为频繁，这是因为这类文体着眼于理论，需要使事物、过程和结果处于句子的中心地位，而被动结构正好能突出说明的对象；再者，客观的表达往往不含有任何的感情色彩，这二者的不相容性在被动结构中能够得到合理的解决。在汉译的过程中，由于汉语语言习惯及结构的要求,常常将被动结构主动化。

例13. Because of the trend toward impulse buying, greater emphasis must be placed on promotional programs to get people into a store.

译文:由于消费者越来越趋向于冲动性购买,销售人员必须注重促销计划,以吸引更多的顾客进入商店。

例14. To accommodate the growing market, modified versions of the basic model are offered, distribution is expanded, different prices are available, and persuasive mass advertising is utilized.

译文:为了适应此阶段的要求,企业应在原样式的基础上改进产品,增加花色,扩大销售,提供不同的价格层次,利用具有说服力的大众广告。

原句是个并列结构,每个分句都是被动语态,都有自己的主语和谓语。当被动语态变为主动语态时,由于语法结构的改变,句子的成分也随之有所增减。其中最为明显的变化是增加了"企业"作主语,原来各分句的主语全部转换为宾语,主语就成了必要且重要的句子成分。

三、市场营销英语翻译中的变通与转换

由于英语和汉语在语言形态、词语表达、句式结构以及衔接手段上存在差异,因此,在英汉翻译中,要采用多种翻译技巧,通过转换词性、调整结构和语序、增词或减词、替代、抽象转具体等变通手段,使译文通顺、达意。

例15. For a fast food restaurant, for example, the training of serving staff would emphasize those items—such as the speed of service and friendliness of staff—that research has found to be most valued by existing and potential customers.

译文:例如,对于一家快餐店而言,对服务人员的培训将着重于那些研究发现最受现有的和潜在的顾客重视的项目,如服务速度和员工的友善程度。

that引导定语从句修饰speed和friendliness。friendliness翻译成汉语时增加"程度"一词,使抽象名词词义具体化。

例16. We now adopt a slightly more sophisticated approach and analyze a product sales model with four stages: introduction, growth, maturity, and decline.

译文:下面采用稍微复杂的表述方法,引用四个阶段来分析产品的销售模型:引入期、成长期、成熟期和衰退期。

原句是由两个简单句构成的并列句,有两个动词谓语、一个介词短语。汉语

译文将介词短语译成了动词短语，four stages（四个阶段）后的四个名词为抽象名词，汉语添加"期"这一概念性词语，以使抽象名词具体化。

例17. To many people, marketing is simply associated with a set of techniques. For example, market research is seen as a technique for finding out about customers' needs, and advertising is thought to be a technique for communicating the benefits of a product offer to potential customers. However, these techniques can be of little value if they are undertaken by an organization that has not fully taken on board the philosophy of marketing.

译文：对许多人来说，市场营销仅仅与一整套技巧相关。例如，市场调研被看作是发现客户需求的一种技巧，而广告被认为是向潜在客户传达产品好处的一种技巧。然而，如果一个企业没有完全接受市场营销的理念，那么这些技巧就没有什么价值。

该段落有三个句子，其中However引导的是一个主从复合句，句子较长，这符合英语的句式特点。而汉语惯用小句、短句，翻译时应采用拆句法。此外，应调整句子结构和语序，将原句的被动语态转换成汉语的主动语态，直接让施事者作主语。

例18. 一是削弱营销计划，相应收缩产品的种类、营销渠道和促销手段；二是通过重新定位、重新包装或重新推销使产品复兴；三是停产退出市场。

译文：They can cut back on their marketing programs, thereby reducing the range of products they make, the outlets they sell through, and the promotion they use; they can revive the product by repositioning, repackaging, or otherwise remarketing it; or they can terminate the product.

原句用"一是""二是""三是"引领的三个句子进行列举。译文将三个句子都转换成有主谓宾结构的句子，并通过分号和表示选择意义的并列连词or将三个句子连接起来，形成并列句，使句子简洁易懂。

第二节　课内翻译任务

一、英译汉　English-Chinese Translation

Market Segmentation

The marketing concept calls for understanding customers and satisfying their needs better than the competition. But different customers have different needs, and it is rarely possible to satisfy all customers by treating them alike.

Mass marketing refers to treatment of the market as a homogenous group and offering the same marketing mix to all customers. Mass marketing allows economies of scale to be realized through mass production, mass distribution and mass communication. The drawback of mass marketing is that customer needs and preferences differ and the same offering is unlikely to be viewed as optimal by all customers. If a firm ignored differing customer needs, another firm would enter the market with a product that serves a specific group, and the incumbent firm would lose those customers. To recognize the diversity of customer needs, it is important to identify different market segments.

A market segment consists of consumers who respond in a similar way to a given set of marketing stimuli. In the car market, for example, consumers who choose the biggest, most comfortable car regardless of price make up one market segment. Another market segment would be customers who care mainly about price and operating economy. It would be difficult to make one model of car that was the first choice of every consumer. Companies are wise to focus their efforts on meeting the distinct needs of one or more market segments.

According to experts, in order to be a good market segment, a group should meet five criteria:

1. It should be possible to identify and measure it.
2. It should be big enough to be worth the effort.
3. It should be easy to reach it.
4. It should not change quickly.
5. And it should be responsive.

Market segmentation strategies that meet these criteria can cover wide range of consumer characteristics. Subsets may be defined by basic demographics like age, race, or gender, for example. Other qualities, like educational background or income can also be used, as can location. Some of the potentially most powerful variables by which to segment a market are behavioral ones, including social class, lifestyle, and interests.

In most scenarios, there will be at least a few established customers who fall into more than one category, but marketing strategists normally allow for this phenomenon. In fact, the overlap in criteria among consumers often leads to additional segmentation and requires adjusted marketing strategies. A marketing plan that targets people who fall into several groups—like women over 30 who earn a high income, for example—may be more successful than one that focuses on just one limited characteristic.

重点解析 Notes and Comments

1. better than the competition 而不是与竞争对手竞争

翻译时采用增词法，增加"与竞争对手"几个字，以使意思更明确、句子更顺畅。

2. Mass marketing refers to treatment of the market as a homogenous group and offering the same marketing mix to all customers. 大众营销是指将市场作为一个同质的群体，并向所有客户提供相同的营销组合。

句中的名词+介词宾语结构（"treatment of"）被转换成动宾结构（"把……看作，将……作为"）。

大众营销又称为广泛市场营销（大量市场营销），是指营销者以相同的方式向市场上所有的消费者提供相同的产品和进行信息沟通，即大量生产、大量分销和大量促销。广泛营销以市场的共性为基础，忽略市场需求的差异，力图以标准化的产品和分销影响最广泛的市场范围。

3. Mass marketing allows economies of scale to be realized through mass production, mass distribution and mass communication. 广泛市场营销允许通过大规模生产、大规模分销和大规模传播来实现规模经济。

原句是被动语态，体现了商务英语惯用被动语态的特点，但译成汉语时要改成主动语态。

4. the same offering is unlikely to be viewed as optimal by all customers 同样的产品不可能被所有客户视为最佳产品

offering 在营销英语里意为"产品"。

5. If a firm ignored differing customer needs, ... 如果一家公司忽视了不同的客户需求，……

differing customer needs 是动名词短语，汉译时转换成名词短语。

6. A market segment consists of consumers who respond in a similar way to a given set of marketing stimuli. 一个细分市场是由对特定促销手段产生类似反应的消费者构成的。

本句翻译时按照原有主从结构,将定语从句译成定语,使句子简短,不必分成两个句子。a given set of marketing stimuli字面意思是"一套给定的营销刺激",译成"特定促销手段"则更显专业性。市场细分(market segmentation,或称市场区分)是指将消费者依照不同的特征和消费需求区分成若干群体,从而形成多个消费群。

7. Companies are wise to focus their efforts on meeting the distinct needs of one or more market segments. 明智的做法是把精力集中在满足一个或多个细分市场的独特需求上。

该句翻译的关键是将作表语的形容词wise拆分出来,转换成定语,增加"做法"二字,构成名词短语,这样才符合汉语的表达习惯。

8. it should be responsive 应该对营销方式反应迅速

responsive如果按照字面意思译成"有响应的"会比较含糊,通过增词法可以使意思更明确。

9. Subsets may be defined by basic demographics like age, race, or gender... 也可以按人口统计因素如年龄、种族、性别细分市场……

Subsets基本意思是"子集""小团体",此处是指细分市场。该句转换了语态,不宜译为"细分市场可以由基本的人口统计定义"。

10. Other qualities, like educational background or income can also be used, as can location. 如同可以按照用户地理位置来划分市场一样,也可以按照其他特征,如教育背景或收入来划分市场。

as can location是倒装句,省略了be used,be used替代前一句的defined。

11. In most scenarios, there will be at least a few established customers who fall into more than one category, but marketing strategists normally allow for this phenomenon. 在大多数情况下,总会有一些老客户同时分属几个类别,但营销策略通常会考虑到这种现象。

established customers应译为"老客户"。marketing strategists译为"营销策略"即可,如译为"战略家,策略家"则不恰当。

二、汉译英 Chinese-English Translation

交换

社会在如何获取商品和服务方面有不同的安排方式。在一些不发达的社会,寻找食物或乞讨可能是一种常态。

在计划经济中，商品和服务可能由政府计划者分配给个人和企业。在现代市场经济中，商品和服务是在交换的基础上获得的。交换意味着一方对另一方作出一些牺牲，以换取一方所看重的东西；另一方也作出类似的牺牲，得到自己认为重要的东西。

当然，所做牺牲和对收到及放弃的商品的价值判断本质上是基于个人的意见和偏好，所以没有客观的方法来定义什么是"公平"的交换，只要双方都对结果感到满意即可。

在市场经济体中，存在这样一种假设：每一方都可以决定是否与另一方进行交易。双方还可以自由选择一些潜在的合作伙伴。虽然在一些交易系统中，商品和服务的交换仍然很常见，但交换通常是以产品换取货币的形式进行的。

可否将交换概念推广至公共服务的提供呢？一些人认为，向政府交税以换取公共服务是一种社会营销的交换形式。在营销框架内，这种交换方法存在的问题是，很难确定政府服务的消费者在决定他们应该进行何种交换时拥有什么权力。

单一的交换不应与交易各方之间的前一次交换和预期的后一次交换分开看待。营销人员越来越注重分析持续的交易关系，而不是一次性的、孤立的交易。

重点解析 Notes and Comments

1. 社会在如何获取商品和服务方面有不同的安排方式。Societies have different ways in which they arrange for goods and services to be acquired.

用in which引导的定语从句修饰the ways。原句中的"在如何获取商品和服务方面……的安排方式"译成arrange for something to be done，使句子结构简洁明了。

2. 在计划经济中，商品和服务可能由政府计划者分配给个人和企业。In planned economies goods and services may be allocated to individuals and firms by government planners.

汉语的"由"字结构在英语中可以用被动结构表达。

3. 以换取一方所看重的东西 in return for receiving something it values

in return for 一般词典解释为"作为……报答、回报"，此处使用非常恰当。

4. 所做牺牲和对收到及放弃的商品的价值判断本质上是基于个人的意见和偏好 the sacrifices and valuations of goods received and given up are essentially

based on personal opinion and preferences

"收到及放弃的"在原句中为前置定语,英文用过去分词短语received and given up作后置定语。句子谓语用被动语态。

5. 在市场经济体中,存在这样一种假设:每一方都可以决定是否与另一方进行交易。In market-based economies there is a presumption that each party can decide whether or not to enter into an exchange with the other.

economy(经济体)在此处为可数名词。原句合并成英语长句,"假设"(presumption)后接that引导的同位语从句。

6. 虽然在一些交易系统中,商品和服务的交换仍然很常见,但交换通常是以产品换取货币的形式进行的。Exchange usually takes the form of a product being exchanged for money, although the bartering of goods and services is still common in some trading systems.

英语与汉语语序不同,汉语中是"尽管(虽然)"在前,"但是"在后;而英语语序则比较灵活。

7. 可否将交换概念推广至公共服务的提供呢?Can the concept of exchange be generalized to cover the provision of public services?

"推广"此处译为be generalized。generalize有"概括,推广,使一般化"之意。

8. 一些人认为,向政府交税以换取公共服务是一种社会营销的交换形式。Some have argued that the payment of taxes to the government in return for the provision of public services is a form of social marketing exchange.

英译时将汉语的两个短句合并成一句,用that引导宾语从句。

9. 在营销框架内,这种交换方法存在的问题是,很难确定政府服务的消费者在决定他们应该进行何种交换时拥有什么权力。Within marketing frameworks, the problem with this approach to exchange is that it can be difficult to identify what sovereignty consumers of government services have in determining which exchanges they should engage in.

原句是由短句组成的长句,这是汉语的句式结构特点。英语是树状语言,多用长句和复合结构。因此,翻译时将汉语的短句合并成英语的长句,就往往需要用复合结构。译文中,主语是the problem,that引导的表语从句中的真正主语不定式to identify后接what引导的宾语从句,宾语从句中的状语是in determining引导的短语,动名词determining后接which引导的名词性宾语从句。

sovereignty本义为"主权""最高权力",此处意指个人至高无上的权力。

第三节 课后翻译训练

一、将下列句子翻译成汉语 Translate the following sentences into Chinese

1. In order to attain the better effect, there are a lot of on-line advertisements which combine with the sale-promotion campaigns to be "on-line advertisement combined with campaign."

2. Even where the subsidiary is selling only locally made products, the tariff can still be a factor in that it helps to keep out low-priced competitors from other countries, giving more pricing freedom to the subsidiary.

3. With cost-based pricing, a firm determines prices by computing merchandise, service, and overhead costs and then adding an amount to cover the firm's profit goal.

4. However, in today's world of floating exchange rates the value of other currencies in terms of home currency is constantly fluctuating and vice versa. Indeed it may fluctuate several percent in a single day.

5. This can have two different impacts on the firm's pricing. The most obvious impact is when the subsidiary is importing products for the local market and paying the duty on top of the transfer price.

6. Consumer products include convenience products, shopping products, specially products and unsought products. These products differ in the way consumers buy them, so they differ in how they are marketed.

7. It is important to realize that whether your firm has enough penetration to maximize sales, fully utilize the media, and pay out the marketing investment in any given market.

8. Brand positioning is a process of establishing and managing the images, perception, and associations that the consumer applies to your product based on the values and beliefs associated with your product.

9. A marketer must highlight the unique selling point of a product instead of overloading consumers with too much information.

10. You need to make sure that your e-mail marketing complies with privacy and data protection rules, and that it is properly targeted on people who want to receive it.

二、将下列句子翻译成英语 Translate the following sentences into English

1. 短期内制约我们在这一地区发展的主要因素是缺少优秀的供货商。
2. 我们必须奋起直追以赶上各竞争对手,否则将得不到任何市场份额。
3. 推出新产品之后,形势得以扭转,我们重新获得了最大的市场份额。
4. 你们要充分利用自身优势,尽快打开市场。
5. 产品定位指的是为某一产品在市场上找到合适的位置。
6. 我们承诺这些产品质量稳定,种类丰富。
7. 低价格加上大力宣传旨在获取较大比例的市场份额。
8. 市场崩盘的规模,无论从成交量还是价格来看,都是出乎意料的。
9. 生产同类产品的厂商通过价格和产品差异的组合进行竞争。
10. 你可以允许别人将你的网页个性化,这样人们就能直接进入感兴趣的商品页面。

三、将下列短文翻译成汉语 Translate the following passage into Chinese

Features of E-marketing

E-marketing means using digital technologies to help promote and sell your goods or service. It is not just about selling goods over the web. These technologies, like mail and website, are a valuable complement to traditional marketing methods whatever the size of your company or your business model.

The basics of marketing remain the same—creating a strategy to deliver the right messages to the right people. What has changed is the number of options you have. Today the buzz words are "multi-channel integration," yet only 6% of businesses are taking advantages of all of the channels available to them.

The 4 main channels today are retail, e-commerce, mail order/telephone order (MOTO) and market places like BT Tradespace, e-bay etc. Simply put, e-marketing gives you lots of new ways to reach your customers, many of them cheaper and more effective than traditional channels. Two thirds of UK shoppers spent more online this Christmas, bringing the total online sales for December 2008 to €4.67 billion. That's up 14.2% on December 2007.

Obviously these figures do not tell the whole story—not all sales made online are the result of e-marketing and not every business has benefited equally.

What is certain, though, is that many businesses are producing great results with e-marketing and its flexible and cost-effective natures make it particularly suitable for small and medium sized companies.

It is no exaggeration to describe e-marketing as a revolution for the marketing industry. For the first time, it gives businesses of any size access to the mass market at an affordable price and, unlike TV or print advertising, it allows truly personalised marketing. Specific benefits of e-marketing include:

Global reach

Lower cost

Trackable, measurable results 24-hour marketing

Shorter lead times

A level playing field

(Andrian Palmer, *Introduction to Marketing*, Oxford University Press, 2009.)

四、将下列短文翻译成英语 Translate the following passage into English

人员推销

作为促销的一种形式，人员推销是指企业的销售人员与一个或一个以上可能成为购买者的人交谈，作口头陈述，以推销其产品。与广告相比，人员推销更依赖人际接触。

与广告的公众性信息相比，人员推销通过单独接触传递信息，提供有说服力的消息。有几个原因能解释为什么人员推销方式有时在海外市场比在美国国内市场起着更大的作用。受教育人口比例低、政府在广告上的限制和媒体缺乏有效性都限制了企业广告的数量，从而使企业强调另一个重要的选择：人员推销。而且，在工资收入较低的发展中国家，人员推销是一种相对便宜的促销方式。

人员推销具有许多积极的和消极的特点。积极的一面是人员推销对每一位消费者给予特别的关注，并传递大量的信息。在买方和卖方之间就存在一个动态的而非被动的交流。广告是做不到这一点的。

人员推销方式灵活，浪费少，能促成销售并快速反馈。人员推销的方式很灵活，能满足特别顾客的需要。一个房地产经纪人会对购买第一处住房的夫妇和对购买第二处住房的夫妇使用不同的促销手段。

人员推销反馈及时清楚。消费者可能被询问关于公司政策和产品特征的看法，或填写对企业及其产品的意见。正如公司的广告活动一样，营销人员能够确定一个营销计划的利弊。

消极的一面是人员推销只接触有限的顾客，单位顾客成本很高，不能在整体顾客中形成产品意识，并可能在一些消费者中留下不良印象。例如，一个家具的推销人员，如果为每位顾客平均介绍15—30分钟，则最多每天只能接待20位顾客。工业品推销人员可能接待的更少。正如前面部分提到的，人员推销的单位顾客成本高，这是由一对一的销售特点所决定的。

本章第一节市场营销相关知识与翻译技巧部分内容选自：莫莉莉的《营销英语的词汇特征及其汉译技巧》、张琳琳的《市场营销英语的语体特点及翻译方法》、肖娴的《市场营销英语的词汇特点与翻译》等论文，以及翁凤翔的《国际营销英语》等专著。本章英汉翻译短文均选自：Andrian Palmer, *Introduction to Marketing*, Oxford University Press, 2009, 并有删减。

第六章 商务合同翻译

商务合同（Business Contract），也称经贸合同，是为了保护买卖双方合法权益和制约双方某些行为而签订的具有法律效力的强制性文件。本章所指的商务合同翻译主要指涉外商务交易中使用的货物买卖合同或协议的英汉互译。涉外商务合同（Foreign Business Contract）是在涉外经贸活动中，自然人或法人之间为实现一定的商务目的，按一定的合法手续达成的规定相互权利和义务的契约，是一种具有法律效力的对外文书，对签约各方都具有法律约束力（legally binding）。英汉两个文本的合同都具有法律文本的严肃性和权威性。准确无误、使用公式化套语是涉外合同翻译的主要特点。（岳峰、刘茵，2014：178）

本章介绍涉外商务合同的构成、基本特征及其翻译技巧，涉及商务合同的基本概念、基本结构、类别、术语以及合同签订的注意事项等方面的知识和英汉翻译相关知识与实践。

第一节 商务合同概述

一、商务合同的概念

合同是两个或多个当事人之间签订的具有法律约束力的协议。但并非所有人与人之间的协议都能称为合同。朋友之间约定在电影院见面，如果其中一位朋友没有出席，他并不会受到法律制裁。商务合同是两个或两个以上当事人之间为实施某种行为或不实施某种行为而订立的具有法律约束力的协议。例如，商务合同可用于约定以一定价格出售货物或提供服务。

商务英语合同包含商务、英语和合同三个方面。"商务"主要涉及与货物买卖、经销代理、加工贸易、劳务出口、国际租赁、补偿贸易等相关的贸易领域专业知识；"英语"则重点关注英文术语、词汇、短语、搭配和英文合同条款、句型等与国际贸易相关的语言领域专业知识；而"合同"指的是为了确定买卖双方的权利和义务关系而涉及的专业术语、条款等法律领域专业知识。商务合同种类繁多，常见的有销售或购货合同（Sales or Purchase Contract or Agreement）、运输合同（Contract of Carriage）、代理协议（Agency Agreement）、技术转让合同（Contract for Technology Transfer）、合资或合营合同（Contract for Joint Venture or Joint Production）、合作伙伴协议（Partnership Agreements）、营业场所租赁合同（Lease of Business Premises）、厂房和设备租赁合同（Lease of Plant and Equipment）、雇佣协议（Employment Agreement）等。

一般来说，合同的订立没有固定的形式，可以通过口头或书面等形式订立。没有固定订立形式的合同称为简易合同或口头合同。然而，某些类型的合同必须以书面等特定的形式签订，才具备法院认可的法律效力。这些类型的合同被称为特殊合同。

二、合同的基本要素

为了使一份合同成立并具有法律约束力，合同必须具备五个基本要素（essential elements）。这五个要素是：

- 协议（Agreement）
- 对价（Consideration）
- 建立法律关系意图（An intention to create legal relations）
- 签约能力（Capacity to contract）
- 符合法律规定的形式（Compliance with required formalities where applicable）

合同协议（Agreement）包含要约和承诺（offer and acceptance）。要约是一方当事人以缔结合同为目的，向对方当事人提出合同条件，希望对方当事人接受的意思表示。发出要约的一方称要约人（offeror），接受要约的一方称受要约人（offeree）。承诺，在商务尤其是国际商务中又称"接盘"（acceptance of offer），是指受要约人同意要约的意思表示。对价是指一方为换取另一方做某事的承诺而向另一方支付的金钱代价或得到该种承诺的代价。

三、商务合同的构成

尽管商务英语合同种类繁多，但其在结构上又具有许多相似性。一般来说，商务合同由标题（Title）、约首（Preamble）、正文（Body）和约尾（Closing）四个主要部分组成。标题用于明确商务合同的性质或者种类，如 sales contract（销售合同），使得主题一目了然。约首主要写明合同生效的基本条件，如合同双方的姓名和国籍、主营业务、合同签订的日期和地点等。正文是商务合同的核心部分，明确地规定了合同双方的权利、义务、责任及风险。为了避免歧义或争议的发生，每条条款都必须清晰、具体、完整。约尾包括合同的合法性及合同效力、合同补充条款、双方的签名等。简而言之，商务英语合同是商务、英语和合同三者之间的有机融合。商务英语合同必须是正式的，正式性主要体现在其内容的特殊性、语言的严谨性和结构的完整性几个方面。

（一）合同标题

标题表示商务合同的性质或者种类，使得主题一目了然。英文合同跟中文合同一样，由于当事人之间的法律关系由合同内容来判断，所以合同的标题也可以没有。但是为了方便识别，一般会在合同首页上方根据合同的性质拟定一个标题。出口合同的标题常常是出口方习惯用的Sales Contract（销售合同），也有的将合同当事人确认的Sales Confirmation（销售确认书）和Proforma Invoice（形式发票）作为合同的标题，也有的用国外买方发出的Purchase Order（购买合同）来表示。除此之外，还可以根据合同的性质和内容拟定其他题目。比如：Property Lease Contract（房屋租赁合同），Contract of Transfer of Technology（技术转让合同），等等。一般在合同标题后面或者右上方的位置写上合同号，如No. 23-455, No. HG236。

（二）合同约首

合同约首也称前言或序言、首部，一般包括合同各方的名称（通常是公司名称）及其国籍（Signing Parties and Their Nationalities）、主要营业场所或住所（Principle Place of Business or Residence Address）、当事人合法依据（Each Party's Authority）、订约时间和地点（Signing Date/Place）、电话和传真（Telephone/Fax）、订约缘由/说明条款（Recitals/Whereas Clause）。

1. 合同各方

合同各方指的是合同买卖双方。买方的英文是"buyer"，如果不止一个买家，可以用复数"buyers"。卖方的英文是"seller"。如果有两个或两个以上的卖家，可以用复数"sellers"。通常英语合同尤其是非买卖合同中的双方，用"Party A"和"Party B"表示，而汉语合同相应译为"甲方"和"乙方"，不能译为"A方"和"B方"。如果原文是汉语合同，交易双方是"甲方"和"乙方"，译成英文就是"Party A"和"Party B"，切不可译为"Party Jia"和"Party Yi"。合同双方的单位要写全称,中英文译文都必须是全称,和约尾的称谓一致。在合同中,称谓和术语要保持一致,以显示严肃性。

2. 陈述订约事由

订约事由是英文协议/合同约首的另一个组成部分,由几个原因从句"whereas clauses"组成。

例1. WHEREAS, Party A possesses exclusive license and represents Licensed Program (both defined here below) for trademarks, copyrights, patents and other certain considerable know-how in the field of design, manufacturing, installation and safety of the Licensed Program and every legal concern regarding this Agreement is fully empowered to ABC and...

译文:鉴于,甲方独家专有许可证和许可证项目(两者定义如下文),包括:商标、版权、专利及其他大量涉及许可证项目的设计、生产、安装和安全等领域的专利技术和合法权益完全授予ABC公司,以及……

(注:以上例子和译文根据岳峰和刘茵主编的2014年版《商务英语笔译》修改)

有的进出口合同比较简单,也有其他类型的合同比如合作经营合同、专利技术使用合同,就没有体现出这个"鉴于从句",有的用了其他类型的句式结构。

(三)合同正文

合同正文部分具体约定了当事人的权利和义务,是合同的核心部分,也是篇幅最大的部分。具体内容包括:合同的类型和合同的种类、范围(the type of contract and the categories and the scope of the object of the contract)、合同标的技术条件、质量、标准、规格、数量(the technical conditions, the quality, the standards, the specifications and the quantities of the object of the contract)、合同履行的期限、地点和方式(time limit, the place and the method of performance)、合同价格条件、支付金额、支付方式和各种附加的费用(the price terms, the amount to be paid, the ways of payment, and the various types of additional charges)、合同能否转让和合同转让条件(whether or not the contract can be assigned or the conditions for assignment)、违反合同的赔偿和其他责任(the compensation and other liabilities for the breach of contract)、合同发生争议时的解决办法(the methods for resolving disputes arising under the contract)、明确风险责任,约定保险范围(the limits of the risks to be borne by the parties in performing the object and the coverage of insurance of the object)合同的有效

期限、延长合同期限和提前终止合同的条件（a period of validity for the contract and conditions for the contractual extension and the contractual termination before its expiration）。（注：以上内容引自徐珺主编的《国际贸易翻译实务》2018年版）

（四）合同约尾

约尾即合同的结尾部分，也称合同的最后条款，写在合同的结尾。其内容一般包括合同的份数（copies of the contract）、合同适用的文字及其效力（the language in which the contract to be written and its validity）、签名（the signature）等。中国人有盖章（the seal）的习惯，外国人只有法人代表签字。

例2. This Contract is executed in two counterparts each in Chinese and English, each of which shall be deemed equally authentic. This Contract is in three copies effective since being signed/sealed by both parties.

译文：本合同为中、英文两种文本，两种文本具有同等效力。本合同一式三份，自双方签字（盖章）之日起生效。

（五）商务合同基本条款

为了避免歧义或争议的发生，每条条款都必须清晰、具体、完整。商务合同的基本条款主要包括：品质条款、数量条款、包装条款、价格条款、支付方式、装运条款、不可抗力等。

1. 品质条款（Quality）

品质条款包括商品名称（Name of Commodity）、规格（Specifications）、货号（Art. No.）等。有的清单上写着货号明细（description of goods），列出各个产品编号。如果是机器，就要列明型号、主要部件和配件。名牌商品因为品质好，通常可以指定品牌销售，质量中等的商品（俗称大路货）则需要写明规格、等级、标准进行买卖，有的凭样品买卖。（岳峰、刘茵，2014：181）

2. 数量条款（Quantity）

数量条款包括购买数量、计量单位等。《联合国国际货物销售合同公约》（The United Nations Convention on Contracts for the International Sale of Goods）规定所交付的货物必须与合同中所签订的数量一致。

3. 包装条款（Packing）

包装条款包含运输标志/唛头（shipping mark）、包装材料、包装方式等。有的产品采用裸装（nude cargo），如汽车、大机器。有的产品不需要或者没必要包装，为了节省运费就采取散装（cargo in bulk）。有的产品需要包装，如鞋子要用纸箱（carton）包装，外面写上正唛和侧唛作为产品的标识。

4. 价格条款（Price）

价格条款包含贸易术语、总值等。

（1）贸易术语

贸易术语也称价格术语。根据《2010年国际贸易术语解释通则》（The Incoterms Rules or International Commercial Terms 2010，简称"Incoterms 2010"，中文又称之为"2010通则"），贸易术语从13个减少到11个。最新的2020通则为出口商、进口商和物流供应商带来了一系列变化。

（2）总值条款

总值是单价和数量的乘积。总值所用的货币必须与单价中的货币和数量单位一致才能得到正确的合同金额。应注意英文大小写的表达。为避免交易一方在金额上进行涂改，汉语除了阿拉伯数字表示小写之外，另外还会用汉字来表示大写，比如：壹、贰、叁、肆、伍、陆、柒、捌、玖、拾。英语的小写也是用数字表示，"小写金额"的表述是total amount in figures，而不是total amount in small letters。英语的大写用英语单词表示，比如：one, two, three, four, 等等。大写金额前一般有个大写英文单词SAY，句末以ONLY结尾，相当于汉语中的"总金额为×××圆整"。"大写金额"用英文表示是total amount in words，而不能译为total amount in capitalized letters。

5. 支付方式（Terms of Payment）

支付方式又称为付款方式。国际贸易支付方式是国际上因商品交换而发生的以贷款为主要内容的债权债务清算方式。不同的支付方式有不同的支付时间、地点和方法。国际贸易中常见的付款方式有汇付（Remittance）、托收（Collection）、信用证（Letter of Credit）三种。汇付是指付款人通过银行，主动把款项汇给收款人（Payee）的一种支付方式。一笔汇款业务涉及汇款人（Remitter）、汇出行（Remitting Bank）、汇入行（Receiving Bank）或解付行（Paying Bank）、收款人（Payee）四个基本当事人。由于国际贸易金额大、时间长、距离远，又涉及不同的国家，合同双方彼此不信任，因此多数利用银行做担保的信用证支付方式，就如同现在的支付宝等网络平台支付功能。

6. 装运条款（Terms of Shipment）

国际货物买卖合同的装运条款，又称交货条款或交货方式，主要指国际货物运输的装运条件和相互责任。从法律上讲，卖方必须按照合同规定的装运时间、装运地、目的地装运和交接货物。FOB，CIF，CFR是三个最常见的贸易术语，即最主要的交货方式。FOB(Free on Board)指"船上交货",CTF(Cost, Insurance and Freight)指"成本、保险加运费",CFR(Cost and Freight)指"成本加运费"。

7. 不可抗力(Force Majeure)

不可抗力又称人力不可抗力,是指在合同签订后,由一些自然因素或社会因素而引发的当事人所不能预见、不能避免和不可控制的意外事件,如水灾、风灾、旱灾、地震、火灾、战争、海盗、检疫、隔离、封锁、政府禁令等(any event beyond control, such as flood, typhoon, drought, earthquake, fire, war, piracy, quarantine, segregation, blockade, government banning, etc.)。

第二节　商务合同的语言特点与翻译

一、商务合同的语言文体特点

（一）词汇特点

商务英语合同用语的特点之一表现在用词上,即选择正式用词和法律用语,使得合同表达的意思准确无误,达到双方均对合同中使用的词语无可争议的程度,词语的使用不带个人感情色彩,以显示合同的严肃和认真。总体上看,商务合同的词汇特点体现在以下几个方面。

1. 使用古体词

商务合同英语属庄重文体(frozen style),是各英语文体中正式程度最高的一种,用词极其考究,具有正式性和严肃性。为了体现庄重严肃的文体风格,商务合同中经常使用古体词,这些词主要来自古英语和中古英语。最常使用的古体词主要包括here, there, where和to, in, of等介词构成的复合副词。here代表this, there代表that, where代表what或which。通常使用的古英语词有:hereafter(此后,今后), hereby(特此,兹), herein(此中,于此,本合同中), hereinafter(以下,此后,在下文), therein(其中,在其中), thereinafter(在下文), thereof(关于,由此,其中), thereto(此外,附随), whereas(鉴于), whereby(因此,由是,据此),等等。

这类复合副词简练、直观,使合同语言显得更为严肃、规范,更能彰显出商务合同的严谨性和权威性。

2. 使用专业术语

在法律语境下,商务合同包含大量的商务专业术语以及法律专业术语。基本的商务专业术语，如ocean bills of lading（海运提单），freight to collect（运费到付），blank endorsed（空白背书）等，常见的法律专业术语，如financial responsibility（经济责任），jurisdiction（司法管辖权），force majeure（不可抗力）等。专业术语意义精确，不带有个人感情色彩，具有国际通用性和鲜明的文体特征，可准确描述商务活动中的各个交易环节和相关的各类单据。一些普通英语词汇，在法律语境当中也会出现特定的含义。以minor和intention为例：在通用的含义当中，minor表示少数或者是更年轻的含义，整体上表达不太严格，但是在法律英语中，该词语则特指18周岁以下；intention一词通常指"打算，意图，目的"，但在法律英语中有其特定的意思，意为"意思表示"。

在法律语境当中，商务合同必须体现出正式以及标准性的特征，这就意味着合同当中必须使用严谨的词汇，体现出商务合同的规范性。因此，商务合同需要使用较多的专业术语以及正式性的词汇。

3. 使用缩写词

商务合同中经常出现缩略词，常见的缩略词多为首字母缩略词和截短词。商务合同中，对于价格、赔偿金以及交货方式的表达，多使用首字母缩略词，如B/L（bill of lading），D/D（demand draft），M/T（mail transfer），FOB（free on board），CIF（cost, insurance, and freight），等等；对于计量单位的表达，通常使用截短词，如CM（centimeter），KG（kilogram），NO（number），PC（piece），T（ton）。同一个首字母缩写词也可指代不同的短语，如P.O.D.既可指交货地点（place of delivery），也可指目的港、卸货港（port of destination, port of discharge）。因此，在翻译具有不同含义的缩略词时，译者必须结合商务合同上下文，准确把握缩略词含义。

4. 使用情态动词

大量使用情态动词是商务合同另一个显著的语言特征。就单词的使用频率来看，shall 出现的频率最高。shall是一个非常严谨的法律专用词，当它作为情态动词与第三人称一起使用时，用于表示命令、义务、职责、权利、特权和许诺等。合同条文中的shall表示对合同当事人在法律上的义务进行了界定和确认，因此通常被译成"应该""必须"，有时也被译成"将""可"。shall not 表示禁止性义务，通常被译成"不得"，语气十分强烈。shall 在合同中可以用于各种时态和人称，带有浓厚的命令性语气和强制性语气，充分体现了商务合同作为法律文件的尊严和不可抗拒性。

此外，will, may, must, should等情态助动词在商务合同中也经常出现。will

也可以表示命令、义务等，但力度要比shall弱很多。may用于约定当事人的权利，没有任何义务的含义，不带有强制性，有时表示允许或许可，通常被译成"可以""得"等，其否定形式may not用于禁止性义务，被译成"不得"，但语气不如shall not强烈。must用于强制性义务，但这一义务不一定具有法律约束力，其否定形式一般不会出现在英文合同中。should一般情况下被译为"应该"，但是在商务合同中，should和if一样，是用较弱的语气来表示假设，所以它大多被译为"万一"或者"如果"，很少译为"应该"。

（二）句法特征

1. 复合长句

商务合同使用较多的长句和复杂句，体现出文本的严谨性，这是商务合同最为明显的句法特征。商务合同的主要用途是明确规定合同双方当事人的权利和义务，因此多使用陈述句用于解释说明。同时，为了避免合同中的条款模糊不清，使得当事人产生误解或引起歧义，商务合同还经常使用含多个从句的复合长句，以至于句子结构长、语法关系复杂。但通过分析不难发现，这些长句脉络清晰，表达准确，逻辑严密。如多个状语从句以及定语从句夹杂其他修饰成分，用于解释或者补充主句的意义。例如：

例3. The Buyer shall pay the Seller US $350,000 within 20 days after the Bank of China has received the following documents from the Seller and found them in order, but not earlier than 12 (twelve) months after the date the Contract Plant for the first time reached 95% of guaranteed capacity of the whole Contract Plant according to the guaranteed quality indices as per Annex VI to the Contract or 65 months after the date of signing the contract, whichever is earlier.

译文：买方须于中国银行收到卖方下列单据，并经审核证实无误后的20天内向卖方支付350,000美元，但此款项的支付不得早于合同工厂第一次达到附件VI所规定之质量保证指标的95%以后的12个月，或本合同签字后的65个月，以早到的日期为准。

这个复合长句中含有一个非常复杂的时间状语，界定了买方承担付款义务的时间。这个句子虽然很长，但从结构上看，主干部分为The buyer shall..., but not...其他均为修饰成分。此处译文将表示补充内容的较长部分转换成汉语的并列句，并将原文中时间状语所修饰的谓语部分的核心，即"支付款项"处理为并列句的主语。因此，对于冗长的状语，译者应考虑英语和汉语行文习惯的差异，翻译时对词序作出必要调整以符合汉语行文规范。

2. 条件句

商务合同主要约定合同各方应享有的权利和应履行的义务，但由于这种权利的行使和义务的履行均附有各种条件，所以条件句的大量使用成为商务合同的另一个句法特点。商务合同中的条件句多由下列连接词引导：if, should, in the event of/that, in case（of）, provided（that）, subject to, unless otherwise等。例如：

例4. 一旦这几个要件达成协议，合同谈判也就"基本"结束了。

译文：Provided that these items have been agreed upon, the contract negotiation "basically" comes to a conclusion.

"一旦……"为条件句，译文可处理为provided that...引导的条件句。

例5. Should all or part of the contract be unable to be fulfilled owing to the fault of one party, the breaching party shall bear the responsibilities thus caused.

译文：由于一方的过失，造成本合同不能履行或不能完全履行时，由过失一方承担违约责任。

3. 被动句

商务合同是以客观公正的词汇、正式的文体和谨慎的措辞来规定双方权利和义务的文件，属于文书性质，其文字叙述应比较客观、公正。而被动句多用于表述客观事实与情景，强调施事的过程和结果，不带主观色彩。因此，商务合同经常使用被动句，用于更好地体现文本的严谨性、客观性和公正性。在商务合同中，与包装、运输、保险、付款等有关的条款大多采用被动句结构。

例6. This is agreed that a margin of 2% shall be allowed for over or short count.

译文：兹同意，允许的数量误差为2%。

为符合汉语的表达习惯，在翻译英文合同时，在不改变主语的情况下，某些英语被动语态可直接译为汉语主动语态，且不必添加任何词语。

二、商务合同翻译原则

（一）准确性原则

商务合同用于界定合同当事人的权利和义务，其文本十分客观、严谨。因此，商务合同的翻译必须以准确性为首要原则。同时，商务合同属于应用文体，而应用文体的翻译不论全译、选译或综译，都应以正确传达原意为第一要义，特别是在表达空间、时间、位置、价值等概念时需更精确，切忌主观臆断。因此，

在理解原文的前提下,须用反映相关概念的术语或专业(行业)常用语来表达。(方梦之、毛忠明,2018:27)

例7. 买卖双方同意按下列条款买卖以下货物。

译文:The Seller agrees to sell and the Buyer agrees to purchase the undermentioned commodity according to the terms and conditions stipulated below.

这个译句中的"条款"一词应译成the terms and conditions。在商务合同中,经常使用成双成对的同义词,同义词之间用and或or连接。成对用同义词是为了避免诉讼时双方律师钻空子,利用词义间的细微差别大作文章。我们知道term和condition是同义词,都表示"条件,条款",它们在合同中经常连用。

例8. 如卖方延期交货超过合同规定20周时,买方有权撤销合同。

译文:In case the Seller fails to make delivery 20 weeks later than the time of shipment stipulated in the Contract, the Buyer shall have the right to cancel the Contract.

商务合同英语中的数字有一系列的规则,有些与汉语的规则有很大差别。一般来说,1至10写成单词,11及以上的数字写成阿拉伯数字。(以上译例及说明选自杨芳,2004:84)

例9. 甲乙双方约定,该房屋每月租金为4000元整(大写:肆仟圆整)。

译文:Party A and Party B have agreed that the total monthly rent shall be RMB 4,000 (SAY RMB FOUR THOUSAND ONLY IN WORD).

在英文合同中,交易金额前必须添加货币(符号),如US($),RMB(¥)等,并添加交易金额的大写。英文金额的大写由四个部分组成:SAY + 货币 + 大写数字(amount in word)+ ONLY/ONLY IN WORD(相当于汉语的"整"),英文大写金额中的所有字母均大写。

(二)忠实性原则

所谓"忠实",即译文所传递的信息同原文所传递的信息要保持一致,或者说要保持信息等值。(刘法公,1999:59)商务合同必然涉及很多数字、日期、单位等内容的翻译,这就要求译者在正确理解合同原文本的前提下将原文信息准确无误地用目的语表达出来,以保障各方的合法权益。因此,商务合同的译文应该从措辞、结构及行文方式上忠实于源语的语言与行文规范,以再现严谨和正式的语篇。(岳峰、刘茵,2014:6)

例10. 单价：每吨成本加运费到黄埔价格2,560美元。

译文：Unit Price：2,560.00 dollars per metric ton CFR Huangpu.

改译：Unit Price：2,560.00 US dollars per metric ton CFR Huangpu.

此句中，将"美元"译为"dollars"不够准确，在措辞上违背了忠实性原则。虽然在狭义的认知中，dollar常常被认为就是"美元"，但dollar并非特指美元，世界上使用"dollar"作为货币单位的国家和地区很多，如加拿大元（Canadian Dollar）、新加坡元（Singapore Dollar）等。因此，为了准确传达原文含义，译文应明确币种，可改译为"US dollars"。此处译文做到忠实于原文，能避免合同当事人因条款指代不明而发生经济纠纷。

商务合同具有法律文本的特点，因此，忠实性原则也体现在术语翻译的准确性以及译文的完整性上。

（三）通顺性原则

所谓"通顺"，是指译文应当符合译入语的语法要求，通顺流畅，清晰易懂。商务合同译文的通顺重点体现在条理清晰上。由于合同订立人希望将信息表达得既完整又严密，不给别人曲解或误解留下可乘之机，因此商务合同的句式结构多为复杂的长句。而中英文在语言结构上存在较大差异，中文注重意合，结构较为松散；而英文注重形合，结构上较为缜密。在翻译英语商务合同中的长句时，要首先找到句子的主干，分析句子各部分之间的逻辑关系，以及各个从句和短句的语法功能，最后按照汉语的表达习惯重新组织成文。（毛慧洁，2018：82）

例11. Generally, an agreement is shown to exist through the presence of offer and acceptance.

译文：一般来说，当事人订立合同采取要约、承诺方式。

英文原文为被动语态，根据"汉语多主动，英语多被动"的语言特点，此处译文将被动语态处理为主动语态。

例12. 从自然关系上说，准合同是合同的前身。

译文：In terms of the natural relationship, a contract grows out of the quasi contract.

"前身"一词指的是事物演变中原来的组织形态或名称，这个词在英文中没有完全对应的词，因此可采用意译法，翻译时将原文的名词转换为动词，译为a contract grows out of the quasi contract，确保译文通顺流畅。

第三节 课内翻译任务

一、英译汉 English-Chinese Translation

SALES CONFIRMATION

Shanghai Foreign Company

1st Happy Road, Shanghai, China

S/C No.：

Date：

Signed At：

To：

ABC Company

1st Garden Road, London, England

Dear Sirs：

　　We hereby confirm having sold to you the following goods on terms and conditions as specified below.

1. Article Number	2. Commodity & Specification	3. Quantity	4. Unit Price	5. Amount
1234567890	White Plush Toys	5,000 PCS	CIF London USD 10.00	USD 50,000.00
Total Value	USD 50,000.00 (SAY US DOLLARS FIFTY THOUSAND ONLY)			

　　1. Packing：In cartons containing five pcs each

　　2. Port of Loading：Shanghai

　　3. Port of Destination：London, England

　　4. Time of Shipment：On or before 20 May 2019

　　5. Partial Shipment：Not Allowed

　　6. Transshipment：Allowed

　　7. Terms of Payment：30% T/T in advance, 70% L/C at sight

　　8. Insurance：To be covered by the Seller for 110% of total invoice value against all risks and war risks as per and subject to the relevant Ocean Marine Cargo Clauses of the People's Insurance Company of China, dated 1/1/1981.

9. Shipping Marks: As per Seller's option

10. Remarks: The Buyers are requested to sign and return one copy of this sales confirmation immediately after receipt of the same. Objection, if any, should be raised by the Buyers within five days after the receipt of this sales confirmation, in the absence of which it is understood that the Buyers have accepted the terms and conditions of the sales confirmation.

The Sellers: The Buyers:

重点解析 Notes and Comments

1. Dear Sirs: We hereby confirm having sold to you the following goods on terms and conditions as specified below. 敬启者：兹确认售予你方下列货品，其成交条款如下。

此句中terms and conditions是一组同义词，terms或conditions单独使用时，在不同的语境中可表示不同的含义。但在商务合同中，并列结构terms and conditions只有一种含义，就是"（合同、协议等的）条款"。

2. CIF London CIF伦敦价，即"成本加保险费加运费到伦敦的价格"。

CIF是Cost Insurance and Freight的缩写，也是国际贸易中最常用的贸易术语之一。按此术语成交，指定目的港，货物自装运港到目的港的运费、保险费由卖方支付。因此CIF报价除成本外，还包括需由卖方支付的运费和保险费。

3. 30% T/T in advance, 70% L/C at sight 电汇支付30%的预付货款，剩余70%的货款采用即期信用证的方式支付。

T/T（电汇），国际贸易中最常用的付款方式之一，是指汇出行应汇款人的申请，采用SWIFT（环球银行间金融电讯系统）等电讯手段将电汇付款委托书给汇入行，指示解付一定金额给收款人的一种汇款方式。L/C at sight（即期信用证），指开证行或付款行收到符合信用证条款的跟单汇票或装运单据后，立即履行付款义务的信用证。

4. To be covered by the Seller for 110% of total invoice value against all risks and war risks as per and subject to the relevant Ocean Marine Cargo Clauses of the People's Insurance Company of China, dated 1/1/1981. 由卖方根据中国人民保险公司1981年1月1日的海洋运输货物保险条款按发票金额的110%投保一切险和

战争险。

subject to在法律文件中通常与agreement, section, contract等法律文件名或文件中特定条款配合使用，通常译为"以……为条件，根据……"等。

5. Shipping Marks指"运输标志"，又称唛头，一般标示于纸箱的正面或侧面，通常由一个简单的几何图形和一些英文字母、数字及简单的文字组成，其作用在于使货物在装卸、运输、保管过程中容易被有关人员识别，以防错发错运。

6. Objection, if any, should be raised by the Buyers within five days after the receipt of this sales confirmation, in the absence of which it is understood that the Buyers have accepted the terms and conditions of the sales confirmation. 如有异议，买方必须在收到本销售确认书5日内提出，否则视买方已接受本销售确认书的各项条款。

此句中if any为插入语，指"如果有的话"，此处用于补充说明插入语之前的objection（"异议"），因此此句译为"如有异议，买方必须……"。

二、汉译英 Chinese-English Translation

销售代理协议

兹有乙方委托甲方为其出口上述货物的代理。为此，甲乙双方经协商，达成如下协议。

乙方应将购销合同提交甲方备案。

乙方负责督促并安排其所指定的生产厂家进行备货。（如乙方出运违禁品，乙方须自行承担一切法律责任。）

甲方负责乙方采购货物的报关、发货、退税工作，主要以FOB交货方式为主。

乙方应在发货前5天向甲方提供准备发货货物的所有细节（包括商品编码、申报品名、金额、数量、装箱尺码、毛/净重、预计开船日期、货运代理等资料）。

由于乙方所指定的生产厂家的原因不能按时按质交货或者提供的货物名称、数量、金额等与实际不符所产生的损失与后果，由乙方自行与生产厂家进行协商或索赔，甲方不承担任何风险与责任。

因乙方原因造成逾期付款的，乙方应承担由此产生的一切责任；除非甲方收到乙方货款，否则甲方不保证将货款支付给乙方指定的生产厂家。

若遇特殊情况，双方另行协商。

乙方委托甲方安排货物运输。

货物出口的相关人民币费用由甲方预付，对该预付款甲方同意不另收利息；货物发运之后，甲方应向乙方提供所有已预付的相关单据凭证复印件。上述货物出口相关费用包括：所有码头费用（船公司收取的）、报关费、商检（报关前1周，乙方必须确认是否需要商检及提供所有资料）、熏蒸费、产地证、银行费用、保险费等。

（此份协议及其译文摘自http://www.kuantianxia.com/webpages/learn/daili-xieyi-hetong-fanyi.html，访问日期：2023年7月10日，有修改。）

重点解析 Notes and Comments

1. 兹有乙方委托甲方为其出口上述货物的代理。为此，甲乙双方经协商，达成如下协议。Whereas, Party B entrusts Party A as its agent to export the goods listed above. Now, therefore, Party A and Party B through consultation hereby agree as follows.

"甲、乙双方经协商，达成如下协议"用于引出合同双方达成的具体协议，译为Now, therefore... hereby是古体词，与by this means意思相同，意为"以此方式，以此，特此"，多出现于合同约首部分。

2. 如乙方出运违禁品，乙方须自行承担一切法律责任。Party B shall bear all legal responsibilities at all its costs for contraband export, if any.

汉语的条件句通常条件在前，结果在后，此句重点强调当条件发生时，乙方应承担的后果。为了使译文达到同样的效果，翻译成英语时将结果前置。英文合同通常使用情态动词shall来规定合同各方当事人的义务，语气较为强烈。

3. ……主要以FOB交货方式为主。...mainly based on FOB basis.

FOB交货方式即FOB贸易术语，是free on board的缩略词，属于国际贸易中最常用的贸易术语之一。类似的还有CIF, CFR等，这些词在英汉和汉英翻译中可以使用零翻译策略。

4. 由于乙方所指定的生产厂家的原因不能按时按质交货或者提供的货物名称、数量、金额等与实际不符所产生的损失与后果，由乙方自行与生产厂家进行协商或索赔，甲方不承担任何风险与责任。In the event that the goods can not be delivered on time or the quality standard, the name, quantity and amount, etc. of the delivered goods do not match the requirement due to the fault of the manufacturer(s) designated by Party B, which further cause a loss and unfavorable

consequence, Party B shall, at all its efforts and discretions, negotiate with or make a claim to the manufacturer(s), and Party A shall not bear any risks and responsibilities in this event.

这句话很长,通过分析句子结构,主干为"(如果)……,乙方……,甲方……",译为In the event that..., Party B shall..., and Party A shall not...其他均为修饰成分,翻译为英文时处理为后置状语、非限制性定语等。另外,英文合同中也常用if, should, in the event of/that, in case(of), provided(that)等短语引导条件状语从句。

5. 货物出口的相关人民币费用由甲方预付,对该预付款甲方同意不另收利息。The RMB expenses relating to the export of the goods shall be prepaid by Party A, and Party A agrees to disclaim its right to charge interest.

合同文体追求客观性和公正性,因此常使用被动句。此句为"由"代替"被"字的隐形被动句,翻译为英文时也应处理为被动句。

第四节　课后翻译训练

一、将下列句子翻译成汉语 Translate the following sentences into Chinese

1. The premium rates vary with differed interests insured.

2. In case the Contract terminates prematurely, the Contract Appendices shall likewise terminate.

3. In processing transactions, the manufacturers shall never have title either to the materials or the finished products.

4. The quality and prices of the commodities to be exchanged between the ex-importers in the two countries shall be acceptable to both sides.

5. The Chairperson may convene an interim meeting based on a proposal made by one-third of the total number of directors.

6. In case one party desires to sell or assign all or part of its investment subscribed, the other party shall have the preemptive right.

7. This Contract can only be altered, amended or supplemented in accordance with documents signed and sealed by authorized representatives of both parties.

8. The formation of this contract, its validity, interpretation, execution and settlement of the disputes shall be governed by related laws of the People's

Republic of China.

9. Contract: an agreement establishing, modifying and terminating the civil rights and obligations between subjects of equal footing, that is, between natural persons, legal persons or other organizations.

注释：
subjects of equal footing：指"地位平等的主体"，即"平等主体"
natural persons：自然人
legal persons：法人

10. The Buyer may, within 15 days after arrival of the goods at the destination, lodge a claim against the Seller for short weight being supported by Inspection Certificate issued by a reputable public surveyor.

注释：
lodge a claim：提出索赔
short weight：短重
Inspection Certificate：检验证书

二、将下列句子翻译成英语 Translate the following sentences into English

1. 双方均应遵守和履行本协议一切条款。

2. 聘方须每月付给受聘方美元500元整。

3. 自9月20日起，甲方已无权接受任何订单或收据。

4. 任何一方不得将本协议全部或部分转让给个人、商号或公司。

5. 本合同使用的FOB，CFR，CIF术语系根据国际商会《2010年国际贸易术语解释通则》所定。

6. 本合同用中、英文两种文字写成，两种文字具有同等效力。本合同一式两份，自双方签字（盖章）之日起生效。

7. 合同在有效期内，双方对合同产品涉及的技术如有改进和发展，应互相免费将改进和发展的技术资料提供给对方。

8. 所有通知用_____文写成，并按照如下地址用传真/电子邮件/快件送达给各方。如果地址有变更，一方应在变更后_____日内书面通知另一方。

9. 买方凭其委托的检验机构出具的检验证明书向卖方提出索赔（包括换货），由此产生的全部费用应由卖方负担，若卖方收到上述索赔后_____天未予答复，则认为卖方已接受买方索赔。

10. 凡因本合同引起的或与本合同有关的任何争议应协商解决，若协商不成，应提交中国国际经济贸易仲裁委员会深圳分会，按照申请仲裁时该会现行有效的仲裁规则进行仲裁。仲裁裁决是终局的，对双方均有约束力。

三、将下列协议翻译成汉语 Translate the following agreement into Chinese

Shareholders' Agreement

The agreement, made this day of 20_____by and between XXX, a corporation duly organized and existing under the laws of Mexico and having its principal office at_____Mexico (hereinafter referred to as "X"), represented by_____and YYY, a corporation duly organized and existing under the laws of_____and having its principal office at_____(hereinafter referred to as "Y"), represented by_____.

WHEREAS, X has been established with the purpose _____among other things, of investing _____ business, and is now desirous of becoming engaged in the manufacturing and selling Contract business.

WHEREAS, Y has for many years been engaged in _____, among other things, research, development and production of certain Contract Products and in the sale of such Products in various parts of the world; WHEREAS, Y has experience in manufacturing Contract PRODUCTS in overseas countries and is therefore capable of furnishing technical assistance for manufacturing such PRODUCTS.

WHEREAS, X and Y are desirous of cooperating with each other in jointly setting-up a new company in Mexico to manufacture Contract PRODUCTS hereinafter more particularly described; and WHEREAS, X and Y are desirous that said new company will obtain technical assistance from Y for manufacturing such PRODUCTS and Y is willing to furnish such technical assistance to the new company; NOW, THEREFORE in consideration of the premises and the mutual covenants herein contained, it is hereby mutually agreed as follows.

（选自岳峰、刘茵，2014：212，略有修改）

四、将下列合同条款翻译成英语 Translate the following contract into English

销 售 合 同

合同编号：
签订日期：
签订地点：

买卖双方同意按照下列条款签订本合同：

1. 货物名称、规格和质量

2. 数量
   允许_____%的溢短装

3. 单价

4. 总值

5. 交货条件

6. 原产地与制造商

7. 包装及标准

8. 唛头

9. 装运期限

10. 装运口岸

11. 目的口岸

12. 保险
    由卖方按发票金额110%投保_____险和_____附加险。

13. 付款条件
信用证方式：买方应在装运期前合同生效后_____日，开出以卖方为受益人的不可撤销信用证，信用证在装船完毕后_____日内到期。

14. 单据
卖方应将下列单据提交银行议付/托收
（1）标明通知收货人/收货代理人的全套清洁的、已装船的、空白抬头、空白背书并注明运费已付/到付的海运/联运/陆运提单；
（2）标有合同编号、信用证号（信用证支付条件下）及装运唛头的商业发票一式_____份；
（3）由_____出具的装箱或重量单一式_____份；
（4）由_____出具的质量证明书一式_____份；

（5）由_____出具的数量证明书一式_____份；

（6）保险单正本一式_____份（CIF交货条件）；

（7）_____签发的产地证一式_____份；

（8）装运通知：卖方应在交运后_____小时内以特快专递方式邮寄给买方上述第_____项单据副本一式一套。

15. 装运条款：FOB交货方式

卖方应在合同规定的装运日期前30天，以_____方式通知买方合同号、品名、数量、金额、包装件、毛重、尺码及装运港可装日期，以便买方安排租船/订舱。装运船只按期到达装运港后，如卖方不能按时装船，发生的空船费或滞期费由卖方负担，在货物越过船舷并脱离吊钩以前，一切费用和风险由卖方负担。

16. 装运通知

经装载完毕，卖方应在_____小时内以_____方式通知买方合同编号、品名、已发运数量、发票总金额、毛重、船名/车/机号及启程日期等。

17. 质量保证

货物品质规格必须符合本合同及质量保证书之规定，品质保证期为货到目的港后_____个月内。在保证期限内，因制造厂商在设计制造过程中的缺陷造成的货物损害应由卖方负责赔偿。

18. 检验

卖方须在装运前_____日委托_____检验机构对本合同之货物进行检验并出具检验证书，货到目的港后，由买方委托_____检验机构进行检验。

19. 不可抗力

凡在制造或装船运输过程中，因不可抗力致使卖方不能或推迟交货时，卖方不负责任。在发生上述情况时，卖方应立即通知买方，并在_____天内，给买方特快专递一份由当地民间商会签发的事故证明书。在此情况下，卖方仍有责任采取一切必要措施加快交货。如事故延续_____天以上，买方有权撤销合同。

20. 附加条款

本合同上述条款与本附加条款抵触时，以本附加条款为准。

买方代表（签字）：　　　　　　　　卖方代表（签字）：

第七章 企业宣传翻译

简介类文本都属于"信息型文本",提供相关机构、学校、人物、图书、产品等的简要介绍。企业介绍类文本是公司塑造形象的重要材料,是企业对自身业务性质、专业水准,以及企业文化、思想、政治等全方位的展示。对内,企业宣传(Corporate Profile)材料对员工的职业理想、道德教育有引导性作用,有助于提高员工归属感和公司凝聚力;对外,企业介绍类文本是客户、消费者认识企业的资料,是公众对企业第一印象的来源,构成了促成合作的纽带。企业宣传文本主要包括两个部分,即公司名和简介。企业简介一般包含以下几个方面:公司概况、发展历程、专业团队、业绩成就、企业文化、发展愿景、联系方式等。

在信息化时代和全球化风潮的大背景下,企业全球化是现代企业正在面临的机会和挑战。商号翻译可以成为企业海外发展的重要推动力,深入人心的翻译如"可口可乐",有人认为这一译名是该公司及其产品在中国风靡的一大原因。由于中西语言和文化的差异,未经深思熟虑的企业名称及简介翻译会造成文化障碍,不利于中国企业在国际市场上的发展。

因此,在此类文本的翻译中,译者应对公司名称和简介有透彻的认识和理解,并灵活使用各类翻译策略进行翻译。

第一节 公司名称与企业商号的翻译

一、公司名称的构成与常用语

公司名称的翻译主要分为两个部分:商号与公司名称后缀,其中商号是企业特定的标志,公司名称后缀表示公司的性质。

表 7.1　常用公司名称后缀及解释

后缀	全称	解释
Co.	Company	泛指公司，不对其法律结构进行指示。
Corp.	Corporation	company 和 corporation 有时可作同义词替换使用。corporation 一般为规模较大的公司；作为后缀时，Corp. 通常指法人团体，公司的所有人为股东。而 company 通常指公司的所有人为公司成员。
Inc.	Incorporated Company	股份有限公司
Ltd.	Limited	（主要用于欧洲国家及加拿大等）有限责任公司
Co., Ltd.	Company Limited	中国常用 Co., Ltd. 表示有限责任公司和股份有限公司的总称，即有限公司。
PLC	Public Limited Company	（主要用于英国）有限公司，根据英国的公司法，公司注册形态主要分为有限及无限公司，而有限公司又分为公开有限公司（Public Limited Company），即上市公司，以及私人有限公司（Private Limited Company），即非上市公司。
LLC	Limited Liability Company	（主要用于美国）有限责任公司
Pty	Proprietary	（主要用于澳大利亚）私人股份公司
Group	—	集团
Holding(s)	—	控股

指代公司时所用称呼还有：firm（公司），enterprise（企业），business（泛指各类商业及商业体）等，在行文中可根据公司性质灵活使用。

提供不同产品或服务的公司在命名中常带有业务种类的特色，举例如下：

1. Line(s)：表示轮船、航空、航运等领域的公司，航空公司也用 Airline(s)、Air Lines, Airways 等。

Hawaiian Airlines 夏威夷航空公司（美国）

British Airways 英国航空公司

2. System(s)：常用于广播、航空等公司。

Tokyo Broadcasting System, Inc. 东京广播电视公司（日本）

Malaysian Airline System 马来西亚航空公司

湖南广播影视集团 Golden Eagle Broadcasting System (GBS)

3. Agency：从事代理业务活动的组织，如代理商、中介公司。

Austin Advertising Agency 奥斯汀广告公司（美国）

中国船务代理有限公司 China Marine Shipping Agency

4. Associates/Union：表示联合公司。

British Nuclear Associates 英国核子联合公司

Dale Carnegie & Associates, Inc. 戴尔·卡耐基联合公司（美国）

5. Service(s)：服务性质的机构，其中包括公司以及政府机构，注意区分。

The United States Postal Service (USPS; also known as the Post Office, U.S. Mail, or Postal Service) 美国邮政署

Airservices Australia 澳大利亚航空服务公司

6. Industries：可用于工业公司，也相当于我国的"实业公司"。在我国，实业公司的英译名称中也常使用"Industry"和"Industrial"。

Mitsubishi Heavy Industries 三菱重工（日本）

Beijing Hongda Industry 北京宏大实业公司

7. Office：有时可指公司性质的组织，单独使用时常指事务所。在指示公司的分部时，head office为总公司，home office为国内总公司，branch office为分公司。注意区别于政府性质的组织机构。

European Patent Office (EPO) 欧洲专利局

航泰律师事务所 Hightime Law Office

8. Insurance/Assurance/Underwriter/Underwriting：表示保险公司。

American International Assurance Co., Ltd. (AIA) 美国友邦保险公司

Swiss Reinsurance Company Ltd. 瑞士再保险公司

中国太平洋保险（集团）股份有限公司（简称太平洋保险）China Pacific Insurance (Group) Co., Ltd. （CPIC; also known as Pacific Insurance）

注：公司名称可能存在相似性，如Insurance Services Office, Inc. (ISO), Insurance Office of America, Inc. (IOA), Insurance Services of America (ISA)都常被译为"美国保险服务公司"，可用缩写来区分这几个公司。

9. Products：用在公司名称中，可译为"产品公司""用品公司"等，也常不译出"产品"。此类公司一般都从事制造、销售产品相关的业务。

Avon Products, Inc. 雅芳公司（美国）

广东欧比个人护理用品有限公司 Guangdong OBEE Personal Care Products Co., Ltd.

10. Laboratories：常用于制药公司、科技研发公司等，翻译中有时也直译为"实验室"。

Abbott Laboratories 雅培公司（美国）

伯乐生命医学产品（上海）有限公司 Bio-Rad Laboratories

11. United/Allied/Consolidated：表示联合。

United Airlines 美国联合航空

Consolidated Coal Company 联合煤炭公司（美国）

12. General：一为"通用"之意，二作"总公司"。

General Electric Company (GE) 通用电气公司（美国）

General Signal Corporation (GSX) 通用信号公司（美国）

注：有时在英文缩写中会用"X"表示"Corporation"。

13. Investment：投资公司。

Apollo Investment Corporation 阿波罗投资公司（美国）

中国投资有限责任公司（中投公司）China Investment Corporation (CIC)

14. Networks：网络公司。

Extreme Networks (EXTR) 美国极进网络

Xena Networks 信雅纳网络（丹麦）

15. Communications/Telecommunications/Mobile：通信公司。

中国电信集团有限公司（中国电信）China Telecom

中国联合网络通信集团有限公司（中国联通）China Unicom

16. Advertising/Media/Communications：广告公司、传媒公司。

Harold Warner Advertising 哈罗德·华纳广告公司（美国）

Dida Media 嘀嗒国际文化传媒（英国）

17. Entertainment/Production(s)/Cinema/Picture(s)/Film(s)/Animation(s)：影视娱乐行业公司、影业公司、动画公司。

Warner Bros. Entertainment, Inc. 华纳兄弟娱乐公司（美国）

Universal Picture 环球影业公司（美国）

Toei Animation Co., Ltd. 东映动画（日本）（注：在对日本公司名称进行翻译时，常沿用日语中对"公司"的提法——"株式会社"，如东映动画全称：东映动画株式会社）

18. Stores：百货公司。

Federated Department Stores 联合百货公司（美国）

Great Universal Stores 大世界百货公司（英国）

二、企业商号翻译策略

企业商号的翻译对公司的宣传可以起到重要的作用，商号是公众识别企业的标志，从而建立起公众与企业的联系，因此，商号的翻译需要经过仔细斟酌，不是所有商号都可以简单音译了事。以下对商号翻译方法进行简要归纳。

（一）音译

当企业商号仅有形式符号的功能，没有实际意义时，一般采用音译法；公司以人名命名时多使用音译；若英文单词过长或者按字面意思翻译不恰当，也可采用音译。中译英时，需注意的是造新词一定要谨慎，充分考虑读者的可接受度。

"同仁堂"全称是北京同仁堂（集团）有限公司。"同仁堂"是极具中国传统特色的对厅堂建筑的命名，相似的如"宝芝堂""六必居"等。此类命名常以文化与文采塑造企业良好形象，但文化内涵在另一个语言环境下通常难以再现，此时多采用音译法，如该公司英文译名为：Beijing Tongrentang (Group) Co., Ltd.。

在翻译外文公司名时，对人名常使用音译，如Mayfield Fund（梅菲尔德风险投资公司），Hotel Ritz（丽兹大酒店）；对不强调词义的名称也可以进行音译，如Canon（佳能公司），Standard Chartered Hong Kong（中国香港渣打银行）。英文公司名称用人名命名的，译成中文时也常用"……氏"来表示，如Wyeth 惠氏（美），Kellogg's 家乐氏公司（美），The Clorox Company 高乐氏公司（美），Koch Industries 科氏工业公司（美）。

（二）音译与缩略

当英文公司名较长或直译为中文后拗口，不适合中国市场对商号的需求时，可以对公司名进行缩略并音译。如：Tate & Lyle 泰莱集团（英），Metro-Goldwyn-Mayer（MGM）米高梅电影公司（美），Procter & Gamble（P&G）宝洁公司（美），Johnson & Johnson 强生公司（美）。

（三）意译

当企业商号的语义占重要地位时，应考虑采用意译法。若名称中带有国名、地名，相应的名称也应使用意译。如：Microsoft（微软），American Express（美国运通公司）。有的带有国名、地名的名称，也可使用缩略形式，如：Arabian American Oil Co.（阿美石油公司），North American Coal Corporation（北美煤炭公司）。

（四）增译

音译或意译后公司名表意不清时，可适当增译。

企业名称翻译中有时增译国家名，以区分英文同名或名称相似的企业，尤其是国有企业或国家重点设施企业常增译国家名。

Thomson SA常译为"法国汤姆逊公司",法国汤姆逊公司是消费类电子产品生产商,后公司破产并重组为现在的Technicolor(特艺集团)。National Railroad Passenger Corporation中文译名为"美国全国铁路客运公司"。有一些公司名中只出现"National",表示其为本国国有企业,这时常需增译出具体国家名称,如此处的"美国"。

(五)音义结合

有些公司名由专有名词与普通名词共同构成,此时常采取一半音译、一半意译。当公司名就是普通名词时,也可进行一定的创新,达到更好的宣传效果。如:Goodyear Tire & Rubber Company(固特异轮胎橡胶公司)。Mobile(美国主要石油公司)中文译名为"美孚",以原英文读音为基础,但又不拘泥于原文。"美孚"的"美"有美国的意思,代表这家石油公司是美国人创立的,而"美"又是"美好"的映射。"孚"字则有"诚信"的意思,在《诗经·大雅·下武》中有云:"成王之孚,下土之式"。因此,"美孚"寓意为"来自美国,创造美好生活,又以诚信经营的公司"。

(六)零翻译

有些商号本身就是英文字母的缩写形式,或者公司名常以其缩写形式出现时,常直接使用字母缩写。BBC全称为British Broadcasting Corporation,正规中文译名为"英国广播公司"。但在实际使用中,BBC这一缩写更为通用,在中文的介绍文本中也经常将其作零翻译处理,直接称BBC公司。

类似的再如:BAE Systems Plc.(英国航太系统公司/BAE系统公司),International Business Machines Corporation (IBM)(国际商业机器公司/IBM公司),United Parcel Service (UPS)(联合包裹速递服务公司/UPS快递)。

有时即使英文公司名不是缩写,但其名称中英文用词较为简单,通俗易懂,不解释也不影响理解,且不译可能比意译或音译更易接受和记忆时,也可采用零翻译。例如:Orange公司(法国电信运营商)。

第二节 企业宣传资料翻译

一、企业宣传文本常用语与语言形式

与产品说明书相似,公司宣传材料有自身的文体特点,并且会涉及公司业务领域的介绍与说明,也就会涉及专业名词、术语的翻译。因此,研究对照平行文本、积累常用句式、熟悉相关领域专有的表达至关重要。

（一）企业性质

企业介绍中对企业性质的表述是对企业最基本的界定，一般都有较为固定的用法，但不同国家、不同体系对相关表述也有一定语言上的差别，需要译者有一定的语言积累，并对企业所在国家语言习惯进行了解，准确翻译。常用的企业性质中英词汇有：国有（government-owned/state-owned）、公众/公开/上市公司（public company/listed company）、私有（private/privately-owned）、私人（privately-held）、个人所有（individual-owned）、外资（foreign-invested/foreign-funded）、外商独资（wholly foreign-owned）、合资企业（joint venture）等。

（二）常用表达

中文和英文的企业介绍类文本各自有一些常用表达，有时是完全对等的，如"本地采购"英文为local procurement；有时并不完全对等，甚至一种语言中的特定表达在另一种语言中完全没有对等物。

应特别注意，术语的对等不等同于词汇的对等，有时中文术语真正的语义不能仅从字面理解。中文中对企业的定位有一种说法为"外向型企业"，此处的"外向"指的是建立在国内、以国外市场为主要销售场所的企业，不同于形容人性格的"外向"（extrovert），若不辩语义直接字字对应地译为extrovert enterprise就会造成理解上的困难。"外向型企业"相对应的英语译文为：export-oriented enterprise。再如：市场化体制（market-driven system）、普遍优惠制（generalized system of preferences, GSP）。

（三）语言形式

中英文介绍类文本在语言形式和习惯上有可直接转换之处，也有一定的差异，这也要求译者关注译文文本整体的语言呈现形式，以适应译文读者的阅读习惯。

譬如，中文中常使用"公司简介"或"企业简介"作为企业介绍页面的标题，英译时若不考虑语言细节差异，可能会译为Brief Introduction to the Company。其实，这种译法冗余、拖沓，英文中比较对应的表达有Company Profile、Corporate Profile，有时也直接用Introduction。此类标题也可借用英文中常用的介宾短语进行处理，英文企业介绍网页标签与手册中常用About...构成词组作为介绍文本的标题，如About Us, Company Profile, About Our Company三种用法。

英文常用标题类型有：1. "5W2H"短语式。常见的有Who we are, Why we do, When we begin, Where we're located, How we work, How much (many) we will complete。不同公司会根据自身特点设置多样化项目，再如What we live by, Why culture matters, Why choose us等。2. "Our..."式。如Our vision, Our philosophy, Our culture, Our locations等。3. "...us"式。如上文提及的About us，类似的表达再如中文中常用的"联系方式"，英文中有Contact us。4. 对话式。有些公司在介绍文本的标题位置不以介绍的口吻指出本文的性质，而是通过对话式的问候，如Welcome to...直接开启下文的介绍。

中文中则多使用名词短语，且偏好四字结构，如"品牌故事""企业文化""公司理念""主要业务""发展愿景""星巴克人""人才培养"等。随着商务交流的日益频繁，中文企业宣传也融入了新的元素，"我们的……"这一模式也逐渐被接受。

二、中英企业介绍文本异同与翻译

（一）中文宣传材料倾向于倾注大词、美词，以铺陈、夸张的手法，善用四字格，在音律上实现朗朗上口的节奏感，在内容上着重建立宣传对象的美好形象。相对来说，英文的宣传文本较少使用华丽的辞藻和冗长的表达，而是以简明易懂的方式呈现信息。宣传材料需要达到交际功能，让读者易于接受，因此，中英文互译时需适当采用归化的手段，避免信息过载，在忠于原文的基础上顺应译文受众的语言习惯。

例1. 我们拥有先进的石斛组培技术，是全国重要的石斛种植基地，年产量占全国市场总量的70%以上，成为行业的标杆和领头羊。

在此类介绍的翻译中应提炼实质性信息，适当缩减描述性语句，翻译时可将几项进行一定的合并。参考译文如下：

译文：As a dendrobe supplier covering 70% of the total domestic production yearly, we hold an industry-leading position in tissue culture technology and boast one of the largest plantation in China.

例2. Our communities connect us. Be part of something bigger and help everyone feel like they belong. Our employee resource groups represent some of the diverse communities that make up who we are as a company. They connect us, empower us, and help us enact change. [Oracle（甲骨文公司）]

甲骨文公司这一段话使用简单有力、有节奏感的动词，如connect, be, help, feel, belong, empower, enact, 加之句式简练，让整句话语义凝练又朗朗上口，能给人直观的体验。

（二）中英文语言塑造的意象常常会有所不同，也会造成有些说法是某种语言中特有的现象，此类话语若不妥善处理会造成企业形象塑造的错位，在翻译中需特别注意两种语言语义内涵转换的适恰和地道性，避免理解与阅读困难。

"拳头产品"不宜译为fist product，可译作core product。"拳头产品"是指企业特有的、别人难以胜过的看家产品，core product指的是与其核心能力最直接相关的公司产品或服务，两者有异曲同工之妙。"龙头企业"不宜译为dragon head enterprise，可译作industry leader。"龙头企业"是指对同行业的其他企业具有很深的影响、号召力和一定的示范引导作用，并对该地区、该行业或者国家作出突出贡献的企业。

（三）中英文企业宣传材料在人称使用上也有一定差异。相对而言，中文善用第三人称进行陈述，而英文更多以第一人称视角拉近与读者的距离。

例3. 中国银行是中国国际化和多元化程度非常高的银行，在中国内地和香港、澳门特别行政区及其他29个国家为客户提供全面的金融服务。

译文：We provide a broad range of financial products and services to customers, corporations and institutions across the Chinese Mainland, Hong Kong SAR, Macao SAR and 29 overseas countries.

（四）行文结构上，英文企业介绍类文本较中文文本更多用概括或罗列式，而中文介绍更讲究面面俱到，以连贯的段落组成，辅以小标题让文章结构更为醒目。

例4. Sinopec公司主营业务范围包括：实业投资及投资管理，石油、天然气的勘探、开采、储运（含管道运输）、销售和综合利用，石油炼制，汽油、煤油、柴油的批发，石油化工及其他化工产品的生产、销售、储存、运输，石油石化工程的勘探设计、施工、建筑安装，石油石化设备检修维修，机电设备制造，技术及信息、替代能源产品的研究、开发、应用、咨询服务，自营和代理各类商品和技术的进出口（国家限定公司经营或禁止进出口的商品和技术除外）。

本段译文若与原文保持相同的结构，字对字地进行翻译，译文会冗长枯燥，可读性低。

译文：Sinopec Group has 6 core activities:

● Petroleum exploration and production.

● Natural gas gathering, processing and marketing.

● Petroleum refining, marketing, supply and transportation.

● Production and distribution of petrochemicals and other chemical products.

● Industrial investment and investment management.

● Petroleum and petrochemical equipment overhaul and maintenance.

（五）中外企业介绍在理念的侧重上有所不同，中文介绍常带有政治性理念，与国家当下的思潮同步，而英文文本着重于公司本身的宗旨。在中译英时，很多带有中国政治特色的内容是英语读者无法理解的，且作为公司简介对英语读者是无用信息，甚至可能造成误解，因此，建议将相关信息进行概括或删减。

例5."十一五"期间，中国海油牢牢把握我国经济社会发展的重要战略机遇期，有效应对国际金融危机带来的严峻冲击，深化改革，创新发展，成功建成"海上大庆油田"，在能源保障能力建设、产业价值链建设、国际化建设、现代企业制度建设和软实力建设等方面取得了优异成绩，进入了一个全新的发展阶段。

本段中"十一五""深化改革""创新发展"都是我国发展战略中常用的理念。"把握……重要战略机遇期""应对国际金融危机带来的严峻冲击"在中文的介绍中也常出现，这几句的作用是相似的，表达的都是公司要积极进取地发展。连续的五个"建设"是典型的中文宣传中使用的并列式。概念使用具有概括性、抽象性，语义有一定的模糊性。如"现代企业制度"是中文中对目前企业经营发展模式的一种概括，不是一个含义明确的"制度"，直译为modern company system无法让译文读者得到与原文相同的理解，且原文的具体意义对建立译文读者对企业的印象没有很大帮助，因此，译文需进行处理，可删去或改写。

总之，本段中很多内容如果直译，恐怕无法让英语读者对该公司有实质性的印象与判断，不符合英文平行文本的要求。

译文：Driven by innovation and technology upgrading, we (CNOOC) have been able to seize opportunities, making constant progress in supplying energy and petrochemical products. We are developing our production capabilities built into offshore installations of Daqing oilfield and growing as a more reliable supplier with a competitive advantage in the industry through our value chain. In securing production and improving management, we strive to stand out in and beyond China.

（六）此处特别要提出介绍类文本汉译英的一大难点：缩略语的翻译。

中、英企业介绍中都会使用缩略语提高语言的简练度与表达力，相对来说，英文介绍中使用的缩略语更为口语化、通俗化，大多简单易懂，而中文中缩略语使用频率更高，且意义更为浓缩精炼，创造性更强，需要读者有一定的语言和知识基础进行理解。有时，中文语言的凝练度也会给翻译造成较大的困难。

缩略语翻译难点尤其体现在中文数字缩略语的翻译。有一些数字缩略语在两种语言中有对等的用法，可直译，如"一刀切"可译为one-size-fits-all；"一站式"可译为one-stop。有一些缩略语是具有独创性的产物，如中文中的"一个中心，两个基本点"，英文企业介绍中也会有类似的说法，如玛氏公司对公司的文化理念的概括为The Five Principles。英文因其语言特点，也常用字母缩略语，如麦当劳的经营理念"QSC&V"（Quality, Service, Cleanliness & Value）。

数字缩略语最常见于政策性文件，其官方译文也可为企业介绍文本翻译提供一定的参考。此处以政府工作报告中提到的部分数字缩略语为例，总结数字缩略语的两种最常见译法——"内容阐释"法与"概念直译"法。如："两个维护"（Two Upholds）、"三严三实"（Three Stricts and Three Earnests）、"四个全面"战略布局（Four-pronged Comprehensive Strategy）、"四个自信"（Four-sphere Confidence）、"四个服从"（Four Principles of Deference）、"五位一体"总体布局（Five-sphere Integrated Plan）、"六稳"（Ensure Stability on the Six Fronts）、"六保"（Ensure Security in the Six Areas）。[概念原文、译文参见党的十八大报告（汉英对照），2014年、2018年、2021年《政府工作报告》（汉英对照），《习近平谈治国理政》（汉英对照）。]

从以上示例可见，中文的数字缩略词可以包含的语义非常广，保留缩略形式往往无法表达出话语含义；"内容阐释"法可以让译文准确严谨，方便理解，但在语义本身特别丰富的情况下，译文所占用的篇幅长，表达繁复，不利于阅读。因此，在一定语境下，国家政策话语可以形成"概念直译"的缩略式译文，更适应外宣要求。此类文本的翻译要求译者在准确理解原文的基础上，根据实际宣传需要，充分照顾到中外文语言文化的差异性，进行适当的处理。

（七）企业宣传材料的翻译应遵循忠实性、通顺性、简洁性原则。

"忠实"是指译者对原文负责。"忠实"并不是说要完全直译，宣传材料的翻译中意译是不可避免且十分必要的，过分拘泥于原文反而无法实现文本的交际目的。"忠实"指的是译文一定要对原文充分地理解和尊重，是用词上的准确、信息上的对等、表达上的专业、风格上的适切，切忌草率下笔、望文生义，甚至产生误译。

"通顺"主要指的是遣词造句要按照译入语的语法和习惯，即内容要"忠实"，表达要"通顺"，需符合译入语习惯，使读者易于接受，杜绝语言结构混乱、逻辑不清。

"简洁"，尤其是指在汉译英时，要语言精练，避免词汇及语义的重复，对冗余信息进行一定的简化和改写。企业宣传材料的译文需突出企业作为商业实体的重点信息。类似的内容若是在政治性文本中，很多概念需要直译且加以解释，但是在企业宣传文本中则需照顾读者的阅读体验和企业宣传效果，进行简化和删减，让译文简洁易懂。

三、企业宣传资料中的标语翻译

企业介绍类文本中除了对企业各项信息的介绍外，也常以标语、口号（slogan）形式对企业文化、宗旨、产品特点等核心内容进行宣传，起到感染大众、深入人心的效果，通常具备广告语功能。因此广告翻译技巧也常适用于此类文本翻译，此处对标语式语言翻译稍作简述。

（一）中英企业标语特点分析

1. 用词特点

中英文标语都常用动态词和形容词及其比较级与最高级在读者心里迅速建立起对品牌和商品的印象，两种语言共通之处为都会大量使用褒义、正向的词汇，但中英标语在选词上也有所差别。中文标语侧重辞藻华丽，尤其体现在选词之"大"，如常用"成就""一流""知名""绚烂""辉煌""无止境""卓尔不群""非同凡响"。英文标语中则更多用简单的单音节词，尤其是简明易懂的日常用词，且会特意选用口语词，整体风格更直观亲和，高频形容词包括good, better, best, easy, fresh, free, clean, nice, rich等，高频动词包括make, do, get, give, have, see, buy, feel, taste等；另外，英文标语还有广泛使用人称代词的特点，以拉近与读者的距离。中文选词更符合中国语言文化与审美习惯，而英文选词更注重快速建立读者与企业、商品的联系，充分发挥英语语言的实用性，达到吸引消费者的目的。

2. 句式特点

中英标语在句式上都表现出多用简单句、省略句、祈使句的特点。中文因语言本身对节奏上的偏好和审美习惯，常用四字短语，且常以四字词铺排形成语言的气势；英文则以节奏轻快流畅为长，常以词或短语构成的平行结构让语言更生动，有节奏感。

句式上的特点从以上可口可乐公司的宣传语中亦可见。中国很多企业文化的介绍中会使用四字词，这种语言形式流行于各类企业的品牌介绍。如国内美妆品牌"毛戈平"的品牌理念是"美至极致，无所畏惧"。可口可乐公司"make mistakes, own them, put them right, learn from them"这句宣传语中以简单句的形式，利用动宾平行结构并列，简明扼要地表达了企业对待错误的态度。

3. 修辞特点

为了提高企业标语与口号的震撼力和可记忆性,中英标语都会巧妙地利用修辞手段产生特殊的效果,再现修辞形成的审美效果也是标语类文本翻译的一大难点。

修辞手段	示例
双关	"心"服务,新体验(中国建设银行) 善建者行,成其久远(中国建设银行) Start ahead. (Rejoice 飘柔) There's a lot in the works. And much more work to do. (Apple 苹果公司)
比喻(明喻、暗喻、换喻)	打造国内优秀文化传播,开启"文化引擎"(川悦文化) Life is a journey. Enjoy the ride. (Nissan 日产汽车)
拟人	让未来生长(中国联通5G品牌口号) The car that cares. (Kia 起亚汽车) Nothing hugs like Huggies. (Huggies 好奇纸尿裤)
排比	随时随地,随心随行(中国移动) 人人想干事、人人能干事、人人干成事(恒力集团) Make them yours, and make something wonderful. (Apple 苹果公司)
对仗	草原仍绿,炉火正红(小肥羊) Integrity first. Excellence always. (Volkswagen 大众汽车)
押韵	爱我中华、振兴石化(中国石化) Good teeth, good health. (Colgate 高露洁)
顶针、回环、拆字等汉语独有修辞手法	轻松上网,易如反掌。(网易) 万家乐,乐万家(万家乐)

(二)企业标语翻译策略与方法

基于企业标语作为宣传企业或商品、刺激消费的工具的定位,标语的翻译主要应遵循翻译目的论的指导,以目的原则作为首要准则,借助不同翻译策略实现翻译目的。常见的标语翻译技巧主要包括直译、意译、套译、直译与意译相结合。

1. 直译

在中英文语言语义可以达到对等替换且在篇章中适恰的情况下,可选择直译,注意适当调整词性、时态、语态等语言形式,符合译入语语法。

示例:

原文	译文
海尔,中国造	Haier, Made in China
海尔,世界造	Haier, Made in the World
海尔,网络造	Haier, Made in Internet

以上是海尔公司在不同阶段提出的口号,三个口号使用相同的模式,通过替换其中的词语表达企业不同时期的目标。该口号可以用直译的方法,保留原文简练的形式,又通过改变语态,用被动形式made in,符合英文语法,形成能够保留宣传功能的口号。

2. 意译

当两种语言的习惯和审美有比较大的差异时,译者需要充分关照译文读者。

示例:

原文	译文
善建者行,成其久远(中国建设银行)	An excellent pursuer, a partner forever.
科技引领,中国智造(GE医疗)	Elevating Health in China
全球厨房的幸福选择(方太)	We bring happiness and health to your kitchen.
Our Mission: Create More Smiles with Every Sip and Every Bite(PepsiCo)	我们的使命:每一口都更多欢笑

上例中建设银行的标语通过把银行的缩写"建行"拆开形成"善建者行",这一拆字效果很难在简短的英文中实现对等,且两个四字短语利用中文语言的凝练形式表达了深厚的含义。译文利用意译的手法摆脱原文语言形式的束缚,用pursuer和partner及修饰语把标语内涵以更符合英文语言的形式呈现出来,同时保留并列结构,既起到了表达企业理念的作用,又能够达到标语的效果。

3. 套译

套译是让译文更加本地化的一种方式,在译文中套用目的语文化中的成语、习语或名句,能更大程度上起到在目标消费者群体中进行宣传的作用。

示例:

原文	译文
Intelligence everywhere.	智慧演绎,无处不在。(Motorola 摩托罗拉)
Always listening. Always understanding.	用心聆听,更知你心。(Prudential 英国宝诚保险)
Think Different.	非同凡想。(Apple 苹果)
Connecting people.	科技以人为本。(Nokia 诺基亚)
OUR VISION Be the Global Leader in Convenient Foods and Beverages by Winning with Purpose.	我们的愿景:秉持"赢之有道"的理念,成为休闲食品和饮料行业的全球领袖。(PepsiCo 百事)

以上几例都是英文标语在汉译中套用四字词的例子。摩托罗拉与宝诚保险公司的英文标语虽形式不同,但汉语译文都采取两个分句形式,以四字短语并

列；苹果公司的汉语译文"非同凡想"改编自中文的"非同凡响"；诺基亚套用中文中"以人为本"的概念；百事公司的标语创译出"赢之有道"的四字短语来表示Winning with Purpose。

4. 直译与意译相结合

很多时候，单纯的直译或意译都不足以兼顾标语的内涵与形式，因此标语的翻译常需要译者灵活使用各种翻译手法，利用直译与意译相结合的方式进行处理。

示例：

原文	译文
智能，为每一个可能（联想）	Smarter Technology for All
爱他未来，有备而来（爱他美）	Raise Them Ready
我们与世界 我们与创新 我们与伙伴（中国银行）	BOC for World BOC for Innovation BOC for Partners

联想公司的标语中"智能"一词在中文中可作为概括性名词使用，而英文中的smart只有形容词的词性，译文需充分考虑中英文语言的差异。该译文结合企业业务范围，增译technology一词，能对企业起到实际的宣传效果，也符合英文的语言习惯。中国银行三个阶段的理念沿用了"我们与……"的形式，英文译文将"我们"显化为BOC，即中国银行的英文缩写，将"与"译为for，并直译后一个名词，译文能够充分体现企业理念，符合英文宣传需要。

第三节　课内翻译任务

一、英译汉 English-Chinese Translation

Starbucks Company Profile

● The Starbucks Story

Our story began in 1971. Back then we were a roaster and retailer of whole bean and ground coffee, tea and spices with a single store in Seattle's Pike Place Market.

Today, we are privileged to connect with millions of customers every day with exceptional products and more than 30,000 retail stores in 80 markets.

● Folklore

Starbucks is named after the first mate in Herman Melville's *Moby Dick*. Our logo is also inspired by the sea—featuring a twin-tailed siren from Greek mythology.

● Starbucks Mission

Our mission: to inspire and nurture the human spirit—one person, one cup and one neighborhood at a time.

● Our Coffee

We've always believed in serving the best coffee possible. It's our goal for all of our coffee to be grown under the highest standards of quality, using ethical sourcing practices. Our coffee buyers personally travel to coffee farms in Latin America, Africa and Asia to select high quality beans. And our master roasters bring out the balance and rich flavor of the beans through the signature Starbucks Roast.

● Our Stores

Our stores are a neighborhood gathering place for meeting friends and family. Our customers enjoy quality service, an inviting atmosphere and an exceptional beverage.

Total stores: 30,000 across 80 markets (as of June 30, 2019)

● Our Partners

We offer some of the finest coffees in the world, grown, prepared and served by the finest people. Our employees, who we call partners, are at the heart of the Starbucks Experience.

We believe in treating our partners with respect and dignity. We are proud to offer several landmark programs for our partners, including comprehensive health coverage for eligible full-and part-time partners, access to full college tuition coverage through the Starbucks College Achievement Plan, and equity in the company through Bean Stock.

● Our Products

Starbucks offers a range of exceptional products that customers enjoy in our stores, at home, and on the go.

Coffee: More than 30 blends and single-origin premium coffees.

Handcrafted Beverages: Fresh-brewed coffee, hot and iced espresso beverages, Iced Coffee, Cold Brew, Nitro, Frappuccino® coffee and non-coffee blended beverages, Starbucks Refreshers® beverages, and Teavana® teas.

Merchandise: Coffee- and tea-brewing equipment, mugs and accessories, packaged goods, books and gifts.

Fresh Food: Baked pastries, cold and hot sandwiches, salads, salad and grain bowls, oatmeal, yogurt parfaits and fruit cups.

● Brand Portfolio

Starbucks Coffee, Seattle's Best Coffee, Teavana, Evolution Fresh, Ethos Water and Torrefazione Italia Coffee.

● Investor Information

Starbucks went public on June 26, 1992 at a price of $17 per share (or $0.53 per share, adjusted for subsequent stock splits) and closed trading that first day at $21.50 per share.

Starbucks was incorporated under the laws of the State of Washington, in Olympia, Washington, on Nov. 4, 1985.

Starbucks Corporation's common stock is listed on NASDAQ, under the trading symbol SBUX.

For more information, please visit Starbucks Investor Relations.

● Being a Responsible Company

At Starbucks, we have always believed in the importance of building a great, enduring company that strikes a balance between profitability and a social conscience.

（本文是2020年星巴克简介，选自 https: //wenku.baidu.com/view/18c83fb7a36925c52cc58bd63186bceb18e8ed13?bfetype=new&_wkts_=1724078082047&bdQuery=Starbucks+is+named+after+the+first+mate+in+Herman+Melville%E2%80%99s+Moby+Dick.+Our&needWelcomeRecommand=1，访问日期：2020年7月13日。）

重点解析 Notes and Comments

1. *Moby Dick* 《白鲸》是19世纪美国小说家赫尔曼·梅尔维尔（Herman Melville, 1819—1891）于1851年发表的一篇海洋题材的长篇小说。小说描写了亚哈船长为了追逐并杀死白鲸莫比·迪克,最终与白鲸同归于尽的故事。

2. ethical sourcing 道德采购

道德采购通常是指企业承诺保证采购物品及原料来源正当,并严格遵守最高标准的社会和环境责任。

3. Our customers enjoy quality service, an inviting atmosphere and an exceptional beverage. 每一位顾客都可以在这里享受优质的服务,感受温馨的气氛,品尝上乘的饮品。

原文中以enjoy一词引导三个部分,即service, atmosphere, beverage,而在中译文中将"enjoy"这个词分配到三个宾语前,分别为"享受服务""感受气氛""品尝饮品"。英文以一个较为笼统的动词后接三个宾语,表达简练,符合英文的行文习惯;作为介绍文体,中文则需要增添一些韵律,因此译文中将笼统的"enjoy"一词具体化为三个动词,以三个并列短句的形式让读者更有画面感。

4. We offer some of the finest coffees in the world, grown, prepared and served by the finest people. 我们供应最好的咖啡,从种植、加工到服务,星巴克人精益求精。

该句可分为两个部分,后半部分"grown, prepared and served..."为非限制性修饰语,翻译中不处理为"的"字构成的前置定语,而是用拆分译法,译为一个短句。本句原文中前后两个"finest"形成呼应,强调咖啡原材料(coffee)以及人工(people)的高质量、高要求,因此在拆分后,短句以"星巴克人"为主语,将"finest"这个形容词意译为该句的主干动词,以"精益求精"表达出英文中的最高级的内涵。

5. stock split 股票分割

股票分割亦称股票拆细,俗称"拆股"或"分股",即将一张较大面值的股票拆成几张较小面值的股票。股票分割对公司的资本结构不会产生任何影响,一般只会使发行在外的股票总数增加,资产负债表中股东权益各账户(股本、资本公积、留存收益)的余额都保持不变,股东权益的总额也保持不变,但股票每股市价降低,投资者持有的股票数增加了。

6. NASDAQ 纳斯达克

全称为美国全国证券交易商协会自动报价表(National Association of Securities Dealers Automated Quotations),是美国的一个电子证券交易机构,创立于1971年,迄今已成为世界最大的股票市场之一。

二、汉译英 Chinese-English Translation

中国空间技术研究院简介

中国空间技术研究院成立于1968年2月20日，隶属中国航天科技集团公司，经过五十多年的发展，已成为中国主要的空间技术及其产品研制基地，是中国空间事业最具实力的骨干力量。主要从事空间技术开发、航天器研制、空间领域对外技术交流与合作、航天技术应用等业务，还参与制定国家空间技术发展规划，研究有关探索、开发、利用外层空间的技术途径，承接用户需要的各类航天器和地面应用设备的研制业务并提供相应的服务。

研究院下设研究机构、卫星制造厂等，拥有一家上市公司和多家全资子公司，建立了多个国家重点实验室和一家以研究生培养、员工培训、客户培训为中心任务的学院，形成了七个产业基地，拥有空间飞行器总体设计、分系统研制生产、卫星总装测试、环境试验、地面设备制造及卫星应用、服务保障等配套完整的研制生产体系。本研究院拥有员工一万余人，其中包括8名两院院士、13名国家级突出贡献专家和5000多名高级专业技术人才。

面向未来，中国空间技术研究院将全面贯彻习近平新时代中国特色社会主义思想和党的十九大精神，坚持"四个全面"战略布局，坚决贯彻落实"创新、协调、绿色、开放、共享"的发展理念，以"发展航天事业，建设航天强国"为己任，大力弘扬航天三大精神，发扬严慎细实的工作作风，不断开拓中国空间事业新局面，为把中国空间技术研究院建成市场化、专业化、产业化、国际化的现代宇航企业而不懈奋斗！

（节选、改编自中国空间技术研究院简介）

重点解析 Notes and Comments

1. 中国空间技术研究院（China Academy of Space Technology，简称CAST），即中国航天科技集团公司五院，是中国主要的空间技术及其产品研制基地。

2. 中国空间技术研究院成立于1968年2月20日，隶属中国航天科技集团公司，经过五十多年的发展，已成为中国主要的空间技术及其产品研制基地，是中国空间事业最具实力的骨干力量。Founded on February 20, 1968, China Academy of Space Technology (CAST), a subordinate of China Aerospace Science and Technology Corporation (CASC), has emerged as a major base of space technology and product development in China, and turned into the most powerful backbone of

China's space industry after more than 50 years of development.

该长句是"简介"类文本经常出现的"表达信息组合",具备现代汉语的典型特征,出现大量无主句。汉译英中处理此类长句通常可以根据信息重心将原文进行拆分重组。在本句中前两个小句是对研究院基本信息的介绍,后三个小句是对其地位的叙述。此处前两个小句以"隶属"为句子的信息中心,"隶属"一词在公司机构的翻译中经常出现,可选词汇有be affiliated to, subordinate/attach等。考虑到前两个小句作为介绍性语言,可以都作为论述对象"中国空间技术研究院"的限定成分,而将整个信息中心放在最后两个小句。为了避免非谓语成分过多而显得结构臃肿,在表示"隶属"的说法中,subordinate可以用作名词,在英译中a subordinate of...作为"中国空间技术研究院"的同位语,自然地与主语衔接。

3. 研究院下设研究机构、卫星制造厂等,拥有一家上市公司和多家全资子公司。The institute has multiple subsidiaries including research institutes, a satellite factory, a listed company and its wholly owned subsidiary companies.

与上段中的"隶属"相似,本句中出现"下设",在翻译中将动词名词化,更有利于英文的行文流畅。

4. 本研究院拥有员工一万余人…… The institute has a staff of over 10,000...
staff表示"全体职员",在表示职员数量时可用a staff of。

5. 两院院士: academicians of the Chinese Academy of Sciences and the Chinese Academy of Engineering。两院院士是中国科学院院士和中国工程院院士的统称。

6. 以"发展航天事业,建设航天强国"为己任 commit to aerospace development and the building of China into a space power

中文善以对仗增强话语的感染力,但在英译中应以简明扼要为基础,不必拘泥于形式,在本小句翻译中即着重表达出汉语所含意义。

7. 大力弘扬航天三大精神,发扬严慎细实的工作作风…… The institute will energetically foster and promote the national character exhibited throughout the course of space exploration and a rigorous and meticulous working style...

中文常以数字化的名词来概括一些概念,如此处的"航天三大精神"。若将"航天三大精神"直译为three space spirits,在没有相关背景知识的英语母语者看来,着实让人摸不着头脑,因此此处采取意译。"航天三大精神"指的是航天传统精神、"两弹一星"精神和载人航天精神,是中国的航天文化在不同历史时期的具体体现和继承发展。

鉴于中国空间技术研究院为国家重要科研机构，在价值取向的介绍中删减与简化应更为谨慎，保留程度应高于一般企业介绍。

第四节　课后翻译训练

一、将下列句子翻译成汉语 Translate the following sentences into Chinese

1. Don't imitate, innovate!

2. Pioneer the future with dreams and curiosity.

3. We at Sanofi are there beside people in need as a health journey partner.

4. The challenge for our generation is to create a world where everyone has a sense of purpose.

5. Sony Corporation is the electronics business unit and the parent company of the Sony Group.

6. Our HR team is aligned to each of our business sectors and functions to deliver strategic solutions at the right levels.

7. We know fairness, respect and courtesy come first. We celebrate individuality and appreciate everyone's contribution.

8. The perfect search engine would really understand whatever your need is. It would understand everything in the world deeply, give you back kind of exactly what you need.

9. Our commitment to the research community is reflected in generous sponsorship of societies and meetings worldwide, our monthly travel award for junior investigators, and excellent bulk pricing.

10. We received ISO9001 certification for our quality management system for the design and manufacture of medical devices and ISO11135 for the development, validation and control of sterilisation process for medical devices.

二、将下列句子翻译成英语 Translate the following sentences into English

1. 关爱生命　呵护健康

2. 使命愿景：用户为本　科技向善

3. 企业宗旨：创造卓越，崇尚文明

4. "个别性"是教育中重要的一环。

5. 自20世纪80年代以来，康菲一直是中国忠诚的合作伙伴，也是中国上游油气行业最大的外商投资者之一。

6. 我们一直致力于将这些方法融入我们的全球业务。有关我们取得的进步和面临的挑战，请详见本公司的全球网站。

7. 网易公司是中国领先的互联网技术公司，在开发互联网应用、服务及其他技术方面，网易始终保持国内业界的领先地位。

8. 未来，海尔集团将继续携手全球一流生态合作方，建设衣食住行康养医教等物联网生态圈，为全球用户定制个性化的智慧生活。

9. 我们信仰清晰而流畅的交互体验，让每一个设计元素出现在它该在的地方。简洁有序的代码，让每一个接口实现正确的功能。

10. 中国中铁业务范围涵盖了几乎所有基本建设领域，包括铁路、公路、市政、房建、城市轨道交通、水利水电、机场、港口、码头等，能够提供建筑业"纵向一体化"的一揽子交钥匙服务。

三、将下列短文翻译成汉语 Translate the following passage into Chinese

Griffin Energy

Griffin Energy is an international company with offices worldwide. Our main operations are managed by our offices in Sana'a, Yemen and in Dubai, UAE. As part of the Griffin Group, Griffin Energy has established itself as a major international company in the oil and gas industry, with extensive experience in oilfield services and project management in remote locations and challenging environments.

Griffin Energy provides the following services:

● Oil and Gas Exploration and Development

● Oilfield Services

Griffin Energy Ltd. has formed strong partnerships with global market leaders in international energy trading. Griffin Energy specializes in international energy trading and has an extended global network serving most of the recognized participants in the industry. Private companies and government agencies use its Inventory Management Service to optimize the value of their crude oil and finished petroleum product stocks.

Key activities

● Supply and trading of crude oil and refined petroleum products

● Direct supply of the full product range, from crude oil and other refinery feed stocks to refined products, including LPG, naphtha, mogas, jet fuel, gas oil and fuel oil as well as bio-fuels

● Physical oil trading, matched by activity in the swaps market to counterbalance the price volatility existing in these markets

● Providing clients with hedging and price management solutions

● Refinery processing and downstream activities, including storage and marketing

● Inventory management

● Storage and storage facilities

● Shipping

● Price risk management

● Asset development

Griffin Energy has a diverse portfolio of customers in the oil and gas industry. Private clients, public companies and government agencies worldwide select Griffin Energy as their partner in the most challenging and complex projects. Although each client has unique needs and goals, they return to Griffin Energy because of our reputation for reliability. Our experience includes assignments in Yemen, Libya, Morocco, Egypt, Algeria, Jordan, Iraq, Saudi Arabia, UAE.

Oman, Sudan, Kenya, Tanzania, Bangladesh, Pakistan and Afghanistan. We are proud of the fact that many of our clients come back to Griffin Energy or have been referred to us by satisfied clients. We have a proven reputation for on time delivery within budget. With several hundred successful projects, we have the experience, resources and credentials to meet the most demanding requirements.

（Griffin Energy公司介绍）

四、将下列短文翻译成英语 Translate the following passage into English

华 为 是 谁

华为创立于1987年，是全球领先的ICT（信息与通信）基础设施和智能终端提供商，我们致力于把数字世界带入每个人、每个家庭、每个组织，构建万物互联的智能世界。截至2023年12月，华为有20.7万员工，业务遍及170多个国家和地区，服务30多亿人口。

我们在通信网络、IT、智能终端和云服务等领域为客户提供有竞争力、安全可信赖的产品、解决方案与服务，与生态伙伴开放合作，持续为客户创造价值，释放个人潜能，丰富家庭生活，激发组织创新。华为坚持围绕客户需求持续创新，加大基础研究投入，厚积薄发，推动世界进步。

（节选、改编自华为公司官网，https://www.huawei.com/cn/corporate-information，访问时间：2024年8月10日。）

第八章 产品介绍翻译

随着中国改革开放的推进,特别是加入世界贸易组织以后,中外双向贸易都呈现蓬勃发展的趋势。国际贸易中,产品介绍(Product Description)文本的翻译是极其重要的一环,产品宣介类文本能让消费者对产品有基本的了解并产生购买的动力,而产品说明书则承担着向消费者介绍产品性能、结构、使用方法、作用、保养、注意事项、质量保证、销售范围等多重功能,准确无误且易于顾客理解的产品说明书对用户体验至关重要。不同类型的产品在说明书的体例、内容和用语规范及习惯上有一定的差异,但都是根据产品自身的特点向消费者全面介绍产品。

本章从中英双语产品介绍文本的语言特点出发,基于此类文本的特点对翻译策略与技巧进行总结。由于篇幅限制,本教材不对产品说明书进行详尽的分类解析,本章各个部分收录了生活用品、电子产品、化妆品、药品、工业材料等多种产品的介绍及翻译练习与讲解,以期提供较广泛的参考。

第一节 产品介绍文本的语言特色

产品介绍文本兼具介绍性与科技性,因此具备了科技和介绍文体的一般性,又表现出自身的独特性,体现在体例、用词、句法、修辞等各个方面。产品介绍文本又可以分为偏重销售功能的产品宣介文本(如产品宣传册、网站等展示的文字介绍)和功能性更强的产品说明书(包括外包装、内包装、标签等部分标注的商品信息)。中文和英文产品介绍文本有明显的共性,同时也存在一定差异,本节首先对两种语言在此类文本中的语言特色进行探究。

一、词汇特点

从词汇方面来看,产品说明书用词具有专业性和一定的固定性,大量使用专有名词、专业术语、缩略词等。这就要求从事产品说明书翻译的译者具有丰富的知识和严谨的态度，在译文达到简练的基础上，还要做到规范、准确、专业。

1. 在长期使用中，各个领域的产品说明中已形成了众多约定俗成的术语和常用表达，翻译时需借鉴目的语中相应的说法或已有的规范。如：skin irritancy皮肤刺激、fragrance-free不含香精、non-comedogenic不致粉刺、anaphylactic reaction过敏反应、warranty card保修卡、abrasion-resistance耐磨性、refer to参看、not applicable to不适用于等。

2. 除了如上所说较为通用的术语外，受物质、地理等语境影响，各地产品可能具备一定的特殊性，存在对事物描述的不统一性，甚至涉及一些在当地语言或使用语言的语境里特有的用语。翻译中，这种语义空缺现象会是翻译的一大难点。

以产品说明书几乎都会涉及的日期表达为例，除了最为常见的失效期（Expiry/Expiration Date）和生产日期（Manufacturing Date/Production Date）外，日期相关常用用法还有：

表 8.1 产品说明书中的期限

英文	参考中文
sell-by date	销售期限 / 销售至……
freeze-by date	冷藏期限 / 冷藏至……
use-by date	使用期限 （注：婴儿配方食品超过标注的 use-by date，即有食品安全隐患。）
best-by date/ best-before date/ best before end (BBE)	最佳食用期限 / 最佳使用期限 /……前食用口感最佳
shelf life	保质期
period after opening (PAO)	开盖保质期

各地对产品日期的规定与规范措施不尽相同，译者首先需要准确理解相关内容的语义，在汉译英中可以适当参照出口国家的用语规范；英译汉中也可适当根据实际需要灵活转换语言形式，除了直接译为"……日期"外，还可用句子的形式，如"……（日期）前食用最佳""……（日期）前食用完毕""开盖……（日）内用完""建议……（日）内……"等。产品标识再如：生产批号（batch number/code, lot number）、产地（made in...）、生产商（manufacturer）、装配工厂（plant of assembly）、型号（model）等。

质、文化语境的差异造成的语义空缺和理解障碍是产品说明书翻译中的难点。下面以中医药相关材料的英译为例。中医是中国特有的医疗手段，传统文化，在英文中的语义空缺极为显著，中药名称、药物功能、生理机制信息都是翻译中的挑战。

中医常用各类草药入药，中药材种类达数百种，中国人耳熟能详的草药名对其他国家的读者来说可能是未知事物。例如植物黄连，学名为Coptis chinensis ranch，网络释义有：Coptis chinensis, the Chinese goldthread, is a species of goldthread flowering plant native to China. 常用的中药"黄连"实为该植物的根状茎，因此在指这种中药材时较正式的说法有Coptis chinensis rhizomes或Coptidis Rhizoma，有时也通俗地称为Chinese goldthread。在翻译中第一次提到时可对其进行增译解释，如：Coptidis Rhizoma, a herbal medicine commonly used in Traditional Chinese Medicine (TCM).

除了物质名称，中医中有诸多概念也是西方文化中缺失的，如"阴阳""五行""太极"。这些词语义丰富，包含了自然科学与人文哲学，在初次传播到西方世界时不可避免地需要补充大量的注释说明才能让读者理解。可喜的是，随着国际交流的日益深入，中医文化已经在世界各国越来越受到关注与认可，在传播中，一些主要术语的音译词已经能为英语使用者所大致理解，并有相关英文的百科说明文章参考，因此在产品说明书中出现此类被普遍知晓的概念时可直接使用通用的音译。中国本土护肤品牌佰草集（Herborist）以"现代中草药古方个人护理专家"为概念推出市场，产品多含中草药成分，在产品命名时也体现出了相应的特点。佰草集官网对某一产品进行的说明直接使用了"Yin"（阴）和"Yang"（阳），后对其进行简明的介绍。

The black mask is Yin. It purifies the upper skin layers and eliminates dust, traces of make-up and dead skin cells.

The white mask is Yang. It soothes, softens and leaves a radiant complexion.

中英文中也各有对某些事物特定的描述语，翻译中常需要对其进行一定的阐释才能表达清晰。譬如中医对药物功能的介绍有"宣肺平喘"。此处的"宣"有疏通之意，"宣肺"说的是疏通肺气，进而"平喘"，即平息气喘的症状。"肺气"也是中医中特有的"气"的一种，目前在相关术语的翻译中普遍支持使用音译，因此"宣肺平喘"可译为：facilitate the flow of the lung-qi to relieve asthma。"宣"这个动词的翻译还可用：dispel（"宣散风寒"dispel wind-cold），clear，ventilate（"宣肺"，医学中更具体的"肺通气"过程可称为ventilate the lung）。

二、句法特点

由于内容一般为解释、说明、规定和建议等，产品说明书的句子结构具有简明扼要的特点，多使用简单句、陈述句和祈使句等。翻译中通常遵照原文句式并以简练、通顺的译入语进行表述即可，以下主要对产品说明书翻译中英汉语言的差异造成的难点进行分析。

1. 英汉互译过程中的词性转换在产品说明书翻译中较为显著。一方面，英文说明书中的非动词成分常需转换为中文中的动词；另一方面，英文常用抽象名词作主语，在汉译时需灵活处理，有时需添加隐含在英文中的主语并将抽象名词转换为动词。

例1. A full charge takes about 16 hours and enables up to 8 days of regular brushing (twice a day, 2 minutes).

译文：牙刷充满一次电需要16小时，电量最多可供常规刷牙使用8天（每天2次，每次2分钟）。

例1中主语为抽象名词charge，并有形容词full对其进行修饰，直译即为"一次满格的充电"，若将其作为中译文的主语，则显得拗口难懂，不符合产品说明书的要求与中文的表达习惯。因此，在译文中增译"牙刷"作为主语，charge名词译作动词，同时full这一形容词转换为副词，修饰充电这一动词。

2. 语态上，中英文产品说明书使用的倾向有所不同：中文产品说明书大部分使用主动语态，而英文产品说明书中被动语态的使用频率较高。这一差异与两种语言的文化与习惯有关，作为科技文体，英文强调事物的发生和存在，而通常隐去施动者，利用无灵主语，表达更为客观，符合英文的语用习惯；而中文中有时引入"有灵"动作发出者可使行文更加流畅、简练，避免"被"字句，即使是在表达被动时也偏向于使用无标记被动句。

例2. 本机采用微电脑控制……

译文：The machine is micro-computer controlled...

例2为中文说明书中描述产品功能时常见的句式，利用"采用"这个万能动词辅助引出产品的各类功能。此类现象在英译中需分类处理，有时省略"采用"这一弱势动词，直接转换为被动形式更为简练且符合英文习惯，如本例的英译中将"控制"作为动词并用被动语态实现语义表达。

3. 句型上，中文常使用无主句；在标准英语中通常需要使用语法正确且完整的句子，但在产品说明书用语中，英语也常可使用不完全句结构，有时也可以直接使用短语（名词、介词短语和不定式短语、分词等）。英汉互译时需根据产品类型不同以及相关要求选择是采取完整形式，还是保留不完全句式。

汉英翻译中将无主句译为完整的句子，首先要确定句子的主语，主要有两种处理方式：（1）使用被动语态；（2）增译主语。

例3. 当不太熟悉的朋友临时借用时，可以添加访客账号。

译文：You can create a guest account for someone who only needs to use your phone temporarily.

例3原句中省略了"手机拥有者"这一主语，即正在阅读该说明书的用户，因此在翻译中直接增译"you"这一主语，即可构成完整的英文语句。另外，在本句的译文中对原文的时间状语进行了调整，用定语从句进行表述，行文更加流畅。

4. 产品说明书中经常需要说明在各种假设的情境中需要采取的措施，翻译中需灵活使用中英文常用的说法，如中文中有"若……""如……""……者"，英文中有"if...""when...""should..."（条件句倒装）"in case of..."，也有隐含在修饰语中的条件。

例4. In case of accidental overdose, get medical help or contact a Poison Control Center right away.

译文：若不慎服用过量，请立即寻求医疗帮助或联系中毒控制中心。

例5. Do not use any opened or torn packets.

译文：若包装开封或破损，请勿使用。

例4原文与译文对应使用表示条件的表达，原文的名词在翻译中转换为动词。例5中原文没有显性的条件，而是用"opened"和"torn"表示两种情况，汉译中将这两个修饰成分译为条件。

三、语体风格特点

产品介绍类文本整体以客观陈述为主，但需要注意的是，中文产品介绍往往带有对产品质量好、功效强的主观描述，这与中文语言和修辞风格有关，卖家常试图刺激消费者的感性体验来宣传产品，放大消费者对产品的期待。这一现象在英文产品说明书中相对不明显，英文的介绍更注重陈述现实，以让消费者了解产品信息为主要目的。在中文说明书英译中应识别客观陈述与主观评论，对主观性强的修辞进行平实化处理。英文说明书中译时要注意措辞迎合中国读者的审美，但也要掌握"度"，肆意夸大绝不可取。

例6.（养生丸）有调理修补机体亏耗之功，延年益寿之效；对肿瘤化放疗术后，亦有促进康复之用。故本品实为男女老少保健养生、延缓衰老必备之妙药。

译文：Vitapill adjusts, invigorates and rejuvenates the body and speeds up the patient's recovery after chemotherapy and radiotherapy of tumor. It is indeed an ideal medicine for the treatment and prevention of diseases and for delaying aging, irrespective of the patient's sex and age.

该例原文为产品功能的介绍，具有鲜明的中文宣传材料的特色，以"……之功""……之效"突出药品的功能，并以"实为""必备""妙药"等中文常用的宣传词增加情态，强调药品功能之优异。该译文没有拘泥于原文的形式，进行了一定的归化。但笔者认为该译文仍不够简明扼要，且在部分用词上仍太注重词的对应（如：indeed对应"实为"，delaying aging对应"延缓衰老"）或表达不易于西方读者理解[如adjusts...the body，在没有更多信息时，adjust the body常指物理上身体体态、姿势的调整，比如在按摩或推拿（chiropractic）时常用此搭配。表示身体对内部及外部状态的适应时主语不宜直接为药物，如The herbal medicines helps adjust your body to stress/external conditions/etc.]。以下提供改译供参考讨论。

改译：Vitapill is an anti-aging herbal health product for everyone. It invigorates and rejuvenates the body and can facilitate recovery after chemotherapy or radiotherapy.

四、中西文化差异的体现

外宣资料非常注意其宣传效果，由于文化差异，很多符合中国人习惯的东西却不符合英语国家人的习惯，"不同文化背景的读者，需要不同的译文"。中药说明书的英译目的是向外国人介绍中药并刺激其购买行为。因此，中药说明书的英译要为受众着想，译文应当符合目标语的表达习惯，尽量做到清晰明了。（罗海燕、邓海静，2017：569）如"京都念慈菴蜜炼川贝枇杷膏"的药名被翻译成 Nin Jiom Pei Pa Koa（Traditional Chinese Herbal Coughs Syrup），采用的是注释法，解释药品的功效和药物成分。（罗海燕、邓海静，2017：569）这是中医药翻译的重要方法。当然，如此翻译也有其弊端。有些药品名的译文过长，这就需要译者进行大胆的创新。如"妇颜宝"这一药名，如果按字面意思采用上面所提到的翻译方法译为Complexion-nourishing Pills for Ladies，则变得冗长，不知所云，无法体现产品的信息，不符合英文产品说明文本的需求。因此，在此类翻译中译者需有一定的创新意识，注重译文的功能，结合英文的命名方法进行翻译。将其处理为Gynecure（gynecological+cure），不拘泥于字面意义，而是利用英文的构词法，用两个部分的语义相结合，明确表达该商品的定位，更符合英文的习惯。（欧阳利锋，2002：17）这一译名可谓既凸显了药品的功效，又做到简洁明了。(罗海燕、邓海静,2017:569)在翻译表达药品功效时还存在语义曲解的问题,如中药中常见的"驱邪"功能,正确翻译方式为"Eliminating Pathogenic Factor",即消除致病因素。如果译者不懂中药文化,很容易翻译成"Exorcism",这个词在英语语境中表达的是驱逐邪恶作祟的东西,更侧重于描述迷信行为。(高春红,2021:78)

相应地,在产品说明类文本中译时也需要符合中国读者的习惯和审美,产品名称译成中文时最常采用的为音译,并根据产品本身的特点采用合适的措辞,如美妆产品常用与"美"或美的事物相关的字眼,富于优雅、柔美之感,譬如美国的Maybelline译为"美宝莲",法国的Guerlain译为"娇兰"。又如目标为男性客户的产品则多表现出刚强、力量等男性的魅力,譬如意大利手表品牌Rolex译为"劳力士"。产品名短小精悍,达到尽善尽美实属不易,但翻译时仍应在贴合产品特点和原名称的前提下,尽量做到音美、形美。Head & Shoulders是宝洁公司的一款洗发产品,其中文译名"海飞丝"兼顾了与原文读音的相似以及意义的表达,"飞"给人以头发飞舞的印象,"丝"则暗示发丝,读起来也朗朗上口,给中国消费者留下了深刻的印象。

产品说明书作为功能性文本,起到跨文化交际的功能,并且需要达到宣传的目的,因此在文化负载词的翻译上应使用英语语言世界习惯的表达与语言结构,摆脱浓重的中国文化色彩,突出商品信息而非文化渲染。

五、产品说明书示例

产品宣介类文本与企业宣传文本在形式和语言上共通之处较多,包括两种语言的命名及翻译也具有相似的特点,故本章不再赘述,请参见本书第七章"企业宣传翻译"相关介绍。本章主要选取产品说明书中专业性和功能性都极强的药品说明书展开介绍,并以中英文对照的形式举例呈现,以供参考。

大多数药品说明书结构基本相似,一般以罗列或表格形式呈现,不同药品的说明书详细程度会有所不同,简短的说明书可能仅有百余字(词),详细的可达上万。药品说明书中可能涵盖的项目如下:

表 8.2　药品说明书介绍项目

英文	中文	英文	中文	英文	中文
(Package) Insert/ Drug Facts/ Fact (Data) Sheet/ Leaflet/ Instructions for Use	说明书/ 药品说明	Drug Name	药品名称	Trade Name/ Proprietary Name	商品名/ 专利药名

续表

英文	中文	英文	中文	英文	中文
Generic Name	通用名	Chemical Name	化学名	Description	性状
Chemical Structure	化学结构式	Molecular Formular	分子式	Strength	规格
Composition	成分	Active Ingredient(s)	活性成分	Inactive Ingredient(s)	非活性成分
Functions	功能主治	Pharmacological Actions	药理作用	Clinical Effect/ Pharmacology	临床效果/药理
Warnings	警告	(Major/ Principal) Indications	（主要）适应证	Contraindications	禁忌
Pharmacokinetics	药物代谢动力学（药代动力学）	Metabolism	药物代谢	Distribution and Elimination	分布与排泄
Drug Interactions	药品交互作用	Potency	药效	Toxicity	毒性
Precaution	注意事项	Side Effects/ By-Effects/ Unwanted or Undesirable Effects	副作用	Adverse Drug Reactions (ADR)	不良反应
Dosage and Administration/ Usage/Directions	用法用量/用法	Overdosage	用药过量	Storage	贮藏
Expiry/Expiration Date (EXP)	失效期	Validity Date	有效期	Manufacturing Date (MFG)/ Production Date	出厂日期
Drug Approval Number	批准文号	Manufacturer	生产商	Packing/Package	包装
Application Number/ NDC Number	药品注册申请号	Marketing Category	市场分类	Start Marketing Date	上市日期

需要注意的是，各国对药品说明书均有自己的规范文件，且相关条款会进行更新。如欧盟国家药品说明书标题偏向使用"Patient Information Leaflet"（PIL）或"Package Leaflet"，美国常用"Package Inserts"（PI），"Patient Package Inserts"（PPI）或"Instructions for Use"；美国药品说明书旧称"Description"或

"Directions"，后经修订为今称；中国《药品说明书和标签管理规定》经过几次修订，对相关措辞进行了修改，相关条款有所增减。因此，译者在翻译前充分了解相关要求，相应熟悉译入语规范是十分有必要的，相关资料如美国食品药品监督管理局（FDA）所作规定、欧盟药品法规、中国《药品说明书和标签管理规定》等。

在每个介绍项目之下对药品的介绍也常包括具有医药产业特征的专业术语和常用表达，译者对相关用语的规范的把握有助于译文的准确性与专业度。表8.3收录了药品说明书中的常用语（中英对照），供读者参考学习。

表8.3 药品说明书常用语

药品类别	generic drug 仿制药/通用名药	brand drug 品牌药	Rx (℞) (prescription) 处方药	OTC (over-the-counter) 非处方药	USP (United States Pharmacopeia) 美国药典	BP (British Pharmacopeia) 英国药典
	immediate-/conventional-release 常释	modified-release 调释	prolonged-/extended-/sustained-release 缓释	delayed-release 迟释	controlled-release 控释	targeted-release 靶向（制剂）
	Federal Law Prohibits Dispensing Without Prescription（美国处方药标签） Adequate Direction for Use（美国非处方药标签）			请仔细阅读说明书并在医师指导下使用（中国处方药说明书标题下方） 请仔细阅读说明书或在药师指导下购买和使用（中国非处方药说明书标题下方）		
剂型	solid (dose) 固体（制剂）	liquid 液体	powder 粉末	aerosol/spray 喷（气）雾剂	inhaler/inhalant 吸入剂	injection 注射剂
	tablet 片剂	adhesive tablet 贴片	scored tablet 刻痕片	effervescent tablet 泡腾片	(sugar-/film-) coated tablet（糖衣片/膜衣片）包衣片	(mineral/olive/snake) oil（矿物油/橄榄油/蛇油）油剂
	capsule 胶囊（剂）	suppository 栓剂	ampoule 针剂	oral solution 口服液	dragee 糖衣丸	emulsion 乳剂

续表

物化性质	odo(u)rless 无臭的	tasteless 无味的	bitter(-tasting) 味苦	sweet(-tasting) 味甘	stable 稳定的	thin 薄的
	insoluble 不溶的	soluble 可溶的	solubility 溶解度	crystalline 结晶的	sterile 无菌的	emplastic 黏性的

成分	formula 配方；制剂	(Sat.) fat （饱和）脂肪	glucose 葡萄糖	lactose 乳糖	starch 淀粉	protein 蛋白质
	sodium 钠	calcium 钙	latex 橡胶	preservative 防腐剂	caffeine 咖啡因	antibiotic 抗生素
	...is a... (e.g. white plain tablet; yellowish to orange, crystalline powder; white opaque fat emulsion; white to off-white solid) which contains/containing 50mg of.../ odourless or almost odourless. ...is a very stable antibiotic, and its activity does not decrease when... that easily dissolves in water or alcohol that poorly solubles in water, delute acid and most organic solents no... (e.g. alcohol; artificial flavor; saccharin) Each... (e.g. tablet; Pulvule®) contains... equivalent to ... (e.g. 10 mg of fluoxetine) in each... (e.g. tablet; pill)			是……（如：白色素片、淡黄色至橙色结晶粉末、白色不透明脂肪乳剂、白色至类白色固体），含有50毫克的……/无臭或几乎无臭。 ……是一种非常稳定的抗生素，其活性在……时不会降低。 易溶于水或酒精 难溶于水、稀酸及大多数有机溶剂中 不含……（如：酒精、人工香料、糖精） 每个……（如：片剂、子弹形胶囊剂） 含有……相当于……（如：10毫克的氟西汀）在每个……（例如：片剂、药丸）中		

适应证与功能	arthritis 关节炎	tonsillitis 扁桃体炎	gastritis 胃炎	meningitis 脑膜炎	bronchitis 支气管炎	stomatitis 口炎
	appendicitis 阑尾炎	dermatitis 皮炎	angina pectoris 心绞痛	diabetes 糖尿病	hypertension 高血压	contact 接触性的
	acute 急性的	chronic 慢性的	antitubercular 抗结核的	vesicular 水泡性	parasitic 寄生（虫）的	menstrual 月经的
	be indicated in (for); be administered in be employed to; be used to (for, as) be recommended for; be helpful/useful in; be intended to be active against; be of value of; be effective in (for, against) for relief of; for/in the treatment/management of for prevention of; to prevent/protect			适用于 用于；被用于 推荐用于；用于……中有帮助/有用 对……有效 对（治疗）缓解……有效；用于治疗/控制…… 用于预防……；防止/保护		

禁忌	allergic/ allergy 过敏的/过敏	hypersensitive/ hypersensitivity 超敏的/超敏	sensitize/ sensitizing dose 使过敏/致敏量	anaphylactic 过敏的	irritable/ irritability 过敏的/过敏	shock 休克	
	damage/ impairment/ impaired 损伤/损害/受损的	failure 衰竭	functional disorder 功能障碍	hepatic 肝的	renal 肾的	cardiac 心脏的	
	cardiogenic 心源性	respiratory 呼吸的	histamine 组胺	sulfonamide 磺胺药物	cephalosporin 头孢菌素	family history 家族史	
	Hypersensitivity to quinolones; severe renal insufficiency Contradicted in the patients with... (e.g. positive penicillin skin test) Patients with a history of.../ with... (e.g. infection) ...is contraindicated in the following patient/in patients with known... (e.g. hypersensitivity to)/ those suffering from... should not be used/employed in/to must not be administered/given to should be used with caution Do not take... if... is not recommended for/the use of...is not recommended It is advisable to avoid the use of... unless... (e.g. clinical circumstances demand such use) Avoid triggers such as spicy foods, caffeinated beverages, and alcohol.			喹诺酮类药物过敏的患者忌用；严重肾机能不全者忌用。 ……（者）禁用（如：青霉素皮试阳性） 有……病史的患者/患有……（如：感染） ……以下患者禁用/已知对……过敏的患者禁用/那些患有……的人 ……（者）禁/忌/慎用。 ……（本品）禁用于/不宜用…… 如果……不推荐使用…… 不建议使用…… 建议避免使用…… 除非……（如：临床情况需要） 避免触发因素，忌辛辣食物、含咖啡因饮料和酒。			
不良反应	prickling/ tingly feeling 刺痛/刺痛感	numbness and tingling 麻木	nausea 恶心	vomiting/ throwing up 呕吐	bloating 腹胀	diarrhea 腹泻	

续表

thirst 口干	tiredness/ fatigue/ drowsiness 乏力/疲惫/ 嗜睡	flush 潮红		dizziness 头昏/眩晕	palpitation 心悸	fever 发热	
dyspnea 呼吸困难	tachycardia 心跳过速	sweating 盗汗		chest distress 胸闷	shortness of breath 气短	coma 昏迷	
burn/ burning feeling 灼烧/灼烧感	pruritus/ itching 瘙痒	rash 皮疹		anorexia 厌食/食欲不振	loss (of appetite) (食欲)减退	inhibition 抑制	
symptom 症状	complication 并发症	(double) infection (双重)感染		transient 短暂的	temporary 暂时的	systematic 全身的	
Feeling... (e.g. dizzy, tired, or weak). pain at site of application ...be (only) observed in...(e.g. isolated) cases In some patients...(e.g. nausea, dizziness, and vomiting) may... In...(e.g. rare) cases...(e.g. a decrease of blood pressure) may appear/ it is recommended that the dose be reduced. ...has been reported to cause... (with an occasionally fatal outcome). The most serious side-effect is... Major adverse reactions include... These unwanted effects/symptoms usually disappear... (spontaneously after 7-14 days or following a temporary reduction in the dosage). These symptoms are usually confined to... (e.g. 7-14 days of treatment) and then tend to disappear.				可见……(如:头晕、疲劳或虚弱)。 给药部位疼痛。 偶有……仅在……(如:个别)病例中观察到。 在一些患者中,可能会出现……(如:恶心、头晕和呕吐)。 在极少数情况下,可能会出现血压下降的情况,建议此时减少剂量。 有报道,极少数患者使用可能会引起某些严重反应(有时可能导致死亡)。 最严重的副作用是…… 主要的不良反应包括…… 这些副作用/症状通常会在……(如:7—14天后)自行消失或在暂时减少剂量后消失。			
用法	administer/ administration 给/用药	inhale/ insufflate 吸入	spray 喷	oral(ly)/ by mouth 口服	sublingual(ly) 舌下(含服)	swallow 吞服	
	chew/ crush 咀嚼/压碎	otic 耳的	nasal/ intranasal 鼻腔/鼻内	apply to 用于、涂于、敷于	rectal(ly) 直肠内	parenteral(ly) 肠道外	

intragluteal(ly) 臀肌内	intravenous(ly) 静脉内	(drip) phleboclysis （点滴）静脉输液	intravenous injection 静注（静脉注射） intravenous infusion (perfusion) 静脉输注	intramuscular(ly) 肌内 intramuscular injection 肌注（肌肉注射）	local(ly) 局部（给药）
take medication... (e.g. during/before/after meals; half an hour before bedtime) Shake well before using. Chew or crush tablets completely before swallowing.			用餐时/饭前/饭后服用；睡前半小时服用。 使用前摇匀。 吞咽前嚼碎或压碎片剂。		

人群与剂量	newborn/ infant/baby/ children 新生儿/婴（幼）儿/儿童	adolescent 青少年	adult 成人	senile/ the elderly/ elderly patients 老年人/老年患者	pregnant women 孕妇	lactation 哺乳期
	women of childbearing age 育龄妇女	nursing mothers 哺乳期妇女	the first trimester (3 months) of pregnancy 妊娠期前三个月	debilitated patients 体弱患者	average/ general/ standard dose/ dosage 平均/一般/标准剂量	high/ maximum/ minimum dose 大/最大/最小剂量（最小有效量）
	indicated dose 有效剂量	maintenance dose 维持剂量	therapeutic dose 治疗剂量	suggested/ recommended dose 推荐剂量	initial/single dose 首次/一次用量	fatal/lethal dose 致死量
	single daily dose; usual... (e.g. adult) dosage for all age groups safe enough for even newest of newborns not recommended for... (e.g. children) avoid when... (e.g. pregnant) use in... (e.g. infants, the elderly)/during... (e.g. pregnancy, delivery, or lactation) in the amount of... (e.g. 25—50 mg daily)			每日单次剂量；通常……（例如：成人）的剂量，适用于所有年龄段 对新生儿也足够安全 不推荐给……（如：儿童）用 在……（如：怀孕）时避免使用 在……（如：婴儿、老年人）中使用/在……（如：怀孕、分娩或哺乳）期间使用		

续表

	Up to... (e.g. twice a day), dep...ending on (e.g. acuteness of the disease). every...hours; at intervals of...; ... (e.g. once; twice) daily (a day); every other day; ... (e.g. 1 tablet) in the morning and... (e.g. 1 tablet) at night, 12 hours apart. Overdosage may give rise to the following signs and symptoms：... divided into...doses; in...divided doses	用量为……（如：每日 25—50 毫克）根据……（如：疾病的急性程度），最多……（如：每天两次）。 每隔……小时；间隔……时间；……（如：一次、两次）每天（一天）；隔天；早上……（如：1 片）和晚上……（如：1 片），每 12 小时一次。 超剂量可能引起下列体征和症状：…… 分……次服用。
包装与储存	airless container 密闭容器 / bottle 瓶 / vial 玻璃小瓶 / ampoule 安瓿 / carton 纸盒 / tube 管 pen 注射笔 / blister pack 吸塑包装 / aluminum-plastic/aluminum foil 铝塑 / strip pack 条状包装 / aseptic pack 无菌包装 / hospital/trade packs 医用/商品包装 Store at or below 25℃ (77 ℉), in a dry area/in the dark... Store at controlled room temperature 59 ℉ to 86 ℉ (15℃ to 30℃)/ between 20℃—25℃ (68 ℉—77 ℉). Keep... (e.g. tightly closed, in the upright position, out of reach of children). Keep away from... (e.g. children). Protect from (excessive) ... (e.g. moisture, heat, light). ...should be stored in the refrigerator, protected against exposure to light. Tamper evident：Carton sealed for safety. Carton containing 12 INBRIJA capsules (3 blister cards containing 4 capsules each). Packaging：Al/PVC film blister pack of 28 tablets × 24 blisters.	存放在 25℃（77 ℉）以下，干燥处/避光，储存在受控的室温下，温度范围为 59 ℉ 至 86 ℉（15℃至 30℃）/ 20℃—25℃（68 ℉—77 ℉）。 保持……（例如密封好，直立放置，放在儿童触不到的地方）。 远离……（例如儿童）。 防止过度接触……（如湿气、热量、光线）。 ……应存放在冰箱中，避光。 防篡改明显：纸箱密封以确保安全。 纸箱内含 12 粒 INBRIJA 胶囊（3 张泡罩卡，每张含 4 粒胶囊）。 包装：铝/PVC 薄膜泡罩包装，共 28 片 × 24 泡罩。

警示语	should be administered under the supervision of a qualified physician (experienced in the use of) ...should be discontinued if/when... Do/Do not..., if... Ask a doctor before use if you have... (e.g. glaucoma; a breathing problem such as emphysema or chronic bronchitis) Stop use and ask a doctor if... ...should be used with caution in... (e.g. epileptics and patients with a history of CNS disorders) Keep out of reach of children.	在医师或药师的指导下使用。 如……，减少本药剂量或停止用药。 本药可能……（如：加剧已存在的局部缺血性心脏病）。 如果……，请/不要……（若患有青光眼或呼吸问题如肺气肿或慢性支气管炎），请在使用前咨询医生。 如果……请停止使用并咨询医生。 ……在……中应谨慎使用（如：癫痫患者和有中枢神经系统疾病史的患者）。 放在儿童接触不到的地方。		
其他常用语	as defined in 按照……（规定）	uncertain/ not known 尚不明确	none reported 未见报道	healthcare professional use only 仅限医疗专业人员使用	administration under medical advice 按医嘱用药	information available at present suggests... 现有资料表明……
	...has not been studied... (in ombination with...) 尚无本品（药）……（与……合用）的研究	no reports of overdose with this drug have been reported 尚缺乏本品药物过量的报道	There is no experiment conducted in this group and no reliable references. 本品未进行该项实验且无可靠参考文献。	No adequate and well-controlled studies of this drug in pregnant women have been done. 尚未对孕妇进行充分严格的对照研究。		

  药品说明书中除了常用术语与句型，还时常会出现缩写形式，尤其是在表格类说明文本中，由于空间限制，缩略程度较高。英译汉时，译者需精准把握缩略词的意义，保证译文的准确性；汉译英时，译者需适当利用英文中常用的缩略形式，加强英文译本的可读性。例如，在说明时间时用hrs，mths和yrs分别表示"小时""月"和"年"，用kg表示重量单位"千克"。

  除了通用单位缩略词，药品说明书中还有很多医学类专业术语缩略词，熟悉相关缩略词对药品说明书译文语言的地道性与可读性十分重要，以下为部分常用缩略形式。

sec(s)=second(s)	秒
min(s)=minute(s)	分钟
hr(s)=hour(s)	小时
d(s)=day(s)	日
wk(s)=week(s)	周
mth(s)=month(s)	月
yr(s)=year(s)	年
kg=kilogram	千克
g=gram	克
mg=milligram	毫克
mcg=microgram（μg）	微克
l/L=liter (litre)	升
ml/ML=milliliter	毫升
c.c.= cubic centimeter	立方厘米
i.u.=international unit	国际单位
ac= atecibum (before meals)	饭前/空腹（例如：空腹血糖）
ic=intercibum (between meals)	饭中
pc= postcibum (after meals)	饭后
po= peros (by mouth)	口服
qh= quaque hora (every hour)	每小时一次
qd= quaque die (every day)	每日一次
bid= bis in die (twice a day)	每日两次
tid= ter in die (three times a day)	每日三次
p.r.n.=pro re nata (Latin)/ when necessary; as needed	必要时/根据情况需要使用（长期医嘱）
s.o.s.= si opus sit (Latin)/ if necessary	需要时（临时医嘱）
ext.	外用

药品说明书是说明类文本中规范性极强的一个品类。相对来说，除医学类外，其他类型产品的说明书在规范上没有那么严格，用语灵活性也更高一些。比如，说明书标题可以有"使用说明""使用指南""用户指南""操作手册"等各种说法，英文中也有Instructions, Manual, Instruction Manual, User Manual, User

Guide等说法。但需要注意的是,虽然各类说明书对规范性的要求不同,但此类文本承担着向消费者介绍产品功能与指导操作的作用,具备较高的科学性和准确性,因此译者需要时刻保持严谨,做到忠实、准确,译前也需仔细阅读相关规范与规定,如国家标准文件《消费品使用说明》,以及相应领域的相关规定,如《医疗器械说明书和标签管理规定》《化妆品标签说明书管理规定》等。

与说明书相比,产品宣介文本对语言规范上的要求更低,但也因专业性、中英语言文化差异等因素,翻译难度高低不等。以下为一份工业材料介绍的中文原文与英文译文,供对比学习。

粉料
产品简介 　　中国石化聚丙烯粉料是采用间歇式液相本体法聚合、不含添加剂的本色粉末状固体,产品质量稳定,种类齐全。 产品用途 　　聚丙烯粉料主要用于制作一般用途制品,如绳索、编织袋、打包带、玩具、日用品、无纺布等。 产品包装及贮运要求 　　本品采用内衬塑料薄膜的聚丙烯编织袋,一般净重20或25kg/袋。 　　产品应存放在通风、干燥的仓库内,远离火源,防止阳光直接照射,不得露天堆放。产品运输时不得在阳光下暴晒或雨淋,不得与沙土、碎金属、煤炭、玻璃等混合装运,更不可与有毒物质、腐蚀性和易燃物品混装。
Powder Grade
Overview 　　Sinopec PP powder grade, produced by the batch liquid-phase bulk polymerization method, is additive-free, powdered solids of natural color. Sinopec provides diverse powder grade products with consistent high quality. Applications 　　PP powder grade is mainly used for general-purpose products including ropes, woven bags, packaging tapes, toys, daily necessities and non-woven fabrics. Packaging, Storage and Transport 　　The resin is packaged in PP(polypropylene) woven bags with thin plastic linings. The net weight is 20 or 25kg per bag. 　　The resin should be stored in a drafty, dry warehouse and protected from fire and exposure to sunlight and shall not be piled up in the open air. It shall not be loaded and transported with sand, soil, scrap metal, coal or glass and mixed loading with toxic, corrosive and flammable substances is strictly prohibited. During transportation, avoid intense sunlight or rain.

第二节　产品说明书翻译原则

一、保证语言的严谨与专业性

译文应体现出对原文相关知识的了解及文本全面的理解，体现专业性、准确性，译者需秉持严谨的态度和责任心，避免常识性或科学性错误，可以参考专业文章，查阅相关专业词典，咨询专业人士。

产品说明书带有科技性，在词汇上具有专业性，切忌望文生义进而导致误译。上文中提到中药"黄连"，与其名称十分相似的还有一款中药制剂名为"双黄连"。该药剂名仅从字面来看会让人误解为由两种黄连制成，但实际上，该药方中并没有黄连，而药剂名是由所用的三种中药名连起来的名称。双黄连全方仅三味药：双花（金银花）、黄芩、连翘，取三味药的第一个字，即为"双黄连"。若将该产品名称译为Double Coptis chinensis无疑会对读者产生误导，绝不可取。这种命名方式与英文的构词法有相似之处，但由于三种中药材本身并不为英语母语者所熟知，且其名称本身具有专业性且较为复杂（金银花Flos Lonicerae，黄芩Radix Scutellariae，连翘Fructus Forsythiae），无法以相似的方法用英语将三种材料名结合成新的药品名。双黄连在国外销售已久，其产品名一般直接采取音译"Shuang Huang Lian"。同样，在翻译英文说明书时也需要注意一词多义，理解单词在语境中的意义，比如：power一词本身有"力量""军队""强国"等意思，而在电器相关说明中很可能表示的是"电""电源""功率"等。

二、直译为主，意译为辅

产品说明书的翻译以直译为主要手段，辅以意译。当中英文术语的相关信息（所指、内涵、用法等）基本吻合时，直译能够实现准确和简明的效果，符合产品说明书作为科技性文本的要求。在专业术语及专业性信息的翻译中要尽量使用直译法，保证译文的准确性和专业性。同时，由于介绍性文本又不同于完全的科技文献，产品说明书又常被赋予一定的文化内涵、语言特点，使用各类修辞让读者对产品或服务形成更具象化、更易于接受、更为深刻的印象，因此，可以借助一定程度的意译，摆脱形式的束缚，发挥译者的主动性，以读者接受为导向，关照译入语语境下的语言特点和表达方式，从而实现产品说明书应该达到的交际目的。

例7. 特级黄山毛峰形似雀舌，白毫显露，色似象牙，鱼叶金黄。

译文：Premium Huangshan Maofeng Tea features leaves resembling

the sparrow's tongue, with distinct white downy hairs on the surface, and is distinguished for its overall yellowish color and fish leaves of a golden tint.

在中文里虽然"白毫"一词有两种含义,但可根据语境清晰地分辨"白毫"为绒毛还是茶名;而在英文中pekoe一词的意义却不那么明晰,虽也有以此指叶片上的绒毛,但并不是普遍用法,甚至是鲜有人知晓的用法。因此,在本句的翻译中基于清晰明了的目标,将"白毫"一词进行释义,译为white downy hairs on the surface。鱼叶亦称"胎叶",是茶树新梢上抽出的第一片叶子,因形似鱼鳞而得名。因此,此处选用直译法翻译"鱼叶"一词。

在句法层面,原文用四个四字短语对茶叶的形状、颜色、外貌进行描述,短小精悍且生动形象。在英文译文中难以完全再现中文之美,若仿照原文句式,以四个短句并列连成一个整句,则显得句式拖沓,且难以连贯。

修辞上,本句使用了比喻和夸张的手法。原文"色似象牙,鱼叶金黄"实为一种略有夸张的形容,通俗来说即该种茶的整体色调偏黄且鱼叶偏亮黄色。ivory确实是有黄色色调,但是以白色与黄色调和而成,与茶叶的黄绿色并不相同。许多网络平台在对本句的英译中,常以ivory直接对应原文的"色似象牙",但常配以黄绿色的茶叶图片,造成了明显的图文不符。而直接称"鱼叶"为gold fish leaf也言过其实。因此,此处采用意译,淡化原文的修辞色彩,只指出整体色泽偏黄且鱼叶有一丝金黄的色调。

三、充分关照读者的阅读习惯,适当归化

产品介绍文本有自身明显的文体特征,不同领域的产品介绍也会有一些约定俗成的模式,中英文文本又会有一定的差异,因此产品说明书的翻译必须对照平行文本,对译文进行适当归化,适应译入语语境中相应的文本特点。

如上文所述,中文在介绍产品时善用中文的各类修辞如对仗、比喻等,在行文中喜用四字词,以铺陈夸张的手法,形成中文特有的韵律和感性审美体验;相反,英文文本则更注重实用性、客观性。另外,中英文在礼貌用语方面也有一定差异,相较而言,英文的产品说明中比较少用敬词please,而是直接以祈使句表达鲜明的指示、警示语气;而中文的产品说明中则贯彻了中文一贯偏向使用敬词来表示礼貌的习惯,尤其是对"请"字的使用,在各类产品说明书中都随处可见。

以下对不同类型的产品说明书中常用的一些表达进行简要举例,仅供参考。

例8. 如不慎入眼,请立即用大量清水冲洗。

译文:In case of contact with eyes, rinse immediately with plenty of water.

例9. 本指南仅供参考，不构成任何形式的承诺，产品（包括但不限于颜色、大小、屏幕显示等）请以实物为准。

译文：This guide is for reference only. The actual product, including but not limited to the color, size, and screen layout, may vary. All statements, information, and recommendations in this guide do not constitute a warranty of any kind, express or implied.

例10. Keep out of reach of children.

译文：请将本品放在儿童接触不到的地方。

第三节　课内翻译任务

一、英译汉 English-Chinese Translation

Oral-B Brush

Welcome to Oral-B!

Before operating this toothbrush, please read these instructions and save this manual for future reference.

IMPORTANT

● Periodically check the cord for damage. If cord is damaged, take the charging unit to an Oral-B Service Centre. A damaged or non-functioning unit should no longer be used. Do not modify or repair the product. This may cause fire, electric shock or injury.

● Usage by children under age 3 is not recommended. Toothbrushes can be used by children and persons with reduced physical, sensory or mental capabilities or lack of experience and knowledge, if they have been given supervision or instruction concerning use of the appliance in a safe way and understand the hazards involved.

● Cleaning and maintenance shall not be performed by children.

● Children shall not play with the appliance.

● Use this product only for its intended use as described in this manual. Do not use attachments which are not recommended by the manufacturer.

WARNING

● Do not place the charger in water or liquid or store where it can fall or be pulled into a tub or sink. Do not reach for it when fallen into water. Unplug immediately.

- This appliance contains batteries that are non-replaceable.
- Do not disassemble the product except when disposing of the battery. When taking out the battery for disposal of the unit, use caution so as not to short the positive (+) and negative (−) terminals.
- When unplugging, always hold the power plug instead of the cord. Do not touch the power plug with wet hands. This can cause an electric shock.
- If you are undergoing treatment for any oral care condition, consult your dental professional prior to use.
- This toothbrush is a personal care device and is not intended for use on multiple patients in a dental practice or institution.

Connecting and charging

Your toothbrush has a waterproof handle, is electrically safe and designed for use in the bathroom.

- Plug the charging unit (D) into an electrical outlet and place the handle (C) on there (1).
- A full charge takes about 16 hours and enables up to 8 days of regular brushing (twice a day, 2 minutes).
- For everyday use, the handle can be stored on the plugged-in charging unit, there is no risk of overcharging.

Battery maintenance

To maintain the maximum capacity of the rechargeable battery, unplug the charging unit and discharge the handle by regular use at least every 6 months.

Brushing technique

- Wet brush head and apply any kind of toothpaste. To avoid splashing, guide the brush head to your teeth before switching on the appliance (B) (2).
- When brushing your teeth with one of the oral-B oscillating-rotating brush heads guide the brush head slowly from tooth to tooth, spending a few seconds on each tooth surface.
- With any brush head start brushing the outside, then the inside and finally the chewing surfaces. Brush all four quadrants of your mouth equally. Brush at

least for 2 minutes. Do not push too hard, simply let the brush do all the work. You may also consult your dentist or dental hygienist about the right technique for you.

● In the first days of using any electric toothbrush, your gums may bleed slightly. In general, bleeding should stop after a few days. Should it persist after 2 weeks, please consult your dentist or dental hygienist.

（Oral-B Brush产品说明书）

重点解析 Notes and Comments

1. If cord is damaged, take the charging unit to an Oral-B Service Centre. 如电源线有损坏，请将充电器送至博朗服务中心。

英文说明书中指明维修点名称为Oral-B Service Centre，为英语国家相应维修点所用名称。而该牙刷在中国销售时与博朗合作，维修由博朗服务中心提供。本参考译文以该产品在中国出售时为中国顾客提供产品说明为目的，因此在翻译中没有直译Oral-B Service Centre，而是相应调整为中文适用的名称。

2. persons with reduced physical, sensory or mental capabilities 身体、感官或精神方面有不便者

该意群作为句子中的一个宾语，结构中心在persons，在修饰成分中with...capabilities为基本结构，而reduced和physical, sensory or mental又对capabilities进行修饰。在翻译中将这个比较长的偏正结构进行了调整，改为动态语句，将离结构中心最远的修饰语physical, sensory or mental放在最前面，而reduced一词动词化，最后通过中文中的名词结构"……者"还原最中心的偏正结构，构成名词成分。

3. Your toothbrush has a waterproof handle, is electrically safe and designed for use in the bathroom. 本牙刷配备防水刷柄，不会导电，可在浴室放心使用。

waterproof adj. 防水的，后缀-proof可表示"防……的"，如：bulletproof 防弹的，airproof 气密的，recession-proof 抗衰退的，childproof 防孩童开启（或使用、损坏）的。electrically safe属于副词修饰形容词，译成中文时采取意译，为"不会导电"。

4. Brush all four quadrants of your mouth equally. 注意均等地清洁口腔内每一个部位。

在此处all four quadrants即指四周，翻译中采用意译，译为"口腔内每一个

部位"。

5. Should it persist after 2 weeks, please consult your dentist or dental hygienist. 若使用两周后仍持续出血,请咨询您的牙科医生或牙科卫生专家。

该句中should在句首构成虚拟语气,表示"万一,如果",相当于If it persists after 2 weeks, please consult your dentist or dental hygienist. 条件句中代词it起到前指作用,指的是上一句中的bleeding,在翻译中还原其指示义。

二、汉译英 Chinese-English Translation

华为Mate 30 Pro用户指南

用户和账户

设置多用户

当他人需要借用您的手机时,您可在手机上添加一个新的访问账号。他人通过该账号登录,将只能使用手机的部分功能,以保护您的隐私和数据安全。

若您开启了健康使用手机,并设置使用者为孩子时,多用户功能无法使用。

手机共有以下几种账号类型:

● 管理员

您的账号默认为管理员账号。

● 用户

可为熟悉的亲人添加用户账号。

使用用户账号时,可使用手机大部分功能,但无法使用恢复出厂设置、手机克隆、更改用户权限、创建隐私空间等影响管理员的功能。

添加新用户或访客账号

1. 进入 ⚙ 设置> 用户和账户 > 多用户,点击**添加用户**或**添加访客**,根据提示添加。

2. 点击切换,进入用户或访客账号。根据提示完成新用户数据配置。

3. 根据需要安装应用。但如果另一个用户已经安装过该应用,且版本高于新用户要安装的版本时,会安装失败。

您最多可添加 3 个用户和 1 个访客账号。

授权用户或访客使用通话和信息

您可以设置用户或访客账户是否可使用通话等功能。

在管理员、用户及访客之间切换

您可以通过以下任一方法切换多用户账户:

- 从顶部状态栏向下滑出通知面板，点击 ，然后点击要登录的用户头像。
- 进入 设置 > 用户和账户 > 多用户，然后点击想要登录的用户名。

删除用户或访客

删除用户或访客账号后，会同步清除该账号下的数据，请谨慎操作。

本指南仅供参考，不构成任何形式的承诺，产品（包括但不限于颜色、大小、屏幕显示等）请以实物为准。

（华为Mate 30 Pro产品说明书）

重点解析 Notes and Comments

1. 他人通过该账号登录，将只能使用手机的部分功能，以保护您的隐私和数据安全。For your privacy and data security, the other user will only be allowed to access certain functions of your phone.

access *n.* 接近，进入，通道，使用机会；*v.* 访问，接近，使用。本句中的"部分"一词没有直译为some of或a part of，而是用certain（某些），既指出能用的不是全部的功能，又很好地对应了内含于中文里的"指定的"部分功能的意思。

2. 从顶部状态栏向下滑出通知面板。Swipe down from the status bar to open the notification panel.

本句中出现了两个在电子产品和程序中常用的对象：状态栏（status bar）和通知面板。本句原文中"顶部"一词对状态栏位置进行标记，但swipe down已经说明了手势方向，"顶部"这一信息隐含其中，不必译为Swipe down from the top status bar。

3. 请谨慎操作。Please exercise caution.

exercise一词在此处意思是"行使，运用"，exercise caution是在给予警告时常用的表达。中文习惯将"操作"作为动作，而"谨慎"作为副词起到修饰作用；而exercise caution将"谨慎"作为名词，强调警告的内容，在英文中起到的警示作用更为鲜明。

4. 产品（包括但不限于颜色、大小、屏幕显示等）请以实物为准。The actual product, including but not limited to the color, size, and screen layout, may vary.

including but not limited to是在各类涉及法律或法律相关文本中常用于表达申明的短语，对应中文的"包括但不限于"，其变化形式还有including without limiting等。including一词本身包含了不完全列举的意思，在普通用语中加上but not limited to会显得重复冗余，但在法律用词中常将隐含义外显，从而避免争端。本句原文中"以实物为准"在中文里表达流畅，但很难直译为英文，因此翻译中使用意译，视角反转，将"为准"改变为"可能有所不同"，对应一个动词vary，简洁明了，且重现原文语义。

第四节　课后翻译训练

一、将下列句子翻译成汉语 Translate the following sentences into Chinese

1. [Storage] below 30℃.
2. Folic acid appears as odorless orange-yellow needles or platelets.
3. The product is white opaque intravenous infusion of fat emulsion.
4. Before operating the system, read the following precautions carefully.
5. Soak a soft cloth in water, wring it out well, and use it to wipe the units and parts.
6. Naloxone is contraindicated for use in patients who are allergic or hypersensitive to it.
7. Safety and effectiveness in pediatric patients younger than 4 months have not been established.
8. Do not use detergents, cleansers, paint thinners, benzene, alcohol or kerosene for cleaning purposes.
9. If you want to install the main unit on a wall, ask an authorized dealer or service personnel to do the job.
10. Do not use well water containing sea water or other salt content (from wells near coastal area) (otherwise trouble may result).

二、将下列句子翻译成英语 Translate the following sentences into English

1. 本产品经环氧乙烷灭菌，无菌、无热源。
2. 开箱时请认真确认在运输中是否有破损现象。
3. 通电情况下不要用手触摸控制端子，否则有触电的危险！
4. 定期吹扫柜内，清除积下的灰尘、杂物，保持柜内卫生。
5. 三角形手握设计，符合人体工学，可以矫正握笔姿势及缓解疲劳。

6. 电源采用美国BCD方案设计，高精度智能控制电路，具有过载、欠压等保护，使用更安全。

7. 佩戴的松紧度以可塞进一个手指头为宜，佩戴位置在腕骨偏左一指宽，以保证心率检测的准确性。

8. 采用最新全自动感应翻盖技术，能准确识别人体目标，实现自动翻盖或闭盖功能，彻底释放您的双手。

9. 产品远销英国、日本、意大利和东南亚，深受消费者欢迎和好评。

10. 爱玛D2电脑全自动钉扣机（双头）是采用电脑数控技术、自动排版、自动送钉、精确定位进行钉合各种各样图案的自动化设备，具有两种钉头选择，通过更换送钉模组可钉合各种规格的四爪钉子。

三、将下列短文翻译成汉语 Translate the following passage into Chinese

DIOR PRESTIGE

DIOR PRESTIGE Le Concentré Yeux

Le Concentré Yeux potentiate the eye contour area regeneration thanks to a unique synergy between skincare and massage.

With the eyes closed, its divinely fresh and enveloping texture rolls out across the whole panoramic eye area for a more complete regeneration. Its action is boosted by the Open Eye™ applicator. This technological wonder reproduces the expert techniques of the Dior Institut thanks to its double-rotating pearls.

Instantly, the eye contour area is smoothed, marks of fatigue disappear. Day after day, the eyes open up, magnified by greater lashes. Full of femininity, they illuminate the face with newfound beauty.

DIOR PRESTIGE La Crème

Its prodigious, unbelievably fine and luxurious texture fuses with the skin and envelops it in absolute comfort. Trapping the Nectar's active ingredients at the heart of the skin, it revitalizes and helps support the homogenous texture of the skin. Upon the first application, the skin feels and looks visibly transformed. Day after day, it is smoother. Its texture is refined and more even. Its radiance is deeply revitalized. Discover the exquisite sensation of rose-petal skin beneath your fingertips.

Dior Prestige La Crème is refillable: a sustainable approach for lasting beauty.

DIOR PRESTIGE La Lotion Essence de Rose

La Lotion Essence de Rose combines the power of a fresh essence with the comfort of a milky lotion. Drenched in hydrating agents, the lotion deeply moisturizes the skin and wraps it in a protective veil all day long. To be used as the first step in your Dior Prestige beauty ritual, La Lotion Essence de Rose doubles the age-defying effectiveness of La Crème to reveal a fresher, even and more luminous complexion.

Through a unique process, Dior Science releases the vital essence concentrated at the heart of Rose de Granville cells and creates the Micro-Reviving Rose Water™. La Lotion Essence de Rose reinvigorates circulation and flow between skin cells. Full of life, the skin is infused with a natural rosy radiance again.

（DIOR PRESTIGE系列产品介绍）

四、将下列短文翻译成英语 Translate the following passage into English

当发生电池电量不足警告时，请在利用输入输出设备保存了加工程序、工具数据、参数之后，更换电池。另外，当发出电池报警时，加工程序、工具数据、参数可能会损坏。在更换电池后，请重新加载各数据。

当存在轴过切或异常声音时，请立即按紧急停止按钮停止轴移动。

连接错误可能会导致设备损坏。请将电缆连接到规定的插座。

请不要在各接口上施加超过本说明书中规定的电压。否则会导致破裂、破损等。

在通电状态下，请不要进行各单元间连接电缆的连接、插拔。

在通电状态下，请不要进行各印刷基板的连接、插拔。

请不要拉拽电缆进行插拔。

请不要对电池进行短接、充电、焚烧及分解。

换下的电池，请按照各地规定的方法进行废弃处理。

请不要在通电状态下更换控制单元。

请不要在通电状态下更换基本I/O单元。

请不要在通电状态下更换控制部分电源基盘。

请不要在通电状态下更换扩展用基盘。

请不要在通电状态下更换内存盒。

请注意不要让金属切削粉末等接触到内存盒与插座的接触部分。

（三菱数控系统说明书）

第九章 商务信函翻译

商务信函（Business Letters）是指企业、政府机关、事业单位、各团体组织之间以推销产品和服务、获取信息、沟通交流、洽谈磋商为目的，以书面文字（纸质信件、电子邮件、传真、电报）为载体的一种文本形式。

商务信函是国际商务来往中经常使用的联系方式，是开展对外贸易业务和有关商务活动的基础及重要工具，贯穿对外贸易的各个环节，能及时、具体、完整、准确地为贸易双方传递商务事务信息以及帮助双方达成最有效的交流与沟通。

商务信函是商家、企业之间进行交流和沟通的必要手段，涉及商贸活动的各个方面，如建立贸易联系、发出邀请、推介商品或服务、提出投诉、解决问题等，在商贸活动中起着非常重要的作用。它既承担了推销商品、传递信息的任务，又是维护客户利益、提升公司形象的重要途径，甚至有时还能作为解决纠纷的重要证据，因此商务信函的写作和翻译要注重语言得体、格式规范、翻译准确。

本章介绍商务英语信函的基本特征及翻译技巧，涉及商务邀约、询盘还盘、催运及投诉等相关内容的知识和英汉翻译实践。

第一节　商务信函的语言特点

一、词汇特点

（一）大量使用专业术语和缩略语

商务信函涉及的领域非常广泛，专业词汇能用最简练的语言做到传神达意。有些普通词汇在商务英语里还有另一层含义，所以译者应该结合不同的语境来斟酌词汇的确切含义，用专业的、精确的商务术语来表达原文的含义，体现信函的专业性。

例1. This price is including CAM and Base rent.

译文：这个价格包括公共区域管理费和基本租金。

例2. We shall be obliged to draw up the contract on the condition that you agree to share the Property Tax of your own parcel.

译文：如果您同意分担你所属地块的土地税，那么我方将立即草拟合同。

上述例子中有一些行业内的术语，如：CAM（Common Area Management公共区域管理费），恰当使用可以便于沟通，但是在不同的语境中有不同的含义，比如CAM亦可指Computer Aided Manufacturing（计算机辅助制造）。

例3. While we appreciate your intention to push the sale of our hardware in your market, we feel very regretful that we are unable to consider your request for payment under D/A terms, the reason being that we generally adopt the method of payment by letter of credit for our exports.

译文：我方感激你方有意在你方市场推销我方五金产品，但我们非常遗憾，不能接受你方提出的以承兑交单的方式付款，原因是对于我们的出口货物，我方通常接受信用证付款方式。

例4. In view of our friendly business relations and to encourage your promotion of our products, we agree to accept, as an exceptional case, payment on a D/P basis for transactions to be finalized between us in the future.

译文：鉴于我们友好的业务关系以及鼓励你方促销我方产品，我方同意此次交易破例接受付款交单方式，下不为例。

D/A全称documents against acceptance：承兑交单，托收支付方式的一种。letter of credit：信用证。D/P 全称documents against payment：付款交单，托收支付方式的一种。以上均为国际贸易专业术语。

（二）大量使用较为正式的词汇

商务信函不同于私人信函，它使用较为中性、正式、书面的词汇来避免传递发函人的感情色彩，避免歧义，即使要表达感谢、不满等情绪，词汇选择也要谨慎，避免使用口语词汇。

例5. Enclosed please find the quotation sheet. All offers and sales are subject to the terms and conditions printed on the reverse side hereof.

译文：随函附上报价单，所有报盘和销售均应以本报价单背面所印条件为准。

商务英语信函中还经常使用here, there和where加上after, by, under, to, with, from, in等组成的复合副词，如hereafter, hereby, herewith, herefrom, thereafter, thereby, thereunder, thereto等古体词。虽然在口语中极少用到，但在

外贸英语信函中会经常出现。该句中的hereof相当于of the quotation sheet。

例6. Your letter of September 15th addressed to our head office asking for the supply of 15 tons peanuts has been passed on to us for attention and reply.

译文：你方9月15日致我总公司关于供应15吨花生的函已转交我方办复。

addressed to...该短语是过去分词短语，修饰letter，意思是"写给，寄给，致函给……"，是信函中较为正式的短语。

（三）常使用一些固定短语

商务信函中，经常会使用一些短语替代完整的句子，以使句子结构简洁。比如in view of, taking into account, in consideration of均表示"鉴于，考虑到"的意思。

例7. In view of the increased demand for our products, we wish to appoint an agent.

译文：鉴于对我方产品的需求有所增加，我们想委派一家代理商。

二、句法特点

（一）大量使用礼貌句式和套话

商务信函的礼貌句式不仅能让收信人感受到尊重，还可以树立良好的企业形象，对顺利开展公司的对外业务有着非常重要的作用。

例8. We really appreciate the additional discount.

译文：我方非常感谢贵公司给予的额外优惠。

例9. We anticipate receiving your further orders.

译文：我们期待你方更多的订单。

例10. We thank you for your letter dated March 15, contents of which have been duly noted.

译文：感谢你方3月15日的来信。信中内容已及时获悉。

（二）大量使用短句

商务信函以直接传达信息为目的，不存在刻意的描绘、形容和修饰，较少叙述主要信息以外的或者相关性不紧密的内容，以内容简单、含义明确为原则。据统计，英语商务信函的平均句子长度为13.4个单词，低于一般句子的平均长度16.7个单词。

例11. We look forward to your favorable reply at an early date.

译文：你方对此作何处置，请告知为盼。

例12. Please let us know what you wish us to do.

译文：请告知为盼。

此句汉语表达也非常简短。

（三）大量使用第一、第二人称代词

商务信函常用第一、第二人称代词，以强调双方的观点和态度。

例13. You earn an additional 5% discount for cash payments.

译文：如果贵方能支付现金，便可享受额外5%的折扣。

例14. We can give you an additional 5% discount for cash payment.

译文：如果贵方支付现金，我方可以给予贵方额外5%的折扣。

虽然两句话表达完全相同的含义，但是例14以对方为主体，体现了"我方"能够站在对方的角度思考问题，让对方感受到"我方"的尊重。

（四）常使用包含"enclose"或其过去分词"enclosed"的句子

例15. Enclosed are two copies of our pricelist.

译文：随函附上两份价目单。

例16. Enclosed, please find a copy of our price list.

译文：随函附上一份价目单，请查收。

例17. We are enclosing our Cheque No. B123 issued by the Barclays' Bank, London, for Stg.£2000 in payment of your Invoice No. 56.

译文：兹寄去伦敦巴克莱银行所开的第B123号支票一张，金额计2000英镑，系付你方的56号发票之款。

第二节　商务英语信函翻译原则

商务信函属于比较拘谨正式的公文体，行文端正，用字洗练，翻译时一般遵循商务英语的翻译原则，即"5C"原则：正确（correctness）、简洁（conciseness）、清楚（clearness）、完整（completeness）、礼貌（courtesy）。具体来讲，有以下几方面内容。

一、遵循"忠实、通顺"的翻译标准

例18. We have obtained your name and address from the Singapore Chamber of Commerce, who has told us that you wish to import electric goods manufactured in China.

原译：我方从新加坡商会处获悉贵方的名称和地址，得知贵方有意进口中国制造的产品。

此句的翻译应该说非常通顺，注重了信函的语言特点，但是它并没有做到忠实的原则，译文中漏译了"electric"。

改译：我方从新加坡商会处获悉贵方的名称和地址，得知贵方有意进口中国制造的电器产品。

例19. I have the honor to notify you that we have commenced a business as commission agents for British goods.

原译：我很荣幸地告知您我们已经开始了一项业务，来作为英国货物的代理。

这句的翻译绝对忠实于原文，却不能够达到通顺的要求，让人读起来感到特别生硬，因此需调整。

改译：我们已经开始了经营代销英国货物的业务，特此通告。

二、注意信函结构程式化的翻译

英汉两种语言在信函结构程式上有一定的差别。如收（寄）信人的地址、写信时间及其位置都是不一样的，需要我们在翻译时作出适当的调整，以适应目的语的格式规范。例如要将英语地址由小到大的顺序译为汉语的由大到小的顺序，或者有时根据汉语的习惯把地址栏省去；时间也由英语当中的日/月/年或月/日/年的顺序改译为汉语中的年/月/日的顺序。

例20. John Wanamaker 68 Fifth street Philadelphia 11 U.S.A.

译文：美国费城第十一邮区第五大街68号约翰·华纳麦克先生

例21. 2 November 2012

译文：2012年11月2日

三、运用套译的翻译方法

（一）称呼语的套译

商务信函最常见的称呼有：Dear Sirs/Madam, My dear Sir, Dear Mr, My dear Ms ×××, Dear Gentlemen 等。在商务英语信函翻译中应注意以下几点：（1）对女性的称呼，无论是已婚还是未婚，都统称为Dear Madam，切忌使用Dear Miss。（2）英国人偏爱使用Dear Sirs，而美国人偏爱使用Dear Gentlemen。（3）Gentlemen仅使用复数形式，不用单数形式Gentleman，也不用Dear

Gentleman。(4) My dear Mrs. Hartley并不意味着比Dear Mrs. Hartley更亲密，相反前者是更为正式的称呼。

所有称呼中的Dear只是一种表示对收信人的尊称，是一种礼貌的习惯性表达方法，并不等同于汉语中的"亲爱的"。因此，根据汉语习惯我们可以套译为"尊敬的阁下/先生/女士/夫人"，有时也可以套译为"敬启者，谨启者，执事先生，尊鉴，台鉴"等。

（二）结尾敬语的套译

英文信函中结尾敬语的表达方式有很多，例如：Yours faithfully, Faithfully yours, Yours truly, Best regard, Sincerely, Best wishes, Yours sincerely, Kind regards, 等等。它们可以直接套译为"谨上，敬上，谨启，顺致敬意"等，而不能直接按照字面意思进行翻译。

（三）信函正文中一些敬辞和谦辞的套译

商务信函的一大特色就是措辞婉约、注重礼节、多用套语。英语商务信函中频繁使用appreciate, esteem, favor, grateful, kindly, oblige, please, pleasure, allow us..., permit us to..., may we...等。而汉语中常用的一些敬辞包括：台鉴、贵方、贵国、贵公司、阁下、敬复、敬悉、惠请、惠函、惠顾、赐复、奉告、承蒙、恭候等；常见的一些谦辞包括：敝人、敝公司、敝处、卑职、愚见、拙见、拙作、拜读、过奖等。

例22. We have pleasure in acknowledging receipt of your esteemed favor of the 8th May.

译文：敬悉贵公司5月8日来函。

例23. Kindly provide us with all possible information on your market.

译文：惠请告知你方市场详情。

四、要注意礼貌原则

礼貌原则分为六大准则：策略准则、慷慨准则、赞誉准则、谦逊准则、一致准则、同情准则。这些准则解释了有的交际语言比较礼貌的原因，当然这并不意味着最礼貌的形式总是最合适的，在商务信函的翻译中我们也要这样对待。礼貌原则还体现在人称代词的翻译方面。英语中的第一人称和第二人称代词，不管单复数，第二人称大多用"贵方""你方"，一般不用"你"或"你们"表示。第一人称一般用"我方"表示。

（一）策略准则和慷慨准则

这两项准则常用于指令和承诺，对于咨询信息、发盘还盘、商议付款条件、索取免费产品以及就赔付方式进行交涉等方面比较适用。

例24. Should you desire, we would be pleased to send you catalogs together with export prices and estimated shipping costs for these items.

译文：若贵方需要，本公司将乐意寄上目录以及这些项目的出口价格以及预估的运输费。

（二）赞誉准则和谦逊准则

这两项准则要求尽量减少对别人的贬损以及对自己的赞扬。在商务信函中这两项准则常见于试探合作意向、商谈合作细节或是感谢信当中。

例25. We were pleased to know in your letter of 24th October of your interest in our products and enclose the catalog and price list you asked for. Also enclosed you will find details of our sale conditions and payment terms.

译文：奉读10月24日来函，欣悉贵方对本公司产品有兴趣。兹附上你方所要求的商品目录和价目表，并附上本公司的售货条件和付款方式。

（三）一致准则和同情准则

根据这一准则，贸易双方应尽量扩大一致，减少分歧。

例26. We have gone into the matter and we are prepared to give you reasonable compensation, but not the amount you claimed, because we cannot see why the loss should be 50% more than the actual value of the goods.

译文：我方已对此事进行调查，愿意对贵方给予合理赔偿，不过不是贵方索赔的金额，因为我方看不出损失何以超过货物实际价值的一半。

写信人在指出对方索赔金额数目不合理之前首先表明愿意承担相应责任，目的在于尽量消除谈判的障碍，确保合作的顺利进行。

例27. At any rate, we deeply regret to learn from you about this unfortunate incident, and should it be necessary, we shall be pleased to take the matter on your behalf with the shipping company concerned.

译文：无论如何，从贵方闻悉发生这一不幸事件，我方深表遗憾。如有必要，我方将很乐意代贵公司向船方提出交涉。

该例句真切地表达了贸易一方对遭受损失一方的慰问及希望给予对方帮助之意，充分体现了同情准则的要求。

第三节 课内翻译任务

一、英译汉 English-Chinese Translation

Counter-offer

Dear Mr Davis,

We wish to thank you for your letter of July 15th, 2022, offering us 10,000 metric tons of the subject goods at US $105.00 per metric ton, CIF London.

In reply, we very much regret to state that we find your price too high and out of line with the prevailing market level. Information indicates that some bags of Korean origin have sold at the level of US $95.00 per metric ton.

Such being the case, it is impossible for us to accept your price, as sugar of similar quality is easily obtainable at a much lower figure. Should you be prepared to reduce your limit by, say, 10%, we might come to terms.

It is in view of our long-standing business relationship that we make you such a counter-offer. As the market is declining, we hope you will consider our counter-offer most favorably and cable us acceptance at your earliest convenience.

We anticipate your early reply.

Yours Faithfully,

Company Name

重点解析 Notes and Comments

1. out of line：不符合，不一致。

2. We very much regret to state... / to inform you / to tell you...

此句是商务信函中常用的句子，可译作"我们遗憾地说明/奉告/通知你们……"。

3. Such being the case, it is impossible for us to accept your price, as sugar of similar quality is easily obtainable at a much lower figure. 由于同等质量的砂糖能以较低价格购进，在此情况下，我方很难接受你方的价格。

翻译该句时要注意翻译的顺序。汉语习惯先说原因，再说结果，因此将as sugar of similar quality is easily obtainable at a much lower figure放在前面进行翻译。

4. Should you be prepared to reduce your limit by, say, 10%, we might come to terms. 若你方有意降价，如降低10%，我们便有望成交。

该句用了虚拟语气，显得较为委婉。汉语通常译作"如果……就……""若……就……"。

come to terms 不可译作"达到条款"，可译为"达成协议"。

5. It is in view of our long-standing business relationship that we make you such a counter-offer.

该句会出现不同的翻译方法，试比较："正是因为我们之间长期的业务关系，所以我们才给你们发出这一还盘"，以及"鉴于我们之间的长期业务关系，特发此盘"。前者比后者更忠实于原文，但不如后者简洁。因此，从正式性和简洁性来考虑，后一种译文更符合商务信函的语言要求。

6. the market is declining 行市不断下跌

我们还可以说：The market is firm 坚挺/steady 稳定/steady quiet 行市稳定但成交很少/barely steady 勉强稳定/quiet 成交清淡/nominal 有行无市/idle 闲散/stagnant 停滞/weak 疲弱/irregular 涨落不定/uncertain 捉摸不定/inactive 不活跃/dull 呆滞。

7. at your earliest convenience（在方便时）尽早，尽快

8. We anticipate your early reply. 期待早日答复。

英语商务信函的结尾常用一些套语。例如：

（1）Your favorable information will be appreciated.

原译：我们期望得到你们的好消息。

改译：恭候佳音！

（2）Your early reply will be highly appreciated.

原译：我们将会十分感激你们的早日答复。

改译：如蒙早复，不胜感激！

（3）Awaiting your immediate reply.

原译：等候你们的早日回信。

改译：请即复！

原译虽说没有曲解原文的意思，却行文啰唆，有失汉语书信的语言风格。实际上，汉语也有类似的客套话，言简意赅，译者可充分发挥译入语的语言优势。

二、汉译英 Chinese-English Translation

催运及回函

敬启者：

关于我方110号订单项下的20,000盒月饼，至今我们没有收到任何关于此货的装运信息，所以希望你方根据合同及时装运。

因为这是季节性货物，所以我方顾客急需整批货物来为销售季节做准备，若货物不能如期进入市场，那么上乘的质量、有竞争性的价格也就毫无意义了。

请务必尽快装运。

感谢你方的合作！

谨上

敬启者：

兹确认已收到你方6月20日关于20,000盒月饼的信函。很抱歉由于我方的装运延迟给你方带来这么大的不便。

现通知你方标题项下的货物已装上"红星"轮，该船将于2022年6月30日左右离开我方港口。

希望货物完好无损到达你方。期待着我们之间有更多的业务。

谨上

重点解析 Notes and Comments

1. 敬启者：Dear sirs/madam

汉语信函中，未知收信人身份时常用"敬启者"作称呼，译成英文时，一般不译作To those who are concerned，译作Dear sirs/madam即可。

2. 关于我方110号订单项下的20,000盒月饼 as regards our Order No. 110 for 20,000 boxes of Moon Cake

"关于"有多种译法，但英语商务信函属于正式文体，因此常译作as regards, concerning, in the case of等。

3. 至今我们没有收到任何关于此货的装运信息。Up to now, we received nothing from you about its shipment.

"装运"在商务英语中可用shipment表示，shipment并非只表示用船运输。

4. 因为这是季节性货物，所以我方顾客急需整批货物来为销售季节做准备，若货物不能如期进入市场，那么上乘的质量、有竞争性的价格也就毫无意义了。Since this is a kind of seasonable goods, our customers are in urgent need of the whole lot to be ready for the selling season. If the goods cannot be put on the market on time, then good quality and competitive price would mean nothing.

该句为复杂句，翻译时，首先应分析句子结构，找出句子关系。该句包含两层关系：一层为因果关系，一层为条件关系。因此翻译时将其分译为两个句子。

5. 请务必尽快装运。

该句在翻译时应进行转换，若翻译为Please dispatch the goods as soon as possible，则有命令对方之嫌，与礼貌原则相违背，因此翻译为Please see to it that the goods will reach us as soon as possible更为合适。

6. 兹确认……

"兹"为商务英语中常见用语，可翻译出来，译为hereby，也可以不译。兹确认……可译为We hereby confirm...或This is to confirm...

7. 现通知你方…… You are informed...或This is to inform you...

第四节　课后翻译训练

一、将下列句子翻译成汉语 Translate the following sentences into Chinese

1. Thank you for your letter of 1st September suggesting that we grant you a sole agency for our household linen.

2. We have heard from China Council for the Promotion of International Trade that you are in the market for electric appliance.

3. If you can accept $275, send us a proforma invoice, and we will open a letter of credit for 1,000 sets.

4. We shall write and ask for their ceiling for the advertising project and then we can budget accordingly.

5. We wonder whether you are satisfied with our quotations.

6. To meet this important client's request for moving up the time of delivery, a special arrangement has been made, and we are now pleased to inform you that the full quantity of your order will be shipped at the beginning of May.

7. Please be informed that, on account of the fluctuations of foreign exchanges, the quotation is subject to change without previous notice.

8. Thank you for the inquiry of May 5, 2022, for 200 Deer Mountain bikes. You can have the lowest price at US $65 for each FOB Los Angeles if paid by cash.

9. We want to notify you that prices of copier parts and components have gone up steadily since the second half of the year. Though we have tried hard to keep our quotations down, we are afraid the margin for keeping on going like this will not last long.

10. We are sorry to inform you that the listed terms of payment do not correspond to our customary business practice.

二、将下列句子翻译成英语 Translate the following sentences into English

1. 现欲扩展业务范围，盼能惠赐商品目录和报价表。
2. 兹通知，标题所述货物已于昨日由"胜利"号货轮运出。
3. 我方望此批订货质量与以前供应的完全一样。
4. 在我方同各国商人的贸易中，一贯坚持平等互利的原则，希望通过双方努力，促进对彼此互利的业务和友谊。
5. 现随函寄上商品小册子和价格表各一份，以便贵公司能对我们出口棉布的情况有一个大概的了解。
6. 兹确认我方今天发出电报装运通知，并通知贵方，本公司已装运贵方订购的5,000吨铁屑，经由"太平洋"号货轮于5月20日载离此处。
7. 按合同条款，6月20日前应交货，我方最迟需在25日前拿到提单。
8. 贵方所提供的包装方式与质量必须完全符合我方的要求。
9. 请将货款汇往中国银行广州分行我方账户，账号为14236538，收款人为广州XYZ公司。
10. 货物将由"东风"号183航次装运，该轮预定于10月31日抵达哥本哈根港，请速订舱。请确认货物将按时备妥。

三、将下列信函翻译成汉语 Translate the following letters into Chinese

Letter 1

Dear Sirs,

We obtain your name and address from www.POCIB.com. We wish to inform you that we specialize in both industrial and pharmaceutical chemicals, and shall be pleased to enter into trade relations with you.

To give you a general idea of our products, we enclose a complete set of leaflets showing various products being handled by this corporation with detailed specifications and means of packing. Quotations and samples will be sent upon receipt of your specific enquiries.

All the delivered goods will be concluded on the basis of shipping quality and weight while testing and inspection will be made by the Shanghai Commodity Inspection Bureau prior to shipment. Necessary certificates in regard to the quality and quantity of the shipment will, of course, be provided.

We look forward to your early reply with much interest.

Yours Faithfully,

×××

Letter 2

Dear Sirs,

Your letter of July 23 addressed to our sister corporation in Shenzhen has been transferred to us for attention and reply, as the items fall within the scope of our business activities.

We are enclosing our illustrated catalogue and pricelist giving the details you asked for. Also, under separate cover we are sending you a full range of samples, when you have a chance to examine them, we feel confident that you will agree that the goods are both excellent in quality and very reasonable in price.

Meanwhile, we would like to invite you to attend Chinese Export Commodities Fair in Guangzhou to be held from October 15 to October 30, 2022. The general manager and sales representatives of our company will be there to meet you and conduct negotiations with you.

We anticipate your enquiry.

Yours faithfully,

(Signature)

China National Light Industrial Products Imp. & Exp. Corp.

四、将下列信函翻译成英语 Translate the following letters into English

信函1

敬启者：

你方8月15日传真收悉，谢谢。

欣悉你方能及时装运我方所定货物。但你方仍要求付款交单，实在令人惊异。我方以为经过多年令人满意的贸易交往，我方有资格要求付款条件。我方绝大部分供货商同我方做60天期承兑交单。如你方也能按此办理，我们将非常感激。

盼复佳音。

敬上

（签名）

信函2

敬启者：

你方第123号订单

兹证实收到你方4月15日关于我方新型自行车的订单。

你方所提到的支付我方货款的安排非常令人满意。我方已按此大意发去电报。你方订单中包括的所有商品均可供应现货，一俟收到电汇的货款当即包装出运。装船之后我方将立即直接空邮下列单据：

提单一式二份

成本加运费加保险费至拉各斯发票一式三份

发票金额110%的保险单

品质证书

请放心，我方将对你方此次及今后所有的订单予以及时办理。一俟所订货物装船，我方当即电告你方。

此致

敬礼

（签名）

中国轻工业品进出口总公司

第十章 招投标书翻译

随着国际贸易一体化的进程不断推进，越来越多的中国企业要参与国际商业竞争，招标、投标这类商务活动也因此显得日益重要。在一项成功的评标活动（包括招标与投标）中，标书的撰写与翻译非常重要。按照国际惯例，运用招标方式采购货物、工程和服务时，与招标采购活动有关的一切文件资料均须用英文编制。即使允许用非英文的语言编制，也须随附一份英文译本备案。当发生分歧时，以英文版本为准。因此招投标文件相关资料的理解和翻译就成了竞标的基础工作，贯穿整个竞标过程，必须予以足够的重视。

本章介绍了国际招标的相关知识，包括国际招投标相关规定、国际招投标文件等，以及国际招标文书的语言特点和翻译技巧。

第一节 国际招标基本知识

一、国际招标基本概念

国际招标，一般是指国际工程招标。国际工程招标，是指在国际工程项目中，招标人邀请几个或几十个投标人参加投标，通过多数投标人竞争，选择其中对招标人最有利的投标人达成交易的方式。招标是当前国际上工程建设项目的一种主要交易方式。它的特点是业主标明其拟发包工程的内容、完成期限、质量要求等，招引或邀请某些愿意承包并符合投标资格的投标者对承包该工程所采用的施工方案和要求的价格等进行投标，通过比价而达成交易的一种经济活动。招标和投标是基本建设领域促进竞争的全面经济责任制形式。一般由需求单位招标，供应/建设单位参与投标，谁的工期短、造价低、质量高、信誉好，就把工程任务包给谁。由需求单位与供应/建设单位签订合同，按交钥匙的方式组织建设。招投标最早起源于英国，作为一种成熟的交易方式，其重要性和优越性在经济活动中日益被各国和各种国际经济组织广泛认可，进而在相当多的国家和国际组织中得到立法推行。

二、国际招标相关规定

目前多数国家都制定了适合本国特点的招标法规,以统一其国内招标办法,但还没有形成一种各国都应遵守的带有强制性的招标规定。国际工程招标,也都根据国家或地区的习惯选用一种具有代表性、适用范围广,并且适用本地区的某一国家的招标法规。如世界银行贷款项目招标和采购法规、英国招标法规和法国使用的工程招标制度等。国际工程招标广泛适用于公私采购上,根据招标标的的性质、国际招标采购的适用范围,大体上包括工程、货物(物资)、服务三个方面。但各国和国际组织对工程、货物、服务的认识和界定并不一样。

国际招标活动必须遵守招标工程所在国政府颁布的招标法规和有关的法律条款,并必须遵守招标工程所在当地地方政府颁布的一切有关的法律、章程和条例。此外,国际招标活动中一般采用国际通用的、由国际咨询工程师联合会(FIDIC)和欧洲建筑工程联合会共同编订的《土木工程施工合同条款》的投标书和协议书格式,一般还采用国际通用的、由英国皇家特许测量师学会制定的《建筑工程量计算原则》。对于是否采用上述两个国际通用的标准文件,完全取决于该国际招标活动中招标文件的有关规定。有些国家在国际招标工程的文件中规定只许采用本国或第三国的合同条款、工程量计算规则以及有关的设计、施工技术规程和施工验收标准,并不采用国际通用的文件标准。由于国际招标活动已有一二百年的历史,以及国际承包市场的竞争日益激烈,所以国际招标要比国内招标复杂一些。但在招标方式和招标程序等方面,大体上是一致的。其具体事务通常由业主委托专业咨询机构办理。

在不同的法规体系下,对招标方式(type of tendering)的规定不尽相同,现归纳如下:

1. 《世界银行贷款和国际开发协会信贷采购指南》重点定义了"国际竞争性招标"(international competitive bidding),指出在国际竞争性招标不是最经济、最有效的时候,还有其他几种更加适宜的采购方式,如"有限国际招标"(limited international bidding)、"国内竞争性招标"(domestic competitive bidding)、"询价采购"(shopping)、"直接签订合同"(direct contracting)等。

2. 世贸组织《政府采购协定》定义了3类招标方式,即"公开招标"(open tendering)、"选择性招标"(selective tendering)以及"局限性招标"(limited tendering)。

3. 中国香港特别行政区政府采购制度中定义了4类招标方式,即"公开招标""选择性招标""资格预审招标"(prequalified tendering)以及"单一招标或局限性招标"（single or restricted tendering）。①

4.《中华人民共和国招标投标法》定义了两类招标方式，即"公开招标"与"邀请招标"。招标类型不同，对投标方的要求也不同。

三、国际招投标文件

（一）标书

标书（Bidding Document）一般是招标文件的简称，是非正式名称。投标书（Bid）则是投标文件的简称。有些人也将投标文件简称为标书。标书的一般内容包括获取招标公告、项目报名、资格预审与后审、备案、组织投标、正式投标等。

标书是由发标单位编制或委托设计单位编制，向投标者提供对拟招标工程的主要技术、质量、工期等要求的文件。标书是招标工作中采购方要遵守的、具有法律效力的且可执行的投标行为标准文件。标书的逻辑性要强，不能前后矛盾，模棱两可；标书用语要精练、简短。标书也是投标和编制投标书的依据，投标商必须对标书的内容作出实质性响应，否则会被判定为无效标（按废弃标处理）。标书也是评标最重要的依据。标书一般有至少一个正本，两个或多个副本。

招标和投标文件里通常有较多的法律用语和与标的项目相关的行业术语，并有一定量的招投标术语。招标文件应包括招标公告或投标邀请书、投标人须知、评标标准和方法、技术条款、投标文件格式、拟签合同主要条款和合同格式、附件和其他要求等。投标文件的主体是对投标人相关资质的介绍，以及对完成拟招标项目的计划方案等。其中，投标函是投标人按照招标文件的条件和要求，向招标人提交的有关报价、质量目标等承诺和说明的函件，是投标人为响应招标文件相关要求所做的概括性说明和承诺的函件，一般位于投标文件的首要部分，其格式、内容必须符合招标文件的规定。

（二）招标预审通告与招标公告的架构

公开招标需要通过媒体或网络发布招标公告，以让公众知晓，赢得尽可能多的竞标人供招标方选择。按照《招标公告发布暂行办法》规定，必须招标的国际招标项目的招标公告应在《中国日报》发布。招标公告或通告主要包括招标资格预审与招标通告。预审通告与招标通告通常包括以下几个部分：

---

① 引自https://max.book118.com/html/2018/1116/8066011050001133.shtm，访问日期：2024年8月10日。

（1）标题

（2）招标单位名称

（3）工程/项目名称

（4）工程/项目招标号

（5）通告正文

（6）附项

（三）我国国际工程招标书实例

以下是我国国际工程招标书（邀请函）实例。限于篇幅，仅保留标书开头部分，其中就包含了标题、招标单位、项目名称、招标号及其他重要事项等。

国际工程招标书

日期：　　　　招标号：

一、中华人民共和国从世界银行申请获得贷款，用于支付　　　　项目的费用。部分贷款将用于支付工程建筑、　　　　等各种合同。所有依世界银行指导原则具有资格的国家，都可参加招标。

二、中国＿＿＿＿公司（以下简称A公司）邀请具有资格的投标者提供密封的标书，提供完成合同工程所需的劳力、材料、设备和服务。

三、具有资格的投标者可从以下地址获得更多的信息，或参看招标文件：中国A公司＿＿＿＿（公司地址）。

四、每一位具有资格的投标者在交纳＿＿＿＿美元（或人民币），并提交书面申请后，均可从上述地址获得招标文件。

五、每一份标书都要附一份投标保证书，且应不迟于＿＿＿＿（时间）提交给A公司。

六、所有标书将在＿＿＿＿（时间）当着投标者代表的面开标。

七、如果具有资格的国外投标者希望与一位中国国内的承包人组建合资公司，需在投标截止日期前30天提出要求。业主有权决定是否同意选定的国内承包人。

八、标前会议将在＿＿＿＿（时间）＿＿＿＿（地址）召开。

（https://jz.docin.com/p-1952011541.html?building=1&fid=4200，访问日期：2020年3月13日。）

译文:

INVITATION TO TENDER

Date: _____   Tender No.: _____

1. The People's Republic of China has applied for a loan and credit from the World Bank towards the cost of _____ Project. It is intended that part of the proceeds of this loan and credit will be applied to eligible payment under various contracts for _____. Tendering is open to all tenderers from eligible source countries as defined under the "Guidelines for procurement" of the World Bank.

2. _____ Company now invites sealed tenders from pre-qualified tenderers for provision of the necessary labour, materials, equipment and services for the construction and completion of the project.

3. Pre-qualified tenderers may obtain further information from, and inspect the tender documents at the office of: _____.

4. A complete set of tender documents may be obtained by any pre-qualified tenderer for the cost of RMB _____ or US $ _____ on the submission of a written application to the above.

5. All tenders must be accompanied by a Tender Security in an acceptable form and must be delivered to _____ Company on or before _____.

6. Tenders will be opened in the presence of those tenderers' representatives who choose to attend at _____ (time).

7. If a pre-qualified foreign tenderer wishes to form Joint venture with a domestic contractor, such a request will be considered if received within 30 days before the closing date for submission of tenders. The selected local contractor shall be subject to approval by the Employer.

8. The Pre-Tender Meeting will be held on _____ at the following address: _____.

标书的正文部分包括"投标者须知""投标文件""投标准备"等部分。

"投标者须知"(Instructions to Tenderers)包括:

1. 工程概述(Description of the Construction)

2. 资金来源(Source of Funds)

3. 资格要求（Eligibility and Qualification Requirements）

4. 投标费用（Cost of Tendering）

5. 现场参观（Site Visit）

"投标文件"（Tender Documents）包括：

1. 投标者须知（Instructions to Tenderers）

投标者须知中还包括合同条款（Conditions of Contract）

2. 技术规范（Specification）

3. 投标表格和附件（Form of Tender and Appendix）、投标保证书（Form of Tender Security）、工程量表（Bill of Quantities）、附录（Schedules of Supplementary Information）。

4. 图纸（Drawings）

"投标准备"（Preparation of Tenders）内容包括很多，其中有：（1）标书文字（Language of Tender）；（2）组成标书的文件（Documents Comprising the Tender）；（3）投标价格（Tender Prices）；（4）投标和支付货币（Currencies of Tender and Payment）；（5）投标保函（Tender Security）；等等。

（四）英文招标书样例

TWO RIVERS DEVELOPMENT

RETAIL, ENTERTAINMENT & LIFESTYLE (REL) TENDER

OCTOBER 2021

MAIN WORKS—RETAIL MALL AND NO.2 OFFICE BLOCKS

EMPLOYER

Two Rivers Development Ltd.

P.O. Box 16429-00100

Nairobi

PROJECT MANAGERS

ARCHITECTS

QUANTITY SURVEYORS

CIVIL / STRUCTURAL ENGINEERS

LETTER OF TENDER

NAME OF CONTRACT: TWO RIVERS DEVELOPMENT

RETAIL, ENTERTAINMENT & LIFESTYLE (REL) TENDER

MAIN WORKS—RETAIL MALL AND NO.2 OFFICE BLOCKS

TO: Two Rivers Development Ltd.

P.O. Box 16429-00100

Nairobi

We have examined the Conditions of Contract, Specification, Drawings, Bill of Quantities, the attached Appendix and Addenda Nos _____ for the execution of the above-named Works. We offer to execute and complete the Works and remedy any defects therein in conformity with this Tender which includes all these documents, for the sum of Kshs_____ (In words) _____or such other sum as may be determined in accordance with the Conditions of Contract. Further we agree to complete the whole of the works within the time as set in Clause 1.1.3.3 of the Appendix.

We agree to abide by this Tender until _____ and it shall remain binding upon us before that date. We acknowledge that the Appendix forms part of this. If this offer is accepted, we will provide the specified Performance Security, commence the Works as soon as is reasonably practicable after the Commencement Date, and complete the Works in accordance with the above-named documents within the Time for Completion. Unless and until a formal Agreement is prepared and executed, this letter of Tender, together with your written acceptance thereof, shall constitute a binding contract between us.

Signature in the capacity of duly authorised to sign tenders for and on behalf of _____

Address：

Date：

参考译文：

两河开发有限公司零售、娱乐、休闲综合体招标书

日期：2021年10月

主要工程（标的）：零售购物中心和二号办公大楼

招标方：两河开发有限公司

邮政信箱：16429-00100

地址：内罗毕

项目经理：

建筑师：

造价师：

土木/结构工程师：

投标函

项目名称：零售、娱乐、休闲综合体项目招标

投标文件接受单位：两河开发有限公司

邮政信箱：16429-00100

地址：内罗毕

我方审查了与实施上述工程相关的合同条件、技术规范、图纸、工程量清单及（标号为_____）附件和附录。我方同意按照本标书及其所有相关文件条款，实施并完成总金额为_____（大写）肯尼亚先令的工程或总金额根据合同条件所确定的工程，并对其中的任何缺陷进行纠正。此外，我方同意在附录1.1.3.3条规定的时间内完成全部工程。

我方同意遵守本标书的条件，直到_____（时间）工程结束。在工程结束日前，该标书对双方均有约束力。我方认为，附录是全部标书的组成部分。如贵方接受我方的投标申请，我方将提供标书规定的履约保证金，在合理可行的情况下，在规定的开工日期后尽快开工，并在规定的时间内按照上述文件完成工程。除非签署正式协议，本投标函连同贵方的书面接受函，均构成双方之间具有约束力的合同。

法定代表签字

    地址：   日期：

该招标书包含了项目的基本信息、招标单位、投标函样本以及其他招标文件（略）。其他招标文件包括Instructions to Tenderers（投标者须知），Conditions of Contract（合同条款），Appendix to Tender（标书附件），Bill of Quantities（工程量表），等等。

第二节　国际标书文本的语言特征与翻译

一、国际标书文本的语言特征

招投标完成后，无论是招标文本，还是投标文本，都是一种商业合同，具有法律效力，须严格执行，一旦遇到纠纷，这些文本就是法律依据。因此，招投标文本具有一般法律文本以及商业合同的基本语言特征，如措辞精当、结构严谨、术语专业、思维缜密、文体正规、语意明确。

（一）大量使用书面化专业术语

招投标文件使用的专业术语近似于行话，尽管具有国际通用性，有明确的特定含义，但一般辞书中往往查不到，不了解招投标业务的译者很难准确理解和翻译。如 procurement 不是一般意义的"获得"，标书中应该理解为"采购"，如 government procurement 表示"政府采购"，pre-qualification 表示"对投标人进行的投标资格预审"，qualification documents 是"投标资格预审文件"，base bid price 不是普通意义上的"价格"，而是招投标过程中非常重要的"标底"。

（二）大量使用情态动词与命令词

招投标文件除了具有招投标所特有的术语外，总体句子与法律合同类文件差不多，大量使用情态动词。如：shall（应该），must（必须），may（可以；可能），will（将）以及其他法律类用词。

在招标采购过程中，招标方在对投标人提出要求时总倾向于使用带有强制性含义的情态动词与命令词，如shall或must。shall 并不是简单的助动词，不是日常生活中的"适宜""将"，而是"应当""应该""应"等意思。值得注意的是，招投标双方的文本对情态动词使用有别，招标方对自己应履行某种义务时，总是极力轻描淡写，淡化语气强度，较多选用will和should，甚至用may，表"愿意"或"可以"。

例1. The Bidder shall carefully check and review the general drawings and Bidding Documents provided by the Bid Inviter, and formulate a detailed plan. The doubts and places needing adjustment shall be reflected in due time, the terms required by the Bidding Documents shall be answered item by item, and the terms failing to be satisfied must be explained in writing, otherwise it will be deemed that the Bidder accept all bidding drawings and all requirements of the Bidding Documents, and assume the consequences resulted in by itself.

译文：投标方应仔细认真核对审阅招标方提供的总图及招标文件，并制订详细方案。对疑问或需调整处应及时进行反馈,对招标文件中要求的各项条款进行逐条对应答复,对于不能满足要求的条款必须给予书面说明,否则将视为对招标图纸及本招标书中所有要求全部接受,并自行承担由此产生的后果。

(三)多用大词、古语词以及外来词(尤其是拉丁语)

招投标文本多使用书面用词,包括大词、古语词和外来词,以体现其权威性和严密性。例如用复杂短语代替简单的介词、连词;用笨重动词代替轻灵动词,如 encourage—urge;用冷僻用词代替日常用词,如 prior to—before, expiry—end;大量使用(here, there)复合词,如hereinafter, hereby, hereto, hereof, therefrom, therein, thereafter, thereinafter, thereby;使用古语词、外来语,如 null and void(无效), nota bene(注), assumpsit(承诺,约定), otherwise(否则)等。

例2. The Bidder must satisfy corresponding qualifications for manufacturing the bidding equipment, and the qualifications to produce and sell these products and provide effective after-services, and submit the list of usage performance of such products during the past two years, otherwise the qualifications will be cancelled.

译文:投标方必须具备制造招标设备的相应资质,必须具备生产和销售该类产品和进行有效售后服务的资格,同时提供该类产品近两年的使用业绩表,否则将被取消投标资格。

例3. The Bidder shall provide a document to certify that the goods and services to be supplied hereunder conform to the specifications of the Bidding Documents; and the certifying document shall form one part of the Bid.

译文:投标人应提交证明文件,证明其拟供的本合同项下的货物和服务符合招标文件规定。该证明文件是投标文件的一部分。

hereunder表示"在此之下""本协议""下文"之意,是典型的法律和合同文本用词,正式、庄重。

例4. Prior to the deadline for submission of tenders, the Employer may, for any reason, whether at its own initiative or in response to a clarification requested by a prospective tenderer, modify the tender documents by the issue of an Addendum.

译文:在提交标书最后期限前,业主可根据自己的意愿,或应回复潜在投标者的解释文件的要求,发布附录修改投标文件。

例4使用了法律英语中常见的术语"prior to",取代日常英语中的"before",用词正式、古雅。

(四)被动句使用频率高

在法律文本和商务文本中,英语习惯用被动结构。国际招标文件既是商务文件也是法律文件。因此,国际招标文件大量使用被动结构。

例5. Comparison and evaluation will be done for the basic offer and alternatives of the lowest evaluated tenderer will be given due consideration. If the alternative offers were to be accepted by the Employer, these will be incorporated into the Contract. Alternative offers which are not priced, or which are not substantiated in sufficient detail, will be rejected.

译文:我们将对基本报价给予比较、评估。评价最低的投标者的供选择方案将得到考虑。如果供选择方案是业主可接受的,将写入合同。未标价或未提供足够细节的供选择方案不予接受。

例6. Bidders are asked to use this specification for the basis of their commercial offer.

译文:投标人须根据本规格书进行商业报价。

本句的字面意思为:"投标人被要求使用本规格书作为其商业报价的基础。"英译中应转换为主动结构。句中offer为"报价/报盘"。

(五)大量使用长句

招投标文本在陈述具体条款的时候,总是把重要的事情说出来,同时,不忘把例外的和次要的事情一并捎上。这类文本注重逻辑联系,不许有联系上的缺环,有什么后果必须探究产生此后果的原因和条件。因此,招投标文件语言结构严谨,长句使用频率颇高。

例7. The Employer or his agent ___A___ Company may, at their discretion, on giving not less than 7 calendar days notice by telex or telegram to all prequalified bidders who have picked up the tender documents, extend the deadline for the submission of bidders by issuing an Addendum in accordance with Clause 8, in which case all rights and obligations of the Employer and the bidders previously subject to the deadline shall thereafter be subject to the new deadline as extended.

译文:业主或其代理人A公司可通过发布条款八规定的附录延长提交标书的最后期限,但至少应在原期限前七天通过电传或电报通知所有已索取投标文件的具有资格的投标者。在此情况下，所有原期限下业主和投标者的权利义务顺延至新期限结束。

例8. The tenderer and any of his representatives will be granted permission by the Employer or his agent ＿＿A＿＿ company to enter upon its premises and lands for the purpose of such inspection by prior arrangement, but only upon the express condition that the tenderer and his representatives, will release and indemnify the Employer or his agent ＿＿A＿＿ Company and its personnel from and against all liability in respect thereof and will be responsible for personal injury (whether fatal or otherwise), loss of or damage to property and any other loss, damage, costs and expenses however caused, which, but for the exercise of such permission, would not have arisen.

译文：业主或其代理人A公司将为投标者提供通行证，允许其到工程现场做安排。如果业主或其代理人因发放这样的通行证，造成投标者或其代理人A公司及其人员遭受人身侵害（致命或不致命的）、财产遗失或其他损害、开支时，业主或代理人不负责。

该句主句很长，除了主谓结构，还有by和for引导的介词短语。主句之后又有一个介词短语but only upon the express condition作状语，该介词短语的中心词express condition后接that引导的同位语从句，同位语结构中既有并列结构，又有which引导的定语从句。整个句子层层叠叠，形成一个结构复杂的长句。

二、招标文件的翻译

随着"一带一路"的推动，越来越多的中国企业会参与国际工程招投标，因此招投标文件的翻译是否准确，会直接关系到企业能否在这个国际项目上中标。

招投标文件翻译是一项系统的、严谨的工程，一方面招标文件的翻译要向投标人传递准确的招标信息和要求，另一方面投标书的翻译又要将投标人对招标文件的响应准确地呈现给招标人。因此，这不仅要求翻译时要做到语言表达准确，而且要求保持招标文件和投标书的术语和文本规范高度一致。相对来说，语言或者语法准确性是较低层次的，一般翻译都能达到要求；而保持招投标文件术语和文本规范的一致性，准确地选用招投标文件的术语，是招投标翻译中需要重点关注的问题。

（一）词语的专业性

作为译者，可以不了解招投标的具体过程，但必须对招投标文件原文有比较高的把握度。其中，最重要的就是招投标相关的专业用词和与法律合同相关的专业用词。下面所列词汇是招投标领域最常见的用词，这些词都是世界银行1992年以后的译法。在1992年以前，以上Bid, Bidder, Bidding等B系列的词分别是T系列的Tender, Tenderer, Tendering，而且，招标人还有另一个单词Tenderee。但这些词语在1992年以后全部改为B系列。

1	the Bid Inviter / the Employer / the Owner	招标人
2	bidder / the Bidder	投标人
3	Invitation for Bid	投标邀请
4	Bidding	招标
5	Bidding Documents	招标文件（标书）
6	Bidding Announcement	招标公告
7	Bid	投标（投标文件）
8	Original Bid	投标文件原件
9	Copy of Bid	投标文件副本
10	eligible Bidders	合格投标人
11	instructions to Bidders (ITB)	投标人须知
12	deadline for submission of Bids	投标截止日期
13	bid price	投标价格
14	bid security	投标保证金
15	bid opening	开标
16	win a bid	中标
17	bid winner	中标人
18	bid awarding	授标
19	individual project / work	单项工程（建设项目的组成部分）
20	unit project / work	单位工程（单项工程的组成部分）
21	fraction project / work 或 sub-unit project / work	分部工程（单位工程的组成部分）
22	constituent project / work	分项工程（工程不可再分的最小部分）

例9. A bid evaluation member shall stay away from bid evaluation process if he or she:

(1) is a close relative to the Bid Inviter or the bidder;

(2) is an official of the administrative authorities or supervising authorities of the Works;

(3) has financial interest in the bidder, and his/her impartial evaluation of bids may be compromised; or

(4) has been administratively disciplined or punished in criminal case due to his/her misconduct or illegal acts during bidding, bid evaluation, or other bid related activities.

译文：

以下评标成员不得参与评标过程：

（1）是招标人或者投标人的近亲；

（2）是工程管理机构或监督机构的行政人员；

（3）与投标人有经济利益关系，从而可能会影响其对投标书的公正评价；或者

（4）由于在招标、评标或其他投标相关活动中的不当行为或非法行为，在刑事案件中受过行政处分或惩罚。

该句中的bid, bid evaluation, bidder等都是招投标文件中的专业词汇。the Bid Inviter不是"招标邀请者"，而是"招标人"。Works在招投标书中首字母大写，意思是项目"工程"。

本例中有几个与法律相关的词，例如：interest 利益（关系）；利害关系。financial interest经济利益。impartial evaluation公正评价。compromise 妥协；折中；危害；达不到（标准等）。compromise在本例中表示"损害"（harm），亦即"造成坏的影响"。

（二）词语的严谨、正式

招投标文件除了具备招投标特有的一些术语和标的项目相关专业知识外，其主体内容基本为法律合同性质。所以，招投标文件跟法律合同文件一样，具有用词严谨、正式、庄重等特点，其中必然涉及大量的法律术语和句式。而在法律合同类词汇中，需要特别注意的是，情态动词或与情态动词用法类似的动词（如fail to）的用法都是有一定讲究的。这些词表示的词意和语气各不相同，这里说明如下。

必须	must	表示很严格，非这样做不可
严禁	must not / strictly prohibit	表示很严格，不能这样做
应 / 应当 / 应该	shall	表示严格，正常情况下均应这样做
不得	shall not	表示严格，正常情况下均不应这样做
宜 / 最好	should	表示允许或有所选择，条件许可时优先这样做
不宜	should not	表示允许或有所选择，条件许可时优先不这样做
可 / 可能 / 可以 / 会	may	表示有选择，一定条件下允许这样做
不可 / 不许	may not	表示严格，一般不允许这样做，常等同于 shall not
能够 / 能	can	通常表示有能力，能够做到
无能力	cannot	通常表示无能力，不能够做到
将 / 将会 / 会	will	通常表示将会发生或出现某种情况
将不会 / 将不 / 不会	will not	通常表示将来不会出现某情况
无法 / 未能	fail to	客观用词，表示因无能力或无意愿而未做到

shall和should的区别：

shall通常与汉语的"应/ 应当/ 应该"对应，是规定应该怎么做，如果没做到，就会被追究相应的法律责任。should通常与汉语的"宜"对应，是推荐对方怎么做；没有做到的话，没人会追究，但可能自己会面临一些不利后果。

may和can的区别：

may通常与汉语的"可/ 可以 / 可能 / 会"对应，表示允许、选择或可能做某事或出现某情况，有时具有某种权利的意思。而can则通常与汉语的"能够 / 能"对应，表示具备能力做某事。

fail to / failure to和may not或cannot的区别：

fail to do…（名词形式为failure to do…）通常与"未能/未/没有（做某事）"对应，指的是最终没有做某事，而不管是不想做还是没做好。may not do… 通常与汉语的"不得/ 不可"相对应，意思与shall not do… 相近，是指不允许做某事。而cannot do… 通常与"不能/不能够"对应，是指没有能力做某事。

以上情态动词的用法都要特别在意，不能弄错；否则，有可能会因为用错词而面临法律纠纷，造成损失，有时候甚至会造成极为重大的损失。

法律术语的正式、严谨、严肃性，也让很多人在书写法律文件时，唯恐法律效力不够，在原本没必要严格规定的动作前面，也加上shall或must，这其实是对情态动词的滥用。情态动词的滥用以shall最为常见。所以，有些文件里shall用得非常多，甚至连"有权"都译成shall have the right to do...。这些实属没有必要的shall，大家在英文文章里碰到的时候，要懂得识别，并根据需要决定是否译出。而在中译英时，则需根据具体情况，决定是否需要用shall，避免滥用shall。

例10. To be qualified for the award of the Contract, bidders shall provide evidence satisfactory to the Employer of their capability and adequacy of resources to carry out the Contract effectively.

译文：为取得授标资格，投标人应向招标人提供充分证据，证明其有效执行合同的能力以及资源的充分性。

除了情态动词之外，招投标文件里还有很多常见的其他法律合同用词，如下表所示。表中列出的其他法律合同用词，其英文也基本都是正式译法，在翻译时一般要优先使用这些正式用词，以免造成纠纷。

中文	英文
甲方/乙方	Party A / Party B（最常见） Side A / Side B （不常见，建议少用） the First Party / the Second Party （不常见，建议少用） the Party of the first part / the Party of the second part（极少见）
丙方，丁方	Party C，Party D
第三方	the third party
该方，当事人	the party
当事人一方，一方	one party
双方	both parties（一般不加 hereto）
双方（当事人）/各方	the parties / all parties
买方	the Buyer / the Vendee / the Purchaser
卖方，供方	the Seller / the Vendor / the Supplier
承包商	the Contractor
分包商	the Subcontractor
以下简称……	hereinafter referred to as... hereinafter called... hereinafter...

中文	英文
鉴于	whereas
权利	right
义务	obligation
责任	responsibilities / liabilities
职责	duties
同意 / 许可	consent / approval
有效	come into force (effect) / take effect/ become effective
无效	become null and void (e.g. ...shall become automatically null and void)
依据，按照	in accordance with / in compliance with / according to
立即	forthwith
具有同等法律效力	possess the same legal validity / be equally authentic
对……具有约束力	be binding upon...
以……为条件，根据	(be) subject to
在……情况下（仅用于不希望出现的情况）	in case of / in case that / in the event that
如果，只要	provided that
属于下列情形之一的，出现以下情况时	under any of the following circumstances（常用于句首主语前）; falling into any of the following categories（常用于主语后）
另有规定的除外	except as otherwise provided for by/in; except where otherwise provided for by/in; unless otherwise specified by; unless otherwise specified herein; unless otherwise agreed upon
除特别许可之外	except as specifically authorized by
有效期	period of validity
期满，失效	expire / expiration
不可抗力	force majeure
违约责任	responsibilities for breach of contract
一式两份 / 三份 / 四份	be made in duplicate / triplicate / quadruplicate

例11. In the event of any doubts or obscurities, it is expected that suitable Requests for Information (RFI) will be raised during the bid period. Otherwise, the entire requirement will be supposed to be accepted.

译文：若投标人对上述要求存在任何疑义或不解之处，可在招标期间提出合理的信息查询要求，否则将默认投标人接受本规格书所有要求。

例12. The Bidder may select alternative standards, brand or models in the bidding, provided that these alternative ones shall substantively satisfy or surpass the requirements of the Technical Specifications.

译文：投标人在投标中可以选用替代标准、品牌或型号，但这些替代要在实质上满足或超过技术文件的要求。

例11中的in the event of短语和例12中的provided that都是商务合同、招标文件等法律文件常用的词语。in the event of短语一般相当于汉语的"万一""若"等；provided that引导一个条件从句，意思是"如果""只要"，但在英译汉时，具体措辞要依具体的语境而定。

（三）术语的专业性

招投标文件不仅具备法律合同属性，会用到大量法律合同术语，还经常涉及产品或服务的质量问题，因此也会用到不少质量管理术语，涉及管理体系、方法、过程、机构、部门、指标与参数等方面，其中不少重要的缩写词，比如TQM、FIFO等。这些管理术语的中英文表达都是相对固定的。所以，译者需熟悉或了解相关的质量管理知识，掌握一定量的质量管理词汇。下面所列为英文招投标文件里常见的质量管理术语，以及一些常见的法律类用词。这些词都是招投标类文件翻译中需熟悉甚至牢记的常见词。

1	acceptance	验收
2	audit	审核，审计
3	correct / correction	纠正，改正，修正
4	modify	修改，变更
5	review	（文件等）评审，审核
6	evaluation	（投标）评审，评标
7	after services	售后服务
8	conforming	（产品或服务）合格的
9	nonconforming	（产品或服务）不合格的
10	conformity / nonconformity (*n.*)	合格 / 不合格

续表

11	qualification	资格，资质
12	qualified	有资格的，有资质的
13	identity / identification	识别，标识，标志
14	warranty	保修单，保证
15	corrective action	纠正措施
16	preventive action	预防措施
17	delivery	交付，交货
18	specification	规范，说明书
19	deviation	偏离，偏差
20	BOM = Bill of Materials	工程量清单
21	TQM = Total Quality Management	全面质量管理
22	FIFO = First In First Out	先进先出（原则）
23	AVL = Approved Vendor List	合格供应商清单
24	ISO = International Standardization Organization	国际标准化组织（视情况不译）
25	OHSAS = Occupational Health and Safety Assessment System	职业健康安全评估体系（通常不译）
26	IATF = International Automotive Task Force	国际汽车工作组
27	SGS = Société Générale de Surveillance	瑞士通用公证行
28	CQC = China Quality Certification Centre	中国质量认证中心

例13. Bidders are required to complete the Cost Analysis Schedule, so that the cost breakdown of their proposed plant can be reviewed.

译文：投标人须填写"成本分析表"，以便对拟定厂房的成本明细进行审核。

Cost Analysis Schedule是典型的财务管理术语。complete在财务会计中意思是"填写"。breakdown在财务金融中是"分类""明细"的意思，因此不能直译为"崩溃""故障"。

（四）避免口语化

招投标文件既属于法律文件，又涉及科学技术内容，逻辑性很强，如《世界银行采购指南》中确定了多条与欺诈、腐败等有关的术语。

例14. "Corrupt practice" is the offering, giving, receiving or soliciting, directly or indirectly, of anything of value to influence improperly the actions of another party.

原译:"腐败活动"意指直接地或间接地提供、给予、收受或要求任何有价财物,以不适当地影响另一方的行为。

改译:"腐败行为"是指直接或间接地提供、给予、接受或索取任何有价值的东西,以不正当地影响另一方的行为。

例15. "Fraudulent practice" is any act or omission, including a misrepresentation, that knowingly or recklessly misleads, or attempts to mislead, a party to obtain a financial or other benefit or to avoid an obligation.

原译:"欺诈活动"意指任何行为,或隐瞒,包括歪曲事实,亦即任何有意或不计后果的误导,或企图误导一方以获得财物或其他方面的利益,或为了逃避一项义务的行为。

改译:"欺诈行为"是指为获取经济利益或其他利益或逃避义务而有意或无意地误导或企图误导一方的任何作为或不作为,包括虚假陈述。

以上二例均有practice,原译"活动"或"实践"均不符合法律用语规范要求。例14中soliciting译为"要求",improperly译为"不适当地"都较口语化、不够专业。例15中financial or other benefit译为"财物或其他方面的利益"也不规范,"财物"过于具体,"其他方面的利益"表达过于通俗、口语化。any act or omission连在一起构成一个固定的法律用语,表示"作为或不作为",而不是"行为或隐瞒"或"行动或忽略"。

(五)词性与句子结构的转换

国际招标文件的用词正式、规范,句子结构严谨、冗长,而英语和汉语在表达方式和结构形式上有很大差别,因此在翻译中,需要进行词性转换,比如抽象名词转换成具体名词,名词转换成动词等。句子结构的转换可以是句子顺序的调整,句子成分的转换、拆分或合并、省略或添加等,应做到通顺达意。

例16. A technical submission detailing key equipment types proposed is also required.

译文:同时要求投标人提交技术文件,详细说明拟定的关键设备。

submission是抽象名词,A technical submission直译就是"技术上的提交",意思不准确。应将submission转换为具体名词,即延伸submission所包含的"提交文件"之意。detailing key equipment types proposed是technical submission的后置定语,其中proposed是types的后置定语。detail在句中作动词,表示详细描述(to describe something completely, giving all the facts)。

例17. The document covers the technical specification and detailed requirements for the design, supply, manufacture, delivery, installation, testing, commissioning and maintenance of the refrigeration plant and associated ancillary equipment for the complex.

译文：本文件包含综合楼制冷设备及其相关辅助设备的技术规格书及其设计、供应、制造、交付、安装、测试、调试和维护方面的具体要求。

本句主干为The document covers the technical specification and detailed requirements，后面for the design, supply, …and maintenance是technical specification and detailed requirements的后置定语；of the refrigeration plant and associated ancillary equipment for the complex则是前面for后面一串并列名词的共同定语。"complex"在本句中意思是"综合设施，综合楼"。

例18. This information will enable an open and transparent assessment of the costs.

译文：此类信息能够确保成本评估公开透明。

本句中"open and transparent"由定语转换成宾语补足语。

综上所述，要做好英文招投标文件的翻译，就必须掌握一定的招投标专业、法律合同专业知识，标的项目的行业知识，质量管理知识，商务、贸易知识等，并了解以上领域所涉及的专业术语。其中招投标和法律合同专业知识必须了解得更多一些。如果对这些相关知识掌握或了解比较少，至少也必须能通过熟练的网络搜索能力（或查找相关书籍）加以迅速了解，并通过网络词典和网络搜索迅速确定相关术语或其他词汇的正确译法。这样现学现卖的翻译，虽然可能不够理想，而且速度也比较慢，但只要译者中英文基本功和翻译基础知识比较扎实，接受新知识的能力比较强，还是可以较快上手的。如果对相关知识掌握比较少，而且网络搜索和网络词典使用能力以及相关书籍查找能力也比较欠缺，就要通过长时间的学习和翻译练习，获得招投标文件的翻译能力。

第三节　课内翻译任务

一、英译汉 English-Chinese Translation

Qualification of the Bidder

To be qualified for the award of the Contract, bidders shall provide evidence satisfactory to the Employer of their capability and adequacy of resources to carry out the Contract effectively. Bidders as part of their qualification document shall submit all the information in the forms included in Volume 3, Section XII, Qualification Questionnaire:

(a) Copies of original documents defining the constitution or legal status, place of registration and principal place of business; power of attorney of the signatory of the Bid, duly notarized, to commit the bidder.

(b) Total annual turnover in the civil works construction business expressed as the sum of payments certified for work performed in each of the last five years.

(c) Performance as prime contractor, management contractor, or proportionately as member of a joint venture or subcontractor, on works of a similar nature and complexity over the last five years, and details of other works in hand and present contractual commitments.

(d) Major items of Contractor's Equipment proposed for carrying out the Contract.

(e) The qualifications and experience of key personnel proposed for administration and execution of the Contract, both on and off site.

(f) Any proposal for subcontracting elements of the Works where the total value to be subcontracted is more than 20 percent of the Bid Price.

(g) Detailed proposals for proposed subcontracting of any highly specialized elements of the Works to named specialist subcontractors.

(h) Reports on the financial standing of the bidder including profit and loss statements, balance sheets and auditor's reports for the past five years, and estimated financial projection for the next two years.

(i) Authority to seek references from the bidder's bankers.

(j) Information regarding any litigation or arbitration resulting from contracts executed by the bidder in the last five years or currently under execution. The information shall include the names of the parties concerned, the disputed amount, cause of litigation, and matter in dispute; and present status of the dispute resolution.

(k) Proposed work methods and program in sufficient detail to demonstrate the adequacy of the bidder's proposals to meet the technical specifications and the completion time referred to in Sub-Clause 1.2 above.

重点解析 Notes and Comments

1. bidders shall provide evidence satisfactory to the Employer是第一句的主句, To be qualified for the award of the Contract是主句的目的状语, of their capability and adequacy of resources是evidence的后置定语, to carry out the Contract effectively则是capability and adequacy的后置定语。

2. Bidders shall submit all the information是第二句的主句, as part of their qualification document是the information的定语, 这一定语本该放在the information之后, 但the information 之后有一个很长的介词短语in the forms included in Volume 3, Section XII, Qualification Questionnaire作submit的方式状语, 为使句子平衡, 此处把as引导的介词短语前置。

3. Qualification Questionnaire（资格审查表）之后(a)至(k)各点都是the information的具体内容, 但都是名词性结构, 而非完整句子。

4. (a)点的核心为Copies of original documents和power of attorney。其中：

（1）defining the constitution or legal status, place of registration and principal place of business是documents的后置定语。

（2）of the signatory of the Bid是power of attorney的后置定语, duly notarized是the signatory的后置定语, to commit the bidder也是the signatory的后置定语。

5. power of attorney of the signatory of the Bid, duly notarized, to commit the bidder经正式公证代表投标人的投标书签名人的委托书

power of attorney在此句中意思是"（授权）委托书"。commit作动词意思是"使承担责任；使表态", 此处可理解成"代表"。

6. (b)点核心为Total annual turnover。其中in the civil works construction business和expressed as the sum of payments都是turnover的后置定语, certified for work是payments的后置定语, 而performed in each of the last five years则是work的后置定语。

7. (c)点核心结构部分为Performance on works of a similar nature and complexity, and details of other works and present contractual commitments（执行具有类似性质和复杂性的工程, 以及其他在建工程和现有合同承诺的详情）, 其中Performance本为名词, 翻译成汉语时转换成动词, 全句形成动宾结构。

8. as prime contractor, management contractor, or as member of a joint venture or subcontractor是performance的方式状语, 译成汉语时置于句首。

proportionately是performance的另一方式状语。

9. (d)点中Major items of Contractor's Equipment的意思是"承包商的主要设备项目",而不是"主要承包商设备项目",因为Major不是Contractor的定语。

10. (e)、(f)、(g)、(h)、(i)各小点中应准确理解和翻译一些专业词汇,如：execution(n. 履行,执行,实施), financial standing(财务状况), profit and loss statements(损益表), balance sheets(资产负债表), auditor's report(审计报告), financial projection(财务预测), bidder's banker(投标人银行)。

11. (j)点第一句中核心词为information。regarding any litigation or arbitration是information的后置定语。resulting from contracts是litigation or arbitration的后置定语, executed by the bidder in the last five years和currently under execution则是contracts的两个并列的后置定语。也就是说,executed和under execution才是并列的动词。

12. Proposed work methods and program in sufficient detail to demonstrate the adequacy of the bidder's proposals to meet the technical specifications and the completion time referred to in Sub-Clause 1.2 above. 拟议的工作方法和计划应足够详细,以证明投标人方案的妥善性能满足上文第1.2款所述的技术规范以及完成时间的要求。

这句英文是不完整的句子,句中没有谓语。翻译成汉语时需要转换成完整的主谓宾结构,相应的词性也要转换。in sufficient detail是methods and program的后置定语,但译为汉语时,介词短语变成谓语, detail转换成汉语的形容词, 形容词sufficient转换成副词。to demonstrate the adequacy是methods and program的目的状语, to meet the technical specifications and the completion time是proposals的目的状语, referred to in Sub-Clause 1.2 above则是the technical specifications and the completion time的后置定语。

二、汉译英 Chinese-English Translation

评　　标

1. 在详细评标之前,评标委员会要审查每份投标文件是否实质上响应了招标文件的要求。实质上响应的投标应该是与招标文件要求的关键条款、条件和规格相符,无重大偏离的投标。对关键条文的偏离、保留或反对,例如关于投标保证金、适用法律、税及关税等内容的偏离将被认为是实质上的偏离。

2. 评标委员会决定投标的响应性只根据投标本身的真实无误的内容，而不依据外部的证据，但投标有不真实、不正确的内容时除外。

3. 实质上未响应招标文件要求的投标将被拒绝。投标人不得通过修正或撤销不合要求的偏离或保留从而使其投标成为实质上响应的投标。在商务评议时，发现下列任何情况的，其投标将被拒绝：

（1）投标人未提交投标保证金或金额不足、保函有效期不足、投标保证金形式或投标保函出证银行不符合招标文件要求的；

（2）投标文件未按照要求逐页签字的；

（3）投标人及其制造商与招标人、招标机构有利害关系的；

（4）投标人的投标书或资格证明文件未提供或不符合招标文件要求的；

（5）投标文件符合招标文件中规定废标的其他商务条款。

4. 在技术评议时，如发现下列情况，则其投标将被拒绝：

（1）投标文件不满足招标文件技术规格中加注星号（"*"）的主要参数要求或加注星号（"*"）的主要参数无技术资料支持的。技术支持资料以制造商公开发布的印刷资料或检测机构出具的检测报告为准。若制造商公开发布的印刷资料与检测机构出具的检测报告不一致，以检测机构出具的检测报告为准。

（2）投标文件技术规格中一般参数超出允许偏离的最大范围或最高项数的。

（3）投标文件技术规格中的响应与事实不符或虚假投标的。

（4）投标文件符合招标文件中规定废标的其他技术条款。

重点解析 Notes and Comments

1. 第1条第一句中，"审查"后的内容宜译成whether引导的宾语从句。

2. 第1条第二句的主干实质上是"投标应该是投标"，其中宾语"投标"前有很长的定语，翻译中，将第一个定语"与招标文件要求的关键条款、条件和规格相符"翻译成分词短语conforming to，将"无重大偏离的"译成without major deviations，作伴随状态。

3. 对关键条文的偏离、保留或反对，……将被认为是实质上的偏离。Deviations from, or reservations or objections to critical provisions, ...will be deemed as major deviations.

"关键条文"可以译为 critical provisions；"被认为是"译为be deemed as。deem（认为，视为）多用于法律文件等比较正式的文体。该句中需注意Deviations from, or reservations or objections to中介词的用法。

4. "评标委员会决定投标的响应性只根据……"本句主干为"评标委员会决定投标的响应性",但后面的条件状语"只根据……,而不依据……"却是很重要的内容,这里可译成后置定语based on...instead of...。不过,这里based on和instead of后面必须是名词形式。后面"但……除外"可以译成except + 名词形式,也可译成unless that...形式。

5. 实质上未响应招标文件要求的投标将被拒绝。投标人不得通过修正或撤销不合要求的偏离或保留从而使其投标成为实质上响应的投标。A bid not substantially responsive will be rejected, and may not subsequently be made responsive by the Bidder by correcting or cancelling the non-conforming deviations or reservations.

这两句内容紧密相关,都有一个关键词"bid",所以可以合译成共用一个主语A bid的句子。当然,也可将后面一句顺译成独立的句子:The Bidder shall not correct or cancel the non-conforming deviations or reservations to turn the bid into a substantively responsive bid.

实质上未响应招标文件要求的投标 = 未实质响应的投标:a bid not substantively responsive。

发现下列任何情况的 = 在以下任何情况下:under any of the following circumstances。

6. 第3条第(1)小点是汉语流水句,主语不统一,所以可将前面部分"投标人未提交投标保证金"译成一个分句,即The Bidder fails to hand in the bid security;将后面所有内容译成以the bid security为主语的另一分句。但要将后面剩余部分的内容整合成一个分句,还要注意选择好用词和句式。

未提交:fail to hand in(注意,"未"宜译成fail to而不是cannot或have not)

金额不足:be of insufficient amount

有效期不足:be of insufficient period of validity

7. 在技术评议时,如发现下列情况,则其投标将被拒绝。During the technical evaluation, the bid will be rejected under any of the following circumstances.

8. 第4条第(1)小点三句都相对较长,其翻译要点是要先弄清楚原文的主干和各修饰成分,先译出主干,然后再把各修饰成分一点点放到合适的位置上,并对用词和句式加以适当调整。第一句主干为"投标文件不满足主要参数要求或主要参数无技术资料支持",句末"的"可以忽略。其中"加注星号的"可译成that

从句,也可省略that are,成为后置定语;另外,"不满足"译成fail to satisfy而不是have not satisfied,显得更简单也更客观。第二句主干为"技术支持资料以印刷资料或检测报告为准",其中"印刷资料"和"检测报告"的定语可译成后置定语。第三句主干为"若印刷资料与检测报告不一致,以检测报告为准",句中的"检测机构出具的检测报告"可译成代词the latter。

第(2)小点中,"超出允许偏离的最高项数"是指偏离项数过多,"项数"宜译为number of items。

第(3)小点中,"或虚假投标"相当于一个独立的句子:"该投标为虚假投标。"

第四节　课后翻译训练

一、将下列句子翻译成汉语 Translate the following sentences into Chinese

1. All this should help speed up the internationalization of China's foreign trade and create a better environment for bringing about our macroeconomics and trade.

2. A complete set of tender documents may be obtained by any pre-qualified tenderer for the cost of RMB _____ or US $ _____ on the submission of a written application to the above.

3. All bidders must be accompanied by a Bid Security in an acceptable form and must be delivered to _____ Company at the above-mentioned address (refer to Item 3) on or before _____.

4. The tender, and in case of a successful tender the Form of Agreement, shall be signed so as to be legally binding on all partners.

5. The bidder shall bear all costs associated with the preparation and submission of his bid and neither the Employer nor his agent_____ Company will in any way be responsible or liable for those costs, regardless of the outcome of the tendering process.

6. Tender documents shall include any addenda issued prior to the closing date of tenders in accordance with Clause 8 and any minutes of pre-tender meetings issued in accordance with Clause 16 of these Instructions to Tenderers.

7. A Prospective tenderer requiring any clarification of the tender documents

may notify _____ in writing or by telex at the following address.

8. Prior to the deadline for submission of tenders, the Employer may, for any reason, whether at its own initiative or in response to a clarification requested by a prospective tenderer, modify the tender documents by the issue of an Addendum.

9. The Employer or his agent _____ will open the tenders, in the presence of bidders' representatives who choose to attend, at_____ on _____ at the offices of _____. Bidders' representatives who are present shall sign a register evidencing their attendance.

10. Tenders for which an acceptable notice of withdrawal has been submitted pursuant to Clause 21 hereof shall not be opened. The Employer or his agent _____ will examine the tenders to determine whether they are complete, whether the requisite tender securities have been furnished, whether the documents have been Properly signed, and whether the tenders are generally in order.

二、将下列句子翻译成英语 Translate the following sentences into English

1. 所有依世界银行指导原则具有资格的国家，都可参加招标。
2. 标书和投标者与业主及其代理人A公司之间的一切联络均使用英文。
3. 应一律使用本文件卷三中的表格、工程量表和目录表。
4. 业主或其代理人A公司将准备一份现场参观交通、食宿安排协议，在标前会议上向投标者宣布。
5. 为此，业主和A公司在公布中标者前，可要求投标者更新其先前提供的资格证明材料。
6. 投标者标书中的一些辅助文件或小册子可使用另外的语言，但与投标有关的段落要有英语译文。
7. 本合同项下的一切货物、服务均应来自上述具有资格的国家。
8. 本合同项下的一切开支仅限于支付这样的货物和服务。
9. 所有标书将在_____（时间）当着投标者代表的面开标。
10. 所有合资人根据合同条款对合同的执行共同负责。

三、将下列短文翻译成汉语 Translate the following passage into Chinese

Bids for Joint Venture

1. Bids submitted individually, as a partner in a Joint Venture or as group as the case may be, must comply with the qualification requirements set in the Bidding Document, Section XII, Qualification Questionnaires.

Moreover, the Joint Venture shall satisfy the following requirements:

(a) The bid, and in case of a successful bid, the Form of Agreement, shall be signed so as to be legally binding on all partners.

(b) One of the partners shall be nominated as being in charge and shall be responsible on behalf of all the partners to the Joint Venture, and this authorization shall be evidenced by submitting a power of attorney signed by legally authorized signatories of all the partners.

(c) The partner in charge shall be authorized to incur liabilities and receive instructions for and on behalf of any and all partners of the joint venture, and the entire execution of the Contract, including payment, shall be done exclusively with the partner in charge.

(d) All partners of the joint venture shall be liable jointly and severally for the execution of the Contract in accordance with the Contract terms, and a statement to this effect shall be included in the authorization mentioned under (b) above, as well as in the Form of Bid and in the Form of Agreement (in case of a successful bid).

(e) A copy of the Joint Venture Agreement entered into by all partners shall be submitted with the Qualification Application. Alternatively, a Letter of Intent to execute a Joint Venture Agreement in the event of a successful Qualification Application shall be signed by all partners and submitted with the bid, together with a copy of the proposed Agreement.

2. For the purposes of this particular Contract, Bidders shall meet the minimum qualifying criteria specified in the Bidding Document, Section XII, and Qualification Questionnaire.

3. The figures for each of the partners of a joint venture shall be added together to determine the bidder's compliance with the minimum qualifying

criteria set out in Sub-Clause 5.3 above.

4. Domestic bidders or joint ventures of domestic bidders applying for eligibility for a 7½ percent margin of preference in bid evaluation shall supply all information required to satisfy the criteria for eligibility as described in Clause 32 of the Instructions to Bidders. The qualifications, capacity, and resources of proposed sub-contractors will not be taken into account in assessing those of individual or joint venture bidders, unless they are named specialist subcontractors and the scope of their specialized participation in the Works is clearly defined in the bid.

注释：

a successful bid 中标　　Form of Agreement 协议书　　nominate 制定
authorization 授权　　Form of Bid 投标函　　be liable jointly 承担连带责任

四、将下列短文翻译成英语 Translate the following passage into English

关于招标文件的说明

1. 招标文件的澄清

（1）招标文件的澄清，采用书面文件或电子邮件的形式进行。

（2）投标人对招标文件如有疑问，可在招标文件规定的投标截止日期4日前，以书面形式（信函、传真）将投标人对招标文件要求澄清的问题清单送达招标单位。

（3）招标人将对按规定提交的、有必要予以澄清的问题给予答复，同时将书面答复发给所有收到招标文件的企业（答复中不包括问题的来源）。

2. 招标文件的修改

（1）在投标截止日期3日前，招标单位可主动或依据投标人要求澄清的问题而修改招标文件，并以书面或电子邮件形式通知每家收到招标文件的企业，拿到招标文件的企业在收到该通知后应立即以传真的形式予以回复确认。

（2）为使投标人在准备投标文件时有合理的时间考虑招标文件的修改，招标人可酌情推迟投标截止时间和开标时间，并以书面形式通知每个投标人。

（3）招标文件的澄清答复文件和修改文件将构成招标文件的一部分，对招投标双方具有同等约束力。

3. 如有需要，投标人可在投标截止日期10日前向招标人提出踏勘需求，招标人根据具体情况，<u>在开标前7日内决定</u>是否组织踏勘。

4. 本招标文件的所有内容，投标人不得用于本次投标以外的任何目的，未经招标人同意，不得泄露给任何第三方，确因投标人泄露的，投标人应<u>负一切责任</u>，情节严重者，将追究其法律责任。

第十一章 国际物流翻译

物流（Logistics）是指物质实体从供应者向需要者的物理性移动，它由一系列创造时间和空间效用的经济活动组成，包括运输（配送）、保管、包装、装卸、流通加工及物流信息处理等多项基本活动，是这些活动的统一。物流是商品流通的一个方面。"物"在这里指一切有经济意义的有形和无形的物质实体；"流"在这里指物质实体的定向移动，既包括其空间位移，又包括其时间延续。

本章简要介绍物流系统的相关概念和知识，从物流英语的词汇特点和句法特点出发，对物流英语的语言特点以及翻译策略与技巧进行总结。通过中、英物流文本材料的呈现，学生可以对物流系统的相关知识有一个大致的了解，并通过相关材料的翻译训练，培养物流材料的翻译技巧和能力。

第一节 物流简述

物流（Physical Distribution）一词于1915年首先出现于美国。美军在二战中提出了"后勤"（Logistics）理论，后成立美国后勤管理协会。七十多年后欧美国家逐渐把物流统称为Logistics。我国20世纪80年代以前多译为"实体分配"，后逐渐引入"物流"概念。物流包括流体、载体和流向三个要素。流体指物流中的物，载体指流体借以流动的设施和设备，流向则指流体从起点到终点的流动方向。三要素之间有极强的内在联系。物流是包括运输、储存、配送、搬运、分拣、包装、加工等多个环节在内的经济活动。城市发展物流，按规模的大小和功能的分工大致可分为物流中心、物流园区和物流配送服务站三种形式，不同的形式有不同的认定条件。

明确的物流概念和理论是二战以后才形成的。不同时期的人们对于物流有不同的定义，反映了物流管理思想发展的大概趋势。《中华人民共和国国家标准：物流术语》对物流的定义为"物品从供应地向接收地的实体流动过程中，根据实际需要,将运输、储存、采购、装卸搬运、包装、流通加工、配送、信息处理等功能有机结合起来实现用户要求的过程"。

为了适应物流的发展,美国物流管理协会(CLM)于1998年修订了物流的定义:"物流是供应链的一部分,是以满足客户需求为目的的,为提高产品、服务和相关信息从起始点到消费点的流动储存效率和效益而对其进行计划、执行和控制的过程。"显然,供应链管理的概念涵盖了物流的概念,用系统的观点看,物流是供应链管理的子系统。

供应链管理(Supply Chain Management, SCM)是一种集成的管理思想和方法,它执行供应链中从供应商到最终用户的物流的计划和控制等职能。从单一的企业角度来看,是指企业通过改善上、下游供应链关系,整合和优化供应链中的信息流、物流、资金流,以获得企业的竞争优势。

当今社会,随着经济全球化的发展、企业的国际化经营与跨国公司的发展,物流的需求和质量从宏观和微观两个方面发生了变化,这导致了国际物流的兴起与发展。广义的国际物流(International Logistics,简称IL)的研究范围包括国际贸易物流、非贸易国际物流、国际物流合作、国际物流投资、国际物流交流等领域。狭义的国际物流主要是指国际贸易物流,即组织货物在国际上的合理流动,也就是指发生在不同国家之间的物流。

国际物流的实质是,根据国际分工协作的原则,依照国际惯例,利用国际化的物流网络、物流设施和物流技术,实现货物在国际上的流动和交换,以促进区域经济的发展和世界资源的优化配置。国际物流的总目标是,为国际贸易和跨国经营服务,即选择最佳的方式和路径,以最低的费用和最小的风险,保质、保量、适时地将货物从某国的供方运到另一国的需方。

根据货物在不同国家间的流动,国际物流可以分为进口物流和出口物流。根据物资输送方式,国际物流可以分为陆运物流(含公路和铁路联运物流)、海运物流、空运物流、管道物流、多式联运物流、邮运物流六种。

物流系统是在一定的时间和空间里,由所输送的物品和其他相关的设施设备、人员以及信息技术等若干相互作用、相互制约的动态要素构成的能实现物流目标的有机整体。

第二节　物流英语的语言特征

一、物流英语词汇的语言特征

（一）有较强的专业性

物流业中的词汇与常见的英语可能存在一定的差异，通用英语中的许多词汇在物流英语中都具有其特定意义。例如，material, drawer, elevator, package, accept, negotiation, collection 在通用英语中分别是"材料""抽屉""电梯""包裹""接受""商议""收集"的意思，但在物流英语中它们分别是"物料""柜式货架""升降梯""包装""承兑""议付""托收"的意思。（黄中军，2016：65）

由于物流英语中词汇含义的专业性，也形成了一些通用英语中不常见的固定搭配。如：material handling 物料搬运、inventory control 库存控制、through transport 直达运输、order processing 订单处理、base stock 基本存货，bonded warehouse 保税仓库，collected and delivered 货款两清，customs broker 报关行，freight broker 货运中介，fixed quantity system 定量订货方式，flow rack 流动式货架，pallet rack 托盘式货架，inventory turns 库存周转，one-off purchase 一次性采购，physical management 实物管理，shipping document 运输单据等。

此外，物流英语的单复数可能会有含义上的差别。例如：imports and exports 可翻译为"进出口商品"或"进出口额"，而 import 和 export 则是"进口业务""出口业务"的意思；shipment 译为"装船，装运"，而 shipments 是"装运的货"；stock 的汉语意思为"库存,存货"，而 stocks 的汉语意思为"库存量"；engagement 可译为"承诺"，而 engagements 意思是"承担的义务"；damage 译为"损坏"，而 damages 译为"损坏赔偿金"。（雷斐，2015：91）

最后，由于目前大量货物在实际运送当中频繁地进行周转，物流英语不断出现大量新的词汇。最为典型的就是电子商务带来的物流英语词汇增加。很多大型企业或公司为了能够提高自身的国际竞争力以及运营效率开始使用 virtual warehousing（VW，虚拟仓库）和 virtual logistics（虚拟物流），这在很大程度上导致物流英语中的新词不断涌现，如 supply-driven inventory control 供应推动式库存管理，visual materials 可视材料，computer assigned ordering 计算机辅助订货系统，bar coding and scanning 条形码扫描技术等。

（二）大量使用缩略语

缩略语属于物流英语中的重要组成内容，具有明显性、简洁性等特点，在物流英语报告中被广泛使用。同时，缩略词具有较多类型，本章主要介绍以下四种：

第一种是首字母缩略语，指由短语中每个词的第一个字母组成的首字母缩写词，这类缩略语在物流英语中最常见、最普遍，具有构词简练、使用便捷、交流方便的特点。如：EOS（electronic order system）电子订货系统，DRP（distribution requirements planning）配送需求计划，VMI（vendor managed inventory）供应商管理库存，CRP（continuous replenishment program）连续库存补充计划，EFC（E Fulfillment Center）电子化运作仓库，IOT（Internet of Things）物联网。

第二种是剪裁缩略语，由后边或中间剪掉几个字母缩略而成。例如：Meas.（measurement）尺寸，CGO（cargo）货物，CTNS（cartons）纸板箱，CNTR（container）集装箱，OFLD（offloaded）卸下，SSPD（shortshipped）漏装，D/Y（delivery）交货，DOZ（dozen）一打，FRT（freight）货物，M/F（manifest）卸货清单，Max（maximum）最大的，MED（medium）中等的，MIN（minimum）最小的，PCS（pieces）只、个、支，PCT（percent）百分比，PKG（package）一包、一件、一捆，PR 或 PRC（price）价格，Recpt（receipt）收据，TTL（total）总共，WGT（weight）重量，G.W.（grass weight）毛重，Whf（wharf）码头。

第三种是由数字、符号、首字母一起构成的缩略语。例如：B2A（business to administration）行业与行政机构的电子商务，B2B（business to business）企业与企业的电子商务，B2C（business to consumer）企业与消费者的电子商务，B2E（business to employee）企业对员工的电子商务，C2C（consumer to consumer）消费者对消费者的电子商务，C/D（customs declaration）报关单，C&D（collected and delivered）货款两清，P/L（packing list）装箱单，T/S（trans-ship）转运、转船，W/T（weight ton）重量吨，3P（pollution prevention pays）防污染投资，3PL（the third party logistics）第三方物流。

第四种是拼缀缩略语，也就是把两个或两个以上的词通过省略字母的方式合成一个新词，例如：advertics（advertising statistics）广告统计，CFR（cost and freight）成本加运费价，SWB（seaway bill）海运单，workfare（work welfare）工作福利制，SPC（special charger）特别附加费，YAS（yard surcharges）码头附加费。

（三）跨行业、跨学科性强

物流英语涵盖众多专业和学科，主要涉及物流管理、交通运输、关税、仓储、装卸、包装、加工、配送、报关等方面，囊括了管理学、经济学、保险学、金融学、法学、文学、互联网等领域的专业词汇和专业术语，因此物流英语词汇来源广泛，覆盖面大。

例如：customs declaration（海关申报），bonded logistics center（保税物流中心）等专业词汇来自报关环节；cross-docking（越库配送）等词汇则来自运输领域；inventory turnover ratio（库存周转率），just-in-time production（准时制生产）等词汇则来自库存管理；film-based packaging和blanket-wrapping应按照包装行业的惯例翻译为"薄膜包装"和"毡布包装"。（杨柳，2013：115）

又如：special drawing rights（特别提款权），negotiating bank（议付行），after-the-fact customs clearance（事后清关）等是金融行业的专业术语；4C（customer, cost, convenience, communication）（营销4C理论），4P（product, price, place and promotion）（4P营销组合），6P（product, price, place, promotion, power and public relations）（大市场营销组合）等是市场营销行业常用的缩略语；booking note（托运单），customs declaration（报关单），delivery order（提货单），document against acceptance（承兑交单），document against payment（付款交单）等是国际贸易行业的常用术语。

再如：Acts of God或Force Majeure（不可抗力）常用于法律文件中，insurance policy是保险业中的术语"保险单"，而不能按字面意思理解成"保险政策"。

二、物流英语句子的语言特征

（一）语态的交替使用

在国际物流英语当中，涉及相关技术时，普遍使用被动语态。通过分析发现，被动语态的使用在一定程度上使得表达的重点更为突出。例如：货物在运输过程中遗失，在未能查明责任方是谁的情况下，使用被动语态较为合适，这句可以翻译为："The Consignment is lost."

例1. The search for suppliers is performed either when a company does not yet have a portfolio of suppliers (e.g. when entering a new market) or when it is about to renew its current pool of suppliers.

译文：当公司尚无供应商组合时（例如，进入新市场时）或即将更新其当前供应商库时，公司应搜索供应商。

例2. Logistics activities can be conducted by the company itself or can be entrusted to a third party.

译文：物流活动可由公司执行，也可委托给第三方。

翻译与物流商务相关的内容时，需要进一步考虑语态的选择，通常情况下，主动和被动语态的使用在表述效果上将产生很大的差异。表达较为中性的内容时，在语态选择上往往更倾向于主动语态；表述可能会导致别人不愉快的内容时，最好选择间接表述，这样更能够体现出事情本身的迫不得已性。

例如在表述别人没有付清账款时可以这样翻译："We found that the bill has not been settled."通过这种方式不仅满足了翻译自身的目的，同时语气较为委婉，不会使别人感到反感。

（二）名词化现象突出

名词化就是用名词或名词短语来代替动词或形容词，表达动词或形容词的意义。名词化结构避用人称主语，其运用能体现文本的客观性和描述的客体性，也能体现语言的经济性，以简单的名词结构表达抽象、复杂的信息和意义，防止句子过于臃肿。物流英语中常有意识地使用名词化结构，用抽象名词代替动词，以表现抽象思维的逻辑性和概念化，从而使语体更加正式，更具书面语风格，更体现正式文体的风格。

国际物流英语的发展可以说是建立在科技发展的基础之上，因此从本质上来说，国际物流英语应当属于科技文体的范畴，同时也应当具备科技文体简洁、客观等特点。

例3. The shipper is responsible for complying with all packing requirements and appropriate marking and labelling of the package, documentation, as well as compliance with all applicable local, state and federal laws, regulations, ordinances and rules.（来自联邦快递标准货运条款）

译文：对于包装的具体要求，托运人需要对其进行负责，在遵守相关法律法规的前提下需要对包装文件的标识进行确认。

例3的英文原句采用了大量的名词化结构，例如packing requirements, marking and labelling等。

例4. The adoption of just-in-time and similar approaches to material supply allied to computer-based information systems that provide up to-the-minute information on stock availability and locations, have certainly challenged the need for holding stock and having warehouses at all.

译文：现在的计算机和信息系统能够及时更新产品的有无和位置信息，以其为基础的准时制和其他类似方法的应用对维持库存和建立仓库的必要性提出了巨大的挑战。

英文原句中，adoption, approaches, availability and locations, holding stock and having warehouses都属于名词化结构。

（三）后置定语较多

物流英语中的后置定语，对名词起修饰、描绘作用，还可以充当表语、补足语、状语等。翻译成汉语时，在遇到形容词、副词、介词短语、动词不定式和分词短语作后置定语时，更多的要把后置定语提到中心词前面去翻译；而遇到定语从句，尤其是非限定性定语从句时则更多地需要用分译法。我们在翻译时不能轻易有所创新，要遵守汉语的表达规则，适当安排其位置。

例5. Very often one area <u>associated</u> with the buying process that is overlooked is the cost of <u>transporting</u> the goods to the buyer's facilities. The companies show a remarkable lack of interest in this area <u>preferring</u> to see it as somebody <u>else</u>'s problem. Unfortunately, the delivered price may hide some extra cost <u>that the buying company could avoid</u>.

译文：通常情况下与购买过程相关的领域是将产品运达购买者的成本。公司一般不注重这一领域，认为这是其他人的问题。但是，运价可能隐藏了一些购买者本可以避免的成本。

这句英文原句中有五个后置定语，其中，associated和preferring为分词作后置定语，transporting为动名词作后置定语，else为代词，that the buying company could avoid为定语从句。这些后置定语都比较短，翻译时按照汉语表达习惯，可以把定语提前到中心词前面。

例6. Other rail services include expedited service to guarantee arrival <u>within a certain number of hours</u>; various stop-off privileges, <u>which</u> permit partial loading and unloading <u>between origin and destination points</u>. Containers <u>that can be loaded two to a railcar in the United States</u> are frequently carried on individual railcars elsewhere.

译文：其他的铁路运输服务包括保证在一定时间到达的快速服务：各种中途停留的优惠待遇，它允许从原发地到目的地部分货物的卸载。在美国，两个集装箱装载到一辆铁轨车上，而在其他地方，一般用私人铁轨车来运送。

这个英文原句中，有两个作后置定语的介词短语、两个定语从句。其中，只有第一处within a certain number of hours翻译成汉语可以放在中心词前面，其他后置定语翻译成中文比较长，按照汉语的语言习惯，可以采用分译法，单独作一个分句。

例7. Logistics was originally a military term encompassing the processes to supply combat and troop support.

译文：起初，物流是一个军事术语，涵盖战斗补给和军队支持的过程。

（四）大量使用复合句

物流英语中常使用结构严谨、语义层次分明、逻辑严密的复合句。复合句往往由独立的主从复合句、并列句、短句、修饰成分（形容词、副词、介词短语、过去分词和现在分词）、时间或条件状语组成，其结构看似松散，但逻辑关系紧密，常采用顺译法、倒译法、分译法（断句法）等译出。

例8. The objective of the industrial firm may be stated as the effective coordination of men, materials, machines and money to provide a product or service <u>when and where</u> needed at a price attractive to the customer, <u>which</u> will provide a profit to the firm and serve the society.

译文：工业公司的目标可以解释为人力、材料、机器和资金的有效整合，以便在合适的时间、地点（适时适地地）为用户提供具有价格优势的产品或服务，使公司盈利，为社会造福。（顺译法）

例9. <u>We regret our being unable to grant your request</u>, as we stated during our negotiations that payment should be made by a confirmed, irrevocable letter of credit payable by draft at sight.

译文：正如在谈判时我方已经说过的，货款必须以保兑的、不可撤销的、凭即期汇票支付的信用证付款。<u>我方很难接受贵方这一要求</u>。

为了符合汉语后重心的表达习惯，采用倒译法将译文的顺序做了调整。

例10. The main stimulus to enterprise is the release of funds, now available for investment in the productive side of a business, <u>which</u> would otherwise need to be held in easily accessible reserves if the firm had not transferred the risk to an insurer.

译文：企业投保的主要动力是他们可以腾出资金留作企业其他生产项目的投资。如果公司不将风险转移给承保人，这笔资金就要留下作为可随时使用的储备金。

which引导的是一个非限制性定语从句，故采用分译法译成两个句子，使意思更加清晰易懂。

例11. According to a widespread definition, logistics (from the Greek term logos, which means "order", or from the French loger, which means "allocate") is the discipline that studies the functional activities determining the flow of materials (and of the relative information) in a company, from their origin at the suppliers up to delivery of the finished products to the customers and to the post-sales service.

(Gianpaolo Ghiani et al., 2013: 1)

译文：广义来说，物流（源自希腊语的logos，意思是"订单"，或源自法语的loger，意思是"分配"）这一学科研究的是公司中决定物料流（及相关信息流）的功能性活动，即从供应商出发，到成品的交付，再到客户以及售后服务的全过程。

第三节　物流英语的翻译策略

一、转换与转译

由于英语重形合，而汉语重意合，即重语句间内在的逻辑关系，而不是形式上的曲折变化，汉语中被动语态和名词化结构使用得都比较少。因此，物流英语汉译时通常要转换语态，把英语被动语态变成汉语主动语态；此外，还要运用一些词汇手段进行转译，把名词化结构转译成汉语中常用的动词形式，来实现英语原文的各种语法结构的语用目的。

例12. Buyer shall be entitled to back charge Seller for any costs of clean-up if Seller fails to clean-up Seller's portion of the job site within 48 hours after demand by Buyer.

译文：卖方不能在买方要求其清洁工作场所后48小时内完成清洁的，买方有权要求卖方退还清洁费。

该句使用了被动语态，shall be entitled to意为"被赋予……权利"，但是在汉译的时候，需要将句子结构进行转换，将shall be entitled to译为"有权"，变被动句为主动句。另外，after demand by Buyer中的名词demand，译成汉语也可以还原为"主语+谓语"的主动形式，即"买方要求"。

例13. Several primary documents (bills of lading, freight bills and shipping manifests) are required to perform each transport movement.

译文：每起运输都需要几种主要单据（提单、运费单和装船舱单）。

英译中多把语句中的关键信息置于句首（前重心），而汉语中多把关键信息置于句尾（后重心）。在本例中，several primary documents是句子的关键信息，所以置于句首。本句若写成To perform each transport movement requires several documents (bills of lading, freight bills and shipping manifests)，句子会显得平铺直叙，没有很好地突出或强调陈述要点的重要性或作用。但翻译成中文时，必须把句子重心（"几种主要单据"）还原到句尾，而目的状语to perform each transport movement可以置于句首，句子使用主动语态，这样转换比较符合汉语的表达习惯。

例14. Logistics is seen as a system (the logistics system), which includes not only all the functional activities determining the flow of materials and information, but also the infrastructures, means, equipment and resources that are indispensable to the execution of these activities.

译文：物流可看作一个系统（即物流系统）。该系统不仅包括决定物料流和信息流的所有功能性活动，而且包括这些活动不可或缺的基础设施、方法、设备和资源。

该句的定语从句可以转移到中心词前面来翻译，其中the execution of these activities是名词化结构，翻译成中文时要转译为动词化结构，"执行活动"。

例15. At each facility the flow of materials is temporarily interrupted, generally in order to change their physical-chemical composition, ownership or appearance.

译文：设备中的物料流通常会为了改变其物理化学成分、所有权或外观而暂时中断。

这句话翻译时可以适当调整语序，保证中文的后重心习惯。

例16. Consumer confidence was shaken and a mild recession intensified in the United States by the terrorist attacks on the World Trade Center and the Pentagon in 2001.

译文：2001年，世贸中心和五角大楼遭恐怖袭击，这使美国消费者的信心开始动摇，也导致美国经济缓步下降。

原句是被动语态，翻译成中文时要把句式还原为主动语态，其中terrorist attacks on...是名词化结构，译文中要还原成陈述语气。

例17. Within a logistics system, with the exception of the cases where recycling of product wrapping is provided or where defective components or products are returned, the flow of materials typically moves from the suppliers to the processing and assembly plants, thence to the sales points and finally to the customers.

译文：在物流系统中，除了提供产品包装回收或退回有缺陷的组件、产品的情况，物料流通常从供应商流向加工厂和组配厂，然后流向销售点，最后流向客户。

该句介词短语带有两个where引导的定语从句，定语从句都是被动结构，汉语译文都是主动结构，不能译为"被……提供""被……回收"。

例18. One recent problem has been the dumping of toxic wastes in nations willing to import those wastes for a fee.

译文：最近的一个问题是，在那些愿意花钱引进有毒废物的国家，还有人倾倒这些废物。

这句的the dumping of toxic wastes也是名词化短语，翻译的时候要转换成动宾结构，并相应补充主语。

二、增词与减词

增词法和减词法的使用使得翻译的内容更加符合原文的意境以及语气，内容上也与原文更符合。这两种方法在选择上通常是根据原文的意境以及所翻译内容所要表达的思想。

在物流英语翻译的具体实践中，在有些情况下，如果仅仅按照英语自身的意思进行翻译，会有很多地方不通顺，也不具备商务英语翻译语言的商务性。因此，需要在一定程度上增加一些词汇和短语，使句子翻译之后的语境更为明显，以此来丰富译文的整体字面含义，而源语言被翻译之后的语境和语言细节都不被改变。比如：

例19. Long-term, outside relationships are at the heart of the strewn lined organization.

译文：与外部企业建立长期关系，是精简组织的关键。

这句话的主语是名词短语long-term, outside relationships。如果按照字面意思，原句会直接翻译成"长期外部关系是精简组织的关键"。但在中文商务语境中，"长期外部关系"所指代的对象并不明确。因此可以增添动词，把名词性短语变成中文常用的动词性短语——"与外部企业建立长期关系"。增词之后，句子变为两个分句，语义也更加明确连贯。

与"增词"对应的是"减词"策略，指的是在物流英语翻译的过程中，将英语语句中不需要刻意翻译出的单词或者短语直接省略，这样使得翻译工作效率大大提升，译文风格也更加简洁明确，符合商务用语的特点。需要注意的是，省略策略的使用要以不改变原句的基本含义为前提。

例20. Will you please inform us the delivery date?

译文：请告知发货日期。

在此例中，原文采用疑问句，按字面意思可以直接翻译为"你能够告知我们具体的发货日期吗？"如果按照这种委婉的语气进行字面翻译，不利于体现商务英语在交涉过程中的客观性，也不符合贸易过程的商务性质。由于在具体的贸易过程中，发货日期是按照合同约定如实履行，所以，翻译过程中为了简约，可以将一些修饰性的形容词、连词、冠词、介词等省略不译。

例21. This added value can be spatial (following e.g. distribution activities) or temporal (owing to storage activities).

译文：增加的价值可以是空间价值（例如由于配送活动）或时间价值（由于保管活动）。

句中spatial和temporal后面要增译省略的value，译为"空间价值"和"时间价值"。

例22. The U.S. currently embargoes trade with the Iraqi political regime now in power in Baghdad.

译文：当前美国对伊拉克政权实行禁运。

该句可以适当采取减词策略，因为巴格达是伊拉克的首都，所以"在巴格达的执政当权"可省略，只译出"伊拉克政权"。

例23. The flow of materials is integrated with an information flow which follows the opposite direction: in the logistics systems of the MTO-type (*Make to Order*), for example, customers' orders influence the production plan and the latter determines the demand for materials and components of the processing and assembly plants.

译文：物料流与反方向流动的信息流是一个整体，例如，在MTO型（按订单生产）的物流系统中，客户的订单会影响生产计划，而生产计划决定了公司对加工厂和组配厂所提供的物料与组件的需求。

该句中"the latter"指代前面的production plan，以避免重复，但汉语中为了使意思明晰化，在后一句中增加了"生产计划"，重复了the latter的意义。

三、句法与逻辑

在物流英语中，为了使所表达的内容具有较强的严密性、准确性和逻辑性，进一步明确事物的内在特性和相互联系，往往使用含有大量复合句和附加成分的简单句长句式，这给翻译工作的理解造成很大困难。翻译长句时，首先要弄清楚原文的句法结构，找出整个句子的中心内容及其各层意思，然后分析几层意思之间的相互逻辑关系，如因果、假设或时间顺序等，再按照汉语特点和表达方式，正确地译出原文的意思，而又不拘泥于原文的形式。

例14. A third-party service provider has one thing in mind when <u>entering</u> negotiations: <u>making</u> the most money while <u>assuming</u> the least amount of risk.

译文：第三方服务提供商在谈判时要牢记一点：争取最大利润和最小责任。

例15. Past experience showed that the sea journey was hard on the cattle, <u>causing</u> either long damage or long delays before the animals could be bred; however, other markets for air cargo charters include famine relief projects in Africa, buyers of textiles <u>trying</u> to meet quota deadlines, and owners of oil fields in Russia <u>needing</u> oversize equipment.

译文：以往的经验表明海运对畜牧业业主是非常痛苦的，在动物可以喂养之前就被伤害和耽搁。包租飞机空运货物在以下情况均有市场：非洲的饥荒援助工程，纺织品购买者为满足限额的最后期限，俄罗斯石油产地的所有者需要超大规模的设备。

如上述两例，动词非谓语形式在国际物流英语中的使用频率高。非谓语动词虽然不能单独作谓语，但仍然保留原有动词的某些性质，可以用状语来修饰。如前所述，物流英语文本行文简练、结构紧凑，为此，往往使用分词短语代替定语从句或状语从句，使用分词独立结构代替状语从句或并列分句，使用不定式短语代替各种从句，使用"介词+动名词"短语代替定语从句或状语从句，这样可缩短句子，又比较醒目。英译汉时，译者必须先明确英文的句法结构，才能准确翻译。

四、拆句与合句

英语重形合，汉语重意合。英语多长句，结构比较复杂。因此，英译汉时，往往要拆分句子，形成汉语短句结构。而汉译英时，则往往需合句，形成英语的复合结构。物流英语多长句、复合句，因此，常常要运用拆句法。

例16. In all cases, each logistic activity carried out involves costs which affect the value of the product, constantly adding to it as it draws nearer the facilities closest to the final customer.

译文：一般情况下，每项物流活动都需要成本，这些成本会影响产品价值；

随着物流活动越来越靠近最终客户,产品价值会不断增加。

costs which...这个定语从句虽然很简单,但可以拆开来翻译,即"每项物流活动都需要成本,这些成本会影响产品价值"。采用分译法,可以使中文的逻辑关系体现得更加清楚,与翻译成定语"每项物流活动都需要影响产品价值的成本"相比,分译之后的中文更加明白通畅。

例17. 物流系统规划越来越重视材料和服务的提供。

译文: In logistics systems planning, an increasing attention is paid to the provision of materials and services.

"物流系统规划"并不是"重视"这个动作的发出者,所以不能作主语,按英文的逻辑将"物流系统规划"译为介词短语作状语,而把中文的谓语动词"越来越重视"转换成名词短语作主语,谓语处理成被动语态。

第四节 课内翻译任务

一、英译汉 English-Chinese Translation

Definition of Logistics

Logistics means the organized movement of goods, services, and, sometimes, people. Logistics was originally a military term encompassing the processes to supply combat and troop support. In trade, logistics handles the physical movement of products between one or more participants in the supply chain. When we speak of international logistics systems, we mean the complex web of carriers, forwarders, bankers, information and communication companies, traders, and so on that facilitate international transactions, trades, and movements of goods and services.

According to a widespread definition, logistics (from the Greek term logos, which means "order", or from the French loger, which means "allocate") is the discipline that studies the functional activities determining the flow of materials (and of the relative information) in a company, from their origin at the suppliers up to delivery of the finished products to the customers and to the post-sales service.

The origins of logistics are of a strictly military nature. In fact, this discipline arose as the study of the methodologies employed to guarantee the correct supply of troops with victuals, ammunition and fuel and, in general, to ensure armies the possibility of moving and fighting in the most efficient conditions. Indeed it was the Babylonians, in the distant 20th century BC, who first created a military corps specialized in the supply, storage, transport and distribution of soldiers' equipment. Logistics was applied exclusively in a military context until the end of Second World War. Subsequently, it was extended to manufacturing companies in order to determine all the activities aimed at ensuring the correct purchasing, moving and managing of materials. Logistics problems are also increasingly present in the service sector, for example in the distribution of some services such as water and gas, in postal services, in urban solid waste collection, in the maintenance of road and electricity networks and in the post-sales activities of manufacturing companies (*service logistics*).

重点解析 Notes and Comments

1. physical movement 为物流术语，可翻译为"实体流动"，不能按字面译为"物理流动"。

2. we mean the complex web of carriers, forwarders, bankers, information and communication companies, traders, and so on that facilitate international transactions, trades, and movements of goods and services. 我们指的是由运输商、货运代理、银行、信息和通信公司、贸易商等组成的复杂网络，它促进了国际交易、贸易以及货物和服务的流动。

这句英文比较长，that引导的定语从句修饰the complex web，翻译时应采用分译法，把从句拆分为单独的分句来翻译。

3. the flow of materials (and of the relative information) 括号中省略了the flow，其中the flow of materials为术语，意思是"物料流"，指原材料、外构件、半成品、零件、组件、部件，从加工、检验、装配、试验、存储、运输直到产品出厂的全过程，不能按字面意思译为"材料流"，the flow of information常常与之并列，译为"信息流"。

4. delivery of the finished products应译为"成品的交付"，其中delivery是物流术语，意思是"交付"，译为"传递"则不专业。

5. The origins of logistics are of a strictly military nature 一句中of a...nature 为固定词组，意为"本质"。例如：The legal concept of insanity is of a different nature from the medical.

6. The origins of logistics are of a strictly military nature. In fact, this discipline arose as the study of the methodologies employed to guarantee the correct supply of troops with victuals, ammunition and fuel and, in general, to ensure armies the possibility of moving and fighting in the most efficient conditions. 物流的起源具有严格的军事性质。事实上，这门学科起源于对保证军队正确供应食物、弹药和燃料的方法的研究，总的来说，是尽可能确保军队能在最高效的条件下行动和作战。

这句的methodologies不应按词典中的解释理解为"方法论"，而可以理解为"一套方法"。employed to...后面都作后置定语，来修饰methodologies。由于后置定语比较长，翻译时可以适当采用分译法，把to guarantee...和to ensure...拆分成单独的分句。

7. Logistics was applied exclusively in a military context until the end of Second World War. 这句可以把"直到第二次世界大战结束"提前到句首翻译，和上一句"在遥远的公元前20世纪"平行。

8. Logistics problems are also increasingly present...中的present不能翻译成"现在，如今"，而应作为形容词理解成"现存的"。increasingly 表示"越来越……"，这里可以翻译成四字词语"日益凸显"。

二、汉译英 Chinese-English Translation

选择供应商

物流系统规划越来越重视材料和服务的提供。在获得利润和提供给客户的服务水平方面，供应商管理是影响公司绩效的一个重要问题。为确保提供足够的物料和服务，公司通常会针对每种供应行为的不同替代方案进行评估。评估考虑的不仅是供应类型，还有公司与各供应商之间的关系。公司与多个供应商（及潜在供应商）就同一产品或服务建立良好的关系会带来便利，因为这样可以监测供应商效率并定期确定是否与之续签现有合同。对于特定产品或服务，选择单一供应商（唯一货源）或多个供应商（多个货源），这两种方案各有利弊。选择单一供应商的优点是鼓励供应商进行有针对性的投资，从而有助于开展有益合作，并使公司与供应商之间的物流流程一体化更加简便。但另一方面，这种方案加大了依赖供应商的风险，且不允许公司与其他货源进行比较。而选择多个供应商则会降低依赖的风险，并允许公司从竞争中获益，但协调多个供应商可能比较复杂。

供应商管理程序由以下主要步骤组成：

1. 定义潜在供应商；

2. 确定选择标准；

3. 选择供应商。

当公司尚无供应商组合时（例如，进入新市场时）或即将更新其当前供应商信息库时，公司应搜索供应商。搜索供应商可以使用多种信息来源：

● 专业期刊，其刊登的文章和广告可以用来收集有用信息，以比较其他供应商；

● 搜索引擎，网络上有关于供应商的大量信息；

● 贸易展览会，这是与潜在供应商会面并分析其产品和服务的良好机会；

● 有组织的会议，可以与供应商代表会面，以商定价格、交货时间和其他相关方面的问题。

对于潜在供应商，工厂的视察访问也可能会有用。

重点解析 Notes and Comments

1. 物流系统规划越来越重视材料和服务的提供。In logistics systems planning, an increasing attention is paid to the provision of materials and services.

"物流系统规划"并不是"重视"这个动作的发出者，所以不能作主语，按英文的逻辑应将"物流系统规划"译为状语，后面的无主句处理成被动语态。

2. 为确保提供足够的物料和服务…… In order to guarantee an adequate provision of materials and services...

原文中的动词"提供"在英译时转换成名词"provision"。该段落中多个"提供"转换成英语"provision"，体现了中文多用动词，而英语多用抽象名词的特点。

3. "这两种方案各有利弊" yields different advantages and disadvantages

该句译文中用了yield，意为"产生（某种结果）"。例如：The search for truth is beginning to yield fruitful results.

4. 选择单一供应商的优点是鼓励供应商进行有针对性的投资，从而有助于开展有益合作，并使公司与供应商之间的物流流程一体化更加简便。The first solution has the advantage of encouraging the supplier to carry on targeted investments, thus contributing to the development of a useful cooperation and simplifying the integration of the logistics processes between the company and the

supplier.

英语译文并未将"选择单一供应商"译为"selecting the sinlge supplier"或"having a single supplier",而是译为"the first solution";"而选择多个供应商"被译为"the second solution"。译文通过"the first ""the second "不仅避免了"选择供应商"字意的重复,而且更好地实现了英文上下文的衔接,使句子更加顺畅。

5. "供应商"的"信息库"可以译为"pool",例如"人才库"可译为a pool of talents。

第五节 课后翻译训练

一、将下列句子翻译成汉语 Translate the following sentences into Chinese

1. Logistics serves as an integrating function in supply chain management.

2. Their ships are the size and type of vessel these companies need, and they have the particular operating characteristics required to support the business of the owners.

3. All nations would like to export more than they import, in order to generate a positive balance of trade, which helps bolster both the country's currency and its employment.

4. They do so in order to control both the availability of carriage and the cost thereof and also to ensure that the right kind of ship is available to meet their special needs.

5. There are several costs associated with international logistics, and they are in addition to the price of the product.

6. What is experienced as the norm of logistics practice in the developed countries is often only an aspirational goal of logisticians in many other places in the world.

7. Port selection choices made by various logistical constituencies can play an integral role in the efficiency of cross-border trade.

8. The emergence of mega-ports for containerized shipments suggests that the relative power in port selection may be shifting to the ocean carriers.

9. The matrix structure(矩阵结构)couples the organization's functional

elements with its divisional elements.

10. The presence of several selection criteria to be jointly considered forces the decision maker to define their relative weights, with the aim of establishing their impact on the supplier selection.

二、将下列句子翻译成英语 Translate the following sentences into English

1. 经济形势和相对经济实力也影响着贸易模式。
2. 国际物流必须考虑文化、货币和运输系统的差异。
3. 隧道和桥梁之间的主要区别在于，隧道是在水道或山脉下方建造的，而桥梁是横跨水道建造的。
4. 发达国家的企业有很好的物流与运输专业人员、系统、基础设施。
5. 运河、隧道和桥梁对国际物流具有重要意义，因为它们减少了运输和贸易的障碍。
6. 私人船队归批发商或制造商所有，供其自主运载货物。
7. 许多国际运输需要决定空运或海运的运输方式。
8. 自由贸易区提供了吸引非国内投资的可能性，以创造就业机会，刺激经济发展。
9. 当一家公司必须同时处理几种产品时，物流系统不可避免地会变得更复杂。
10. 通常，在使用新产品期间，项目包含诸如规划、制造、物料流、交付和客户支持等活动。

三、将下列短文翻译成汉语 Translate the following passage into Chinese

Objectives of Logistics

The objectives of logistics can be characterized by three variables: costs, profits and service level.

Costs. The costs of logistics activities are the financial resources consumed by the company when carrying out these activities. They are divided into fixed and variable costs.

Profits. Logistics activities affect company profits, even though, contrary to costs, the impact of logistics operations on sales is difficult to quantify. For this reason, the sole objective of profit maximization is not very practical from the point of view of logistics.

Service level. The service level encompasses the overall degree of customer satisfaction and depends on numerous factors (indicated collectively as *marketing mix*), connected to the product characteristics, price, promotional offers and mode of distribution. It is possible to quantify the service level, as will be shown in this chapter, by using suitable indicators.

Company profits are directly connected to the service level offered to customers. For example, it has been experimentally tested that an effective and efficient organization of the distribution service yields a direct increase in market share. One possible objective of logistics is to minimize costs in a reference time horizon (e.g. a year), while keeping the service level unchanged. Alternatively, the objective could be to determine the optimal service level for maximum profit (difference between revenues and costs) in a reference period. In general, the maximization of profit is obtained for high (but less than maximum) values of service level.

The most widespread way of measuring the service level of a logistics system is through the quantification of the order-cycle time, defined as the time interval from the issuing of an order (or request of service) to the delivery of the product (or completion of the service). The main logistical components of the order-cycle time are the order processing time (checking for errors in the order, preparation of the shipping documents, updating of the store inventory etc.), the availability of the products in the warehouse, the assembly time of the products making up the order (withdrawal from a storage point or creation of packaging for transport) and the shipping time (movement of products from the storage point to delivery point, including loading and unloading of the goods).

四、将下列短文翻译成英语 Translate the following passage into English

物流系统的管理

在公司内部，物流系统的管理是指规划、组织和控制的横向过程。

规划是指根据物流系统的预定目标作出最佳决策。

组织是指组织公司结构图中直接参与物流活动的人力资源，以便有效、高效地实现公司目标。

控制是指按公司管理要求的质量、数量标准，测定物流系统的性能。若结果与目标不符,应采取纠正措施。

组织阶段

公司的组织决策决定了其责任和任务的分配。这些决策受不同因素的影响,例如其运营部门、公司文化(组织成员共同的信念、价值观和期望)、采用的技术(先进技术的使用越多,组织结构越精简)和公司规模(小公司通常有唯一的决策者,而中型公司则必须下放权力,通过职能来建立权力关系)。

公司的物流是公司的主要活动,可以采用组织结构的传统解释方法来说明:功能、部分和整体。

规划阶段

物流系统的规划通常考虑以下**决策领域**:预测、选址、供应、存储和配送。

预测是估计物流系统的不确定特征参数的过程。预测有助于正确确定物流系统的规模、生产能力和正确的库存水平,也有助于规划和制订生产计划、组织运输等。

选址是指确定设施最佳位置的活动,不论是物流系统的规划阶段,还是现有系统的重新组合,都需要选址。

供应是涉及购买原材料、半成品或供应服务的所有物流活动的决策范畴。这一范畴的决定很大程度上取决于公司的具体情况。

存储和配送是决策领域最重要的物流活动。物流规划可以在三个不同的决策层面上组织:战略、战术和运营。

控制阶段

控制物流系统效率,需要定义监控物流活动的指标,即**关键绩效指标**(KPI)。

应该注意的是,通常不会预先设定有效的KPI组。但这些指标的选择要取决于特定的物流系统,尤其取决于公司物流活动的重要程度,以及物流活动的目标性质。

本章课内翻译任务和课后翻译训练中的英汉和汉英翻译短文均选自:Gianpaolo Ghiani et al., *Introduction to Logistics Systems Management*, John Wiley & Sons, Incorporated, 2013; Donald F. Wood et al., *International Logistics*, AMACOM, 2002.

第十二章 财务会计翻译

财务会计（Financial Accounting）是对企业会计信息的核算与监督，对企业的财务状况与盈利能力等经济信息进行分析，为企业提供有效的决策信息，并积极参与企业管理，提高企业的经济效益。

国际会计是西方企业会计的一个最新发展。它是第二次世界大战以后，随着跨国公司的蓬勃发展、国际贸易的日益频繁和资本投资的日趋国际化而产生并日益发展起来的。它的最终目标是建立一套适用于全世界范围的会计原则和方法，实现各国会计的标准化。

财务会计在企业管理、成本核算、国际结算等方面都是不可缺少的内容。

本章简要介绍会计英语的概念、会计英语的语言特点以及翻译原则，涉及财务会计的基本概念以及现金流量表、平衡表等与财务会计相关的知识及其翻译实践。

第一节 会计英语的语言特点

"会计英语"包含会计与英语两个方面。会计有两层意思：一是指会计工作，二是指会计工作人员。我国的会计工作是指根据《中华人民共和国会计法》《中华人民共和国预算法》《中华人民共和国统计法》核对记账凭证、财务账簿、财务报表，从事经济核算和监督的过程，是以货币为主要计量单位，运用专门的方法，核算和监督一个单位经济活动的一种经济管理工作。会计工作人员是从事会计工作的人员，有会计主管、会计监督和核算、财产管理、出纳等人员。会计英语作为专门用途英语的一个分支，以英语为载体解决与完成会计实务中涉外的专业性问题和任务，以实现会计理论方法的交流与传播。

一、词汇特点

(一)专业术语丰富

大量会计术语的存在是会计英语词汇的第一大特点。术语(terminology)是在特定学科领域用来表示概念的称谓的集合,是各门学科中的专门用语。会计术语具有单义性、相对性与时代性等特点。

单义性是指在会计学科领域内,一个术语只表达一个特定的意思,即词义的单一特性。如:net assets, long-term liabilities, unearned revenues, contingent liabilities, retained earnings等,分别指净资产、长期负债、预收收入、或有负债、留存收益等。这些词意思相对固定,且只在会计英语中存在并使用。

相对性是指词语所表示的意思在逻辑上相对或相关联。如:debit/credit 借/贷, debtor/creditor 债务人/债权人, gains/loss 收益/亏损, revenue/expenses 收入/费用, preferred stock/common stock 优先股/普通股, assets/liabilities 资产/负债, current assets/fixed assets 流动资产/固定资产, appreciation/depreciation 升值/贬值, trade deficit/trade surplus 贸易逆差/贸易顺差, net weight/gross weight 净重/毛重, notes receivable/notes payable 应收票据/应付票据,等等。

时代性是指随着时代的发展和科学技术的进步,一些新思想、新观念和新产品不断涌现,会计英语里出现了大量新术语,如:electronic funds transfer 电子资金转账, electronic commerce 电子商务, future transaction 期货交易, supply chain management 供应链管理, online transaction processing 线上交易处理,等等。

(二)缩略词多

大量使用缩略词是会计英语词汇的第二大特点。有的缩略形式形成了紧密结构,凝固成为一个能自由运用的语言单位,叫作缩略词。会计英语中的缩略词具有含义明确、使用相对规范的特点。缩略词的表现形式很多,但主要有两种:一是首字母缩写词,如:BS(balance sheet资产负债表), FIFO(first-in, first-out先进先出分步成本法), FASB(Financial Accounting Standards Board财务会计准则委员会), IPO(initial public offerings首次公开募股发行), VAT(value added tax增值税), GST(goods and service tax货物和劳务税), CPA(certified public accountant注册会计师), ABS(asset backed securities资产支持证券),等等;二是截短词,如:Dr.(debit借), Cr.(credit贷), Acct.(account账户), Bal.(balance余额), Lia.(liability负债), Rev.(revenue收入), Exp.(expenses费用), Net inc.(net income净收入)和Cap.(capital资本),

等等。

(三) 派生词与复合词较为常见

派生词和复合词的使用是会计英语词汇的第三大特点。派生词是英语主要的构词法。此方法是借前缀或后缀制造出派生词，主要有名词、形容词和动词三种。会计英语中的前缀以表"否定"的为主，表示"前或再"的为辅。如：non-current assets非流动资产，non-current liabilities非流动负债，non-interest bearing note不带息的票据，non-operating revenues and expenses营业外收入和费用，unrecorded未入账的，prepaid预付，preferred stock优先股，repurchase回购，refund退还，等等。后缀以动词变化成名词和形容词为主，如：bank statement银行对账单，appropriation分拨，distribution分配，accounts receivable应收账款，bonds payable应付债券，taxable income应纳税所得额。还有表示身份的后缀，如：auditor审计员，cashier出纳员，creditor债权人，debtor债务人，issuer发行人，consignee承销人，consignor寄销人，等等。复合词就是将两个或三个单词以某种形式结合起来构成的词，会计英语中复合词也较为常见，如：paid-in capital实收资本，direct write-off method直接冲销法，double-entry accounting复式会计，first-in, first-out method先进先出法，going-concern assumption持续经营假设，long-term liability长期负债，short-term loans短期贷款，straight-line depreciation method直线折旧法，等等。

(四) 多数字表述

财务会计是对企业财务状况的记录、核算和监督，必然涉及大量的数字、百分比以及数学计算等。下列段落包含了数字、金额、百分比、货币单位以及表示成本、增加或减少等短语。

例1. HSBC has outlined plans to cut costs by as much as $3.5bn over the next three years as an attempt to boost its returns to shareholders. Analysts at Bank of America, Merill Lynch, said the envisaged cuts could shave close to 10pc off the bank's total cost base. Among the businesses that will benefit from the plan is wealth management, with HSBC targeting annual revenues of $4bn as it looks to grab a large slice of the profits from managing the money of the world's richest people, HSBC aims to shave costs by up to $3.5bn in three years.

译文：汇丰银行已制订计划，拟在未来三年内削减成本，金额多达35亿美元，以提高股东回报率。美国银行分析师梅里尔·林奇表示，预期的削减幅度可能会使该行的总成本基础削减近10%。汇丰银行的目标是三年内削减35亿美元的成本，年收入达40亿美元。汇丰管理着世界上最富有的一部分人的金钱，其目的就是希望从这项管理中获取大笔利润，因此，各项业务中，财富管理业务将受益于该计划。

二、句法及语篇特点

（一）陈述句为主，常使用祈使句和定语从句

会计是一门商业语言，也是现代商业的复杂性所必需的信息体系，其目的是为决策者作出商业决策提供信息。会计英语需要详细准确地记录和阐释商业交易的效果，所以以叙述事实的陈述句为主，表示建议、假设的祈使句多在举例时使用。

例2. Assume that a business owns assets of $1,000,000, borrows from creditor $200,000, and the owner invests $800,000.

译文：假设公司拥有资产 $1,000,000，向债权人借款$200,000，公司所有人投资 $800,000。

例3. Classify the effects of similar transaction in a manner that permits determination of the various totals and subtotals useful to management and used in accounting reports.

译文：按照一定的方法将相似商业交易的影响进行分类，并将其加总或部分加总，以便提供给管理层和编制会计报告。

此句还用了一个限制性定语从句that permits determination of the various totals and subtotals修饰manner。定语从句和非谓语动词作后置定语在会计英语中很常见，为的是准确客观地传递会计信息，也为了使句子结构紧密且意思明确。

例4. Decision made on information provided by accountants can materially affect the lives of clients and others, often referred to as third parties, which include employees, creditors, investors, supplies, customers, government and the general public.

译文：会计决定披露哪些信息可能对企业客户或其他人（我们称之为第三方）的生活产生重大影响。第三方包括雇员、债权人、投资者、供应商、顾客、政府和公众。

made on information作decision的后置定语，provided by accountants又作information的后置定语。third parties之后还有which引导的非限制性定语从句。

（二）多用现在时和被动语态

会计英语需要对会计领域的会计准则、客观事实和相关信息理论进行客观

描述，在描述的过程中强调的是某个行为或动作的发生过程、方式和产生的结果，而不强调行为者，所以在语篇中多使用现在时和被动语态。

例5. Bonds secured by pledge of specific assets are called mortgage bonds.

译文：以某种资产作保的债券称为抵押债券。

例6. Accounts receivable are classified as current assets.

译文：应收账款被归为流动资产。

例7. Cash discounts are used primarily to induce prompt payment by customers.

译文：现金折扣主要是为了吸引顾客尽早付款而提供的折扣。

第二节 会计英语的翻译原则

一、专业准确

会计英语中有大量的专业术语和缩略词，翻译工作者须具备基本的会计专业知识，也要多阅读有关会计的英汉语言文献，熟悉相关翻译技巧，多采用约定俗成、普遍认可的译法。平时多积累会计专业领域知识，在无法确定准确译文的时候，一定要查询会计专业词典，做到表达准确、清晰。

例8. Normally, a company may account inventories under the following methods:

A. Specific identification;

B. First-in, first-out (FIFO);

C. Last-in, first-out (LIFO);

D. Weighted average.

译文：通常，公司可以用下面的存货计价方法：

A. 个别计价法；

B. 先进先出法；

C. 后进先出法；

D. 加权平均法。

account作名词时在会计英语中的意思是"账目，账户"；作动词时是"计算，计费"的意思。所以这里翻译为"计价"。

例9. ABC Company is not able to say how much of $2,000 would be collected. But the accountants can estimate that clients could not pay $500 of accounts receivable. ABC Company should recognize the anticipated future write-off of receivable in the current accounting period. So the accountants need an adjusting entry.

译文：ABC公司不能说清2000美元能收到多少。但会计员能估计到客户不能支付500美元的应收账款。ABC公司应确认在当前会计期间应收账款未来的预计坏账核销。所以会计员需要调整分录。

accounts receivable和write-off都是会计英语专有词汇。entry在日常英语中是"进入"的意思，在会计英语中是"记录，分录"的意思。

例10. A note receivable usually includes the maturity date and rate of interest.

译文：应收票据通常包含到期日和利率。

note receivable是会计英语专有词汇。maturity和interest在日常英语中分别是"成熟"和"兴趣"的意思，而在会计英语中则是"到期"和"利息"的意思。

例11. This is a special offer and is not subject to our usual discounts.

译文：这是特惠报盘，我方通常的折扣不适用于此盘。

offer在日常英语中是"提供，提议"的意思，而在会计英语中，则是"出价，报价"的意思，而且有固定的汉语译法——报盘。

例12. By contrast, management accounting deals with similar activities, but is geared to providing information about the organization to its managers to help them run it.

译文：相比之下，管理会计虽然也处理与财务会计类似的科目，但其目的是向管理人员提供有关企业的信息，以帮助他们管理企业。

similar activities不能译成"类似的活动"，而应根据财务会计的专业性特点，译为"类似的科目"。be geared to 意思是"使适应"，这里表示目的。

例13. Financial accounting is concerned with the recording, processing and presentation of economic information after the event to those people outside the organization who are interested in it.

译文：财务会计是在会计事项发生后，记录和处理经济信息，供企业外部与企业利益相关的人查看。

be concerned with 意为"与……有关"，该句可以采取省译的方法，不把is concerned with直接翻译出来。the event 指的是会计事项，按照汉语习惯，时间状语需要前置。who引导的定语从句修饰前面的people，这里不是指感兴趣的人，而是指利益相关方。

例14. A statement of financial position records the assets, liabilities and equity of a business at a certain point in time.

译文：财务状况表（资产负债表）是反映企业在某一特定日期资产、负债和所有者权益情况的会计报表。

资产负债表又叫财务状况表，体现了一个企业在一定时期的财务状况。资产负债表中包含的会计要素有：资产、负债和所有者（股东）权益。资产负债表的编制运用了会计等式的概念。资产列在左边，相加得出资产合计；负债和所有者权益列在右边，相加得出负债与所有者权益合计。资产合计应等于负债和所有者权益之和。也就是说，会计等式必须平衡，因此取名平衡表（Balance Sheet）。asset 和 liability 使用复数时通常是资产和负债的意思。

二、结合语境

在语言翻译的过程中，语境的意义在于帮助阅读者理解词语和句子。结合语境的翻译，才能更好地传达原文的意思，能够让读者真正理解表述的内容。为了结合语境，有时需要实现语态的转化，有时需要实现词性的转化。

鉴于会计学科的科学性，被动句在会计文献里占据主导地位，无论是用英语表述会计理念时，还是在翻译会计信息和文献时，都应突出被动句的重要地位。但汉语中主动句更常见，所以翻译的时候除了可以结合语境，将被动句翻译成主动句，还可以少用"被"字句，而用别的词替代，如"所""受""遭""由""予以""加以"等被动表达方法，选择恰当的用词。

例15. Bonds can be sold or transferred before maturity. When the bonds are sold, the book value should be firstly confirmed at that very day, especially for those purchase data premium or a discount, and the actual purchase cost must be exactly determined with the premium or discount being amortized till the transferring date and the difference between investment revenue from sales of the bonds and their actual cost.

译文：长期债券可以在未到期之前（被）出售或转让。企业出售长期债券时，应当先确定转让日债券的账面价值，尤其是溢价或折价。购入的债券要把溢价或折价摊销到转让日为止，从而正确地确定各种债券的实际成本。然后按出售或转让的收入与出售债券实际成本的差额来确认价差损益。

本段的第一句翻译成被动语态，符合信息的客观性。第二句的前半部分如果还是直译成被动语态,会显得很生硬:"长期债券被出售时,债券的账面价值应当在转让日首先被确定,尤其是溢价或折价。"所以加上动作的执行主语"企业",更符合汉语习惯。而后面部分更不能直译成被动语态,用被动语态会造成语序不通、表达不清的情况。

例16. Assets are economic resources, which are measurable by money value, which are owned or controlled by an enterprise, including all property, rights as a creditor to others, and other rights.

译文:资产是以货币计量的由企业所拥有或控制的经济资源,包括各种财产、债权和其他权利。

本句由两个which引导的非限制性定语从句组成。定语从句中都用了被动语态,但在翻译的时候,没有直接用"被",而是用"以"和"所"来表示被动,更符合汉语习惯。

例17. A corporation is formed, or incorporated, under the laws of a state as a separate legal entity.

译文:股份公司是依据政府的法令,作为一个单独的法律实体而组建的。

本句中be formed和be incorporated,都不能直接翻译成"被"字句,form意思是"形成",incorporate意思是"并入",连在一起翻译成"组建"更为贴切。

结合语境,除了语态有时在主动和被动两者间转化外,词性也是如此。英语中习惯用名词来表达动作,而汉语中则多使用动词。

例18. Purchase of real estate and certain types of equipment often are financed by the issuance of mortgage notes payable.

译文:企业在购买房地产和某些固定资产时,常常是通过发行抵押票据的方式来筹集资金的。

原句是被动语态,purchase和issuance都是名词,结合语境,需要转化成主动语态,而这两个名词也应转化成动词。

例19. Depreciation means the allocation of the cost of a fixed asset to expense in the periods in which services are received from the asset.

译文:折旧是指将固定资产的成本分配到该资产提供服务期间的费用中。

allocation是名词"分配"的意思,翻译时应转化为动词。

例20. Accounting is the provision of financial information to managers and owners so that they can make business decisions.

译文:会计就是为了企业管理者和企业所有者能够作出经营决策,向他们如实提供财务信息的管理活动。

the provision of financial information 不能译为"财务信息的提供",而要把名词转化为动词,译为动宾结构"提供财务信息"。

例21. Accounting is the process of identifying, measuring and communicating economic information to permit informed judgments and decisions by users of the information.

译文:会计是甄别、计量和传达经济信息的过程,以便信息使用者作出明智的判断和决策。

to permit 不定式表目的,permit是"准许"的意思,这里不能直译,可以依照汉语惯用动词的特点翻译成动词短语"以便"。

三、顺畅达意

为了实现翻译的顺畅,要充分了解英汉两种语言的差异性。会计英语中复合句居多,复合句中定语从句和状语从句最为常见。根据英语语言习惯,定语和定语从句均后置,但状语和状语从句位置不固定,而汉语中的定语和状语往往置于被修饰词之前,即前置定语和状语。所以翻译时需要重新调整语序,以符合两种语言的习惯,从而使语句通顺、意思明确。

例22. Inventories refer to merchandise, finished goods, semi-finished goods, goods in process, and all kinds of materials, fuels, containers, low-value and perishable articles and so on (that stocked for the purpose of sale, production or consumption) during the operational process.

译文:存货是指在企业生产经营过程中,为销售或耗用而储存的各种资产,包括商品、产成品、半成品、在产品及各类材料、燃料、包装物、低值易耗品等。

that stocked for the purpose of sale, production or consumption 为 that 引导的定语从句,during the operational process 为时间状语,在翻译的过程中,应充分考虑中英两种语言的差异,调整语序,以达成译文的顺畅性。

例23. Current assets are assets that are expected to be converted to cash, sold, or consumed during the next 12 months or within the business's normal operating cycle if longer than a year.

译文:流动资产是预计在一年或长于一年的一个营业周期内变现、出售或消耗的资产。

that are expected to be converted to cash, sold, or consumed 为 that 引导的定

语从句，during the next 12 months和within the business's normal operating cycle都是时间状语，if longer than a year为if引导的条件状语从句，在翻译成汉语时都需要前置。

四、地道专业

在会计英语中，有大量表达数字的词语和数学表达式；有的词语只是普通词汇，并非会计专业词汇。翻译转换时用词要地道专业，同时还要对句子结构进行适当调整。

例24. Assets less liabilities will equal equity.

译文：资产减去负债等于所有者权益。

less表"较少，更少"。这里用作介词，表示"减去，除去"。表减法的词还有subtract, minus。

例25. Here the assets are added together and then the liabilities are taken away.

译文：表中资产相加，负债减除。

liabilities are taken away直译为"负债被拿走"，被谁拿走呢？此处应意译为"减除"。

例26. The net assets (i.e., assets less liabilities) equals the total equity employed by the business.

译文：净资产（即资产减去负债）等于企业拥有的总权益。

total equity意为"总权益"，而不要译为"全部权益"。employed by the business作为后置定语修饰前面的句子，翻译成汉语时需前置。employ 意为"雇佣"，这里应意译为"拥有"。

例27. This is prepared using a format where the total assets are totaled, these then equal total equity and liabilities.

译文：编制该表时，使用算式：资产金额总计=股东权益金额合计+负债金额合计。

This指财务状况表，total assets are totaled：资产总计。

这里是用语言描述一个等式，直接翻译成等式更一目了然。

例28. A statement of financial position (balance sheet) in a listed company format following international accounting standards is presented for Volkswagen in Appendix 2.5.

译文：附录2.5是大众公司的财务状况表（资产负债表），该表是依照国际会计准则，采用上市公司算式编制的。

此处 is presented 译为"编制"而不是"呈现"。

提升会计英语的翻译技巧，不仅需要熟悉既定的会计表达方式，包括专业术语，常见的缩略词、派生词和复合词；还需要了解在特定的会计语境中，会计英语所表现出的句法和语篇特点。在翻译英语句子的时候，需要结合语境，理解并拆分句子的语法结构和逻辑结构，理清句子的结构层次，并注意两种语言的差异性，力求做到译文专业准确，表达地道顺畅。

第三节　课内翻译任务

一、英译汉 English-Chinese Translation

Financial Accounting

The objective of general purpose of financial reporting is to provide financial information about the reporting entity that is useful to existing and potential investors, lenders and other creditors in making decisions about providing resources to the entity. Those decisions involve buying, selling or holding equity and debt instruments, and providing or settling loans and other forms of credit.

Financial accounting meets the common needs of a wide range of users. It does not, however, provide all the information users may need. An important additional role of financial accounting is that it shows the stewardship of management (i.e., how successfully they run the company). Shareholders may use this information to decide whether or not to sell their shares.

Financial accounting, along with management accounting, is one of the two main branches of accounting. Its main objective is to provide financial information to users for decision making. Shareholders, for example, are provided with information to assess the stewardship of managers so that they can then make decisions such as whether to buy or sell their shares. Understanding the accounting language is a key requisite to understanding accounting itself. Four accounting conventions (entity, money measurement, historical cost and periodicity) and three accounting concepts (going concern, accruals and consistency) underpin financial accounting. In addition, many people believe prudence is an important accounting concept.

At a still broader level, accounting allows managers to assess their organization's performance. It is a way of seeing how well they have done or, keeping the score. The main financial statements for sole traders, partnerships and companies are the income statement (profit and loss account) and the statement of financial position (balance sheet). These contain details of income, expenses, assets, liabilities and equity or capital. For companies (and often for other businesses), these two statements are accompanied by a statement of cash flows (cash flow statement), which summarizes a company's cash flows. Generally, the principal user is assumed to be the shareholder. These three statements are sent to shareholders once a year in a document called an annual report. However, managers need more detailed and more frequent information to run a company effectively. Monthly accounts and accounts for different parts of the business are, therefore, often drawn up.

Classification and recording of the monetary transactions of an entity in accordance with established concepts, principles, accounting standards and legal requirements by means of income statements, balance sheets (statements of financial position) and cash flow statements (statements of cash flow), during and at the end of an accounting period.

重点解析 Notes and Comments

1. Those decisions involve buying, selling or holding equity and debt instruments, and providing or settling loans and other forms of credit. 这些决定涉及股票和债务证券的购买、出售或持有，以及贷款和其他形式信贷的提供或结算。

debt instruments 在经济学中指的是债务证券，credit 在会计英语中意为"贷方、贷记"，与它对应的是debit，意为"借方、借记"。复式记账的英文为double entry bookkeeping，依据"有借必有贷，借贷必相等"的规则记账，无论是发生额还是余额都保持借贷平衡关系。

2. Shareholders, for example, are provided with information to assess the

stewardship of managers so that they can then make decisions such as whether to buy or sell their shares. 例如，向股东提供评估管理者管理才能的信息，以便他们随后可以作出决定。

stewardship 的本来意思是管理方法或组织方式，但评估的应该是经理的才能，而非方法或方式。then 为"随后，然后"的意思，可以省译。

3. It is a way of seeing how well they have done or, keeping the score. 这是一种查看他们的成绩或记分的方式。

how well they have done：做得有多好，可以精简翻译为"成绩"。

keeping the score：记分

4. sole traders, partnerships and companies

公司主要有三种形式：sole traders 独资企业，partnerships 合资企业，companies 股份公司。

5. income statement (profit and loss account) and the statement of financial position (balance sheet) 损益表和资产负债表

财务报告中有三个基本报表：损益表、资产负债表和现金流量表。收益表（income statement），公司的一种报表，报告某时期（通常为一年）的销售收入或所获收益，所售商品的合理的成本，还有剔除成本后所剩的利润（净收入），又称损益表（statement of profit and loss）。资产负债表（balance sheet）是反映企业在某一特定日期（如月末、季末、年末）全部资产、负债和所有者权益情况的会计报表，是企业经营活动的静态体现，根据"资产=负债+所有者权益"这一平衡公式，依照一定的分类标准和一定的次序，将某一特定日期的资产、负债、所有者权益的具体项目予以适当的排列编制而成。现金流量表（cash flow statement）是反映一定时期内（如月度、季度或年度）企业经营活动、投资活动和筹资活动对其现金及现金等价物所产生影响的财务报表。现金流量表是原先财务状况变动表或者资金流动状况表的替代物。它详细描述了公司的经营、投资与筹资活动所产生的现金流。

6. Monthly accounts and accounts for different parts of the business are, therefore, often drawn up. 因此，通常会编制月账和企业部门账目。

本句为被动语态，如果直译为"每月账目和企业不同部门的账目因此需要经常被制定"显得很生硬，可以改用符合汉语习惯的主动语态并调整语序。

7. Classification and recording of the monetary transactions of an entity in accordance with established concepts, principles, accounting standards and legal

requirements and their presentation, by means of income statements, balance sheets (statements of financial position) and cash flow statements (statements of cash flow), during and at the end of an accounting period. 在一个会计期间内和结束时，需要根据通行的财务概念、原则、会计准则和法律要求，使用损益表、资产负债表（财务状况表）和现金流量表对企业的现金交易进行分类和记录。

本句的主句为Classification and recording of the monetary transactions of an entity, in accordance with和by means of引导方式状语，during and at the end of 引导时间状语，根据汉语中状语前置的特点，翻译的时候需要调整语序。

二、汉译英 Chinese-English Translation

资金来源和用途

资金来源可分为两大类：权益（也称为资本）和债务。这些都是企业的负债，因为企业有最终偿还债务的义务。如果企业终止，则必须偿还贷款，甚至还必须偿还企业所有者投资的资本。同样，利润最终也不属于企业，而是属于所有者，因为整个企业都属于所有者。因此，获得的利润必须由企业支付给所有者。换句话说，过去赚取并由企业留存的利润是企业的负债。与此同时，企业可以将股本和债务资金用于购买各种商品和服务。有些购买的东西是暂时存在的，例如劳动力。购买员工一小时的时间所获得的直接收益随着一小时的结束而结束。而同样，用于支付电费的金额也不会列出来。请注意，劳动力和电力很可能已用于生产企业的产品，并且该产品的任何库存（股份）都将持续存在。但是，我们要区分的是，劳动力和电力不再以劳动力和电力的形式存在，而是作为存货价值的一部分。为了进行比较，企业将其资金用于某些项目的例子将持续存在。我们已经看到，这样的例子可能是库存。其他的例子还可能是建筑物、车辆或机械。这些本身持续存在并在未来为企业带来利润的项目称为资产。

重点解析 Notes and Comments

1. 资金来源可分为两大类。There are two broad classifications of funding sources.

这里的两大类，不能直译为two big classifications，应该是表示宽泛的broad。

2. 如果企业终止，则必须偿还贷款，甚至还必须偿还企业所有者投资的资本。Loans will have to be repaid and even the capital invested by the owners of

the business will have to be repaid to them if and when the business comes to an end.

本句强调的是偿还贷款和投资者资本的必要性，因此需要调换语序。

3. 过去赚取并由企业留存的利润是企业的负债。The profits made in the past and retained by the business are a liability of the business.

翻译成英文时"过去赚取并由企业留存的"应为profit的后置定语。

4. 企业可以将股本和债务资金用于购买各种商品和服务。The business can spend the equity and debt funds on buying a range of goods and services.

股本也可以用capital来表示，但capital比equity的适用范围小，一般像公司成立时的注册资本等称为capital，而equity则是公司运行过程中的资本，这里用equity更准确。

5. 购买员工一小时的时间所获得的直接收益随着一小时的结束而结束。The immediate benefit that comes from buying one hour of an employee's time ends at the end of that hour.

"直接收益"为主语。"购买员工一小时的时间所获得的"作后置定语，用that引导。

6. 为了进行比较，企业将其资金用于某些项目的例子将持续存在。For comparison, some of the things the business applies its funds to will have a continuing existence.

这里的"例子"不能直译，应该意译为泛指一些事情。"应用"是apply to，"持续存在"为continuing existence。

7. 这些本身持续存在并在未来为企业带来利润的项目称为资产。Items like this which have a continuing existence in themselves, and are of future benefit to the business, are called assets.

主语为"项目"，which引导定语从句，本句应使用被动语态。

第四节　课后翻译训练

一、将下列句子翻译成汉语 Translate the following sentences into Chinese

1. Current liabilities are obligations that must be paid within one year or within the operating cycle, whichever is longer.

2. The second and third digits in an account number indicate where the

account fits within the category.

3. The types of special journals used depend largely on the types of transaction that occur frequently in a business enterprise.

4. The way to save the labor is to divide the transactions into groups of like nature and to record them respectively in special journals.

5. Credit sales: a sale made on terms in which cash is to be paid at an agreed future date. At the debtors, who are customers to whom credit sales have been made, pay, the debtors' control account balance will be reduced.

6. Accountants have a responsibility to report favorable as well as unfavorable information and to refrain from taking actions which undermine an organization's legitimate and ethical objectives.

7. When this method is used, however, it is very difficult to follow individual transaction with the debit recorded in one account and the credit in another.

8. The quality of debits and credits in the ledger is tested periodically by preparing a trial balance, which lists the balance in each account after the posting process has been completed.

9. The first digit refers to the major financial statement classifications. Assets are often numbered beginning with 1, liabilities with 2, owners' equity with 3, revenue with 4, and expense with 5.

10. A control account is an account in general ledger that shows the total balance of all the subsidiary accounts related to it. Subsidiary ledger is a group of related accounts showing details supporting the related general ledger control account balance.

二、将下列句子翻译成英语 Translate the following sentences into English

1. 损益表有两种常见的格式：多步式损益表和单步式损益表。

2. 权责发生制要求会计员在提供劳务和发生费用时记录经济交易。

3. 就某一项经济业务来说，收入的金额相当于从客户那里收到的资产的价值。

4. 公司的现金流一般包括经营行为现金流、投资行为现金流及融资行为现金流。

5. 公司在由两人或更多的人所有且不以单独的法律实体形式组织时，被称为合伙。

6. 在调整分录全部记入日记账并过账后，需要编制调整后的试算平衡表。

7. 为了衡量收入，企业必须采用一些会计原则和概念，如会计期间、权责发生制、收入原则、配比原则。

8. 在传统的手工记账系统中，T字分类账经常被用到。T字分类账有两栏，借方在左，贷方在右。

9. 普通日记账（或称日记账）是按时间顺序在同一地方提供每一笔业务的完整记录与具体业务的借贷双方相联系的原始分录的记录。

10. 在实践中，工作底稿是为了便于编制正式的财务报表而编制的，是用以归集财务报表所需的账户余额及调整信息。

三、将下列短文翻译成汉语 Translate the following passage into Chinese

Accounting Assumptions or Concepts

There are four generally recognized potential accounting concepts. The international Accounting Standards Board recognizes two overriding underlying assumptions (going concern and accrual). The UK Companies Act, however, recognizes in addition two extra assumptions consistency and prudence. However, the IASB has severe reservations about prudence which is the most contentious of the concepts.

Going Concern

This concept assumes the business will continue into the foreseeable future. Assets, liabilities, income and expenses are thus calculated on the basis. If you are valuing a specialized machine, for example, you will value the machine at a higher value if the business is ongoing than if it is about to go bankrupt. If it were bankrupt the machine would only have scrap value.

Accruals

The accruals concept (often known as the matching concept) recognizes income and expenses when they are accrued (i.e., earned or incurred) rather than when the money is received or paid. Income is matched with any associated expenses to determine the appropriate profit or loss. A telephone bill owing at the accounting year even if it is paid in the next year. If the telephone bill is not received by the year end, then the amount of telephone calls will be estimated.

Consistency

This concept states that similar items will be treated similarly from year to year. Thus, consistency attempts to stop companies choosing different accounting policies in different years. If they do this, then it becomes more difficult to compare the results of one year to the next.

Prudence

This is the most contentious of the four accounting concepts. Indeed, the IASB in the latest version of its Conceptual Framework in 2010 has replaced it completely. Prudence introduces an element of caution into accounting. Income and profits should only be recorded in the books when they are certain to result in an inflow of cash. By contrast, provisions or liabilities should be made as soon as they are recognized, even though their amount may not be known with certainty. Prudence is contentious because it introduces an asymmetry into the accounting process. Potential incomes are treated differently from potential liabilities. Some accountants believe that prudence is an out-of-date concept, while others feel that it is needed to stop management providing an over-optimistic view of the accounts. However, the IASB feels that prudence conflicts with a neutral view of accounts. It is, therefore, undesirable as it introduces bias into accounting.

四、将下列短文翻译成英语 Translate the following passage into English

损 益 表

损益表，最简单地说，就是超时记录企业的收入和支出。收入减去支出等于利润。如果支出大于收入，就会发生损失。重要的是（如《真实世界观察》所示），即使对于世界上最大的公司，也要确保收入（或利润）超过支出（或成本）。损益表中的净利润（或净亏损）被添加（或从中减去）成为财务状况表中的权益。多年来，公认的术语已经发生了变化。利润表被正式称为损益表。根据国际财务报告准则，持续经营产生的利润，如销售和其他综合性收益[例如，外汇换算收益、财产估价和精算收益（源于养老金）]是分开的。

国际会计准则1批准两类报表。一类报表称为"综合收益表"（将持续经营的利润和其他综合收益结合在一起）。另一类可以提供两份表格。首先是一份关于持续经营的损益表,然后是一份综合损益表。鉴于这本入门书的性质,我通常使用损益表,因为小型企业(独资经营者、合资企业和非上市有限公司)通常没有其他综合性收入。但是,对于上市公司,即使我在本书中未对"其他综合收益"进行任何深入的探讨,我有时也会使用"综合收益表"作为一份单独的报表,显示诸如外币收益之类的项目。

本章课内翻译任务和课后翻译训练中的英汉和汉英翻译短文均选自:Michael Jones, *Accounting for Non-Specialists*, John Wiley and Sons Ltd., 2002.

第十三章 电子商务翻译

电子商务（E-Business/E-Commerce）通常是指在全球各地广泛的商业贸易活动中，在因特网开放的网络环境下，基于浏览器（服务器）应用方式，买卖双方不见面地进行各种商贸活动，实现消费者的网上购物、商户之间的网上交易和在线电子支付，以及各种商务活动、交易活动、金融活动和相关的综合服务活动的一种新型商业运营模式。

电子商务，是融计算机科学、市场营销学、管理学、经济学、法学和现代物流于一体的新型交叉学科。联合国国际贸易程序简化工作组对电子商务的定义是：采用电子形式开展商务活动，它包括在供应商、客户、政府及其他参与方之间通过任何电子工具，如EDI、Web技术、电子邮件等共享非结构化商务信息，并管理和完成在商务活动、管理活动和消费活动中的各种交易。

本章介绍电子商务英语的基本特征及其翻译技巧，涉及电子商务的基本概念、电子支付方式、电子商务模式和电子商务集成等方面的知识和英汉翻译实践与技巧。

第一节 电子商务的语言特点

一、词汇特点

（一）词汇的跨学科性

电子商务英语词汇涉及众多的行业领域，除了计算机和网络技术的大量专业术语外，还包括商务贸易、广告、银行、零售、旅游、出版、证券等诸多行业的专业词汇，以及电子商务本身的专业术语。因此，它具有明显的跨学科性。例如，常见的词汇有registration（登记）、rate sheets（房价表）、tariff（旅馆、饭店或服务公司的价目表）、cancellation（取消预订）等；还有频繁出现的经济学术语，例如，demand curve（经济增长分析中的需求曲线）、price index（价格指数）、

inflation（通货膨胀），fluctuation（价格浮动），Gross Domestic Product（GDP，国内生产总值）等。

（二）新词语的创造

虽然电子商务英语大多具有较强的专业性，语言比较正式，但是由于当今的电子商务以网络媒体为支撑，受到网络语言追求新奇独特和轻松活泼特点的影响，出现了一些复合变异的新词语，例如，加前缀构成的单词，如multi-（多，如multimedia，多媒体），hyper-（超级，如hypercard，超级卡片），super-（超级，如super-pipeline，超流水线），缩写E-和其他词语结合构成新词（如E-retailing，电子化零售），online-（网上的，如online publishing，网上出版），cyber-（网络的，如cybersquatting，抢注域名）；加后缀构成的单词，如-able（可能的，如portable，便携），-ware（物件，如hardware，硬件）。

（三）名词连用

所谓名词连用是指名词中心词前可有许多不变形态的名词，它们是中心词的前置形容词修饰语，被称为扩展的名词前置修饰语。电子商务英语中出现大量名词连用，是为了避免使用过多的从句结构或介词短语结构，有效地简化语言结构。例如：quantity discounts（数量折扣）相当于discounts which are calculated in proportion to the quantity of the products purchase, logistics network（物流网络），order initialization（订单初始化），internet procurement system（因特网采购系统），transport level protocol reliability（传输层协议可靠性），approval cycle/channels（受理周期/渠道），availability check（有效性核查）。而有些名词连用需要根据各个名词之间的内在逻辑关系和名词连用所表达的整体意义灵活翻译，例如：theft and fraud losses相当于losses caused by theft and fraud（on the internet）[由于（网上）盗窃和欺诈行为造成的损失], order fulfillment cycle time（根据订单交货的周期）。

（四）使用缩略术语和简略词

电子商务英语中有许多缩略词，它们由主干单词的首字母组成。这些词的词义单一、简洁明了、使用规范，同时又在表达上节省时间，提高了效率。如：AWB（air waybill, 空运提单），A/W（actual weight, 实际重量）。在贸易实务中，缩略词和简略词表明了双方在合同中一般会明确使用的解释规则，使合同标准化；同时，用简短的文字说明买卖双方在货物交割中的责任、费用和风险划分，从而易于划分交易双方的责任，解决纠纷；另外，还省略了长篇的说明文字，使合同简洁明了。但需注意，同一写法的贸易术语的解释也会不尽相同，有时甚至出入很大,因为存在几个不同的《国际贸易术语解释通则》的修订版本,因此需对合同的附加语句加以注意。

(五)符号词

电子商务英语中有时将数字与英语字母连用,以数字代表相应的英语词来构成新词,最常见的是以"2"代表"to"。例如:B2B(Business to Business,企业与企业之间的电子商务),B2C(Business to Consumer,企业面向消费者的网上零售业务),C2C(Consumer to Consumer,消费者之间的电子商务),C2B(Consumer to Business,消费者通过互联网向企业出售个人物品)。

(六)合词法

合词法是把两个或两个以上的词语按一定的顺序组合构成新词。合词法构成的新词称为复合词。电子商务英语中有不少复合词,这类词语信息量大、形式简练且大都为分写式(有连字符)复合词。例如:EC-enabled(已经实施电子商务的),EC-friendly(有良好电子商务环境的),point-to-point(点对点的),end-to-end(终端到终端的),just-in-time(manufacturing)[零库存(生产)],value-added-service(增值服务),store-and-forward(存储转发),return-on-investment(metric)[投资回报(体系)],brick-and-mortar(离线经营的),click-and-mortar(混合经营的),front-user(前端用户)。

(七)用词生动活泼

电子商务英语虽有较强的专业性,语言比较正式,但因为电子商务是以网络媒体为支撑而发展起来的,所以电子商务英语也受到网络语言轻松活泼、追求新颖独特等特点的影响。

例1. The network needs greater capacity to deal not only with increased traffic but also with the advent of **bandwidth hungry service**.

译文:电子商务网络系统需要更大的带宽容量,以便容纳更多的网络流量和对带宽要求较高的服务。

原文用bandwidth hungry service来表示service that requires greater bandwidth, hungry一词用在这里不仅生动形象,而且轻松诙谐。

例2. A corresponding fear is that such trends could lead to an economy of information "haves" and "have nots" on a national, regional, and global scale.

译文:随之而来的担心就是这样的趋势可能会导致因信息技术发展水平不同而在一个国家、一个地区和全球范围内造成贫富不均的情况。

原句中"'haves' and 'have nots'"是一个非常生动形象的短语,意思是

"穷人和富人"，而在这句话中，an economy of information "haves" and "have nots" 指的是"因信息技术发展水平不同而……造成的贫富不均的情况"，可谓言简意赅、形象直观，而又新颖独特、富有创意。

（八）词项重复

电子商务英语中，词义相同或相近的词汇经常重复出现，中间用and, or或者and/or连接，例如，all and any（全部），null and void（无效），terms and condition（条款），losses and damages（损失）等。这种重复能使句意得到强调，并在上下文之间建立联系，达到准确无误的目的。通过这些词汇之间的词义相互补充和完善，保证了表述的准确性和严密性。重复关键词也有助于提高准确性，即避免使用代词来指代前面提到的人或事物，这一点与汉语非常相似。例如，除了在it is important that之类的结构中，代词it几乎见不到。

二、句法特点

（一）一般现在时的出现频率较高

电子商务英语所描述的多为一些事实，陈述客观现象或解释科学术语、贸易行为等，因此多使用一般现在时。

例3. In the United States, there are a number of hubs where the backbone intersects with regional and local networks and where the backbone owners connect with one another.

译文：美国有许多网络中心，因特网主干与区域性网络、地方性网络交叉，主干网络拥有者也在此处彼此连接。

（二）常用被动语态

被动语态也是电子商务英语中一种常用的句式形态。

例4. The firms that provide the lowest level of service in the multi-tiered Internet architecture by leasing Internet access to home owners, small businesses, and some large institutions are called Internet Service Providers (ISP).

译文：在多层次因特网体系中，通过向家庭出租因特网访问通道提供最低水平服务的公司、小型企业和一些大机构叫作因特网服务提供商（ISP）。

此例中的被动语态用来解释"因特网服务提供商"。

（三）条件从句的使用率较高

电子商务英语中的条件从句用来表示在某种条件下某事发生后可能产生的后果，常用连词if引导。

例5. If customers trust that the web is safe and that personal and transactional information remains private, they will gather to E-commerce in large groups.

译文：如果顾客相信某个网站是安全的，且能保护个人隐私和交易信息隐私，这个网站就会有很多顾客进行电子商务交易。

例6. On condition that yours is an E-business, your relationship with your customers will be altered.

译文：如果你的生意成为电子商务，那你和客户的关系将会发生变化。

（四）常用情态动词

电子商务英语中常用的情态动词主要有can, must等，用在比较正式的句子中，所述内容与法律法规相关或陈述某些客观事实。

例7. In addition to these professional bodies, the Internet must also conform to the laws of the sovereign nation-states in which it operates, as well as the technical infrastructures that exist within the nation-state.

译文：除了这些专业团体，因特网还必须符合所在的主权民族国家的法律，以及这个民族国家现有的技术基础。

例8. Any method that can address the lower or higher end of the price continuum or that can span one of the extremes and the middle has a chance of being widely accepted.

译文：任何支付方式都应该有消费最低或最高的限用额度，或是能够超出一个极值点和中间点，这样的支付方式才能被广泛接受。

第二节　电子商务英语翻译技巧

在翻译电子商务文本时，除了具备一定的电子商务知识，还需要根据电子商务的词汇特征和句法特征，合理运用英汉翻译的一般技巧，如词性转换、顺译法、逆序译法、分译法和合译法以及省译等翻译技巧。

一、词性转换

例9. The impact of E-commerce is especially expressed in industries engaged in the production of computers, software and computer equipment and other elements necessary for realization of E-commerce.

译文：电子商务的影响尤其表现在从事计算机、软件和计算机设备生产的行业上,以及实现电子商务所需的其他要素方面。

realization of E-commerce为名词短语,由于英语为静态语言,使用名词较多,翻译时可转化为动词,译为"实现电子商务",这样更符合汉语的表达习惯。

例10. Promotion is much cheaper. It is easier to achieve publicity on the Internet. There are more opportunities to adapt to customer needs, and with all that, the customer is enabled easier purchases carried out from an armchair, with no time limit (nonstop), without affecting the sales staff in the decision-making and various other benefits.

译文:在互联网上宣传更容易,有更多的机会适应客户需求,而且客户坐在椅子上即可进行购买,没有时间限制(不间断),不影响销售人员的决策,另外还有各种其他好处。

promotion和purchases都是名词,此处译为动词。publicity为抽象名词,意为"公开性",该句如直译为"网络上更容易达到公开性",则不符合汉语表达习惯。汉语中倾向于使用具体名词或动词,因此,将publicity译为"宣传",动词achieve省略不译。

例11. For example, a person can pay their bill electronically or transfer money electronically among their accounts to their child's college fund.

译文:例如,可以通过电子的方式支付账单,或进行转账,或将钱转到孩子的学校账户上。

该句中副词electronically不宜直译为"电子方面地"或"电子方式地",应进行词性转换,译为"以电子的方式"。

例12. 电商直播增长主要是由于直播在中国三线、四线城市消费者中具有强大的吸引力。

译文:The growth of E-commerce livestreaming is largely due to its strong appeal among consumers in lower-tier cities in China.

该句原文中有三个动词,分别为"增长""是"以及"具有",翻译时只能保留一个主要动词,另外两个则要进行词性转换,"增长"转化为名词,译为growth,"具有"则省略未译。

二、顺译法

当英语长句的表达顺序与汉语的表达习惯相同时,按照动作发生的时间顺序,可以考虑按照原文的顺序进行翻译。

例13. In the Internet Era, any company or person with little investment, such as a computer, a browser software, a modem, and an Internet account can soon get into the virtual market on the web to compete with any other company, no matter how far distance, how large scale, or how successful the other companies are.

译文：在互联网时代，任何公司或个人只需要极少的投资，比如，一台计算机、一个浏览软件、一个调制解调器和一个互联网账号，就可以迅速地进入网上的虚拟市场，与任何其他的公司竞争，无论他们离你有多远，规模有多大或者运作有多么的成功。

三、逆序译法

当有的英语长句的表达顺序与汉语表达习惯不太相同，甚至完全相反时，可以考虑逆着原文的顺序进行翻译。

例14. A number of companies are attempting to ensure the security issues involved in handling payments on the Internet by establishing electronic clearing systems.

译文：许多公司正在试图通过建立电子转账系统以确保处理网上支付等问题的安全性。

需要逆序翻译的句子中通常含有各种状语从句，如原因状语从句、时间状语从句或由介词短语构成的状语成分，或含有后置定语成分，需要将状语或定语部分提前，适当调整语序。

四、分译法

当英语长句的主句与其从句或其修饰词语之间的关系不是非常密切时，可以把从句或修饰词语部分分解成很小的短语来翻译。但是在将长句拆开翻译时，中文应加上"这""其""它们"之类的关联词，使句子前后连贯、通顺流畅。

例15. A splash screen is an initial Website page used to capture the users' attention for a short time as a promotion or lead-in to the site's home page or to tell the users what kind of browser and other software they need to view the site.

译文：Splash屏幕是一个初始的页面，用来在短时间内引起用户的注意。它可作为一种提升工具，也可以用来介绍网站主页，或者告知用户该使用何种浏览器以及他们浏览网站所需要的其他软件。

此例句在as处将全句分为两个分句，前句提出splash屏幕这个概念，后句具体解释它的作用，分句之间用指示代词"它"来衔接。

例16. Today, companies have a lot more information than before, which allows them to take advantage of this information as efficiently as possible, to segment the market, and to adapt their products or services to potential customers or service users as well as possible.

译文：如今企业的信息比以前多得多，因此能够有效地利用这些信息，细分市场，并尽可能地使其产品或服务适应潜在客户或服务用户。

该句中包含一个非限定性定语从句，表示因果关系，其中，动词allow有三个宾语，分别为to take advantage, to segment the market以及to adapt their products。翻译时，需化整为零，单独翻译定语从句。

例17. Unfortunately, paying online with some instruments that people use offline, namely cash, credit card, debit card, or paper check, may be too slow, inefficient, or expensive for online payment.

译文：很遗憾，使用和线下同样的支付媒介，如现金、信用卡、借记卡或纸质支票进行线上支付可能会很慢、效率低或者很贵。

该句中主语较长，翻译时需将其单独处理，翻译为句子，这样更符合汉语的表达习惯。

五、合译法

当英语的长句不太适合按照上述某种方法进行翻译时，可以着眼篇章，以逻辑分析为基础，综合使用顺译法、逆序译法、分译法，按照汉语句子的表达习惯翻译英语长句。

例18. Packet switching is a method of slicing digital messages into parcels called "packets", sending the packets along different communication paths as they become available and then reassembling the packets once they arrive at their destination.

译文：分组交换是传输数据的一种方法，它先将数据信息分割成许多称为"分组"的数据信息包；当路径可用时，通过不同的通信路径发送；当到达目的地后，再将它们组装起来。

此例句将一个长的定语从句sending the packets along different communication paths as they become available, and then reassembling the packets once they arrive at their destination拆分成几个并列的分句，可翻译为："当……""再……"。

例19. Behind this formal definition are three extremely important concepts that are the basis for understanding the Internet: packet switching, the TCP/IP communications protocol, and client/server computing.

译文：在这个正式定义的背后，隐含着三个极其重要的概念：分组交换、TCP/IP（传输控制协议/网际协议）通信协议和客户机/服务器计算技术，它们是理解因特网的基础。

本句在翻译时综合使用了顺译法、分译法，将Behind this formal definition are three extremely important concepts that are the basis for understanding the Internet从that从句处拆开，前面用顺译法翻译，中间插入三个concepts的译文，最后翻译that从句。

六、结构调整

由于英汉思维的差异，英语和汉语的句子结构顺序也存在着差异，不仅英译汉需要进行结构调整，汉译英也需要进行结构调整，可采用分译、合译、顺译、逆译等手段，有时候还要根据句子的特点增减词汇，补充句子结构中的缺损，使句子含义明晰化。

例20. 虽然电商直播在中国已经存在了好几年，但它是在2019年开始腾飞的。很能说明问题的情况是，在去年的双十一购物节中，阿里巴巴的淘宝电商直播就产生了28.5亿美元的销售额——占这一天总销售额的7.5%左右。

译文：While E-commerce livestreaming has existed in China for several years, it took off in 2019, which was made clear during this year's Singles Day shopping festival when livestreaming on Alibaba's Taobao livestreaming platform generated $2.85 billion in sales — around 7.5 percent of the day's total sales.

该句原文由两个句子构成，第二句用数据进一步解释第一句，因此，翻译时要对句子结构进行调整，将第二句处理成定语从句。同时，将第二句的时间状语"去年的双十一购物节"处理为定语从句中的中心词，主句处理为该中心词的定语从句。结构上如此转换，译文更符合英语的表达习惯。

例21. ……通常从多家供应商招标购买间接材料和机器配件，属于大批量、单品价值低的业务。

译文：...It usually solicits bids from a variety of suppliers for indirect materials and machinery replacement parts, which is a business of large scale and low single value.

原句由两个句子构成，译文中将两个句子的隐性关系显性化，将第二个句子处理为非限定性定语从句。其中"大批量""单品价值低"两个定语用with处理成两个并列的名词短语。

例22. 每项交易都需要调出相关的设计图纸，影印后和其他规格文档一起邮寄给对招标感兴趣的供应商。

译文：The relevant blueprints, photocopy, and other material specification documents need to be sent to the suppliers who might be interested in the bids in every transaction.

原句为汉语中较为典型的无主句，翻译时可选择以下方法：（1）运用被动结构；（2）名词结构作主语；（3）运用there be结构；（4）使用形式主语。本句中，采用了第（1）种处理方式。

例23. 从应标到确认是否获得GE照明的合同时间缩短，供应商非常满意，这使得他们更容易制订生产计划。

译文：Suppliers welcome the reduced time lag between submitting the bid and learning whether GE Lighting will award them the contract; this makes their production planning easier.

汉语为意合语言，句中若有叙事部分和表态部分，往往叙事部分（事实、描写等）在前，表态部分（判断、结论等）在后，英语的顺序往往相反。因此翻译该句时，将"供货商非常满意"放至句首。

例24. EDI是一项涉及面极广、影响极为深远、在世界范围内蓬勃发展的电子应用技术。

译文：EDI is an electronic application technology of booming development in the world, which involves wide scope and professional influence.

句中如有描写性或限制性部分，汉语多用作谓语，少作定语，而英语则常常用作定语，少作谓语。

第三节　课内翻译任务

一、英译汉 English-Chinese Translation

Guide to E-Business Integration

Building an E-business is a complex undertaking. The key to long-term success is an agile E-business infrastructure that can quickly and easily accommodate changes in business processes and technology. Creating such an infrastructure demands the integration of diverse technologies, applications, and business semantics.

While many vendors claim to have a "comprehensive, end-to-end solution", in reality most offer functionality in specific areas. E-business infrastructures will commonly be multi-vendor solutions. The challenge is to match your individual business requirements to specific vendor offerings. This, however, is no easy task when all the vendors and their products sound alike.

×××has developed an E-business Integration Road Map to guide companies in distinguishing among the vendor offerings. The road map is based on stringent criteria in various technology areas.

Enterprise Application Integration

An EAI solution integrates different applications through a common API. It includes data translation and transformation, rules-and content-based routing, and application connectors or adaptors to packaged applications such as SAP and PeopleSoft. Some EAI vendors have more support for legacy integration than others do. Many legacy integration tools require custom programming and are responsible for most of the cost of implementation. Companies should evaluate performance and adaptability requirements before choosing a legacy integration solution.

重点解析 Notes and Comments

1. building an E-business表示要建立起一个电子商务的环境或公司，business一词当复数用时应指实体。另外，E-commerce和E-business概念不同，前者只包含买卖的部分，但后者则包括所有商务流程，不过两个词一般都翻译成"电子商务"。

2. infrastructure在本文中属于专业技术词语，要按规定的译法翻译，不能自创译法，如此处就应翻译成"基础结构"或"基础设施"，而且下面再出现时也应该用同样的词，保持一致。

3. integration在计算机文本的语境中一般翻译成"集成"，所以"结合""整合"，以及国际政治经济领域常用的"一体化"之类的译法在计算机和网络语境中都不合适。也就是说，只要这个词用在这个场合，都是译为"集成"，当然如果不用在技术语境中则另当别论。

4. application在计算机领域，作为单数使用时，一般情况下表示"应用"之意，如application software（应用软件，应用程序）；作为复数时（applications），一般翻译成"应用程序"。

5. While many vendors claim to have a "comprehensive, end-to-end solution"…尽管许多供应商声称自己具备"综合全面的端对端解决方案"……

这里的专业术语必须按规定翻译，end-to-end就是"端对端"，solution就是"解决方案"，没有什么通融的余地。其他的"点对点""解决办法"等译法都不合适。

6. …and application connectors or adaptors to packaged applications such as SAP and PeopleSoft.

这里的to packaged applications是表示与打包应用程序连接的连接器或适配器，而SAP and PeopleSoft是这种打包应用程序的例子，该句应理解为包括连接诸如SAP及PeopleSoft等打包应用程序的程序"连接器"或"适配器"。

7. Many legacy integration tools require custom programming and are responsible for most of the cost of implementation. 许多旧系统集成工具需要自定义编程，因此会占用大部分实施成本。

这里的legacy integration表示现在已在使用的或已经老旧的系统的集成，此处其实省略了system，翻译时加进去才更清楚。responsible for不宜按字面意思翻译成"负责承担"。responsible for most of the cost of implementation的大意一看就懂，翻译时应摆脱原文的束缚，译为"占用了大部分的实施成本"。

二、汉译英 Chinese-English Translation

B2B模式

B2B模式指的是企业间利用互联网技术进行的交易。其交易活动的内容主要包括企业向其供应商进行的采购、企业向其客户进行的批量销售、企业与其合作伙伴之间的业务协调等。从实现方式来看，企业可以通过自建网站直接开展B2B交易，也可以借助电子中介服务来实现B2B交易。自建网站开展B2B的企业多为产业链长、业务伙伴多或自身专业性强的大企业、跨国公司，如飞机、汽车、计算机等行业的制造商以及大型批发、零售企业等，主要用于公司自身的业务和对供应商、销售商的服务；而借助中介服务实现B2B的企业则多为中小型企业。在表现形式上，B2B主要分为以企业为中心的B2B和电子市场两种。以企业为中心的B2B模式又分为卖方集中模式和买方集中模式。由卖家企业面向多家买家企业搭建平台销售其产品称为卖方集中模式。而由买家企业面向多家供应商搭建平台采购原材料、零部件、经销产品或办公用品则称为买方集中模式。而电子市场的B2B模式则可分为垂直和水平两种类型。垂直市场专门针对某个行业，如电子行业、汽车行业、钢铁行业、化工行业、纺织行业等。水平市场则是普遍适用于各个行业的宽泛的交易平台。

B2B模式自产生至今，无论是实践还是理论的发展都日益成熟，其交易额和交易量也远远大于其他四种电子商务模式，因而在电子商务中占据着重要的地位。无论是生产制造型企业还是流通贸易型企业，B2B电子商务在帮助改善信息、物流和资金管理以及降低生产、经营和管理成本等方面都发挥着显著作用。

重点解析 Notes and Comments

1. B2B模式指的是企业间利用互联网技术进行的交易。

进行交易，常见搭配有conduct transactions或carry on transactions。该句中，"利用互联网技术进行的交易"如直译为use Internet technology to conduct transactions，显得累赘，译为conduct transactions with the help of Internet technology更为自然。

2. 自建网站开展B2B的企业多为产业链长、业务伙伴多或自身专业性强的大企业、跨国公司，如飞机、汽车、计算机等行业的制造商以及大型批发、零售企业等，主要用于公司自身的业务和对供应商、销售商的服务……Most of the enterprises who host the website in-house to serve for their own business and their suppliers and sellers are generally large enterprises or multinational companies with a long industry chain, or with many business partners, or engaging themselves in specialized areas such as manufacturing planes, automobile, computer as well as large wholesaling and retailing, etc.

该句原句为长句，翻译时如按照原来的结构翻译，则不符合英语的表达习惯。译文以"企业为大型企业、跨国公司以及大型批发、零售企业等"为主要结构，将"自建网站开展B2B"及"主要用于公司自身的业务和对供应商、销售商的服务"合并作定语置于主语之后，译文主次分明，结构清晰，体现了英语的表达特点。

3. 改善信息、物流和资金管理improve information management, logistics, and finance management

第四节　课后翻译训练

一、将下列句子翻译成汉语 Translate the following sentences into Chinese

1. Few innovations in human history encompass as many potential benefits as E-commerce does to organizations, individuals, and society. These benefits are just starting to materialize, but they will increase significantly as E-commerce expands.

2. E-commerce is perceived not as a product but rather as an agent that will transform every way products and services are created and sold.

3. Banner advertising is the most commonly used form of advertising on the Internet. There are two types of banners: keyword banners and random banners.

4. A number of factors come into play in determining whether a particular method of E-payment achieves widespread acceptance.

5. When a credit card is used for payment, the merchant pays a transaction fee of up to about 3 percent of the item's purchase price (about a minimum fixed fee).

6. With the development of our society and productivity, especially with the continuous innovation of science and technology in different periods, the forms and contents of commerce are changing constantly based on the demands of the market.

7. Electronic commerce expands the marketplace to national and international markets. With minimal capital outlay, a company can easily and quickly locate more customers, the best suppliers, and the most suitable business partners worldwide.

8. Electronic commerce allows reduced inventories and overheads by facilitating pull-type supply chain management. In a pull-type system, the process starts with customer orders and uses just-in-time manufacturing.

9. Although establishing and maintaining a Website on the Internet has costs of its own, the price of using the Web versus other sales channels is substantially reduced. As an advertising medium, promotion using a Web site results in the sale of ten times the number of units with one-tenth of the advertising budget.

10. One of the biggest commercial advantages of the Internet is a lowering of

transaction costs, which usually translates directly into lower prices for the consumer.

二、将下列句子翻译成英语 Translate the following sentences into English

1. 电子商务，顾名思义就是建立在电子技术和网络技术基础上的商业运作，是利用电子技术所提供的工具手段实现其操作过程的商务活动。

2. 完整的电子商务内涵包括：前提条件、信息内容和集成信息资源、人的知识和技能、系列化系统化的电子工具、以商品交易为中心的各种经济（商业）事务活动。

3. 支持大数据、云计算、人工智能、量子计算（quantum computing）等新技术应用，不断塑造亚太（the Asia-Pacific region）发展新动能新优势。

4. 1991年，由国务院电子信息系统推广应用办公室牵头，发起成立"中国促进EDI应用协调小组"，标志着电子商务已经在我国起步。

5. 电子商务扩大了企业的竞争领域，使竞争从常规的广告、促销、产品设计与包装等扩大到无形的虚拟市场的竞争。

6. 电子商务的安全是个非常重要的问题，只有网上交易做到了安全可靠，客户才能接受和使用这种交易方式，电子商务才能顺利开展下去。

7. 电子商务最明显的优势就是增加了贸易机会，降低了贸易成本，提高了贸易效率。它大大改变了商务模式，带动了经济结构的变革，对现代经济活动产生了巨大的影响。

8. 发展电子商务需要政府的推动，必然对政府的管理工作提出新要求和新改变，电子政务的发展正成为政府提高管理效益，实现公平、公正和公开政务的重要形式。

9. 互联网实际上是一个"网络的网络"，它由网络路由器及通信线路组成，基于一个共同的通信协议（TCP/IP），将位于不同地区、不同环境的网络互联为一个整体，形成全球化的虚拟网络，是共享资源的集合。

10. 在11日的"双十一"购物节落幕后，本周快递行业将迎来一年中最繁忙的时间。邮政部门预计，11—18日期间，邮政及快递公司处理的包裹数量将达28亿件。

三、将下列短文翻译成汉语 Translate the following passage into Chinese

E-commerce

E-commerce can be viewed from the narrower and wider point of view. In the narrow sense, electronic commerce involves buying and selling through the Internet, and in a broader sense, it includes the exchange of business information, maintaining business relationships, and conducting business transactions by means of telecommunications networks. In fulfilling tasks, it uses electronic communication media such as the Internet, extranets, e-mail, databases, and mobile telephony. Electronic commerce includes several activities, such as electronic sales and purchases of goods and services, online delivery of digital content, electronic funds transfer, public procurement, direct consumer marketing, and other after-sales services. The basis of E-business is often called a fully digital business, and it contains three components: product, process, and participants. Everything that can be sent and received via the Internet is considered to be a digital product.

Electronic commerce creates new markets and economic activities, which are characterized by rapid information processes and market dynamics. Electronic networks provide the infrastructure for collecting and disseminating information. They also serve as a new channel for the sales, promotion of products, and services delivery. Moreover, the network integrates information for managing business activities at all levels of the company and provides new electronic connections with customers and partners in the supply chain. An increasing number of activities that add value to the economy take place in cyberspace through globally connected electronic networks. The Internet has expanded the premises to which companies reach. Managers can detect a greater number of business opportunities due to obtaining many additional business information from the Internet.

四、将下列短文翻译成英语 Translate the following passage into English

互联网与购物

互联网正深深地改变着消费者的消费行为。目前，有1/5的美国人在去商店购买电子产品前，会先到网上去查询其最低价，以节省哪怕一毛钱。更让人吃惊的是，有3/4的美国人在购买新汽车时也会首先想到互联网，即使最后成交仍可能是用传统的方式——从经销商那儿购买，但他们会到网上去了解有关要购买的汽车的各种信息，并选定网上推荐的最好的经销商。有时，他们还会到相关网站上去打印自己感兴趣的汽车的图片等资料作参考。

弗雷斯特(Forrester)，一家研究咨询公司提供的数据显示，在欧洲6亿消费者中，有半数采取先在网上查询商品信息，然后线下购买的方式来消费。当然不同国家又有不同的消费习惯，例如在意大利和西班牙，采取在网上查询然后线下购买的人数大约是网上直接购买的两倍。但在德国和英国这两个网络更发达的国家里，二者基本相当。弗雷斯特称，人们在网上购物一般都是从一些简单的物品开始的，然后向较复杂的商品过渡。在美国，二手汽车是网上购物增长最快的一个领域。

第十四章 知识产权文献翻译

知识产权（intellectual property，或intellectual property rights）是指人们就其智力劳动成果所依法享有的专有权利，通常是国家赋予创造者对其智力成果在一定时期内享有的专有权或独占权（exclusive right）。

随着经济全球化的发展和我国法律制度的逐步完善，知识产权的保护越来越受到广泛重视，知识产权领域的文献也越来越多，相关的文献翻译也与日俱增。

知识产权从本质上说是一种无形财产权，它的客体是智力成果或是知识产品，是一种无形财产或者一种没有形体的精神财富，是创造性的智力劳动所创造的劳动成果。它与房屋、汽车等有形财产一样，都受到国家法律的保护，都具有价值和使用价值。有些重大专利、驰名商标或作品的价值也远远高于房屋、汽车等有形财产。

知识产权主要有两类：一类是著作权（也称为版权、文学产权，copyright or author's right），另一类是工业产权（也称为产业产权，industrial property）。工业产权主要包括专利权（patent）与商标权（trademark）。本章所探讨的知识产权翻译主要是指专利和商标的翻译。

第一节　专利文献语言特点与翻译

专利（patent），从字面上是指专有的权利和利益。"专利"一词来自拉丁语 *litterae patentes*，意为公开的信件或公共文献，是中世纪的君主用来颁布某种特权的证明，后来指英国国王亲自签署的独占权利证书。

在知识产权中，专利通常包括三种含义：1. 法律层面的专利权，即国家依法在一定时期内授予专利权人或者其权利继受者独占使用其发明创造的权利，具有排他性；2. 受到专利法保护的发明创造，即专利技术；3. 专利文件，即专利局颁发的确认申请人对其发明创造享有的专利权的专利证书或指记载发明创造内容的专利文献。在我国，专利分为发明、实用新型和外观设计三种类型。

一、概述

世界知识产权组织发布的报告显示，在2019年中国已经超越美国成为《专利合作条约》框架下国际专利申请的第一大来源国。专利文献是记载专利申请、审查、批准过程中所产生的各种有关文件的文件资料，是一种典型的科技型文本。狭义的专利文献主要指在受理、授权过程中产生的官方文件，包括专利请求书、说明书、权利要求书、摘要在内的专利申请说明书和已经批准的专利说明书的文件资料。广义的专利文献是一种集技术、经济、法律三种情报为一体的文件资料，包括专利公报、专利文摘、专利索引等。在本节主要对专利说明书这一重要专利文献进行探讨。

专利文献的特点主要表现为：1. 数量浩瀚。据统计，每年出版的专利文献约占世界科技出版物的四分之一，且仍以每年100多万件的速度增长，涵盖了人类活动的所有科技领域。2. 形式规范。各国出版的专利说明书文件结构一致，均包括首页（front page）、摘要（abstract）、说明书（specification）、权利要求书（claim）、附图（figure）等几部分内容。在国际专利申请过程中，语言翻译是重要的一环，针对专利的翻译有着独特的规则和规律，要突出显示信息传递型文本的语言特点。

二、专利文献的词汇特点

专利中有着大量的专业术语，具有单一性、专业性和规范性的特点，它对于词语的选择非常重视，力求用词准确、精练，在选择词语对应的翻译时，要及时查阅专业词典和书籍，根据词类和上下文选择词义。

（一）大量使用技术词汇

专利文献涉及的通常是某一专业领域的发明创造、新技术、新材料、新方法、新产品或新设备，要求发明人必须将发明的内容充分公开，并达到该专业领域的技术人员凭借其内容即可基本上将其付诸实施的程度。专利文献是一种专业技术性很强的科技文献，其词汇呈现高度专业化的特点，包括各专业通用的一般技术词汇和某些专业专门使用的技术词汇。例如化学领域的一些词汇：

peroxides 过氧化物

bittern 盐卤

saponification 皂化

talc 滑石

glyceryl monostearate 甘油单硬脂酸酯

cellulose 纤维素

fermentations 发酵

phenyl 苯基

glyceryl ester 甘油酯

需要特别注意的是，同其他科技文体一样，专利文献中同样存在普通词汇专业化的现象。因此，翻译时要对专利文献所涉及的专业领域有一定了解，根据专业属性确定词义，避免望文生义。

（参见上海合同专利翻译网：http://www.locatran.cn/patentview.aspx?ProductID= 519，访问日期：2022年2月3日）

（二）大量使用复合词

专利翻译涉及的专业面很广，例如化学类就有化工、食品、化学药品、生物药品、材料等主要分支。译者对翻译的专利所涉及的技术领域往往是既有所了解，实际上又知之不深。翻译时除先查阅有关资料，了解相关知识之外，还要勤查专业词典，切莫望文生义。

专利文献的专业词语很多是复合词，译者或许认识复合词中的每个单词，但如果按单词的表面意思来翻译复合词，而不用专业词典加以查证，往往会发生错误。例如，number theory（数论），不可按单词number（数字）和theory（理论）各自的词义译成"数理"。又如在食品工程中，protein isolate意思是"分离蛋白"，切勿望文生义地译成"蛋白分离物"。因此，对专业复合词，如果没有见过或不确定，要将其作为整体来查专业词典，以确定其准确词义。

专利文献涉及大量的新技术，而新技术往往会涉及新名词，译文是否规范到位，新名词的处理至关重要。不过很多新名词产生后不久便会有权威的译文，译者应参照经过权威审定的译法。在我国，该项工作由全国科学技术名词审定委员会负责，委员会由各领域的权威专家组成，定期公布各个领域的新名词。

三、专利文献的句式特点

科技人员在研究和解决科学技术问题时，总是要从客观事物出发，力求作出客观准确的陈述或论证，所以专利文本的语句结构的主要特征是复杂多样。在句子层面，专利文献中经常会出现被动语态或复杂从句，因此在翻译前要了解中英文的语言特点,认真分析句型,划分成分。例如:Fluorescent tags can be detected using fluorescence microscopy or cytometry, and colorimentric dyes can be detected visually or using absorbance spectroscopy. 本句使用被动语态,但中文经常使用主动语态,被动语态相对较少,因此在翻译时要将被动转化为主动。本句可译为:"利用荧光显微法或细胞计数法可以检测荧光标记,通过视觉观察或吸光度光谱法可以检测比色燃。"

四、专利文献的翻译原则

（一）忠实于原文

专利文献翻译最重要的就是要忠实于原文。忠实于原文是指,从技术的角度和法律的角度看,译文的内容要和原文的内容完全一致,不得不同,不得增加,不得减少。例如,原文是"the circle has a diameter of 6cm",应译成"该圆有6cm的直径",而不是"该圆的直径为6cm"。这两种译法看起来几乎没差别,但是为了避免在译法有差别的情形下无意犯错,建议按照原文表达,采用逐字对译。

逐字对译与原文最为一致,可以帮助译者免责。但清晰、通顺的语言更有利于读者正确理解专利文件的内容。因此在翻译专利文件时,如果逐字对译能清楚地表达原文的内容和意思,就优先采用逐字对译;如果逐字对译的译文不清楚、不易理解,甚至可能产生歧义,那么译者就需要在正确理解原文之后,再进行适当的词性转换、语态变化、长句拆分等工作。例如:However, the door 20 of the related washing machine and the dryer is disposed low as compared with the user, and the door 20 is perpendicular to a floor. That is, the door 20 is horizontal with the user and the front surface of the cabinet 2, so that the user has to bend over for putting the laundry into the inside of the drum, thereby generating user's inconvenience. 如果逐字翻译,该句可译为:"然而,现有洗衣机和烘干机的门20布置得比较低,相对使用者来说,而且门20是与地面垂直的。换句话说,门20与使用者和箱体2的前表面平行,因此,使用者不得不弯腰将衣物放入滚筒内部,因此产生使用者的不便。"这种完全按照英文语序对原文的每部分进行翻译使得译文读起来不够通顺,读者需再次结合原文进行理解。这就需要译者对译文略加调整,从逐字翻译转换成字面翻译,改译为:"然而,相对使用者来说,现有洗衣机和烘干机的门20安装较低,且门20是与地面垂直的。换句话说,门20与使用者和箱体2的前表面平行,这样使用者不得不俯身将衣物放入滚筒内部,因而给使用者带来不便。"在这个字面翻译过程中，我们进行了语序调整、动词替换等，让译文读起来更顺畅。

（二）一词一译

为了保证全文技术内容的统一和明确，每一个原文词汇（尤其是重要名词、术语）要有一个唯一对应的译文。例如原文中连续出现"apparatus, means, device, equipment, facility, tool"，要对应翻译成"部件、装置、设备、装备、设施、工具"，不能混用。

（三）尊重目标语言习惯

不同国家或地区的语言不同，对具有相同含义的技术术语的表达也存在差异。例如，汉语中的技术术语"等离子"，在英文中的表述为"plasma"，即便都属于汉语体系，在中国台湾地区的表述是"电浆"。虽然都表示"等离子体"的含义，但在翻译过程中，如果不尊重目标语言的表达习惯而造成翻译偏差，那么在世界专利文献中获得较为全面的与"等离子体"相关的专利申请是有困难的。

（四）非语言内容照搬

原则上，数字、元素符号、公式等不需要翻译，可按原文照抄，切记不可出错。

专利翻译相对于普通文本翻译来说，涉及专业领域多，使用的专业术语和法律术语多，文献形式规范，语言严谨，因此具有很大的难度，需要译者熟悉专利特点，了解常用表达，扩大知识面，反复练习。

第二节 商标语言特点与翻译

商标是商品和企业的一种符号或标识。品牌商标的塑造对于产品和企业的成功至关重要，而商标文字是商标各个组成部分的核心。全球化竞争如此激烈，要能够在全球市场占有一席之地，商标名字的选择及翻译十分重要。商标词汇是一种特殊的词汇，有其鲜明的特点：标志性、简明性、适应性、艺术性、严肃性和稳定性，需要与众不同、传达信息、营造美感、唤起消费、易读易记，从而实现商标的商业功能。同时商标是一个受到法律保护且使用权归所有者独有的品牌，因此商标也是法律语言，具有其独特性。

一、商标文献的语言特点

（一）简洁易记

好的商标一般比较简短，朗朗上口，容易被大众熟记。如风靡全球的碳酸饮料"Coca-Cola",仅有简单的四个音节,却既有头韵,又押尾韵。在汉译时,采用音译法,翻译为"可口可乐",同时保留了原商标的音韵美和对称美,实现了吸引消费者的目的。

（二）含义美好

优秀的商标能反映商品的属性,体现商品的特性和优点,从而迎合消费者的购物欲,这些商标充满寓意,能激发丰富的联想。例如,中国品牌"双喜牌"乒乓球,符合中国的文化风俗,满足中国顾客追求双喜临门,对美好生活的向往。在英译时,采用直译法,译为"Double Happiness",同样也会引起国外消费者的幸福联想,使人倍感亲切。再如,世界著名汽车品牌"Benz"的汉译也是一个典型例子。汉译名"奔驰"既采用了音译法,保留了原商标的音,又寓意丰富,传神地体现了汽车的属性,给人如骏马奔驰的联想。

（三）创意新奇

商标有一个常用的设计理念,即标新立异,与众不同,让读者印象深刻。一个创意独特的商标就等于一笔巨额财富。例如,美国美孚石油公司起初使用"Esso"（埃索）作为商标。为了更改该商标,组成了一个由经济学、心理学、社会学、语言学、商品学等方面的专家组成的研究小组,研究了世界上许多国家的语言和风俗习惯,前后历时六年,耗资1.22亿美元,最后从一万多个候选的商标设计方案中确定"Exxon"（埃克森）作为商标。由此可以看出一个优秀的商标对企业的重要程度。

二、商标的翻译技巧

（一）音译

音译,顾名思义,是指在翻译过程中,按照源语发音采取的一种直译方法。Catford（1965）和Aixela（1996）认为,音译在专有名词的翻译中能催生目的语中最近的音位对等词。其主要特点是通过分析商标在源语言中的发音,再在目的语中找具有相同或类似发音的字或词。一般而言,当原商标构不成完整的意义,属新奇型或专有独用的,或是人名地名时,可采用音译。如以下直接音译的商标名都是包含地名或人名的：

青岛啤酒——Tsingtao Beer（啤酒品牌）

李宁——Lining（运动品牌）

Lincoln——林肯（轿车品牌）

Champagne——香槟（酒品牌）

Adidas——阿迪达斯（运动品牌）

Lux——力士（香皂品牌）。这个闻名全球的香皂商标没有任何含义，却展示出商标简明、响亮、易记的特点，对应的中文商标采用音译法，译为"力士"，也能使人产生清洁有力的积极联想。

但商标翻译中的音译远远不止同音或近音这么简单。译者不仅要深刻了解商标语言中的内涵，还需要在目的语中找到发音相似、意义对等的词汇。因此，译者要熟悉双方的文化差异性与相似性，选取富有创意、诠释商品特性的音译名。例如：

海尔——Haier（电器品牌）。海尔的英译名对于国外消费者来说，既易读，又能联想到"higher"（更高）一词，体现出海尔品牌向更好、更高发展的壮志雄心。

香格里拉——Shangri-la（豪华酒店名称）。这个名称来自20世纪30年代英国作家詹姆斯·希尔顿的著名小说 *Lost Horizon*（《消失的地平线》），被描述为世外桃源而为世人所向往，也使得该酒店闻名于全世界。

在采用音译时还要注意目标市场消费者的发音特点。例如汉语中的c、x、q等发音与英语发音存在差异，因此诸如山西汾酒杏花村（Xing Hua Cun）、北京烤鸭全聚德（Quan Ju De）等的音译，外国消费者读起来存在困难，也无法理解其本身传达的传统文化内涵。

（二）意译

意译是按源语基本词义直接翻译的一种方法，作为商标翻译的一个重要手段，能较好地体现商标设计者的初衷和意图。例如，

雪中飞——Snow Flying（服装品牌）

狮——Lion（文具品牌）

雅致——Elegance（服装品牌）

熊猫——Panda（电子产品品牌）

Time——《时代周刊》（杂志品牌）

Apple——苹果（电子产品品牌）

意译也要遵循易读、易记、好懂、产生积极联想的原则。比如运动品牌骆驼，翻译为"Camel"，给消费者传递一种耐用的信号，永久牌自行车翻译为"Forever"，寓意经久耐用。

在汉译英时，使用意译法不能仅依照中国的民族文化，还要考虑外国的文化和消费者心理，否则会影响产品销售。比如中国名牌产品白象牌电池，若直译

为"White Elephant",在国外市场肯定无人问津。因为在西方文化中,"White Elephant"指的是昂贵的无用之物,因此要意译为"Silver Elephant",既保留了原文的核心词,又避免产生不好的联想。

（三）音义双关

音义双关即兼顾音译法和意译法,属于补偿式翻译手法,是把与原文相近的谐音变成有意义的译名,用目的语的多义信息来补偿翻译过程中的语义损失。采用这种方法既能做到译名的读音与原商标的读音相似,又能激发消费者的联想,达到形神兼备的效果,所以是几种翻译方法中技巧性要求较高的。例如：

Budweiser——百威（啤酒品牌）

Ericsson——爱立信（手机品牌）

Johnson's——强生（婴儿用品品牌）

Gillette——吉列（剃须刀品牌）

可伶可俐——Clean and Clear（祛斑霜品牌）

乐凯——Lucky（胶卷品牌）

西山——Sunshine（瓷砖品牌）

Colgate——高露洁（牙膏品牌）。这个汉译商标名不仅音韵相似,而且露字是中国女生取名的常用词,代表着美丽优雅,洁字体现了牙膏的性能,具有点题的作用。

舒肤佳——Safeguard（香皂品牌）,英译商标含有中文商标中s, f, a三个字母读音,其发音接近原商标名,同时又属于复合词,由safe（安全）和guard（保护）合成,放在一起意为保护安全,使人联想到使用该香皂既安全又护肤。

译者在翻译商标时必须注意商标的语言功能、文化功能和社会功能,要提升语言表达能力,熟悉目标市场文化背景,掌握恰当的翻译技巧,做到商标翻译的音美、意美,准确传递商品信息。

第三节　课内翻译任务

一、英译汉 English-Chinese Translation

Official Examination and Publication of Trademark Application

The application will be examined by OHIM for compliance with the absolute and relative grounds of refusal, much as in the UKIPO. If a mark is descriptive in one Member State, or lacks distinctive character in more than one Member State, the applicant will have to prove acquired distinctiveness to overcome the difficulty. An application for a CTM will be refused if an absolute ground for refusal exists in only part of the Community. OHIM may seek a disclaimer in an appropriate case as a condition of registration.

OHIM will search for conflicts between the mark applied for and prior CTM registrations and applications; for absolute objections it will examine the facts of its own motion, but for relative grounds it is restricted to considering the facts and evidence from the parties. The substance of such conflicts is, of course, much the same as in the UK, but with the added complication of language to contend with. If the applicant asks for national searches to be carried out, this will be done by some but not all of the Member States' national trade mark offices and the results will be sent to OHIM. The applicant is informed of all of the conflicts found, and on publication of the application (at least a month later) the proprietors of any conflicting earlier CTMs and CTM applications (but not national marks) will be informed of the pending application. It is up to the proprietors of any conflicting marks to file an opposition if they wish to prevent the application from proceedings to registration. As with UK marks, a CTM application may be divided or amended in the same limited way, to correct obvious errors, etc.

重点解析 Notes and Comments

1. The application will be examined by OHIM for compliance with the absolute and relative grounds of refusal, much as in the UKIPO. 类似于英国知识产权局那样，内协局会基于是否符合驳回的绝对理由和相对理由对申请进行审查。

2. absolute and relative grounds of refusal 绝对和相对的驳回理由。

ground在这里不是"地面，土地"的意思，而是"根据，充分的理由"的意思，常用作复数形式。

3. UKIPO：UK Intellectual Property Office 英国知识产权局

英国知识产权局是一家负责英国知识产权的机构，该机构根据1852年专利法修正案成立，并于同年10月1日起提供服务。

4. If a mark is descriptive in one Member, or lacks distinctive character

in more than one Member State, the applicant will have to prove acquired distinctiveness to overcome the difficulty. 如果商标在一个成员中具有描述性，或者在一个以上成员中缺乏独特性，申请人必须证明自己的商标具有独特性才能克服被驳回的问题。

此句中，descriptive在商标领域的意思是描述性或具有描述性词汇或语言。描述性商标是指该商标使用的词汇属于对商品或服务的质量、功能、用途等特点的描述性表达，由于该词汇属于公有领域，本身并不具有区分商品或服务来源的作用，只是由于通过使用获得了显著性（可以区分商品或服务来源的作用）。描述性标志对商品或服务信息的传递往往是直接的，在消费者意识中该标志应当被认为是对使用该标志的商品或服务的描述，从而与借助联想才能获得商品或服务信息的"暗示性商标"构成差别。

difficulty本义是困难，但结合上文提到的如果商标属于描述性的或缺乏显著特色这些问题，申请人就要证明必要的商标特点可知，overcome the difficulty翻译为"克服问题"更合适。在进行英译汉时，看到常见词汇切不可望词生义，需结合上下文进行恰当的翻译。

5. OHIM will search for conflicts between the mark applied for and prior CTM registrations and applications...

本句中applied for 是过去分词作为后置定语修饰the mark。过去分词作为后置定语一般表示被动和/或过去。

6. The substance of such conflicts is, of course, much the same as in the UK, but with the added complication of language to contend with. 此类冲突的实质当然与英国相同，但要应对的语言却更加复杂。

with the added complication of language to contend with是介词with引导的状语结构，表示这种冲突所具有的特点，即具有应对的语言更加复杂的特点。

二、汉译英 Chinese-English Translation

案 例 分 析

例如，在Heidelberger Bauchemie一案中，一项彩色商标的申请被驳回了。该商标的复制品只是一张纸，纸的上半部分是蓝色，下半部分是黄色，并附有关于该商标的描述："所申请的商标由申请人的公司颜色组成，这些颜色以各种可能的形式被使用，特别是在包装和标签上，都会使用这些颜色。"尽管已确定所使用的色调，但欧盟法院（CJEU）认为该描述过于模糊，无法明确地识别该标志，这会引起不公平竞争的风险。

2013年10月，上诉法院合并裁决了两起上诉案件，因为它们都涉及注册对象是不是标志的问题。第一起案件涉及吉百利（Cadbury）牛奶巧克力产品的标志申请。该标志由一个长方形的紫色块所标识，并描述为"该紫色，如申请表所示，应用于商品包装的整个可见表面，或者是应用于整个可见表面的主要颜色。"吉百利通过提交长期大量使用该标志的证据证明其显著性。雀巢反对该项注册，认为该商标不是由标志构成，也无法以图形的方式表示出来。英国知识产权局（UKIPO）驳回了反对意见，第一次上诉的法官也作出了同样的裁决。但是，在向上诉法院提出的第二次上诉中，法院认为，如果在包装上使用的紫色仅是"主要的"颜色，那么该申请就要包含与紫色搭配的其他要素，而这些内容没有以"具体、确定、自含和精确的方式"进行图形表示或语言描述。由于这些标志的外观和数量对于注册局或公众都是未知的，该申请违反了"确定性原则"。

上诉法院审理的第二起案件是 J W Spear 公司起诉 Zynga 公司的案子。该案涉及一个含拼字游戏磁贴图案的商标，并附以下文字描述："该商标由一个三维象牙色磁贴组成，在其顶部展示了罗马字母表中的一个字母和1至10范围内的一个数字。"在这起侵权诉讼中，该商标的有效性受到反诉。在上诉中，商标所有人辩称，法官对该商标是不是标志的判决是错误的，因为该判决没有考虑到其已获得的显著性。上诉法院驳回上诉并完全维持了 Arnold J.（阿诺德法官）的判决。

拼字游戏案例表明，如果商标申请没有描述一个可正确识别的标志，则无法通过表示该"标志"在使用中已获得显著性来挽救该申请。在戴森案例中，欧洲联盟法院同样认为，没有必要考虑"垃圾桶"标志是否获得显著性，因为它根本就不是一个标志。

重点解析 Notes and Comments

1. 所申请的商标由申请人的公司颜色组成，这些颜色以各种可能的形式被使用，特别是在包装和标签上，都会使用这些颜色。The trade mark applied for consists of the applicant's corporate colours which are used in every conceivable form, in particular on packaging and labels.

该句主要描述被驳回商标的颜色及其使用位置，反复重复"颜色"一词。在翻译成英文时，应避免重复翻译，可将颜色说明部分处理成定语从句的形式，如此一来，句子结构清晰，逻辑紧凑。

2. 上诉法院the Court of Appeal

3. 上诉法院合并裁决了两起上诉案件the Court of Appeal decided two appeals which were heard together

"裁决"一词有以下表达方式：arbitrate（vt.），decide（vt.），adjudicate（vt.），其中arbitrate（in/on sth.）表示仲裁，用来调解矛盾；adjudicate（on/upon/in sth.）后常搭配dispute，用来解决争执；decide（for/against sb）表示司法裁决、判决（to make an official or legal judgement）。因此本句中的裁决翻译成decide更合适。译文中的hear在《牛津词典》中解释为to listen to and judge a case in court，此处采用了增译法，凸显是审理后裁决的。

4. 雀巢反对该项注册，认为该商标不是由标志构成，也无法以图形的方式表示出来。Nestlé opposed the registration, arguing that it did not consist of a sign, nor was it capable of being represented graphically.

本句中两个主要动词为"反对"和"认为"，经分析可以看出，两句之间的关系是因果关系，因此"认为"处理为分词形式承担状语更恰当，同时使用argue更好地表达使用理由论证，以理服人。

5. 这些内容没有以"具体、确定、自含和精确的方式"进行图形表示或语言描述 which was not graphically represented or verbally described in the requisite "specific, certain, self-contained and precise manner"

本句中"具定、确定、自含和精确"是商标中标志的必要特点，可译为"specific, certain, self-contained and precise"。

6. 显著性distinctiveness

显著性是商标特点之一，《中华人民共和国商标法》第九条规定，申请注册的商标，应当有显著特征，便于识别。

显著性意指某一标志可以让消费者识别销售的商品来自某一特定，虽然有时是匿名的来源的属性。商标的显著特征，是指商标应当具备的足以使相关公众区分商品来源的特征。简言之，商标具有显著性意味着该标志具有区分商品来源的能力。《中华人民共和国商标法》所要求的显著特征包含两方面内容，即标志本身的构成要素以及标志与其使用的商品或服务之间的联系和程序。商标的这种属性取决于商标标志与产品属性之间的联系。同时，显著性强的商标对相近似标志的排斥力较强；反之，显著性弱的商标则对相近似标志的排斥力较弱。

有研究者表示商标图样存在瑕疵而不能对商标标志加以确定的，虽然不属于《商标法》第四十四条第一款规定的应予无效的情形，但应当认定其不具备商标注册所需的显著特征，从而予以无效宣告。本案例中，法院就是基于商标缺乏显著性对吉百利商标作出判决的。

7. CJEU: Court of Justice of the European Union，欧洲联盟法院

第四节　课后翻译训练

一、将下列句子翻译成汉语 Translate the following sentences into Chinese

1. The user of a trademark shall be responsible for the quality of the goods on which the trademark is used.

2. By signaling a reliable level of quality coming from a single source, a trademark can protect consumers against deception.

3. In the application for registration or use of a trademark, the principle of good faith shall be followed.

4. A trademark registrant shall have the right to use the words "registered trademark" or a sign standing for registration.

5. The trademark for registration shall be distinctive for easy identification, and may not be in conflict with any prior legal rights acquired by others.

6. The holder of a trademark well known by the relevant public may file a request for well-known trademark protection under this Law if believing that there is any infringement upon its rights.

7. Actions for trade libel or malicious falsehood (a form of defamation) may sometimes also arise out of trade mark disputes, in particular where the case involves comparative advertising.

8. Where a registered trademark must be used on the goods prescribed by any law or administrative regulation, trademark registration must be applied for, and such goods may not be marketed without approval of trademark registration.

9. The preparation of an application for patent and the conducting of the proceedings in the United States Patent and Trademark Office to obtain the patent is an undertaking requiring the knowledge of patent law and rules and Office practice and procedures, as well as knowledge of the scientific or technical

matters involved in the particular invention.

10. Applications for patents, which are not published or issued as patents, are not generally open to the public, and no information concerning them is released except on written authority of the applicant, his or her assignee, or his or her attorney, or when necessary to the conduct of the business of the USPTO.

二、将下列句子翻译成英语 Translate the following sentences into English

1. 商标应作为质量担保。
2. 注册商标需要改变其标志的，应当重新提出注册申请。
3. 各级工商行政管理部门应当通过商标管理制止欺骗消费者的行为。
4. 人们倾向于把一个特定品牌与质量和价格之间的既定权衡联系起来。
5. 如果两个或两个以上的人合作完成了发明，他们应以共同发明人的身份一起申请专利。
6. 商标所有者有既得利益，那就是打击那些使用混淆或欺骗性标志来兜售竞争商品的无赖。
7. 由于商标可以识别和区分市场上供应商的产品和服务，商标已成为品牌身份的关键和大多数广告及促销活动的核心。
8. 涉及专利的函件（除了用于缴纳维护费之外）应写明专利权人姓名、发明的名称、专利号以及发布日期。
9. 根据法律规定，发明人或其受让人，或者有义务将发明让予他人的人，可以申请专利，但某些情况除外。
10. 发明名称应尽可能简短和具体（不超过500个字符），如果申请文件开头没有出现，则应作为标题出现在说明书第一页。

三、将下列短文翻译成汉语 Translate the following passage into Chinese

Novelty and Non-Obviousness, Conditions for Obtaining a Patent

In order for an invention to be patentable it must be new as defined in the patent law, which provides that an invention cannot be patented if:

"(1) the claimed invention was patented, described in a printed publication, or in public use, on sale, or otherwise available to the public before the effective filing date of the claimed invention," or

"(2) the claimed invention was described in a patent issued [by the U.S.] or in an application for patent published or deemed published [by the U.S.], in which the patent or application, as the case may be, names another inventor and was effectively filed before the effective filing date of the claimed invention."

There are certain limited patent law exceptions to patent prohibitions (1) and (2) above. Notably, an exception may apply to a "disclosure made 1 year or less before the effective filing date of the claimed invention," but only if "the disclosure was made by the inventor or joint inventor or by another who obtained the subject matter disclosed...from the inventor or a joint inventor."

In patent prohibition (1), the term "otherwise available to the public" refers to other types of disclosures of the claimed invention such as, for example, an oral presentation at a scientific meeting, a demonstration at a trade show, a lecture or speech, a statement made on a radio talk show, a YouTube™ video, or a website or other on-line material.

Effective filing date of the claimed invention: This term appears in patent prohibitions (1) and (2). For a U.S. nonprovisional patent application that is the first application containing the claimed subject matter, the term "effective filing date of the claimed invention" means the actual filing date of the U.S. nonprovisional patent application. For a U.S. nonprovisional application that claims the benefit of a corresponding prior-filed U.S. provisional application, "effective filing date of the claimed invention" can be the filing date of the prior-filed provisional application provided the provisional application sufficiently describes the claimed invention. Similarly, for a U.S. nonprovisional application that is a continuation or division of a prior-filed U.S. nonprovisional application, "effective filing date of the claimed invention" can be the filing date of the prior filed nonprovisional application that sufficiently describes the claimed invention. Finally, "effective filing date of the claimed invention" may be the filing date of a prior-filed foreign patent application to which foreign priority is claimed provided the foreign patent application sufficiently describes the claimed invention.

四、将下列短文翻译成英语 Translate the following passage into English

如何选择商标

理想情况下，商标应与所标记产品的形象和属性相适应。描述性商标可以反映商品或服务的性质、内容或品质，因为它们能够自我宣传而具有吸引力。然而，带有强烈信息的商标可能描述性过多，以至于无法注册或作为商标受到保护。在特定行业中，常用的词语或图案可能会吸引商标所有者，但可能没法注册且难以防止竞争对手使用类似标志。如果商标要暗示商品或服务的性质或其他品质，得巧妙地做到这一点；巧妙的暗示可以增强商标的记忆性。许多商标都由一个日常词汇组成，这些词虽然没有实际描述产品，却唤起了人们对产品品质的强烈主观印象。比如"闪电"这个词代表了家用清洁剂的速度。

文字商标还必须易于发音，尤其是在选择外来词时。如果要出口商品，或者希望在多个国家使用商标，则应谨慎选择一个适合所有相关语言的商标。

本章课内翻译任务和课后翻译训练英汉和汉英翻译短文均选自：Amanda Michaels & Andrew Norris, *A Practical Guide to Trade Mark Law*, 5th ed., Oxford University Press, 2014.

第十五章 国际商事法律翻译

根据John Shijian Mo编写的《国际商法》(*International Commercial Law*)，国际商法包含以下十二个方面的法律内容：本国国际货物买卖法律、联合国国际货物买卖合同公约、知识产权合同法、海陆空运输合同法、国际贸易支付法、国际银行和融资法、国际贸易海运和空运保险法、外资法、世贸组织法、地区贸易组织法、国际商务诉讼法和法律冲突、国际贸易争端解决机制。

上述国际商事法律法规（也称为国际商务法律法规）的笔译属于法律翻译大家族的一个重要成员，翻译职业类型上又属于专门职业翻译。这种法律职业翻译是一种专业化翻译，要求译者必须准确把握商事法律专门知识，同时又具备商事法律语言服务的实践经验，尤其具备语言和法律的交叉学科能力。能胜任涉外商事法律翻译服务的职业译员是高端翻译人才，称为复合型国际化法律翻译人才。

学习和研究国际商事法律翻译，是了解国际商事规则，准确适用准据法，为涉外商事法律诉讼服务的一个基础教学环节。这正是我国高校法律专业、法律英语专业、商务英语专业以及国际商务或贸易专业教学走向应用化、国际化的必然选择。本章结合美国合同法、美国《统一商法典》、《中华人民共和国民法典》、《中华人民共和国外商投资法》、《联合国国际货物销售合同公约》、美国《无尽前沿法案》之国际商务的法律规定，对国际商法翻译进行一般性的翻译理论和实践的探讨，重点探讨国际商事法律语言的特点以及翻译技巧。

第一节 国际商事法律英语语言特征

国际商事法律文本是国际商事法律法规、国际商事法律文书、国际商事诉讼文书、国际商事会议和研究成果的总称。国际商事法律文本有它们的共同特征——定义句、授权句、确认句、宣称句（definition statement, authorization statement, confirmation statement, declaration statement），学习者抓住这几个基本语句特征，再对相关术语和行话进行平行语料库对照学习和研究，就会收到与"产出导向法"一样的学习效果。

一、国际商事法律英语的用词特征

首先，国际商事法律词汇是法律语言的基本组成部分，有必要在了解其法律词汇分类的基础上进一步探讨其翻译原则。根据国际商事法律词汇构词结构、意义结构、语义来源、使用特征等，国际商事法律词汇可分为：商事法律术语、商事法律行话、商事法律含义普通词汇、商事法律古旧词汇、商事法律外来词、商事法律并用近义词、商事法律模糊词语和法律专用词语等。

（一）使用国际商事法律术语

1. 国际商事法律常用术语包括：日常词汇法律化术语、法律术语日常化术语。

（1）不明确表示特定商事法律概念，常用于商事法律语言中，也在日常生活中普遍使用的固定意义词语。如：review of international banking and financing system国际银行和融资体系的审查，complete perform完全履行，enforceable conduct法律强制力行为，corresponding parties对方，third party第三方，goods商品，representing conduct 代理行为，principle-agent relationship委托代理关系，等等。

（2）原来仅表示特定法律概念，后来扩展到常用词汇领域。如：international sale of goods国际货物销售，formation of contract合同的成立，passing of risk风险转移，application to UCC《统一商法典》的适用，due procedure正当程序，creditor and debtor债权人与债务人，dying words临终遗言。

常用国际商事法律术语的特点还表现为国际商事法律行为中的常用性、强大构词性、意义固定性。例如：meeting of minds意思表示一致，last decision最终裁决，noncriminal agency非刑事代理，gratuitous agency无偿代理，contract capacity合同能力，civil procedure民事诉讼程序，applied law准据法。人类文明的进步与法律的现代化进程，使这些词汇走进人们的社会生活，并使这些法律语义常用化。

2. 排他性专门国际商事法律含义术语

这类国际商事法律术语，排除了非法律概念的一般含义，保留了特定的法律含义。这类术语的多义是历史发展形成的，词义外延或扩大或缩小，法律固定含义是法律和法制发展的必然结果。这类术语可分为两类：

（1）词义外延扩大产生的术语：许多法律专门术语，随着人们法治观念的不断发展，其适用范围也扩大到日常生活中，具有了普通含义。例如：mirror rule principle镜像规则——不变规则；licensing agreements许可协议——颁发执照协议书；distribution agreement分销协议——分配方案；transfer of technology技术转让——让与技术；company code公司章程——公司规定。但是，在国际商事法律文本及其翻译中，我们要取其前面的法律含义。

（2）词义外延缩小产生的术语：许多原来的日常用语，随着国际商务实践规模的扩大、国际商务全球化的发展和法律文化的拓展，其含义越来越固定，其外延逐渐缩小，变成了国际商事法律文本的专门用语，用来专指国际商事法律含义。例如：means and ways方式方法——筹款；real rights真正的权利——物权；mutual assent双方同意——双方意思表示一致；consumption complaint消费投诉——消费诉讼；carriage of goods by sea货物海运——海上货物运输；marine insurance海洋运输保险——水险；marine risks海上风险——海险；just consideration公平考虑——法律上的充分对价。

排他性专门法律含义术语因其表示的法律概念构成固定、意义固定、使用频率高，故而构成法律术语的主体。

3. 专门法律术语

这类术语具有术语的概念准确、单义、表意严格等三个基本特征，属于严格意义上的标准法律术语。这类特征术语的使用构成了法律行文的特色，也是翻译的难点。例如：subscribing witness具名见证人，UCC美国《统一商法典》，plaintiff原告，defendant被告，subsidiary company子公司，crime against property侵犯财产罪，droit de suite追索权，droits civils民事权利，equity of redemption衡平法上的回赎权，general warranty一般担保，licensing许可证贸易，recidivism累犯，bigamy重婚罪，negligence疏忽，homicide杀人，burden of proof举证责任，voidable contract可撤销合同。对这些法律专门用语的学习，必须借助专门的法律词典和工具书。

4. 借用术语

随着社会分工的细化和社会关系的复杂化，法律调整的内容越来越复杂，涉及的领域在急剧膨胀，新的法律分支和边缘学科应运而生，相关领域内的专门术语大量涌入，成为法律英语专门术语。例如：narcotic act（毒品法）来自现代毒品分类，no-action clause（无诉条款）来自保险规定，negotiable bill of lading（可流通提单、可转让提单）来自现代商务结算，sadism（性虐待狂）源自心理学，

abortion（堕胎）源自医学，internet tort（网络侵权）来自互联网，artistic work（艺术作品）源自艺术，accord and satisfaction（和解与清偿）来自破产管理，heredity（遗传）源自生物学，incest（乱伦罪）源自社会学，monogamy（一夫一妻制）源自人口学，tariff（关税）源自经济学，umpire（独立仲裁人）来自现代仲裁实践，average（海损）源自运输，claims（索赔）源自外贸业务，life insurance（人寿保险）源自保险单，means of dispute settlement（争议解决条款）来自民事诉讼，等等。

（二）使用国际商事法律行话

为了突出行业特点，常使用法律行话。比如：duty to communicate告知义务，evidence in support of alibi 不在场证据，business compulsion商业胁迫，letters patent专利证书，negotiable instrument流通票据，reasonable doubt合理怀疑，等等。

"法律行话"与"法律术语"都是法律专业性用语，但两者又有不同。"法律术语"是法律文本规范性专业用语，比"法律行话"更适用于书面用语和书面表达。"法律术语"是法律工作者间使用的专门用语，也可以是对客户的专业表述。"法律行话"是属于法律工作者内部的行话。

在日常用语中可能有几种含义的词，用到法律文本或庭审中，意思就明确而单一了。如minors指"未成年人"，capacity指"签约能力"，exemption clauses指"免责条款"，winding up指"结案"，work product指"（律师）工作成果"，express terms指"明示条款"，power of attorney指"委任书"。法律行话的使用避免了法律职业者交流过程中意思的曲解。

（三）普通英语词汇表示国际商事法律含义

随着法制的沿革和法律法规的丰富、判例的大规模积累、诉讼制度的完善、司法制度的逐步健全，以及人们法治观念的增强和法律文化的形成，有些法律英语词汇根据立法、司法等工作的实际需要，不仅保留了在日常交流中的普通词义，还在国际商事法律英语中形成了一种固定的法律含义。在汉语国际商事法律和司法审判实践中，也形成了自己的一套较为固定的法律词汇、句式和语篇表达，使法律法规、审判实践用语具备了各自法律语言的一系列固定用法。在英译汉或汉译英时，在充分把握英汉两种语言和法律语言习惯和规律的基础上，必须尽量找到对应的国际商事法律语言，才能达到国际商事法律翻译准确、规范和专业化的要求。

某些普通词汇在法律语言中具有特殊的法律意义。例如：cross hearing字面含义是"交叉听觉"，但是法律含义是"交叉听证"；dead freight 字面含义是"死亡货运"，但是法律含义却是"空仓费"；duties of agent to principal原义是"经纪人对主角的责任"，商法含义为"代理人对委托人的职责"。所以，法律术语的翻译必须专业。

另外还有一些常用词，意思很明了，但是具有特殊的法律意义。例如：good faith原义是"诚意"，而在商事法律里含义是"善意"；real action的字面含义是"真干"，但是法律含义却是"不动产诉讼"；damage是"损坏"的意思，而"damages"就成了法律上的"损害赔偿金"；calendar day意思是"日历日"，但其复数calendar days含义却是"工作日"；consideration通常含义是"考虑""体贴"，在合同法中特指"对价"；infant在美国合同法中指"未成年人"。普通词汇的法律含义需要结合所处的语境确定。

（四）古旧英语词汇应用在规范的国际商事法律文书中

古旧词汇主要指古代英语和中世纪英语沿用至今的词语。其中，从拉丁语、法语和希腊语中借来的外来词形成的法律词语大部分至今仍在使用。

使用古体词不仅使合同语言更为简练、规范、严肃，文体更为正式、庄重、严谨，而且避免了用词重复和句子冗长。

但是，为了使国际商务当事人更加容易理解把握国际商务规则，更加便利地进行交流和规范，无论是美国宪法修正案、美国合同法、美国《统一商法典》、美国贸易法，还是英国合同法、澳大利亚合同法等成文法律，都严格限制使用以here, there, where为词根的古体词，拉丁词也进行了严格限制。herein, hereafter, hereinafter, hereunder, thereof, therefor, thereafter, whereof, whereafter, whereby, whereas等在成文法中已经严格限制使用频率，但有些大型合同使用上述古体词较多。

这类词的含义和用法大体相同，一般可以互换，在汉语中表示"在此""自此以后""此后下文中""由此""为此""此后""随后""反之"等意思。

例1. Words "**herein**" and "this Act", referred to in the three paragraphs of subsec. (a), mean the Clayton Act. For classification of the Clayton Act to the Code, see last paragraph **hereunder**.（2019USC15, p. 18）

译文：在本条第三款提到的"在此"和"本法"意思是《克莱顿法》。有关《克莱顿法》在本法典的分类，请参阅下文最后一项。（2019年美国法典第15卷第18页）

本法条中，herein有"此中""于此"的含义，结合上下文可译为"在此"。

hereunder有"在此之下"或"在下文"两种含义,但是结合本文语篇,应翻译为"在下文"。法律行文的这种古旧连词的使用,是坚持法律行文严肃性的结果,须结合文本内容,进行正确理解,才能做到正确翻译。

例2. That the person so conveying has not executed or done, or knowingly suffered, or been party or privy to any deed or thing, **whereby** or by means **whereof** the subject-matter of the conveyance or any part thereof, is or may be impeached, charged, affected or encumbered in title, estate, or otherwise, or whereby or by means whereof the person who so conveys is in anywise hindered from conveying the subject-matter of the conveyance, or any part thereof, in the manner in which it is expressed to be conveyed. [*Commercial Tenancy (Retail Shops) Agreements Act 1985*,104, Third Schedule amended by No. 24 of 1990s. 123.]

译文:转让人未履行、未完成履行、明确放任不履行的,或已成为契约的当事人或参与人而转让或部分转让该标的物的,转让人转让或部分转让的标的物所有权、不动产权因此受到质疑、指控、影响或阻碍的,或转让人对标的物的明示转让或部分转让因此受到阻碍的。(《1985年商业租赁(零售店铺)协议法》附件3第123条,1990年第24号法令修改,第104条)

whereby:由此;whereof:在此。

例3. Whereas, Company A is a manufacturer of Automobile Machine and has certain technical information and experiences which may be useful in developing the Product as hereinafter defined, the parties hereto agree as follows.

译文:鉴于公司甲是汽车发动机制造商,并拥有有助于开发下列产品的特定技术资料和经验,双方特此达成以下协议。

日常用语中whereas为连词,意为"而,却,反之",表示语气的转折。在合同中通常译为"鉴于""有鉴于"。

例4. This contract is made in a spirit of friendly cooperation by and between Party A and Party B, whereby Party A shall invite Party B for service as a foreign staff on the terms and conditions stipulated as follows.

译文:甲、乙双方本着友好合作的精神签订本合同,甲方依本合同如下条款聘请乙方为外籍工作人员。

whereby在日常语言中是"凭此""借以"的含义,在语法上是定语从句的引导词,在法律行文中含义为"依……""据……"。

（五）国际商事法律英语中使用外来词

1. 拉丁语

拉丁语在法律语言中处于权威性地位。很多拉丁语法律格言反映了法律背后的价值规范，有些涉及实体价值，例如："Contra bonos mores"英语解释为"contrary to good morals"，意即"违背善良风俗的"。有些涉及程序价值，例如："Accusare nemo se debet"英语解释为"nobody is bound to incriminate himself"，意即"一个人不应被强迫去提供对其不利的证词"；conciliation and mediation固定指破产程序里的"调解与调停"；nunc pro tunc原义是"现在替代过去""事后补救"，后来固定到商事行为的法律责任上，指"溯及既往"。

2. 法语

11世纪至15世纪，法国威廉家族统治英格兰，法语取代英语成为英国的统治语言和官方语言，政府行政和立法、司法语言改为法语。此后，尽管法语逐渐退出英国政府行政和司法领域，但很多法语法律词语被保留下来，而且形成和发展为英语的基础法律语言。

有些法律法语词汇，如"action"（诉讼），"suit"（诉讼），"alien"（转让），"issue"（子女），"bona fide acquisition"（善意取得），"pour autre vie"（for another's life）（他人生存期的）等，已经变成了英语词汇，成为英语法律常用语言。

（六）国际商事法律文书中常出现近义词的并用

英美法规和法律文件中经常有一个句子中出现几个近义词并列的情况。近义词的使用可以分为求异型近义词和求同型近义词两种。

1. 求异型近义词

这种类型的近义词着眼点是各近义词的意义差别部分。

例5. In the course of interpreting or constructing the contract, ...

interpret 与 construct 两词都有"解释"的意思，但意义有差别。interpret 是指意图解释法，即依文件起草背景来确定起草者真实意图的解释；而construct 是指文意解释法，即严格按字面意义进行解释。并列使用这对近义词是为了区分它们的意义差别。翻译时不能拘泥于表面含义，而要使用能体现出其差别的合适的中文词，可翻译为："解释合同目的和合同含义时，……"

2. 求同型近义词/异态的同义词

例如：

（1）acknowledge and confess 承认和供认

（2）adjust, compromise, and settle 调整，妥协，和解

（3）agree and covenant 协议与契约

（4）all and every 全部/每一项

（5）alter or change 修改和变更

（6）any and all 所有/全部

（7）sole and exclusive 单一

（8）each and every 各自

（9）assume and agree 认为和同意

（10）bind and obligate 约束和负有义务

（11）by and with 随同

（12）null and void 无效

此类近义词的连用，是法律英语严密性、庄重性和规范性的重要表现。

二、国际商事法律英语的句法特征

不同于普通英语的句式表达，国际商事法律英语句式表达具有精确、严密、清晰的特征，而且大多数是以复杂的从句和短语并列、递进、转折等特征表现出来，被动句、叠加句、列举句成了法律英语的语言特色，较少出现简短句。为了使法律条款表达的意思更准确、界定适用范围更严格，立法者还常常使用特定的语言结构，由特定词引导，具有特定的语言含义。法律文件特有的固定句式只在法律英语中出现，因此也更能反映法律英语的特点。

根据法律英语的句式特点、句式功能可以把法律句式分为以下几种：

1. 概念确定式，例如：A contract is...。

例6. <u>A contract is</u> a promise or a set of promises for the breach of which the law gives a remedy, or the performance of which the law in some way recognizes as a duty. [§1, Chapter 1, *Restatement (Second) of Contracts*]

译文：合同指的是一个允诺或一组允诺，如果违反此允诺，则法律给予救济；如果其履行了允诺，则法律以某种方式将其视为一项义务。（《美国合同法（第二次）重述》第一章第1条）

2. 条件引导式，例如：when distributed, when issued。

例7.（e）This section does not affect the right of a party to cancel a contract for a security "<u>when, as and if issued</u>" or "<u>when distributed</u>" in the event of a material change in the character of the security that is the subject of the contract or in the plan or arrangement pursuant to which the security is to be issued or distributed. (§8-202, UCC)

译文：(e)"凡是"或"如果发行的"或"已发行了的"证券，性质上发生实质性变化的，且这种变化归咎于合同本身条款的变化，或证券发行计划或协议发生变化的，本条款不影响当事人取消证券合同的权利。（美国《统一商法典》8—202条）

3. 意义递进复合式，例如：When leasing house to Party A, or Party A is transferring to Party C, even when restoring the house...both parties shall negotiate the terms of performance...。

4. 目的表达式，例如：in order to protect...; for the purpose of...。

例8. <u>For the purposes of</u> Article 20 and Article 21(a) of the Convention as given the force of law by this section, a statement to the effect that the Centre has waived an immunity in the circumstance specified in the statement, being a statement certified by the Secretary General of the Centre, or by the person acting as Secretary General, shall be conclusive evidence of such waiver. [Article 8(3), *The Arbitration (International Investment Disputes) Act*, 2011]

译文：为依本节规定使公约第20条和第21(a)条产生法律效力，本仲裁中心声明在符合规定的情况下放弃豁免权，该声明由仲裁中心主任或其代理人审核后作出，可视为放弃豁免权的证据。[2011年《仲裁（国际投资纠纷）法》第8条第3款]

5. 授权式和权利限制式，例如：The buyer may, unless seller...。

例9. <u>Unless</u> a statute provides otherwise, a natural person has the capacity to incur only voidable contractual duties until the beginning of the day before the person's eighteenth birthday. (14, *Restatement (Second) of Contracts*)

译文：除非法令另有规定，自然人在18岁生日之前只具有创设可撤销合同义务的行为能力。（《美国合同法（第二次）重述》，第14条）。

另外，在国际商事法律文书的书写实践中还有：

6. 限定条件式，例如：If Party A breaks...; In case of...; In respect of...。

7. 由特定词引导的句式，比如：notwithstanding 引导的特色法律句式、where 引导的条件状语从句、without prejudice to 引导的条件句式等。

第二节　国际商事法律翻译

一、国际商事法律翻译的原则

近些年来，我国法律翻译学者对法律翻译原则进行了积极的探讨，以期找到法律翻译的衡量准绳。邱贵溪第一次较全面地归纳并论述了法律文件翻译的五大原则：1. 使用庄严词语的原则；2. 准确性原则；3. 精练性原则；4. 术语一致性原则；5. 使用专业术语的原则。（邱贵溪，2000：2）

张法连教授主编的《法律英语翻译教程》及其所开展的法律翻译研究，将法律翻译的基本原则归纳如下：清晰准确原则（clear and concise）、严谨规范原则（strict and formal）、文化对应原则（cultural equivalence）、灵活对等原则（dynamic equivalence）、术语一致原则（legal terms coherence）、法律专业化原则（legally professional）。

国际商事法律翻译不同于其他文体的翻译，尤其与文学翻译大相径庭。

1. 目的不同。国际商事法律文书翻译的目的是实现语码转换和语义对等转化，与激情没有关系，和个人情感也没有关系；而文学翻译则是在目的语中找到相对应的激情表达，是感情交融的体现。文学翻译弥合了文化和语言之间微妙的情感联系；而法律翻译则是在另一种语言中复制一种特殊的社会制度、无情感的规则和条例，根本不可以把个人感情带进法律翻译中来。

2. 两种翻译的判断标准不同。文学翻译旨在实现源语在译入语中音乐般的、有节奏感和视觉冲击的可能性，不需要精确的等价性；而国际商事法律翻译则是在法律上实现术语的准确对应、规定和制度的再现。

二、国际商事法律翻译方法

要想落实国际商事法律翻译的原则和翻译理论的指导，找到国际商事法律翻译的途径和方法很重要。

法律翻译研究的流行观点认为，法律翻译方法主要有直译、意译或兼译（literal translation, free translation, or simultaneous translation）。从实践来看，法律语言的特点决定了法律文件多用直译。但在法律语言翻译过程中，由法律文化性差异造成的翻译问题，要求译者具备一定的创造性，要灵活对应，而此时意译是不可避免的选择。

（一）国际商事法规词汇的翻译

由于英美的判例法系法律与属于大陆法系的中国的法律在制度、思想理念上有很大差别，作为法律载体的法律词汇在两种法律体系之间存在较大的差别。但是随着国际经贸往来的不断深入，以及英美法律对全世界的国际商事法律制度的影响，中国国际商事法规和英美国际商事法规又有很多相同、相似之处。

首先应该把法律语言做好分类，这是做好法律词汇翻译的基础。按照法律语言的法律属性，法律语言可分为：立法语言、司法语言、审判语言（legislative language, judicial language, trial language）。我国著名法律语言学家杜金榜教授明确地把法律语言从功能上分为指向性（explicitly directive）法律语言、宣称性（declarative）法律语言、陈述性（narrative）法律语言。（杜金榜，2004: 105—112）

Deborah Cao在其著作 *Translating Law* 中对法律语言进行进一步划分，认为法律词汇可分为规定性（prescriptive）、执行性（performative）、强制性（imperative）、管理性（executive）、强有力实施性（enforcing）、确定性（defining）、规范性（normative）等类别。

所以，法律词汇翻译时只要达到上述特征性要求，译文就是合格的，是为法律界所能接受的翻译。另外，法律词汇翻译不可以离开语篇翻译，否则就是词典对应式翻译，就不是合格的翻译。

例10. Notwithstanding the provisions of subsection (3), a person who conveys or distributes any real or personal property to or amongst the persons entitled thereto without having ascertained that there is no person who is or may be entitled to any interest in that property by virtue of that subsection is not liable to any such person of whose claim he did not have notice at the time of the conveyance or distribution.

译文：尽管第三款作出法律规定，但向主张权利方转让或交付未提前查明根据本款没有任何人可以对该财产享有权益的动产或不动产的，转让人不对受让人或受交付人负责，受让人或被交付人之不知情的主张无效。

这里有notwithstanding这个让步条件从句的引导词，一般翻译为"尽管"。subsection (3)必须看法律原文确定section和subsection在本法所指，有的译为"节"和"条"，但是有的英语法律法规把我们汉语法律里的"条"用section来表达，那么subsection就只能翻译为"款"，本法翻译就属于这种情况。real or personal property指不动产和动产，personal property不可以译为"个人财产"，这是根据英、美财产法律制度正确判断出来的。thereto是其前面的persons entitled的后置修饰词，三个词一起翻译为"享有财产权的"。by virtue of是"根据……"的意思，不可翻译为"按照……美德"。is not liable to是"对……负有法律责任"的意思。claim是民事诉讼中的"诉讼请求"的意思。notice是"通知"的意思,这里灵活地翻译为"知情"。

所以,法律词汇的翻译是一个综合把握法律语篇能力的反映。

(二)国际商事法规短语结构的翻译

法律翻译是两种法律文化和体系的转换,在了解源语与目标语的法律制度和法律文化的基础上,除了不能发挥译者的话题主体性和追求情感的一致外,其他翻译技巧比如顺译、倒译、拆分、重构、变更主题、创设对应等都适用于法律翻译,只不过法律翻译技巧主要是对法律文本的逻辑解读和句式的转换。在此基础上,掌握一些常用法律文本句型成了提高法律文本翻译效率的有效途径。

常用法律句型举例:

1. otherwise 除非

例11. Unless displaced by the particular provisions of this Act, the principles of law and equity, including the law merchant and the law relative to capacity to contract, principal and agent, estoppel, fraud, misrepresentation, duress, coercion, mistake, bankruptcy, or other validating or invalidating cause shall supplement its provisions. (*Uniform Commercial Code* 1912)

译文:除非被本法特定条款排除,法律原则和衡平法,包括商人法以及与缔约能力、本人与代理、禁止反言、欺诈、不实陈述、强迫、威胁、错误、破产有关的法律,或者其他生效或没生效的案件判决,都可作为本法该条款的补充。(1912年美国《统一商法典》)

2. subject to 属于,依据;subject only to 只限于

例12. Transferee of land subject to encumbrance to indemnify transferor. (*Transfer of Land Act* 1893, Westen Australia)

译文:土地受让人(属于)妨碍对土地转让人的保护。(1893年西澳大利亚州《土地转让法》)

3. where + clause 凡……的

例13. Where in an instrument the absolute vesting either of capital or income of property, or the ascertainment of a beneficiary or class of beneficiaries, is made to depend on the attainment by any person of an age exceeding 21 years, and the gift to that beneficiary or class or any member thereof, or any gift over, remainder, executory limitation or trust arising on the total or partial failure of the original gift, would, but for this section, be rendered invalid as infringing the rule against perpetuities, the instrument takes effect for the purposes of that gift, gift over, remainder, executory limitation or trust as if the absolute vesting or ascertainment had been made to depend on the person attaining the age of 21 years, and that age shall be substituted for the age stated in the instrument.

译文：凡契据中有资本或财产收入绝对授权，或需确定受益人或受益人等级的，均要求上述当事人年满21岁；向该受益人、该等级及其成员赠予的，或因全部或部分赠予不能实现而出现转赠、剩余权利、赠予限制或信托的，除按本条规定外，因为违反禁止永久权规则，而属无效；凡为赠予、转赠、剩余权利、赠予限制或信托而签订的契据皆为有效，效力如同绝对授权或确定的受益人或受让人年龄已满21岁，契据须一律遵从该年龄限制。（executory limitation = executory interests 期待利益，将来利益）

本款的翻译用上了法律翻译的全部6个原则和长句翻译的几种方法。

4. notwithstanding 尽管

介词notwithstanding 在普通英文中的使用极为罕见，但在法律英文中被频繁使用。它的译法跟although/though/even if 引导的状语从句没有太大分别，基本上可以译成"尽管……""即使……"，表示让步。但习惯上该词之后不跟句子，只跟一个名词性短语。

5. provided that 句式

"provided that..."在普通英文中很少使用，但在法律文书中广泛使用。其用法与if或but非常类似，汉语中的意思相当于"倘若/如果"或"但"。该短语放在句首，引导的是一个条件分句，与if, when或where引导的法律条件句没有本质上的差异；但如果该短语之前存在一个主句，则它表示的是一个与之前的陈述相反的"例外"，相当于"with the exception of..."，可译成"但"或"但是"。

例14. However, permanent residents of the Region who are not of Chinese nationality or who have the right of abode in foreign countries may also be elected members of the Legislative Council of the Region, provided that the proportion of such members does not exceed 20 percent of the total membership of the Council.

译文：但是，非中国籍的香港特别行政区永久性居民和在外国有居留权的香港特别行政区永久性居民也可以当选为香港特别行政区立法会议员，但其所占比例不得超过立法会全体议员的百分之二十。

（三）国际商事法规句子的翻译

国际商事法律英语和法律汉语的句子都有其复杂的句式表达习惯，复合句是基本特色,长句是表达复杂法律关系的常用语篇习惯,复合句的概念确定式、行为引导式和语义的递进或转折式、条件设定和结果引导式等是法律法规语言的主要表现形式。法律汉语中"……的"或"凡……的"就是法律英语的where, if, when引导的法律英语句式。法律英语中的并列形容词、并列动词或并列名词引导的句式经常在法律汉语中用"凡……,或……,以致……的,应……"来对应。

1. 典型法律英语句式的翻译及解析

(1) 概念确定式

例15. A contract is an exchange of promises between two or more parties to do or refrain from doing...

译文:合同是指两个或两个以上的当事人之间为或不为一定行为的承诺的交换……

这样的句式,译文必须符合目标语下定义的模式。

(2) 行为引导式

例16. When selling goods, a taxpayer shall issue a VAT invoice...

译文:纳税人销售货物的,应当开具增值税发票……

本结构可译为"……的"或"……时"。

(3) 意义递进复合式

例17. (a) Laws of important wholly state-owned enterprises, wholly state-owned companies, and state-owned capital, Administrative regulations and the provisions of the people's governments holding companies at the corresponding levels on major matters...

译文:(a)关于重要的国有独资企业、国有独资公司和国有资本的法律,各级人民政府对其控股公司重大事项的行政法规和规定……(holding companies/corporations控股公司)

例18. (b) It shall apply to the competent tax authority..., and shall declare and pay taxes..., the tax payment shall be filed with the competent tax authorities...

译文:(b)应当向其机构所在地的主管税务机关申请……,并申报纳税;向……主管税务机关申报纳税……

这类句式一般译为"……应当……,并……","……的,还应……,并……"。

(4) 目的表达式

例19. In order to protect the lawful civil rights and interests of citizens and legal persons, this law is enacted...

译文：为了保护公民和法人的合法民事权益，制定本法……

这类句式译为"为了……而……""为维护……的利益，而……"，一般用来表示立法、合同签订或其他行为的目的。

（5）授权式和权利限制式

例20. The buyer may fix an additional period of time of reasonable length for performance by the seller of his obligations.

译文：买方可以规定一段合理时限的额外时间，让卖方履行其义务。

例21. Unless the buyer has received notice from the seller that he will not perform within the period so fixed, the buyer may not, during that period, resort to any remedy for breach of contract.

译文：除非买方收到卖方的通知，声称他将不在所规定的时间内履行义务，买方在这段时间内不得对违反合同采取任何补救办法。

情态动词may在法律语言中表示授权，可译为"有权……"；will表示"将要"进行的法律行为，是有权采取行动的意思；unless表示"除非……"，是一种权利或行为的限制性用语。

（6）限定条件式

例22. If the failure by the seller to perform any of his obligations under the contract or this Convention amounts to a fundamental breach of contract; or...

译文：卖方不履行其在合同或本公约中的任何义务，等于根本违反合同；或者……

例23. In case of non-delivery, if the seller does not deliver the goods within the additional period of time fixed by the buyer in accordance with paragraph (1) of article 47 or declares that he will not deliver within the period so fixed...

译文：如果发生不交货的情况，卖方不在买方按照第四十七条第（1）款规定的额外时间内交付货物，或卖方声明他将不在所规定的时间内交付货物……

（7）一些特定词引导的句式

notwithstanding引导的特色法律句式，翻译为"尽管……"。where引导的条件状语从句，翻译为"凡……的"或者"如果……的"，与if引导的从句翻译相似。without prejudice to引导的条件句式，翻译为"不影响……"。

2. 国际商事法律汉语句式的翻译及解析

（1）表示法律目的的"为了"句式

例24. 为了保护合同当事人的合法权益，维护社会经济秩序，促进社会主义现代化建设，制定本法。

译文：This Law is formulated in order to protect the lawful rights and interests of contract parties, to safeguard social and economic order, and to promote socialist modernization.

"为了"译为"in order to"，有时也译为"for the purpose of"。

（2）定义式句式

例25. 本法所称合同是平等主体的自然人、法人、其他组织之间设立、变更、终止民事权利义务关系的协议。婚姻、收养、监护等有关身份关系的协议，适用其他法律的规定。

译文：For purposes of this Law, a contract is an agreement between natural persons, legal persons or other organizations with equal standing, for the purpose of establishing, altering, or discharging a relationship of civil rights and obligations. An agreement concerning any personal relationship such as marriage, adoption, guardianship, etc. shall be governed by other applicable laws.

定义式句式可译为"...is..." "...is defined as..."。

（3）"不得"引导的禁止性句式

例26. 当事人依法享有自愿订立合同的权利，任何单位和个人不得非法干预。

译文：A party is entitled to enter into a contract voluntarily under the law, and no entity or individual may unlawfully interfere with such right.

"不得"引导的禁止性句式一般译为"neither...may..."或"no...may..."，表示法律的禁止性规范或禁止性行为。

（4）"应当"引导的行为引导句式

例27. 当事人行使权利、履行义务应当遵循诚实信用原则。

译文：The parties shall abide by the principle of good faith in exercising their rights and performing their obligations.

行为引导句式一般译为"shall..."，但是不可以译为"should..."，"应当遵守"译为"shall abide by"。

（5）"……的"类型概念句式

例28. 要约以信件或者电报作出的，承诺期限自信件载明的日期或者电报交发之日开始计算。

译文：Where an offer is made by a letter or a telegram, the period for acceptance commences on the date shown on the letter or the date on which the telegram is handed in for dispatch.

"……的"类型概念或定义可译为"if the X",或者"where an X is…",或"those…are…"

（6）条件+授权句式

例29. 只有那些预期的受益人有权起诉，以强制执行合同双方之间的协议。意向受益人必须符合下列要求：

（1）给予意向受益人起诉的权利会使合同当事人的合同意向得以实现；并且

（2）履行承诺将履行向受益人支付款项的承诺义务，或

（3）合同签订的情形表明，承诺意向是给予受益人承诺履行的利益。

译文：Only those intended beneficiaries are entitled to sue to enforce an agreement between two other parties. The test of an intended beneficiary must satisfy the following requirements:

(1) Giving the party (intended beneficiary) the right to sue would effectuate the intentions of the parties; and

(2) The performance of the promise will satisfy an obligation of the promise to pay money to the beneficiary, or

(3) The circumstances indicate that the promise intends to give the beneficiary the benefit of the promised performance.

"只有"是法律汉语常用的条件句式，英文一般译为only或unless引导的句式。"意向受益人"是涉及第三方受益人合同常用的表达方式，译为intended beneficiaries，这是美国合同法里的固定表达式。"符合下列要求"是合同条款常用术语，译为satisfy the following requirements。"承诺履行"是合同中设定条件的常用术语，译为the promised performance。

第三节　课内翻译任务

一、英译汉 English-Chinese Translation

Uniform Commercial Code

(9) "**Buyer** in ordinary course of business" means a person who in good faith and without knowledge that the sale to him is in violation of the ownership rights or security interest of a third party in the goods buys in ordinary course from a person in the business of selling goods of that kind but does not include

a pawnbroker. All persons who sell minerals or the like (including oil and gas) at wellhead or minehead shall be deemed to be persons in the business of selling goods of that kind. "Buying" may be for cash or by exchange of other property or on secured or unsecured credit and includes receiving goods or documents of title under a preexisting contract for sale but does not include a transfer in bulk or as security for or in total or partial satisfaction of a money debt.

(10) "**Conspicuous**", a term or clause is conspicuous when it is so written that a reasonable person against whom it is to operate ought to have noticed it. A printed heading in capitals (as: NONNEGOTIABLE BILL OF LADING) is conspicuous. if it is in larger or other contrasting type or color. But in a telegram any stated term is "conspicuous." Whether a term or clause is "conspicuous" or not is for decision by the court.

(11) "**Contract**" means the total legal obligation which results from the parties' agreement as affected by this Act and any other applicable rules of law. (Compare "Agreement.")

(12) "**Creditor**" includes a general creditor, a secured creditor, a lien creditor and any representative of creditors, including an assignee for the benefit of creditors, a trustee in bankruptcy, a receiver in equity and an executor or administrator of an insolvent debtor's or assignor's estate.

重点解析 Notes and Comments

1. "Buyer in ordinary course of business" means a person who in good faith and without knowledge that the sale to him is in violation of the ownership rights or security interest of a third party in the goods buys in ordinary course from a person in the business of selling goods of that kind but does not include a pawnbroker. "正常经营过程中的买受人" 是指买受人善意购买，并且对向其出售的商品侵犯第三人对该商品所有权或享有的担保物权不知情，并且购买是按正常买卖程序从出售人处购得，而不是从当铺老板处购得。

该句运用了法律翻译中的拆分手法，即把一个包含了很多语法结构和复句的长句子，按照逻辑、意群进行适当的切分和重构（restructure），变成一系列目标语容易接受的句式和语义，再分别进行翻译。在使用这个方法的时候，译者一定要搞清楚长句子的逻辑线索，不然的话，翻译稿可能会和原文的意思相差甚远，有的时候甚至相悖，造成严重的后果。该句将a person的定语和"不是从当铺老板处购得"分别切为小句，是采用了灵活对等（dynamic equivalence）的翻译方法。

2. buyer 在法律英语中意思是"买受人"，在合同中一般译为"买方"，和seller（"卖方"）意思相对。

3. good faith善意，指购买人或其他民事参与人，对标的物或民事行为参与人的瑕疵不知情，从而认定己方行为或应合法取得的标的物合法。good faith就是法律术语bona fides third party中的bona fides。民法上的善意第三人（bona fides third party），指的是该第三人不知道法律关系双方的真实情况，通常是指非法交易中，不知情的、已经办理了登记的权利人。无权处分他人动产或不动产的占有人，将动产或不动产非法转让给第三人以后，如果受让人在取得该动产或不动产时出于善意，就可以依法取得对该动产或不动产的所有权。受让人在取得动产或不动产的所有权以后，原所有人不得要求受让人返还财产，而只能要求转让人（占有人）赔偿损失。

4. violation of the ownership rights or security interest侵犯所有权或担保物权，违反所有权或担保物权的规定

5. legal obligation法律责任，具体指duty, liability, damages等。

6. "Creditor" includes a general creditor, a secured creditor, a lien creditor and any representative of creditors... "债权人"包括普通债权人、获得担保的债权人、留置债权人和债权人的任何代表人……

法律翻译力求准确，常有一些固定搭配的词语，general在此处译为"普通"。此处应该省略"a"。

7. 多用shall代替will或should，前者代替后者加强语气和强制力。在合同行文中，shall并非单纯表示将来时，而常用来表示法律上可强制执行的任务，具有约束力，宜译为"应""应该""必须"；will无论语气还是强制力都比shall弱，宜译为"将""原""要"；should通常只用来表示语气较强的假设，可译为"万一"。

二、汉译英 Chinese-English Translation

外商投资法

第二条

在中华人民共和国境内（以下简称中国境内）的外商投资，适用本法。

本法所称外商投资，是指外国的自然人、企业或者其他组织（以下称外国投

资者）直接或者间接在中国境内进行的投资活动，包括下列情形：

（一）外国投资者单独或者与其他投资者共同在中国境内设立外商投资企业；

（二）外国投资者取得中国境内企业的股份、股权、财产份额或者其他类似权益；

（三）外国投资者单独或者与其他投资者共同在中国境内投资新建项目；

（四）法律、行政法规或者国务院规定的其他方式的投资。

本法所称外商投资企业，是指全部或者部分由外国投资者投资，依照中国法律在中国境内经登记注册设立的企业。

重点解析 Notes and Comments

1. "在中华人民共和国境内"必须英译为"within the territory of the People's Republic of China"，不可以省译为China。"以下简称中国境内"译为"hereinafter referred to as within China"，"以下"译为英文常用古体词"hereinafter"，该译法既在成文法中，也在合同、协议、章程中经常使用。"适用本法"译为"This Law applies"，成文法中的"适用"，在英语中不用被动语态，但是司法文书中可以使用被动语态，比如："Article 2 of Foreign Investment Law is applied in the decision of the case."国际私法中的准据法，就译为applied law。所以"在中华人民共和国境内（以下简称中国境内）的外商投资，适用本法"英译为"This Law applies to foreign investment within the territory of the People's Republic of China (hereinafter referred to as 'within China')."此句采用了逆译、"重构"（Restructure）和动态对等的翻译方法。注意：如果不是上一条、前款或前面已经提到"以下简称中国境内"，那么"中国"必须翻译成"the People's Republic of China"。此处采用动态对等的翻译方法。

2. 外国投资者, a foreign investor; 股份、股权、财产份额或者其他类似权益, stock shares, equity shares, shares in assets, or other like rights and interests。

3. "单独或者与其他投资者共同"译为individually or collectively with other investors。

第四节　课后翻译训练

一、将下列句子翻译成汉语 Translate the following sentences into Chinese

1. The offer shall be sufficiently definite and indicates the intention of the

offeror to be bound in case of acceptance.

2. The interest of a lessor or a lessee under a lease contract entered into before the goods became accessions is superior to all interests in the whole except as stated in subsection.

3. "Employee" includes an independent contractor and employee of an independent contractor retained by the employer.

4. A draft may be accepted although it has not been signed by the drawer, is otherwise incomplete, is overdue, or has been dishonored.

5. If the holder assents to an acceptance varying the terms of a draft, the obligation of each drawer and indorser that does not expressly assent to the acceptance is discharged.

6. This section does not apply to cashier's checks or other drafts drawn on the drawer.

7. The person manifesting the intention is the promisor.

8. The person to whom the manifestation is addressed is the promisee.

9. A promise may be stated in words either oral or written, or may be inferred wholly or partly from conduct.

10. If the goods do not conform with the contract, the buyer may require delivery of substitute goods only if the lack of conformity constitute a fundamental breach of the contract.

二、将下列句子翻译成英语 Translate the following sentences into English

1. 撤回要约的通知应当在要约到达受要约人之前或者与要约同时到达受要约人。

2. 只有在法律正义中法律和道德才非常接近，几乎合而为一。

3. 承诺是受要约人同意要约的意思表示。

4. 承诺生效时合同成立。

5. 当事人在订立合同过程中有下列情形之一，给对方造成损失的，应当承担损害赔偿责任。

6. 申请注册的商标，应当有显著特征，便于识别，并不得与他人在先取得的合法权利相冲突。

7. 法人在法律上被视为一个实体。

8. 对于合同中这一条款的确切释义他们的看法不一样。

9. 国家建立外商投资安全审查制度，对影响或者可能影响国家安全的外商投资进行安全审查。

10. 当事人未选择法院的，应由被告住所地或合同履行地法院管辖。

三、将下列短文翻译成汉语 Translate the following passage into Chinese

How a Promise May Be Made

4. How a Promise May Be Made

A promise may be stated in words either oral or written, or may be inferred wholly or partly from conduct.

5. Terms of Promise, Agreement, or Contract

(1) A term of promise or agreement is that portion of the intention or assent manifested which relates to a particular matter.

(2) A term of contract is that portion of the legal relations resulting from the promise or set of promises which relates to a particular matter, whether or not the parties manifest an intention to create those relations.

6. Formal Contracts

The following types of contracts are subject in some respects to special rules that depend on their formal characteristics and differ from those governing contracts in general:

(1) Contracts under seal,

(2) Recognizances,

(3) Negotiable instruments and documents,

(4) Letters of credit.

7. Voidable Contracts

A voidable contract is one where one or more parties have the power, by a manifestation of election to do so, to avoid the legal relations created by the contract, or by ratification of the contract to extinguish the power of avoidance.

8. Unenforceable Contracts

An unenforceable contract is one for the breach of which neither the remedy of damages nor the remedy of specific performance is available, but which is recognized in some other way as creating a duty of performance, though there has been no ratification.

9. Parties Required

There must be at least two parties to a contract, a promisor and a promisee, but there may be any greater number.

10. Multiple Promisors and Promisees of the Same Performance

(1) Where there are more promisors than one in a contract, some or all of them may promise the same performance, whether or not there are also promises for separate performances.

(2) Where there are more promises than one in a contract, a promise may be made to some or all of them as a unit, whether or not the same or another performance is separately promised to one or more of them.

11. When a Person May Be Both Promisor and Promisee

A contract may be formed between two or more persons acting as a unit and one or more but fewer than all of these persons, acting either singly or with other persons.

注释：

"How a Promise May Be Made"（"如何作出承诺"）为《美国合同法（第二次）重述》的一部分。

四、将下列短文翻译成英语 Translate the following passage into English

外商投资法

第四条　国家对外商投资实行准入前国民待遇加负面清单管理制度。

前款所称准入前国民待遇，是指在投资准入阶段给予外国投资者及其投资不低于本国投资者及其投资的待遇；所称负面清单，是指国家规定在特定领域对外商投资实施的准入特别管理措施。国家对负面清单之外的外商投资，给予国民待遇。

负面清单由国务院发布或者批准发布。

中华人民共和国缔结或者参加的国际条约、协定对外国投资者准入待遇有更优惠规定的，可以按照相关规定执行。

第五条　国家依法保护外国投资者在中国境内的投资、收益和其他合法权益。

第六条　在中国境内进行投资活动的外国投资者、外商投资企业,应当遵守中国法律法规,不得危害中国国家安全、损害社会公共利益。

第七条　国务院商务主管部门、投资主管部门按照职责分工,开展外商投资促进、保护和管理工作;国务院其他有关部门在各自职责范围内,负责外商投资促进、保护和管理的相关工作。

县级以上地方人民政府有关部门依照法律法规和本级人民政府确定的职责分工,开展外商投资促进、保护和管理工作。

本章中的UCC指美国《统一商法典》(*Uniform Commercial Code*),U.S. CODE或UC指《美国联邦法典》(*The United States Code of Federal Regulations*),相关例句均选自美国联邦最高法院官方网站,网址:www.supremecourt.gov/oral_arguments/argument_audio/2018,访问日期:2024年6月30日。

第十六章 国际旅游翻译

根据联合国世界旅游组织(UNWTO)公布的资料,到2030年,全球旅游人数预计达到18亿。旅游产业与各行各业息息相关,如通信、时尚与休闲、大型赛事等。旅游行业正在迅速而灵活地适应新市场的需求变化。在经济全球化的背景下,这一行业不仅吸引着越来越多的外国游客前来游览,为本土市场带来丰富的投资机会;同时,也有大批本国游客走出国门,探索外面的世界。以中国为例,不仅来华旅游的外国游客人数不断攀升,中国游客出境游的数量也在逐年增长。中国,作为世界文明古国,凭借独特的历史文化、民族风情和山水风光,吸引着全球旅游爱好者。进入21世纪,中国已成为热门投资地和安全旅游胜地,旅游业成为重要的支柱产业。旅游翻译作为沟通桥梁,对国人了解世界、世界了解中国至关重要。本章介绍了旅游翻译的概念、功能与原则,以及英汉旅游文体的差异,着重探讨了中文旅游文本英译的主要文体与翻译方法。

第一节 旅游翻译的概念、功能与原则

一、旅游翻译的概念

本章所讲的旅游翻译(tourism translation)指的是专注于人们出行和旅游相关内容的英汉互译活动。由于旅游文化涵盖了不同国家的物质与非物质文化精髓,旅游翻译相较于其他翻译类型,展现出跨语言、跨社会、跨时空、跨文化及跨心理的鲜明特点,成为一种独特的交际活动。

陈刚教授深入剖析了旅游翻译的这些特征,并进行了多维度的分类和说明:

从翻译手段来看,旅游翻译可分为导译、口译(涵盖视译、交替传译、同声传译等多种形式)、笔译以及机器翻译等四种类型。

一、按照涉及的符号和语言划分,旅游翻译包含语内翻译、语际翻译以及符际翻译三种形式。

二、按照译出语和译入语的不同，旅游翻译可以分为外语译为本族语和本族语译为外语两种类别。

三、从题材角度看，旅游翻译既体现了专业性翻译的特点，又兼具一般性和文学性翻译的特质。

四、按照翻译方式的不同，旅游翻译既包括全译，也涵盖部分翻译的方式。

这些分类方式为我们更全面地理解旅游翻译的多样性和复杂性提供了有力的工具。（陈刚，2004：20—25）

二、旅游翻译的功能

旅游资料的翻译需将资料功能与翻译技巧相结合，无论何种类型，其目的均为吸引游客。其核心功能包括信息提供、美感传递与"诱导"游客。资料必须详尽介绍风景名胜，宣传其魅力，从而激发人们的旅游兴趣，并增进对中国历史文化的认识。因此，在旅游翻译中，为有效传递信息、感染受众，译者必须顾及译文读者的欣赏习惯和心理感受，在译文中尽量使用他们所熟悉的语言表达形式（至少不能因方式不当而造成理解上的障碍），尽可能地使译文获取近似原文的读者效应。从这个意义上来说，旅游翻译注重的应是原文与译文间信息内容和交际功能的对等，而不是语言形式上的对应，更不是展示源语语言文化的异质性。它的功能更像商品广告，目的就是要吸引游客，最大限度地取得旅游产品的预期效果。（方梦之、毛忠明，2018：230）因此，旅游资料翻译应全面传达原文信息，反映其功能，以达到原文的交际目的。

三、旅游翻译的原则

方梦之教授提出了"达旨、循规、共喻"的应用翻译原则。旅游翻译在遵循这一原则的基础上，还需根据旅游翻译的特性、功能及目的，制定一套专门指导其研究与实践的具体性原则。

夏康明与范先明（2013）认为，旅游翻译应遵循三大原则：一是信息内容与文本功能对等，二是贴近译语的语言和文化习惯，三是具备跨文化交际意识。

（一）旅游文化翻译应做到信息内容和文本功能对等

旅游翻译应注重原文和译文中所传递的内容和作用的对等，换句话说，应具有准确传递信息，吸引游客和打动读者的功能。这就要求旅游翻译应做到准确、通俗、易懂，具有吸引力，且能被不同文化水平的游客所接受和理解。

旅游资料翻译的成功与否，首先取决于效果，即是否达到宣传的目的。美国当代著名翻译理论家尤金·奈达（Eugene Nida）和查尔斯·泰伯（Charles R. Taber）指出："所谓翻译，是指从语义到语体用最切近而又最自然的对等语再现原文的信息。"（Nida and Taber, 1969: 12）这里的"对等"指的是译文对目的语读者所产生的效果大致相等。译者必须把重点放在译文的读者上，充分考虑到译文的可读性和读者接受能力，使读者理解并接受信息，达到旅游资料翻译的最终目的。

（二）旅游文化翻译应贴近译语的语言和文化习惯

为了使读者能够通过本国的语言来了解其他国家的文化，译者在翻译内容时不仅要遵循译文的信息内容和文本功能对等原则，还要考虑翻译方法和形式是否符合目的语的语言结构。

由汉语译为其他语言的方式在我国的旅游翻译中占了很高的比例，而旅游翻译又属于对外翻译，因此黄友义教授对对外翻译的译者提出了更高的要求和原则，即"外宣三贴近（贴近中国发展的实际，贴近国外受众对中国信息的需求，贴近国外受众的思维习惯）的原则"（黄友义，2004: 27）。旅游翻译是外宣翻译的关键一环，若翻译内容或方式稍有不妥，其错误和缺陷会被国际社会放大审视。因此，译者在翻译时需格外注意文化差异，深入研究并了解外国语言习俗，力求避免歧义，以免被他人诟病。

（三）旅游文化翻译必须具备跨文化交际意识

跨文化交际是不同文化背景的人之间的信息交流过程，这一过程常受到双方文化、价值观及思维方式差异的影响，进而影响信息理解的深度。在全球化的今天，语言翻译作为各国文化交流的桥梁，在各民族文化的交流过程中起着十分重要的作用。翻译标准的设定需要以跨文化交际为依据，对确定翻译标准的适度性、翻译技巧选用的策略性、翻译过程的合理性、翻译质量的优质性，以及翻译传播的实效性提供了定性或定量的支撑。（夏康明、范先明，2013: 45）因此，译者在旅游翻译中扮演着促进文化交融的关键角色，必须具备跨文化交际意识，深刻理解原文与译文背后的不同文化意蕴。

总之，旅游翻译作为一种跨文化交际活动，涵盖了旅游者的衣食住行及丰富多样的文化内容。翻译过程涉及不同文化的特殊性，因此译者须具备强烈的跨文化意识，确保旅游文化信息能准确传达给海外游客。

第二节　英汉旅游文体的差异

一、行文习惯不同

在汉语表达中，一般习惯将重要的信息放在最后，而在英语表达中，则习惯于将重要的信息放在最前面，这与两种不同的文化背景有关。中国人说话、写文章有时喜欢"卖关子"，将重要的信息最后传达，所以在听人说话或阅读文章时，我们中国人一般会特别关注最后出现的信息；而英美人一般会直截了当将他们的目的或意图首先说出，然后再作具体的阐述说明。在有些旅游景点资料汉译英的过程中，为符合英美人的表述习惯，可将次序调整，起到开门见山、突出重点的作用。

例1. 在四川阿坝藏族羌族自治州的南坪、松潘等地的交界处，有一片纵深30余公里的风景区，那就是举世闻名的大熊猫的故乡——九寨沟自然保护区。

译文：Jiuzhaigou, a 30-kilometre-long scenic gully, lies on the border between Nanping and Songpan in the Aba Tibetan and Qiang Autonomous Prefecture, Sichuan Province. It is the natural range of the world-known giant panda, as well as a nature reserve designated by the state.

原文"九寨沟"在最后出现，译文句首就出现Jiuzhaigou，可谓开门见山，突出重点信息。此外，把"有一片纵深30余公里的风景区"这句变成Jiuzhaigou的同位语，做补充说明，简化了句子结构。同时，"风景区"也没有直译为scenic area或scenic attraction，而用了gully这个表示"冲沟、水沟"的词，突出了"沟"的内涵。

二、表达形式不同

汉语和英语源自两种完全不同的文化背景，而且由于中国人和英美人生活的社会结构、历史条件、地理环境等方面存在差异，形成了两种不同的思维方式和审美观点。汉语表达委婉含蓄，意境悠远；英语表达思维缜密，结构严谨。汉语为了加强文章的力度，往往不惜使用大量的修饰词汇和动词密集句子，这与英语的习惯和风格相去甚远。英语最忌表达繁复，加上英语句子是以主谓结构为主干，如果译文不分主次一味堆积动词，就会破坏英语的习惯表达，与英美人的审美方式和欣赏习惯背道而驰。例如：

例2. 西湖犹如明镜，千峰凝翠，洞壑幽深，风光旖旎。

译文：The West Lake is like a mirror embellished all around with green hills and deep caves of enchanting beauty.

英语忌讳"形式流散",遣词讲究逻辑性,造句推崇组织性。翻译该句时,首先,不宜同时并列使用几个主语,须辨其主次,确立这句话的主语是the West Lake;其次,再分析千峰、洞壑、风光与西湖的关系,寻找它们的联系词;最后还应注意名词的单复数形式等问题。在上述译文中,虽然"千峰""凝翠"的诗情画意消失了,"洞壑""幽深"的语境不见了,但译文在语言的地道性上更符合英美国家的习惯,也较好地传达了语言信息。

例3. 姑苏城外,湖泊河流,星罗棋布,河泽纵横,各具特色的桥梁鳞次栉比,举目入画。建筑傍水而立,幽静雅逸,形成了水乡城市的独特风貌。

译文:Outside Suzhou, rivers, lakes and artificial waterways spread all over the place. The canals are spanned with small bridges with distinct features. If you look round, you will enjoy the view of picturesque beauty. The quiet elegant waterside buildings have assumed the unique feature of a water city.

在汉语表达中,为了起到言简意赅、生动形象的效果,我们常用"四字格"语言来表达。以上一段短短的旅游介绍文字涉及的就有"湖泊河流""星罗棋布""河泽纵横""鳞次栉比""举目入画""傍水而立""幽静雅逸"。在直译表达不符合英美人欣赏习惯的情况下,我们应该采用简洁的意译方式,将原有文字在理解之后重组。

旅游景点的汉语英译有别于文学翻译,它只是一种介绍性的文字,目的是让国外游客能够理解。在翻译时只有善于抓住主旨,去繁就简,才能译出符合英语表达方式的文章。

三、句式结构不同

在将中国的旅游景点资料译为英语时,句式结构的处理尤为重要。汉语句子信息的传达主要通过语言环境和语言内在关联来体现——"以意统形"。句中任何相关结合部分只要搭配合理就能够组成句子,因而句子反映的是整体思维的多维性特征,带有很强的模糊性。而英语则注重形态变化,句界分明,以动词为核心,主谓结构为主干,形成空间组合,句子结构层次分明,表现为一种严密的逻辑性思维。

例4."人间仙境"桃花源,位于湖南省常德市西南40公里处,南倚武陵,中贯国道,北临沅水,居湖南省诸风景名胜区之枢纽,系湖南省十大风景名胜区之一。

在当地的旅游景点资料中是这样翻译的：

The Peach Blossom Spring which is situated about 40km to the southwest of Changde City, Hunan Province has the Wuling Mountains towering over at its south and Yuan River flowing by at its north. The thorough fare runs through the land. It is a pivot of the scenic spots and the one of the famous ten regions of scenery in Hunan Province.

这段英语文字，主干部分明显偏离汉语的重心，与其他部分关系不清，构句行文纯属汉语思维方式，因而结构散乱。按照句子层次结构，该例句主干应该是汉语文字的画线部分，其余只是辅助成分，英译时可用分词短语和介词结构来表示，显得主次分明。修改后的译文为：

Taohuayuan (Peach Blossom Spring), located about 40km to the southwest of Changde City, is among the ten well-known scenic spots in Hunan Province. It is a thoroughfare to other places with Mount Wuling on the south, the Yuan River on the north, and the national roads through its area.

四、文化渊源不同

汉语旅游资料常常会涉及一些具有中国特色的人名、地名、朝代以及度量衡，外国游客中，许多人对中国的情况知道甚少，或者根本不了解。在翻译时，我们应该"以服务为本"，注意适当添加辅助信息，将这些知识补充出来。

例5. 颐和园历史悠久，早在金朝时便是完颜亮的行宫。元朝官员郭守敬在北京时，又加以扩建，他将玉泉山和昌平县的泉水引入了今昆明湖。

译文：The Summer Palace boasts a long history. It began to serve as a temporary palace as far back as the reign of Wanyan Liang (1149—1161), ruler of the Jin Dynasty (1115—1234). Guo Shoujing (1231—1316), an official in the Yuan Dynasty (1271—1368), built more palatial buildings temples and flower gardens around Kunming Lake in the palace.

翻译过程中，应注明人物所处时代和相关信息。与此同时，汉语旅游资料有时会涉及文化味浓但又不是非有不可的词语或典故，如果强行翻译，会使译文显得拖泥带水、松散乏力，反而失去原文特色。一些典故和引用对本国读者来说，可以加深他们的印象，从中获得艺术的享受，而在外国游客看来也许就是画蛇添足。对理解原文没有帮助的部分，可以考虑省去不译，或者加以压缩。

例6. (天津独乐寺)门内两侧是两座民间称为哼哈二将的泥塑金刚力士像，

紧跟着是四幅明人所绘的"四大天王",即<u>东方持国天王、南方增长天王、西方广目天王、北方多闻天王</u>的彩色画像。

译文:(In Dule Temple) Behind the gate stand two powerful-looking clay statues of warrior attendants, one on either side. Further behind are four colored pictures of heavenly Kings by a Ming Dynasty painter.

画线部分文字,对外国游客来讲意义不大。可以将其作删减处理。

中国旅游景点资料英译属于对外宣传文本,它的主要目的是让外国游客能够理解。翻译时要从文化角度入手,符合英语使用者的思维方式、文化传统和审美习惯。翻译旅游资料要有针对性,忠于原文的同时,在不影响原文意思表达的前提下,为符合英美人的欣赏习惯,可以对段落文字进行次序调整、内容添加或删减。

西方传统哲学思维偏重理性、突出个性、主客观对立的特点,使得英语表达具有客观、简约的风格,语言上追求一种自然理性之美,表达逻辑严谨,思维缜密,行文用字最忌重复堆砌。

例7. Tiny islands are strung around the edge of the peninsula like a pearl necklace. Hunks of coral reef, coconut palms and fine white sand.

译文:座座岛屿玲珑小巧,紧密相连,像一串珍珠缀成的项链,环绕着半岛边缘。岛上椰树成片,沙滩如银,四周满是红色的珊瑚礁,景色如诗如画。(方梦之、毛忠明,2018:237)

这句话看起来就像一张实地拍的照片,几乎全是景物的罗列:镶嵌在边缘的一串珍珠、大片的珊瑚礁、椰树、白色的沙滩,整个场景构成了一幅生动鲜活的海岛风光图。

例8. The harbor looked most beautiful in its semi-circle of hills and half lights. The color of a pearl gray and a fairy texture soft, melting halftones. Nothing brittle of garish.

译文:只见海港被环抱于半圆形的小山丛中,煞是好看,朦朦胧胧,一片银灰,宛若仙境——它浓淡交融,光影柔和,清雅绝俗。

全文句式简洁,译文中"朦朦胧胧"等表达十分直观精细,一景一物,栩栩如生,按汉语的行文方式译出,显得越发音韵和美、意境交融。

第三节　旅游资料英译的主要方法

旅游文本翻译涉及旅游景点介绍、广告、告示标牌、民俗风情画册及古迹楹联解说等多方面内容。其中，景点介绍翻译尤为凸显旅游文体特色，也是翻译中的重点和难点。中文旅游文本在推广中国丰富的人文、历史、自然与文化旅游资源时，扮演着举足轻重的角色。优秀的翻译不仅能吸引更多外国游客前来中国，还能让中国深厚的文化内涵传扬四海，进而树立中国作为旅游大国的良好形象。

在英译旅游资料时，译文应自然流畅、清晰易懂、简洁直观且富有感染力。这需要采用多种翻译方法，并对译文进行适当调整，以达到最佳效果。

旅游资料翻译不是表面文字上的吻合，而是信息和语言内涵上的契合。鉴于以上英汉旅游文体的差异，在进行具体的翻译操作时应针对不同的语言现象采取灵活的翻译策略，如"直译""直译加注释""增补""省译""意译"和"类比"等。旅游资料的翻译只有把握翻译的基本原则，采取多种翻译方法有机结合，对译文进行适当的调整，才能取得更好的效果。在翻译实践中，应根据旅游资料不同的侧重点，进行必要的变通和处理，对译文进行调整。既不能一味地追求"忠实"，也不能一味地追求通顺。

一、直译

例9. 紫禁城分成两部分，前面部分有三大殿。皇帝在这里处理朝政，主持重要仪式。紫禁城内大部分建筑物的屋顶都是黄瓦，黄色只有皇帝才能使用。

译文：The Forbidden City is divided into two sections. The front part has three large halls, where the emperor dealt with the state affairs and conducted important ceremonies. Most buildings in the Forbidden City have roofs of yellow tiles, for yellow was the colour for the emperor.

二、直译加注释

例10. 当时在城西南的锡山开采出了锡矿，锡矿发现后，人们就把这个地方称为"有锡"。天长日久，锡矿挖完了，"有锡"便改成了"无锡"。

译文：Then on the Xishan Hill to the southwest of the city, a tin mine was discovered. After that, the city was named "Youxi" (which means "having tin"). As time went by, the tin mine was exhausted, and the city was renamed "Wuxi" (which means "having no tin").

三、增补

增补,也可称为增词或加注,就是在翻译有关人名、历史事件、地理名称、风俗、典故、诗词等内容时予以简要的说明、解释或补充,增加一些信息和背景知识,也称为增译。例如,在介绍桂林风土人情的文章中,把"三月三节"翻译成San Yue San Festival还不够,因为外国旅客对此一无所知,不能唤起他们的兴趣和共鸣,所以应该加上适当的解释,比如译成: The festival usually takes place on the third day of the third lunar month, when the ethnic minority, especially the young get together for folk song contests to make friends with each other.

中文习惯于用朝代来记录和表述历史事件发生的时间,提到某个朝代,就能让人想起相应的历史文化背景以及与现在的距离感,然而外国人是不可能有这样的感受的,更不用说记得每个朝代的皇帝了。如果不加以解释的话,外国游客就无法感受其历史的悠久和文化的深远,因此在翻译这类时间时,都会用公历年份加以解释。(桑龙扬、赵联斌,2017: 51)

例11. 大观楼位于滇池北岸,修建于清朝康熙二十九年。

译文: The Grand View Pavilion, located at the lake's northern bank, was built in the 29th year of Kangxi Reign in the Qing Dynasty (1690 AD).

四、类比/归化

类比,即用人们所熟悉的事例说明或解释未知的或较难理解的道理。运用类比,不需要长篇大论就可以把难以表达的概念或道理表达清楚。类比的方法不仅有助于外国游客克服文化差异,更好地理解译文,更能拉近彼此之间的距离,产生亲切感,激发游客的兴趣,使译文收到良好的效果。

例12. 济公劫富济贫,深受穷苦人民爱戴。

译文: Jigong, the Chinese "Robin Hood", robbed the rich and helped the poor.

译文将济公比作外国游客非常熟悉的罗宾汉,不用更多的笔墨就可以让外国游客了解济公是什么样的人和他在人民心中的地位,产生很好的效果。

类比可以是多方面的。它可以使外国游客将他们感到陌生的中国历史年代、人物和事件等与他们熟悉的人物、事件等联系起来,便于理解。

五、省译

汉语在描写景物时,主观色彩极浓,辞藻华丽,文笔夸张。如果将汉语原文逐字译出，与英语简洁明快、直观理性的欣赏习惯不相符合。刻意追求原文之美，会使外国游客感到语言啰唆，华而不实，根本无法领略其中的美感。在翻译这类资料时，需要译者仔细推敲原文，透过其华丽的外表，抓住实质具体的内容，译出符合英语表达习惯的译文，只有这样才能使译文读者获得与原文读者相同或相近的审美反映。

例13. 这里3000座奇峰拔地而起，形态各异，有的似玉柱神鞭，立地顶天；有的像铜墙铁壁，巍然屹立；有的如晃板垒卵，摇摇欲坠；有的若盆景古董，玲珑剔透……神奇而又真实，迷离而又实在，不是艺术创造胜似艺术创造，令人叹为观止。

译文：3000 crags rise in various shape-pillars, columns, walls, shaky egg stacks and potted landscapes, conjuring up fantastic and unforgettable images.

译文删掉了原文堆砌的辞藻，根据原文内容译出了具体的实物，符合英语的表达习惯。

例14. 这儿的峡谷又是另一番景象：谷中急水奔流，穿峡而过，两岸树木葱茏，鲜花繁茂，碧草萋萋，活脱脱一幅生机盎然的天然风景画。各种奇峰异岭，令人感受各异，遐想万千。

译文：It is another gorge through which a rapid stream flows. Trees, flowers and grass, a picture of nature vitality, thrive on both banks. The majestic peaks arouse disparate thoughts.

汉语为了增加原文的色彩，用了"葱茏""繁茂""萋萋"三个词。若按照英语思维，这三个词表达同一个意思——"生长茂盛"，可以用一个vitality概括，再结合"树、花、草"等实物，语言练达，直观简洁，符合外国游客的审美习惯。

六、意译

汉语描写景色的词汇丰富，多用对偶、排比，翻译成英语可能很困难，因此多采用意译。如果勉强逐字逐句照译，可能反而伤害原意。

例15. 境内西湖明镜，千峰凝翠，洞壑幽深，风光旖旎。

译文：The West Lake is like a mirror embellished all around with green hills and deep caves of enchanting beauty.

原文用了"千峰凝翠""洞壑幽深""风光旖旎"等四字词，翻译时切忌死译，应根据英语习惯，译出其意义。

总之，译文应考虑外国游客的特点和中外文化差异，在达意的基础上，务求语言的简明，努力唤起外国读者的兴趣，并使他们了解一些中国文化。

七、音译

音译法多用于旅游翻译中的专有名词，如地名和人名的翻译。这符合国际惯例所要求的地名、人名单一罗马化，即使用普通话中的汉语拼音。大部分的旅游景点名称都是采用的音译法，如：北海公园（Beihai Park）、苏州园林（Suzhou Gardens）、滇池（Dianchi Lake）。当然，不是所有的景点名称都适用于音译法。有些景点名称含有特别寓意时，需要采用意译的方法，例如故宫的正大门"午门"，这里的"午"是有其含义的，代表的是"子午线"的意思，因此"午门"的译名是Meridian Gate，而不是Wu Gate。这就要求译者对我国的文化古迹、风景名胜的历史非常了解。

八、综译

综译就是综合运用各种译法，根据特定条件下读者的特殊需求，对旅游文本语篇采用摘译、编译、译述、缩译、综述、述评、译评、改译、阐译、译写和参译等"变译"方式进行翻译。从旅游文本整体语篇效果来看，汉语文本使用四字格词语及修辞手法较多，气势磅礴，场面大气。英语文本场景描述简单朴素，语气客观真实。因此在进行旅游文本语篇的汉英翻译时，要抓住语篇实质性的信息进行重点翻译。（高飞雁、王莲凤，2019：39—41）

例16. 与东海岛相映成趣的是吉兆湾海滩旅游区，它距离湛江市区仅65公里，并被誉为"南国风光经典"。那里的海滩十里九湾，湾如新月，沙似浇金。水清、沙莹、石美、林密，一湾一景，真不愧为南国风光的"经典"。吉兆湾甚至还被人们美称为"小三亚"。每逢正月元宵佳节，湾里还可观赏到闻名中外的"吴川三绝"——花桥、泥塑与飘色。

译文：Jizhaowan Beach Resort forms a delightful contrast with Donghai Island and is only 65 miles from Zhanjiang City. It is called "the classic sample of southern scenery." The beach looks like a crescent shaped turning and is with golden sand. It is also famous for clear water, beautiful sands and stones and heavy forests. Surely it is the "classic" of southern scenery. Jizhaowan has even gained the reputation of "Small Sanya in Hainan Island." Well, you can enjoy the three wonders of Wuchuan here—flower bridge, clay sculpture and wooden images of local opera during Lantern Festival in the first month of lunar year.

译文在翻译第一句时抓住了文中实质性的信息，省略了汉语渲染性的词汇"相映成趣"。"南国风光经典"属重复的表述，以示强调。翻译时作为总结性的句子放在了景点介绍之后。"吴川三绝"中的"飘色"采用了释义的方法，便于读者更好地理解。此外，为避免重复，译文中多次用代词it代替主语Jizhaowan Beach Resort，既符合英语语言习惯，又能达到更好的语篇衔接效果。

例17. 柳州市区青山环绕，水抱城流，被誉为"世界第一天然大盆景"。唐代诗人柳宗元诗中"岭树重遮千里目，江流曲似九回肠"，便是柳州城市风貌最为形象的写照。

译文：With green mountains standing around the city, and a crystal river meandering through, Liuzhou gets a fine reputation of "the biggest natural bonsai in the world" for its unique geographical scenery.

译文采用了摘译的翻译方式。进行摘译时，首先应仔细阅读原文的内容，在对其内容进行准确、充分的理解后，再将重点以简短句翻译出来，尽量删去不必要的内容，保留重要的概念。本段译文重点表述柳州的地理风貌，删除了译文读者不容易理解的诗句，用介词短语for its unique geographical scenery一笔概括柳州被称为"世界第一天然大盆景"的原因，言简意赅，通俗易懂。

旅游文本的功能是信息性、情感性和诱导性，其中诱导性为主导功能。因此，翻译旅游文本时要认真分析、掌握读者的文化心理和审美习惯，使译文所表达的信息易于被游客理解、接受。同时，旅游文本翻译应遵循适宜原则和对等原则，应充分理解和尊重中西方文化差异，适当调整翻译方法，可采用直译、直译+注释、增译/释义、省译/删减、音译+意译、归化/类比或者"变译"等方法进行翻译。如此，才能达到吸引外国游客，同时向世界传播中国文化的目的。

第四节　课内翻译任务

一、英译汉 English-Chinese Translation

The Cambridge University Botanic Garden

Plants from all over the world in one great garden, one great day out.

- A 40 acre oasis of beautiful gardens and glasshouses
- A Grade II heritage landscape, with the best arboretum in the region
- All-year interest & seasonal inspiration

"This exceptionally attractive botanic garden is essential visiting for any garden lover."

This heritage-listed Garden opened in 1846 through the vision and drive of Professor John Henslow, mentor to Charles Darwin. Today the Garden is a showcase for over 8000 plant species from around the world, including nine National Plant Collections, all immaculately displayed amongst the finest arboretum in the region.

Designed for both year-round interest and seasonal inspiration, highlights include the beautiful new herbaceous plants around the Garden Cafe, designed by Bradley-Hole Schoenaich Landscape Architects; the renowned Winter Garden, a masterclass in combining foliage, flower and fragrance; the Rock Garden, with its kaleidoscopic early-summer flowers and vantage point over the Lake; the Dry Garden, an inspirational experiment in water-wise gardening; the Scented Garden, richly-fragranced with herbs and roses; and, the unique, historic Systematic Beds, that demonstrate plant groupings across an unparalleled three-acre site. The magnificent Glasshouse Range offers year-round warmth in which to explore habitats ranging from arid lands of architectural cactus to flamboyant, tropical rainforests.

The beautiful Garden Cafe is situated at the heart of the Garden, part of the Stirling Prize-winning Sainsbury Laboratory complex, and serves delicious homemade food locally sourced where possible, and teas and coffees. The Botanic Garden Shop is the perfect place to pick up a gift, memento or reference work, including the new Guide to the Botanic Garden.

Opening daily at 10am, the Cambridge University Botanic Garden is an inspiration for gardeners, an exciting introduction to the natural world for families (children can borrow our free Young Explorer backpacks from the ticket offices) and a great day out for all our visitors.

重点解析 Notes and Comments

1. 本篇短文是剑桥大学植物园的简介，是典型的旅游简介文本，文体风格上体现了信息型文本和呼唤型文本的特征：既要提供植物园的基本信息，又要有吸引游客和植物爱好者的感召力。

2. Plants from all over the world in one great garden, one great day out.观赏世界各地植物，享受一天美好时光。

原文是名词短语，可以译为动感较强的动宾结构。汉语旅游文本句子并列时惯用对称结构，若要保留原文词性特征，依然译为对称结构，可译为：天下植物荟萃，一天美好时光。

3. A 40 acre oasis of beautiful gardens and glasshouses

A Grade II heritage landscape, with the best arboretum in the region

占地40英亩的绿洲，处处是美丽的花园和温室

属二级遗产景观，是本地区最美植物园

两句英文均为名词短语，译为动宾结构，尤其是第二句with引导的介词短语，也译为"是"字句。

4. All-year interest & seasonal inspiration全年胜境，四季皆景

原文两个并列的名词短语，译为汉语的两个四字结构，符合汉语的语言特征。

5. This heritage-listed Garden opened in 1846 through the vision and drive of Professor John Henslow, mentor to Charles Darwin. 1846年，这座登上遗产名录的花园，在查尔斯·达尔文的导师约翰·亨斯洛教授的推动下开园。

原文"through the vision and drive of..."句如译为"通过……的愿景与推动"则搭配不当，应将"drive"转译为动词，而把"vision"一词移到下一句翻译。

6. Designed for both year-round interest and seasonal inspiration, highlights include...

主体部分"highlights include..."是一个主谓宾结构，"designed for..."是过去分词短语，修饰主体部分。"highlights include..."中的动词谓语include后接一系列并列的名词宾语，有的宾语后面带介词短语，有的宾语后面带that引导的定语从句。这些宾语成分都是植物园内的著名景点，而且又分别带有附加和修饰成分。因此，为突出原文的主旨，翻译时要凸显这些景点特征，采取拆句的方法，将各个景点名称分别译出，这样读起来才清晰、通顺，也符合中文的表达习惯。

7. The Botanic Garden Shop is the perfect place to pick up a gift, memento or reference work, including the new Guide to the Botanic Garden.植物园商店里，礼品、纪念品或《植物园指南》，任君选取。

根据旅游景点的实际情况，有些纪念品是免费的，旅游手册和指南之类的材料，一般也是免费的。所以，这里的pick up不要译得太具体，可以译为"选取""挑选"等。

二、汉译英 Chinese-English Translation

庐山

庐山，位于江西省北部，北濒长江，东南临鄱阳湖。自然风光奇特秀丽。"匡庐奇秀，甲天下山"。方圆302平方公里的风景区内，有16个大自然奇观，474处景点。171座山峰逶迤相连，峰峦叠嶂。

庐山奇峰幽险，瀑飞泉鸣；云蒸雾涌，气象万千。3000余种植物分布在云山锦谷，苍翠斑斓，争奇斗艳。独特的第四纪冰川遗迹，使其平添几分神秘色彩。山麓的鄱阳湖候鸟多达百万，世界上最大的鹤群在水天之间翩翩起舞，构成了鹤飞千点的天下奇观。

庐山，历史文化悠久丰厚。早在远古时期，庐山就曾出现在我们祖先的遗迹中。西汉历史学家司马迁南登庐山，将庐山之名载入《史记》至今已有2000多年。白鹿洞书院为我国古代四大书院之首，在中国教育史上享有盛誉。东晋高僧建造的东林寺，是佛教净土宗的发源地。历史上先后有众多名人登庐山，为庐山留下了4000余首诗、900余处摩崖石刻和浩如烟海的著作、画卷及书法作品。现在的600余栋风格迥异、造型别致的别墅，反映了16个不同的国家和民族的文化底蕴。

重点解析 Notes and Comments

1. 庐山，位于江西省北部，北濒长江，东南临鄱阳湖。自然风光奇特秀丽。Mount Lushan is situated in the north of Jiangxi Province, with the Changjiang River (the Yangtze River) flowing by in the north and Poyang Lake in the southeast, featuring unique and charming natural scenery.

表达"位于"之意，英语可以用be situated, be located, lie作句子的谓语，如本句译文。很多情况下，"位于"句可译成分词短语，句子结构也随之改变。本句也可以译为：

Mount Lushan, situated in the northern part of Jiangxi Province, is bordered by the Yangtze River to the north and Poyang Lake to the southeast.

也可以将"位于"句置于句首，译为：

Situated in the northern part of Jiangxi Province, Mount Lushan is bordered by the Yangtze River to the north and Poyang Lake to the southeast.

"自然风光奇特秀丽"在原文中是独立的句子，但译文与前句合并翻译，以使句子更加紧凑,更具有衔接性。

2. 匡庐奇秀,甲天下山。Known as "the most beautiful mountain in the world."

"匡庐奇秀,甲天下山"还可以译为"renowned for its exceptional beauty, ranking first among all mountains in the world"。采用这两种译法,既体现了庐山风光的卓越,又避免了直译可能带来的歧义。注意不能直接译成"Mount Lushan is the most beautiful mountain in the world."国内不少名胜、名山冠以"天下第一、江南第一、甲天下"等美誉,一般不能从委托者的角度直接表达"天下第一"等意思,因为这样有自吹自擂之嫌。"桂林山水甲天下"曾征集译文,吴伟雄的译文获得最佳译文奖:"East or West, the landscape of Guilin is the best."该译文既朗朗上口,又避免了自我吹嘘的尴尬。

3. ……171座山峰逶迤相连,峰峦叠嶂。...171 peaks standing on rolling mountain ranges

该句可以简化译为:171 peaks。"逶迤相连,峰峦叠嶂"是中文旅游文本中对山的典型描述,但英文一般比较简洁,不必把中文里色彩比较浓厚的描述性词语完整翻译出来。

4. 庐山奇峰幽险,瀑飞泉鸣;云蒸雾涌,气象万千。The landscape of Mount Lushan is characterized by its rugged peaks and deep valleys, where waterfalls roar like thunder cascading down precipitous cliffs, and streams meander through serene nooks and gurgle over rocks. Clouds and mist float and envelop the surroundings, creating an ethereal atmosphere.

中文重意合,英文重形合。原文多用四字格形式,对仗工整,在翻译成英文时,应将句内逻辑关系补充完整,如"奇峰幽险,瀑飞泉鸣"为"庐山"之特点,所以英文译文可补充be characterized by/features这一表达。此外,译文使用了许多生动形象的词语和短语,如"waterfalls roar like thunder","cascading down precipitous cliffs","streams meander through serene nooks and gurgle over rocks","creating an ethereal atmosphere"等,这样的表达更具有感染力和吸引力,读者能够更加身临其境地感受到庐山的美丽景观。

5. 白鹿洞书院为我国古代四大书院之首 the White Deer Cave Academy, foremost among the four ancient academies of China

这句译文准确地传达了白鹿洞书院在中国古代书院中的重要地位。

6. ……东林寺,是佛教净土宗的发源地。The East Forest Monastery, founded

by a prominent monk during the Eastern Jin Dynasty (317—420), serves as the birthplace of the Pure Land Sect of Buddhism.

译文不仅增补了东林寺的建造者和建造时间,还指出其在佛教中的重要地位,让外国读者一目了然。其中西汉也增译了年代。

第五节 课后翻译训练

一、将下列句子翻译成汉语 Translate the following sentences into Chinese

1. You can learn something about a place by reading a travel book, but you learn more when you actually travel there.

2. There is a combination of enthusiasm and excitement that is felt while travelling. New foods, different faces, foreign languages, and interesting customers all fascinate the travelers.

3. In January New England was covered with thick snow and ice while Miami was warm with flowers in blossoms.

4. The Mogao Caves, hewed from a desert cliff-side, tell the story of the great flowering of Buddhist art in China.

5. The environment is friendly. The physical beauty of Hawaii is almost unparalleled. Majestic mountains were created millions of years ago by volcanic activity that thrust islands three miles from the ocean floor.

6. With a dragon head fixed in the front of the boat and a dragon tail at the end, the narrow long boat resembles a dragon.

7. The island continent of Australia offers an enormous array of scenic variety and you can take the opportunity of enjoying just about every adventure you've ever dreamed possible.

8. Now a World Heritage Site, Stonehenge and all its surroundings remain powerful witnesses to the once great civilization of the Stone and Bronze Ages, between 5,000 and 3,000 years ago.

9. The reason for Disney's success are varied and numerous, but ultimately the credit belongs to one person—the man who created cartoon and built the company from nothing.

10. The Australian continent has many different climatic zones ranging from

tropical in the north, leading to subtropical and savanna, to arid deserts in the centre and temperate in the south.

二、将下列句子翻译成英语 Translate the following sentences into English

1. 旅游是人类对美好生活的向往与追求,是认识新鲜事物和未知世界的重要途径。

2. 中国人自古就有旅游的文化传统,先贤们"读万卷书,行万里路",留下了无数脍炙人口的旅游名篇佳作。

3. 徐霞客一生游历四方,"达人所之未达,探人所之未知",经三十多年旅行,撰写了《徐霞客游记》,该书有着广泛而深远的影响。

4. 生态旅游是中国西部和其他欠发达地区发展的一个至关重要的领域。

5. 平遥有着2000多年历史,在明清时代商业非常繁荣。当时的人不知道平遥,就如同现代人不知道深圳一样不可思议。

6. 九寨沟的瀑布也让人神往。这里河道纵横,水流顺着台阶形的河谷奔腾而下,构成数不清的瀑布。

7. 这些瀑布从绝崖顶部而下,从茂密的林间穿越直泻,如珠帘垂空,如玉帛迎风,如天女散花。

8. 在广袤无垠的中华大地上,有着无数绚丽多姿的自然景观。

9. 在过去20年间,中国的旅游业与经济发展齐头并进。

10. 随着中国旅游市场迅速扩大,人们正在创造更好的环境,以促进旅游市场进一步发展。

三、将下列短文翻译成汉语 Translate the following passage into Chinese

Delta

The large river best known to the ancient Greeks was the Nile of Egypt. They spoke of the river with admiration and called Egypt "the gift of the Nile." The reason for this was, first, that the Nile brought water to a rainless desert and, second, that once a year, the river overflowed its banks, leaving, as the water went back, a new layer of fertile soil.

The flood waters carry in them soil (called silt) from the upper parts of the river valley to the lower parts, and so to the sea. But as the river meets the sea, the sea acts as a barrier and forces the river to drop the silt it is carrying.

There are no tides in the Mediterranean to carry the silt away, so year after year it collects at the mouth of the Nile, and the river must find its way around islands of silt to the more distant Mediterranean. In this way, a vast area of fertile soil has been built up at the mouth of the Nile and out into the sea. The river water splits up to form small branches winding across the area. To the ancient Greeks, the mouth of the Nile looked like the drawing.

Now we sometimes name things after the letters of the alphabet they resemble: a U-turn, an I-beam, a T-square, an S-bend, and so on. The Greeks did the same. The triangular area of land built up at the mouth of the Nile looked like the fourth letter of the Greek alphabet delta (Δ) and so this was the name they gave it. The word is now used for all areas of land formed at the mouth of rivers which flow into tideless seas, even when they are nor triangular in shape. The Mississippi delta, for example, is not shaped at all like the Greek delta, as you will see if you look at a map.

四、将下列短文翻译成英语 Translate the following passage into English

杭州——"人间天堂"

意大利著名旅行家马可·波罗曾这样叙述他印象中的杭州:"这是世界上最美妙迷人的城市,它使人觉得自己是在天堂。"在中国,也流传着这样的话:"上有天堂,下有苏杭。"杭州的名气主要在于风景如画的西湖。西湖一年四季都美不胜收,宋代著名诗人苏东坡用"淡妆浓抹总相宜"的诗句来赞誉西湖。在杭州,您可以饱览西湖的秀色,也不妨漫步街头闹市,品尝一下杭州的名菜名点,还可购上几样名土特产。

苏堤和白堤把西湖一分为二,仿佛两条绿色的缎带,飘逸于碧波之上。湖中心有三个小岛:阮公墩、湖心亭和小瀛洲。湖水泛着涟漪,四周山林茂密,点缀着楼台亭阁。西湖是我国最有名的旅游景点之一。

杭州人观西湖有种说法:"晴湖不如雨湖,雨湖不如夜湖。"您在杭州,一定要去领略一下西湖的风韵,看看此说是否有道理。

杭州是中国著名的六大古都之一,已有两千多年的历史。杭州不仅以自然美景闻名于世,而且有着传统文化的魅力;不仅有历代文人墨客的题咏,而且有美味佳肴和漂亮的工艺品。

　　杭州是中国的"丝绸之府",丝绸产品品种繁多,其中织锦尤为引人注目。杭州还专门生产黑纸扇和檀香扇。其他特产有西湖绸伞和中国十大名茶之一的西湖龙井。

　　杭州有许多有名的餐馆,供应各种菜点,还有很多旅馆酒店,为游客提供舒适的住宿。

　　一般来说,游览西湖及其周围景点花上两天时间较为合适。到杭州旅游,既令人愉快,又能得到文化享受。

第十七章 公示语翻译

公示语(Public Signs),又称"标志语""标识语""标语"等,指公开和面对公众的告示、指示、提示、警示以及与生活、生产、生命、生态等休戚相关的文字及图文信息,是用于公共场所以达到某种特定交际目的的一种特殊应用文体。英语中最广为接受的表示方法为public signs;凡公示给公众、旅游者、海外宾客、驻华外籍人士、在外旅游经商的中国公民等,涉及食、宿、行、游、娱等行为与需求的基本公示文字信息内容都在公示语研究范畴之内。

第一节 公示语的类别与功能

2004年外语教学与研究出版社出版的 *English Vocabulary in Use* 一书的Notices and Warnings单元中,将languages of notices(公告语言)分为Informational notices, Do this, Don't do this和Watch out四大类。根据公示语具体内容,我们将公示语分为六大类,即提示性公示语(informational notices, reminder signs)、指示性公示语(instructive/directive/guiding notices)、限制性公示语(regulatory notices)、警示性公示语(warning notices)、强制性公示语(mandatory notices)和宣传性公示语(publicity notices, public slogans)。

1. 提示性公示语具有提示功能,往往体现为公共场合为公众所提供的服务信息水平,主要为公众提供方位、地点等信息。提示性公示语仅起提示作用,但用途广泛。常见的提示性公示语有:Sterilized(已消毒)、Out of Order(系统故障)、Wi-Fi Zone(无线网络覆盖区)、Escape Route/Emergency Evacuation Passage(疏散通道)和Clearance Sales Starts Today(今日起清仓大甩卖)等。

2. 指示性公示语体现的是周到信息,功能在于指示性服务,常见的指示性公示语有:Waiting Room(候车室)、First Aid(急救)、Filling/Cargo Station(汽车加油站)、Cargo Lift/Freight Elevator(货运电梯)、Teacher's Lounge(教师休息

室), Car Rental (租车服务), Courtesy Seats/Priority Seats (爱心专座, 老弱病残孕专座), Cycles for Hire or Sale (租售自行车), Admission to Ticket Holders Only (凭票入场) 和 Please Queue the Other Side for Taxis (排队等候出租车请到另一边) 等。

3. 限制性公示语通常对人们的行为予以限制和约束, 但语言不生硬。常见的限制性公示语有: No Vacancies (客满), Private Road, No Parking (私家路段, 禁止停车), Please Do Not Disturb (请勿打扰), Please Do Not Feed the Animals (请不要投喂野生动物), Dogs must be kept on a leash (须用皮带牵着您的爱犬) 以及 Dogs Must Be Carried on the Escalator (乘坐电梯时请抱好您的爱犬) 等。

4. 警示性公示语, 顾名思义, 起到警示作业, 提请公众注意的作用。常见的警示性公示语有: Mind/Watch Your Head (当心碰头), Hands Off (请勿触摸), Handle with Care (小心轻放), Do Not Leave Luggage Unattended (请注意保管好您的行李, 以免遗失) 和 Beware of Sharks (当心鲨鱼) 等。

5. 强制性公示语, 顾名思义, 具有强制性要求, 语气直白, 没有商量余地。常见的强制性公示语有: Overtaking Strictly Prohibited (严禁超车), No U-turn (禁止掉头), No Thoroughfare (禁止通行), Don't Drink and Drive (禁止酒驾) 和 No Fire (严禁烟火) 等。

6. 宣传性公示语是向公众就特定事情进行宣传的公示语, 比如 "新北京, 新奥运" (New Beijing, Great Olympics) 和 "城市, 让生活更美好" (Better City, Better Life) 等。

公示语在使用中的功能不同, 所展示的信息状态既有 "静态", 也有 "动态"。突出服务、指示功能的公示语广泛应用于旅游设施、旅游景点、旅游服务、商业设施、体育设施、文化设施、卫生设施、科教机构、涉外机构、街区名称、旅游信息咨询, 以及一些具有公示意义的职务、职称等方面。如 Smoking Seat (吸烟席), Drinking Water (饮用水), Express Way (高速公路) 和 Shopping Mall (购物商城) 等, 往往展示的是具有 "静态" 意义的信息。

强制性公示语广泛应用于公共交通、公共设施、紧急救援等方面, 更多地使用展现 "动态意义" 的语汇表达, 如: Turn Right, No Photographs/No Photos (严禁拍照), Hold the Hand Rail (拉好扶手), Fasten Seat Belt While Seated (坐稳后请系好安全带) 等。

第二节 英语公示语的语言特点与翻译

英语公示语的特点是语言比较简洁明了、正式规范。比如公共汽车上的提示语"老弱病残孕专座",如果用英语公示语,可以表达为Courtesy seats。而"本店有权要求购烟者提供年龄证明"的英语译文是:We are authorized to demand proof of buyer's age. 这类英语表达都比较拘谨,这是由词汇的语域功能所决定的。所谓语域(register),是指根据语言使用的社会情景定义的一种具有某种具体用途的语言变体,如科技语体、艺术语体、政论语体、公文语体等。一般来说,法律、科技方面的材料,以及新闻报道、讲演词、政论文,包括公示语,其表达都比较正式。(丁衡祁,2006:63—67)

一、英语公示语的词汇特点与翻译

(一)字母常用大写。

英文公示语广泛使用全部字母大写或者首字母大写,以使公示语正式、醒目,从而引起公众的注意。例如:

EXIT/ENTRANCE 出口/入口

NO U-TURN 禁止掉头

DETOUR 请绕行/道路施工,请绕行

OPENING/BUSINESS/OFFICE HOURS 营业时间

(二)广泛使用名词和名词短语

这两种结构常见于静态公示语中,起着提示和指示功能。因为这样的结构使得公示语短小、简洁、清晰,人们只需一瞥就可以了解主要意思。一些典型的例子如下:

Information Desk 问询处

Staff Only 员工专用/顾客止步

No Admission 禁止入内

Big Sale 大甩卖

(三)广泛使用动词和动名词

不同于静态公示语使用名词和名词短语,动态公示语会使用动词和动名词,起着告示和警示功能。动词和动名词的使用使公示语显得正式,并且很有力量。比如:

Keep Clear 保持畅通

Please pay here 请在此付款

Buy One and Get One Free 买一赠一

No Jaywalking 禁闯红灯

（四）广泛使用缩略语

缩略语的使用令公示语变得更为短小和简洁。人们通常会在公共设施和服务场所看到这些缩略公示语。因为这些缩略语对我们来说都很熟悉，所以我们很容易就能抓住这些缩略语所蕴含的信息。例如：

P（Parking）停车场

WC（Water Closet）厕所

3-D（Three-Dimensional）Movie 立体电影

VIP Suite（Very Important Person Suite）贵宾套房

（五）多用常用词语和短语

公示语多使用常用词语和短语，避免使用生僻词语、古语、俚语和术语等。例如：

No Littering 请勿乱扔废弃物

Occupied（厕所）有人

Fragile 易碎物品，小心误碰

Private Parking 专用车位

二、英语公示语的句法特征及其翻译

句法指的是连词成句的规则。句法使得有效语言沟通具有多种可能。公示语英语的句法具有以下几种特征：

（一）主要采用一般现在时

时态是时间在语法上的表现。人们用一般现在时来表达现在或者不远的将来的单个动作或者状态。中文句子没有时态上的差异，而英文句子中可以用不同的动词形式来表达不同的时态。因为公示语具有告示、指示、提示、警示某人现在或者在不远的将来做某事的功能，所以使用一般现在时就尤为重要。例如：

Periodicals Are for Library Use Only. 期刊概不外借

Tickets Are Non-refundable and Non-changeable. 票一经售出概不退换

Your Safety Is Our Priority. 您的安全，我们的天责

It Is Forbidden to Drive Without a License. 禁止无证驾驶

（二）常使用祈使句

祈使句短小、精练、醒目，让人们第一眼见了就能够获取想要或者需要的信息，

从而增加公示语的有效性。用祈使句来表达限制、强制或者禁止的信息，语气很强，能够让目标读者看到公示语之后就采取相应的举措。以下是一些典型的例子：

Don't Drink and Drive! 请勿酒后驾车！

Don't Touch the Exhibits! 请勿触摸展品！

Please Take Care of Your Valuables/Belongings! 请保管好您的贵重物品/随身物品！

Please Do Not Lean Against the Door in the Train! 请勿倚靠车厢门！

（三）常使用省略句

英语公示语词汇简洁，措辞精当，只要不影响公示语准确体现特定的意义、功能，可以仅使用实词、关键词、核心词，而冠词、代词、助动词等一概可以省略。（吕和发，2004：40）例如：

Passengers Only 送客止步

Beverage Not Included 酒水另付

Ticket Holders Only 凭票入场

Registration Office 挂号处

三、英语公示语的语篇特征及其翻译

公示语的语篇总的来说有三个主要特征，即简洁性、规约性和醒目性。下面，我们将分别进行描述。

（一）简洁性（Conciseness）

由于公示语一般写在小木板上，或者刻在公共场所的金属物品上，空间较小，因此公示语的表达都是很简洁的，只用短短几个字就把核心意思表达出来。这些公示语多半会使用关键词，并且往往会省略冠词、代词、助动词等，以便人们在短时间就可以获取最准确、最直接的信息，如Suggestions & Complaints Box（意见/投诉箱）和Dangerous Section/Area（危险地带）等。但是具有警示和告示功能的公示语通常使用动词短语和祈使句，以便让公众能够注意到指令，从而采取被要求或期待的动作，如No Visitors/No Admittance/Staff Only（谢绝参观）和No Photos Allowed（未经允许，不得拍照）等。大多数情况下，公示语的字数越少越好。有的时候只用两三个字就可以把意思清晰地表达出来，如：City Bus Only（市内公共汽车专用）和Admission Free（免费入场）。

（二）规约性（Conventionality）

规约性涉及公示语翻译的规则问题，尤其是特定表达方式或特定场所、

地名的翻译。由于历史沿革和语言文化习惯的影响，很多公示语的翻译都已约定俗成，不能随意变更，否则会产生歧义。例如：Pagoda, Dagoba, Tower的中文都译作"塔"，但此"塔"非彼"塔"。Pagoda指多层佛塔，如杭州的雷峰塔（the Thunder Peak Pagoda）、苏州的虎丘塔（the Tiger Hill Pagoda）以及西安的大雁塔（the Great Wild Goose Pagoda）都用Pagoda。Tower则泛指塔或塔状的建筑物，如瞭望塔（Watch Tower）、森林火灾瞭望塔（Forest Fire Lookout Tower）、意大利的比萨斜塔（the Leaning Tower）和英国的伦敦塔（the Tower of London）。但"白塔寺"译名则用the Temple of the White Dagoba，因为这里的塔指的是舍利佛塔，此时不再用Pagoda。

（三）醒目性（Conspicuousness）

人们通常会用大写字母并且省略标点来组织公示语，从而引人注目。例如PRESS（按）和STOP（停）等。此外，一些公示语还和图片与符号相结合。标志上的图片或者符号是高度概括的图像，不仅生动形象，引人注目，也简单易懂，公众能很方便地识别、理解和接受公示语。有时候，单单靠图片或者标志就可以让公众理解他们的含义。

理论上，公示语在汉译英的过程中应当保持语言前后一致（consistency），比如，同一个地方若将"禁止吸烟"翻译为No Smoking，同地点的"禁止乱丢垃圾"便宜译作No Littering。再比如，同一地点的"出口"和"进口"，不宜将其分别译作Way In和Exit，而应当译作Way In和Way Out，或Exit和Entrance。

第三节　公示语错译误译解读

随着我国对外开放的不断深入，人们在日常生活中与不同种族、宗教与国籍的人的交往日益增多。为了国际友人出行方便，提高我国形象，我国很多城市的公共场所均使用了英汉双语标识。然而，公示语英译中的错误却比比皆是，有损我国的国际形象。正如黄友义、黄长奇（2005：8）所指出："我们的外宣翻译确实仍然存在不少问题，有不少亟待解决和改进的地方。在宾馆饭店、旅游景点或博物馆等窗口行业，在公园、街头、商场等公共场所，错误或不规范的外文随处可见。"

一、常见误译现象

汉译英公示语的常见错误可归纳为四种：

（一）望文生义，生搬硬套

例如：将"禁止拍照"译成Don't take pictures! 通常应译为：No photographs! /No photos! 将"小心地滑"译成Slip carefully!（意为"小心地滑倒！"）通常应译为CAUTION：Wet Floor!（地面有水或者地板刚拖过）或CAUTION：Slippery!（地段本身或地表材质容易让人摔跤）将"女厕所"译成Female Toilet，这种生硬的翻译令人捧腹，通常应译为Ladies' Room, Women's Room或Ladies' Lounge等。将商店"打八折"或"八折优惠"误译作"80% Discount"，其实"打八折"或"八折优惠"意味着少收20%或优惠20%，故应译为"20% Discount"或"20% Off"。

（二）只管字面意思，不顾特殊含义

例如：误将"教师休息室"译成Teachers' Restroom，可改为Teachers' Lounge。不同的场合下，英语中表示休息室的词可能有不同的表达方法，如旅馆的大厅（休息室）常用lobby一词表示。而英文中的restroom与分开写的"rest room"通常都是指厕所（当然，表示厕所的方法还有很多，如washing room, bathroom, public lavatory和public rest room等）。

有人将"相约九月（参加会议之类）"译成Dating this September，显然这里的"约"被误译成"男女之间约会"的"约"，应译作Let's Meet together this September。再比如，将"龙头企业"译成a dragon-headed enterprise。西方通常将dragon视作怪兽，同时也很少这样比喻，不妨将其改译为a flagship enterprise，用人人皆知的旗舰作比喻，当然，译作a leading enterprise也未尝不可。

（三）过度音译

例如：把"新天地"译成Xin Tiandi，将"理工"译作ligong，这等于根本没翻译。翻译的目的是让目的语读者看得懂，而不是学习汉语拼音。比如，有人将拙政园中的"枇杷园"译成Pipa Garden，这显然是不对的，此"枇杷"非"琵琶"，而是果树枇杷，故应将其译作Loquat Garden。

如果我们将"社稷坛"译作the Altar of Sheji显然不够友好，可以考虑将音译改成意译，译作the Altar to the God of the Land and Grain。

（四）语气或口吻不恰当

有些宾馆饭店的旅客须知以居高临下、盛气凌人的口气说话，这种宣传材料就很可能给人留下不好的印象。

例如：

一、旅客登记时，须凭足以证明本人身份的有效证件，并说明住宿原因；

二、旅客必须遵守宾馆饭店的规章制度，服从工作人员的管理，爱护饭店的公共财物；

三、对违反上述规定的旅客，饭店有权责成其改正。

其英译文的口气当然也是十分生硬：

1. Guests are requested to show **their own valid papers to prove their identities** and to **tell the reason for lodging** when they check in at the hotel.

2. Every guest **has the obligation to abide** (by) the rules and regulations of the hotel, cooperate with the personnel in carrying out their duties and **take good care of the property** in the hotel.

3. The **authority** of the hotel **has the right to reason** with anyone who has violated (the) regulations mentioned above.（黑体系编者后加）

上述公示语是改革开放初期某些宾馆制定的（且是针对"内宾"的），显然已经不能适应改革开放以来环境的需要。如今的宾馆应该用非常客气的语气对客人说话，包括要求客人遵守有关的规定，语气也应该很客气。试比较下面的几种表达方法（参考英语国家饭店的有关规定）。

1. Please **help** us to **speed up your check-in** by **presenting your ID**.

2. Our guests are kindly expected to heed the rules and regulations. Your cooperation will be **appreciated** in making our services effective.

3. **In the unlikely event** that something in the room is broken or damaged, please let the Floor Desk know immediately.

4. If you **find the robe** in the bathroom **to your liking**, you **are welcome to contact** the Front Desk for a purchase deal.

5. If your departure time **does not coincide with** our 12 Noon checkout timing, please call our Reception Desk and **every effort will be made to accommodate you**.（丁衡祁，2002：46）

二、误译出现的原因

通过以上分析，我们能够意识到公示语的误译主要是由以下三个方面的原因引起的。

（一）不理解公示语的功能和文本类型

上面提到过公示语主要有提示性、指示性、告示性、警示性、强制性和宣传性六种功能。根据赖斯的文本类型理论，公示语隶属"语用"或"非文学文本"，赖斯认为，语用文本的目标文本应该传播原文本全部概念性内容，并且在目标读者中产生预期的反应。因此，原文本的语言形式或者原来的文体就没有必要保留在原文本中，因为目的文本实现了预期的目的或者功能。但是我们通常也会碰到一些双语公示语，这些公示语的英文翻译从字面上来说忠实于原文，但无法像原文一样影响目标读者或者听众。译者应该了解公示语的文本类型和功能，灵活采用各种翻译策略实现目标文本预期的功能。

（二）缺乏合适理论的指导

公示语翻译研究始于20世纪90年代。进入21世纪之后，公示语翻译逐渐成了翻译圈子的一个热门话题和翻译研究的新兴领域。长时间以来，公示语研究一直停留在数据收集和错误纠正层面，缺乏系统深入的研究。因此，公示语研究急需可行、合适的理论给予指导。中国传统的翻译理论，不管是严复提出的"信、达、雅"，还是鲁迅提出的"忠实"而不是"通顺"，都强调如何实现形式和内容的统一。这些理论并不完全适用于语用或者非文学文本的翻译。因此，对公示语的翻译研究急需相关理论的支持和指导。

（三）缺乏文化差异意识或者不了解文化差异

第六版《牛津高阶英汉双解词典》（2004）将文化定义为"某一国家或团体的习俗和信仰、艺术、生活方式和社会组织"。不同国家的人有着不同的文化背景，或许会支持不同的社会组织、价值体系和世界观。此外，他们可能拥有不同的认识、不同的行为模式、不同的习俗和规则。语言是文化的一面镜子，深受文化影响。翻译不仅涉及两种语言，也涉及两种文化。近年来，人们越来越关注翻译中的文化交互，因为成功的翻译要求二元文化原则比双语原则更加重要。译者如果缺乏对这些文化差异的了解或者压根不知道文化差异，或许会使得目标文本不被接受或误解，从而影响公示语翻译实现预期的效果。因此，对中西两种文化中的差异敏感对公示语翻译至关重要。

第四节　汉英公示语语言的区别

汉语和英语公示语之间虽然有许多相似点，但两者毕竟属于不同的语言文化传统，受各自语言表达习惯和思维方式的影响，因此，汉语和英语公示语之间又存在许多不同之处。

一、对名词中心词的不同形式的修饰

公示语中常有以名词为中心词的名词性短语，用来说明所标识事物的性质、目的和用途，以便与其他同类事物相区别。汉英两种语言中这类名词性短语的表达方式并不相同：汉语公示语中都是修饰成分在前直接修饰名词中心词，是"名词+名词中心词"的结构，中间没有其他成分；而在英语公示语中则是名词中心词在前，修饰成分在后，中间还需要其他词来连接，通常是"名词中心词+介词+名词"的结构。中心词重心的不同，是汉英两种语言表达不同的一个较明显的特点，是汉民族环形思维模式和英语民族直线型思维模式不同的一个表现。例如：

汉语公示语	英语公示语
儿童外借部	Book Borrowing for Children
出租公寓	Apartments for Rent
本站最后一班车时间	Last Train from This Station
乘务人员工作守则	Rules for Crew

二、不同的表达角度

汉英两种语言表达方式虽然有一致的一面，即汉英两种语言都可能用否定形式表示禁止某种动作或行为，但汉英两种表达往往词性不一样。汉语偏向用动词，英语偏向于用名词，但不限于名词，有的也直接用形容词等，如"易碎物品"英语便可直接表示为"Fragile"。汉英两种语言表达方式也有不一致的一面，汉英两种公示语有时也采用相反的表达角度：汉语通常直接表达禁止某种动作或行为，英语则会直接用肯定形式表达禁止某种动作或行为。另外，汉语通常用祈使句提示公众对某事物作出反应，而英语则习惯直接用名词短语进行提示。例如：

汉语公示语	英语公示语
贵宾休息室	VIP Lounge
送客止步	Passengers Only
当心触电	Danger！High Voltage
严禁携带易燃易爆物品	Inflammables and Explosives Strictly Prohibited

三、对称结构与非对称结构

由于汉民族的综合型思维模式，其语言表达常用四字格，且四字结构之间往往不用任何连词、介词等虚词连接，语句简洁匀称；而西方人由于其分析型思维模式，句子结构之间往往由介词、不定式等连接，句式结构比较严密完整，但不一定对称。例如：

汉语公示语	英语公示语
水深危险 注意安全！	Danger：Deep Water！
小草青青 足下留情	Please give me a chance to grow！
上下台阶 注意安全	Watch your steps
注意安全 小心滑坡	Warning：Slippery slope

四、"禁止/请勿+动词"结构与"No+名词或动名词"结构

汉语表示禁止的公示语一般用"禁止/请勿+动词"结构，而在英语公示语中常用"No+名词或动名词"的形式。例如：

汉语公示语	英语公示语
禁止摆摊	No Vendors
游客止步	No Visitors
禁止随地吐痰	No Spitting
禁止乱涂乱画	No Graffiti

五、主动形式与被动形式

英语民族因其客观思维习惯的影响，语言表达上常用被动结构，公示语也不例外；而汉语公示语的表达上惯用主动语态，很少看到汉语公示语中出现被动语态。例如：

汉语公示语	英语公示语
车位已满	Occupied
已预订	Reserved
暂停服务	Service Temporarily Closed

六、语法省略与语法完整

由于英语为形合语言，汉语为意合语言，因此，英语句子在语法上往往更完整，而汉语则不一定如此。例如：

汉语公示语	英语公示语
欢迎下次光临！	We look forward to seeing you again！
工地上须戴好安全帽！	Safety helmets must be worn on this site！
儿童乘坐时必须有成人陪护。	Minors must be accompanied by an adult.

由以上对比可知，由于文化和思维习惯的差异，汉英公示语在词汇、语法、语义以及表达方式上的差异很大，这就要求我们在翻译过程中超越纯语义和语法翻译的手段，而在更为广阔的文化视野下，采用交际功能对等的基本翻译方法。

第五节 公示语的翻译原则与方法

一、公示语的翻译原则

公示语的社会功能决定了公示语的英译必须从根本上遵循以受众为中心的基本原则，并尊重英语公示语的语言习惯。鉴于汉英公示语各自的特点，我们在公示语的英译过程中应遵循以下原则。

（一）准确性原则

汉语公示语译成英文时要达到交际目的，信是翻译的底线，换而言之，翻译就应该首先保证其准确性，否则就无法实现翻译的目标。比如有人将"110一拨就灵"译作"110 one dial is magical"，这样的英文公示语让英语为母语的读者见了，根本无法知道110指的是什么意思，但若译成"For help, call the police at 110"，意义便一目了然。

（二）简洁性原则

公示语的语言特点是言简意赅，翻译时也应使用简洁的语言。一般来说，公示语的译文应选用通俗易懂的词语、简短的句子或短语，甚至单个词来快速传递信息。如将"请保持安静！"译作"Silence, please!"便可把原祈使句的意义表示出来。虽然"禁止泊车"可以用句子表达（"Parking is forbidden here."），但用两个词"No Parking"表达更为简洁。

（三）语境性原则

公示语通常被固定在特定的使用场所，与其所在的环境一起构成其言语行为。同一个公示语在不同的场所使用便传达不同的意思，因此，翻译时应考虑其使用的环境。比如，"小心路滑"可能会在多种情况下使用：若指的是地面太滑，人走在上面容易滑倒，这时只需翻译成"Caution: Slippery!"即可；若是刚拖过地板，地面因为潮湿而滑，天干燥时并不滑，这时应该根据具体情况译作"Caution! Wet Floor"为宜。苏州园林中，"网师园"的译名为"Master-of-Nets Garden"，由于现代英语中"Nets"更多指各种网络，基于"网师园"中的"网师"指的是渔夫，故此，译作"Master-of-Fishing Nets Garden"或许更准确。

（四）礼貌性原则

公示语属于社会性标志语，社会文明的发展要求它趋向于多元化和人本化。礼貌原则在公示语翻译中的应用体现了对受话人的尊重与宽容、平等与信任。"指令类"公示语以"盛气凌人"的姿态对受话人直截了当地作出强行指令或警示，会有损受话人的尊严或"面子"，其结果往往降低了公示语的交际功效。针对外国人的公示语当然也应该遵从礼貌原则，展示我们礼仪之邦的精神面貌，使公示语所发出的限制、禁止指令更容易被外国人愉快地接受。体现礼貌原则的手段很多，而最明显、最直接的手段无疑是礼貌标志语的使用，如Please等。

（五）文化性原则

公示语翻译是让不同语言、不同文化的人们相互沟通，不仅应该体现出原文的意图，而且应该考虑到接收者可能作出的反应，并理解为何在那种语境下会作出那样的反应。要达到上述目的，译者除了要很好地掌握两种语言知识之外，还必须了解两种文化及其思维上的差异，翻译时顺从受众的文化习惯和思维方式，使他们减少理解上的困难，这样才能使译语公示语起到和源语同样的作用，也使公示语的交际意图更容易实现。例如，公交车上广播里经常说的"贵重物品，请您随身携带"应直接套用英语中现成的表达方式，译成"Please don't leave valuables unattended"，而不应按字面顺序译成"Valuable things, please take them with you!"再如，不应将"航友宾馆"译成"Hang You Hotel"，而应考虑Hang You在英语中恰好也是两个常见词，其搭配意义为"吊死你"或"绞死你"，因此，为了避免歧义，宜译作"Aviation Friendship Hotel"。

（六）警示性原则

公示语不仅有提示作用，警示作用也是其社会功能的重要组成部分，以便人们一看到就能够警惕潜在的危险，并迅速作出反应和采取有力措施避免危险的发生。例如，在海边有深水和易产生大浪的地方，为了提示游人，管理机构做了"浪大危险，注意安全"和"注意潮汐"等相关标识。为了加强其警示作用，翻译时开头可以加上Caution一词。上述几个标识可以分别译成"Caution: Huge Waves!"和"Caution Dangerous Waves at High Tide!"一些类似的公路交通标识牌也需要做同样的处理，例如"转弯慢行"虽然在汉语中没有"小心"的字眼，英译时还是加上Caution一词为好，可以译成"Caution! Turn Ahead-Slow Down!"以突出其警示作用。

（七）保护性原则

英译的公示语是我国文化、传统和日常行为规范向外国人的一种传递，也必然会在外国人心中产生反应。因此，在公示语的翻译过程中必须意识到，英译的公示语本身即是对我国思想文化的一种宣传，要注意维护本国的良好形象。

（八）流畅性原则

公示语的目的是广泛流传，这就要求翻译要发挥译语优势，力争翻译流畅，朗朗上口。比如，翻译"桂林山水甲天下"时，翻译家吴伟雄便模仿英语中的谚语"East or west, home is best"，将其译作"East or west, Guilin landscape is best"。汉语公示语"机房重地，非请莫入"体现了汉语四字格的鲜明特征，翻译成英语时要体现出英语中名词比较突出的特征，可模仿Staff Only（闲人免进，非请莫入），仿译作"Machinery Room, Staff Only"。以上这样的翻译不仅语言地道，而且朗朗上口。

二、公示语的常用翻译方法

公示语的范围非常宽泛，因此很难在有限的篇幅内全面讨论公示语的翻译问题。我们暂且把内容集中在四个方面，即关于禁止吸烟、零售商业设施、禁止践踏草地和禁止停车的用语，从这几个方面来确定参照性的标准翻译文本。围绕这几个方面，我们可以采取三种不同的翻译方法：如果英语中有现成的对应的表达，我们就可以直接套用；如果英语里有类似的表达，我们就可以参照加以改造，即模仿；如果前两种情况都不存在，那么我们就按照英语的习惯和思路进行创译，即进行创造性翻译。我们可以把这三种翻译方法归纳为"套译""仿译""创译"三种模式。对于公示语的英译，有一条十分重要的原则必须遵循，那就是要充分考虑英语的表达习惯。

（一）套译

"请勿吸烟"和"严禁吸烟"这类公示语的翻译非常简单，可采用套译。直接从下面现有的几种表达方法中加以选择。

比如，要翻译汉语中的"严禁吸烟"，可以直接套用英语的No Smoking或Smoking Strictly Prohibited。

（二）仿译

中国文化要走出去、走进去，不是说将中国的作品翻译成外语就万事大吉了，而应翻译得让外国人知之，甚至乐之、好之方可，而要取得这种效果，翻译时要尽量模仿或者说采用目的语的行文方式。（张顺生，2015：93）

翻译"司机一滴酒，亲人两行泪"时，可以部分套用英语里drink and drive这种的说法，模仿英文的行文译作："If you drink and drive, it may well cost your life."模仿英语中的习语"Seeing Is Believing"（百闻不如一见）可以仿写出"Tasting Is Believing"和"Wearing Is Believing"等广告词。

（三）创译

如果找不到能够直接供模仿的译语结构，或者虽然有直接可以模仿的译语结构，但是译者希望实现一定的突破，而不是直接照搬具体框架时，可以采用创译。严格意义上说，创译是仿译的延伸。（张顺生，2015：93）但创译是隐形的仿译，由于模仿的是译语的行文方式，故而显得非常具有创意，算得上创译。如天津名小吃"狗不理"包子的商标英译一直都让人犯难，但公司正式注册的英文商标名Go Believe就很有创意，此译名不但发音和"狗不理"很接近，同时含义也很好，与"狗不理"的质量以及一贯倡导的诚信服务吻合。（张顺生，2015：93）

当然，无论直接套用、结构模仿还是融会创新，都需要一个前提，那就是大量的英语、汉语输入，因为有大量的输入才能正确地输出，因此平时要勤于阅读，勤于积累，勤于思考，这样才能达到"触类旁通"的效果，尽量减少"书到用时方恨少"的尴尬局面的出现。（张顺生，2015：94）

第六节　课内翻译任务

一、英译汉 English-Chinese Translation

1. All passengers are strongly advised to obtain travel insurance.
2. Tickets Are Free from the Admission Desk.

3. Dental Clinics Closed on Sunday and Public Holidays.

4. No Re-entry Once the Ticket Is Marked or Punched.

5. Keep Gateways Clear

重点解析 Notes and Comments

1. 英语公示语常用被动结构，而汉语公示语惯用主动语态。例如：Safety helmets must be worn on this site工地上须戴安全帽

2. free在英语公示语中使用频率很高，可以与众多名词组合。例如：tax free（免税），free of charge（免费），for free（免费），smoke free（禁止吸烟），smoke-free area（无烟区）。

3. 上面第3条公示语没有完整的谓语，谓语的位置只有过去分词Closed，省略了be动词are，表示"关闭""停业"的意思。公示语的主要特征就是简洁、地道，能省则省。这类省略，有的省略谓语的be动词，有的把主语和be都省略。例如Lost and Found（失物招领处）就是由两个并列的过去分词组成。

4. 英语中有大量的使用"No+动名词"或No+名词"的公示语。No可表示"禁止""不得""不要""没有"等意思。而大多数表示同样概念的汉语公示语则使用"禁止"等动词结构，例如：No Parking（禁止停车），No Horn（禁止鸣笛）等。

5. 公示语的主要功能就是提醒或要求受众遵循某种规矩、规定，语气客气而坚定，尽可能简单明了、简短干脆，因此，常使用祈使句，起着告示和警示功能。例如：Please Take Care of Public Facilities！（请爱护公共设施！）Please Show Your ID Card and Boarding Pass！（请出示身份证和登机牌！）Stand Clear of the Closing Doors Please！（车门正在关闭，请勿站在门口！）

二、汉译英 Chinese-English Translation

1. 桂林山水甲天下！

2. 来也匆匆，去也冲冲

3. 激情盛会，和谐亚洲

4. 分享青春，共筑未来

5. 当心路滑

重点解析 Notes and Comments

1. 来也匆匆，去也冲冲 Come in a rush, leave after a flush.

这句话是公共卫生间最常见的公示语，巧用了中文的四字格与叠词，对仗工整，"匆匆"与"冲冲"也十分押韵，读起来朗朗上口，流传度很广。英译不仅完美地呈现了四字结构，也保留了押韵效果。

2. 激情盛会，和谐亚洲 Thrilling Games, Harmonious Asia

这句话是2010年广州亚运会的主题宣传语，"亚组委对这一理念的基本内涵进行了阐释：'激情盛会，和谐亚洲'既把握了时代的主题，又体现了亚运会的宗旨，表达了亚洲各国人民的共同愿望。"（陈京京，2014：190）其英文翻译"Thrilling Games, Harmonious Asia"做到了意义传达准确与形式上的对等。在选词上，该翻译没有选择用exciting, passionate和inspiring，是因为thrilling不仅有exciting之意，还有enjoyable的意思，更加契合亚运会想让亚洲人民享受这场盛会的主旨。

3. 分享青春，共筑未来 Share the Games, Share our Dreams

这句话是2014年南京青奥会的主题宣传语。"该标语想要传达的是青奥会旨在聚集世界各地青少年，通过分享体育运动、文化交流，使体育回归生活，从而共同创建更美好的未来，实现奥林匹克运动的大同理想。"（陈京京，2014：191）若直译，翻译成"Share the Youth, Build the Future"较为抽象，并没有准确传达青奥会主旨，不如直接把the Youth换成the Games，与赛事呼应。而后半句话，"共筑"如果只译成build就丢掉了"共"这个核心，不如与前面的"分享"保持一致，翻译成share；而"未来"如果处理成future同样十分宽泛，不如将"未来"具体化为our dreams，体现一起实现梦想的理念，不仅结构工整，也十分押韵。

4. 当心路滑 (1) Caution! Slippery（2）Caution! Slippery When Wet

公示语或标识语通常被固定在特定的使用场所，与其所在的环境构成其言语行为。相同的一个公示语，适用场所不同便传达不同的意思，因此翻译时应优先考虑其使用环境。（黄忠廉、任东升，2014：103）"当心路滑"可能会在多种情况下使用，若是在商店中使用，可能指的是地面太滑，人走在上面容易滑倒，这时只需要翻译成"Caution! Slippery"即可。若是在公路上使用，则可能指的是雨雪天路面湿滑，而不是雨雪天时并不滑，这时应译作"Caution! Slippery When Wet"，否则就会误导交通。

第七节　课后翻译训练

一、将下列公示语翻译成汉语 Translate the following public signs into Chinese

1. Toilet Engaged
2. Danger: Falling Rocks!
3. Admission by Ticket Only
4. Do Not Overtake Turning Vehicle
5. Look Around and Cross
6. Please Check Your Change Before Leaving
7. Tickets Are Non-refundable and Non-changeable
8. What Happens Here, Stays Here（拉斯维加斯广告语）
9. Please Buy Your Ticket Before You Board The Train
10. Fasten Seat Belt While Seated

二、将下列公示语翻译成英语 Translate the following public signs into English

1. 饮用水
2. 专用车位
3. 收费站
4. 新品上市
5. 请勿让儿童在电梯上或周围玩耍
6. 限速每小时60公里
7. 国家级文物保护单位
8. 创绿色文明城市，为家乡添彩
9. 身高1.3米（含）以下儿童免票
10. 五岳归来不看山，黄山归来不看岳

三、将下列短文翻译成汉语 Translate the following passage into Chinese

14 Wall Street[①]

The Mausoleum of Halicarnassus piled on top of the bell-tower of St. Mark's in Venice, at the corner of Wall and Broad — that's the design concept behind 14 Wall Street. In its day the world's tallest bank building, the 539-foot-high skyscraper originally housed the headquarters of Bankers Trust, one of the country's wealthiest financial institutions.

Many early skyscrapers took the Venetian bell-tower as a logical model for a modern office tower, but 14 Wall Street was the first to top it off with a temple in the sky, a seven-story stepped pyramid modeled on one of the seven wonders of the ancient world. The bank then adopted the pyramid as its trademark, and took as its slogan "A Tower of Strength."

Instantly a standard-bearer in the fabled Downtown skyline, 14 Wall Street went on to become a widely recognized symbol of Wall Street and American capitalism.

四、将下列短文翻译成英语 Translate the following passage into English

紫禁城简介[②]

紫禁城始建于明永乐四年（1406年），建成于明永乐十八年（1420年），占地面积约72万平方米，建筑面积约15万平方米，房屋8700余间，高约10米的城墙和宽达52米的护城河环绕四周。紫禁城是我国现存最大、最完整的木质结构古代宫殿建筑群。

紫禁城分为外朝和内廷两大部分，外朝以三大殿即太和殿、中和殿、保和殿为主体，文华殿、武英殿为两翼，主要是皇帝举行盛大典礼的场所。内廷以乾清宫、交泰殿、坤宁宫为主体，东、西六宫为两翼，是皇帝处理日常政务以及皇帝和后妃们生活的地方。此外，还包括外东路太上皇宫殿及皇子居住的南三所和外西路太后宫院。

---

① 选自吕和发，2013：251—252。

② 引自王玉娥，2018：25—29。

参考文献

外文文献

Aixela J F. Culture—specific items in translation[C]// Alvarez, R. and Vidal, M.C.-A. Translation, Power, Subversion. Topics in Translation. Bristol: Multilingual Matters, 1996: 52—78.

Cao D. 法律翻译[M]. 上海: 上海外语教育出版社, 2008.

Catford J C. A Linguistic Theory of Translation[M]. London: Oxford University Press, 1965.

Devinney T M, Pedersen T, Tihanyi L. Institutional Theory in International Business and Management[M]. London: Emerald Publishing Limited, 2012.

Ghiani G et al. Introduction to Logistics Systems Management[M]. London: John Wiley & Sons, Incorporated, 2013.

Heffernan S. Modern Banking[M]. London: John Wiley & Sons, Incorporated, 2005.

Ho G. Translating Advertising across Heterogeneous Cultures[A]. Key Debates in the Translation of Avertising Materials. Manchester: St. Jerome Publishing, 2004: 233—237.

Jones M. Accounting for Non-Specialists[M]. London: John Wiley and Sons, Incorporated, 2002.

Nida E A, Taber C R. The Theory and Practice of Translation[M]. Leiden: E. J. Brill, 1969.

Palmer, A. Introduction to Marketing[M]. New York: Oxford University Press, 2009.

Parkin M. Economics, Global Edition[M]. London: Pearson Education Limited, 2016.

Powell H et al. The Advertising Handbook[M]. London, New York: Routledge, 2009.

Somashekar N T. Banking[M]. New Delhi: New Age International Ltd., 2000.

Thorson E, Rodgers S. Advertising Theory[M]. London, New York: Routledge, 2012.

Toni A F De. International Operations Management: Lessons in Global Business[M]. Oxford: Taylor & Francis Group, 2011.

Venkateswaran N. International Business Management[M]. New Delhi: New Age International Ltd., 2011.

Wood D F et al. International Logistics[M]. New York: AMACOM, 2002.

Yang X et al. Encyclopedic Reference of Traditional Chinese Medicine. Berlin

Heidelberg: Springer, 2003.

中文文献

鲍文, 刘云. 物联网文本专业词汇英汉翻译精确性研究 [J]. 中国翻译, 2021（03）: 150—156.

陈刚. 旅游翻译与涉外导游 [M]. 北京: 中国对外翻译出版公司, 2004.

陈京京. 生态翻译学视角下的公示语翻译: 以南京青奥会和广州亚运会主题标语为例 [J]. 辽宁行政学院学报, 2014（10）: 190—192.

丁衡祁. 对外宣传中的英语质量亟待提高 [J]. 中国翻译, 2002（4）: 44—46.

丁衡祁. 努力完善城市公示语 逐步确定参照性译文 [J]. 中国翻译, 2006（06）: 42—46.

杜金榜. 法律语言学 [M]. 上海: 上海外语教育出版社, 2004.

方梦之, 毛忠明. 英汉—汉英应用翻译综合教程 [M]. 2版. 上海: 上海外语教育出版社, 2018.

方梦之. 应用（文体）翻译学的内部体系 [J]. 上海翻译, 2014（02）: 1—6.

方梦之. 应用翻译研究: 原理、策略与技巧(修订版)[M]. 上海: 上海外语教育出版社, 2019.

冯长甫, 李文中. 金融英语术语的特征及其翻译 [J]. 河南广播电视大学学报, 2011（01）: 46—48.

冯长甫, 孙小兰. 金融英语长句翻译探讨 [J]. 河北广播电视大学学报, 2011（02）: 61—63.

高春红. 中药产品出口贸易中商务英语应用面临的问题与改进策略 [J]. 对外经贸实务, 2021（04）: 77—79.

高飞雁, 王莲凤. 旅游文本翻译策略与实例解析 [J]. 广西教育学院学报, 2019（06）: 39—42.

顾维勇. 实用文体翻译 [M]. 北京: 国防工业出版社, 2005.

管妮. 金融英语词汇的特点及其翻译 [J]. 高教学刊. 2015（18）: 73—75.

黄友义, 黄长奇. 翻译质量与翻译协会的责任: 在第17届世界翻译大会公开论坛上的演讲 [J]. 中国翻译, 2005（05）: 8—9.

黄友义. 从翻译工作者的权利到外宣翻译: 在首届全国公示语翻译大会上的讲话 [J]. 中国翻译, 2005（06）: 31—33.

黄友义. 坚持"外宣三贴近原则", 处理好外宣翻译中的难点问题 [J]. 中国翻译, 2004（06）: 27—28.

黄中军. 浅析物流英语的词汇特征及翻译[J]. 北京宣武红旗业余大学学报, 2016（04）: 59—63.

黄忠廉, 任东升. 汉英笔译全译实践教程[M]. 北京: 国防工业出版社, 2014.

黄忠廉, 余承法. 英汉笔译全译实践教程[M]. 北京: 国防工业出版社, 2012.

黄忠廉. 应用翻译学名实探[J]. 中国外语, 2013（04）: 93—98.

雷斐. 浅谈物流英语翻译中应注意的若干问题[J]. 英语教师, 2015（18）: 91—93.

李建蓉. 专利文献与信息[M]. 北京: 知识产权出版社, 2002.

李玉良, 于巧峰. 汉语标识语的英译原则[J]. 上海翻译, 2008（01）: 42—45.

梁金萍. 现代物流学[M]. 大连: 东北财经大学出版社, 2003.

梁雪松. 实用商务英语翻译教程[M]. 北京: 北京大学出版社, 2013.

廖国强. 商务英汉互译理论与实践[M]. 北京: 国防工业出版社, 2014.

刘法公. 商贸汉英翻译专论[M]. 重庆: 重庆出版社, 1999.

刘季春. 实用翻译教程（修订版）[M]. 广州: 中山大学出版社, 2007.

刘丽芬. 中国公示语研究进展与前瞻[J]. 中国外语, 2016（06）: 53—58.

罗海燕, 邓海静. 文本类型理论指导下的中医外宣资料英译[J]. 中国中医基础医学杂志, 2017（04）: 567—569.

吕和发, 单丽萍. 汉英公示语词典[M]. 北京: 商务印书馆, 2004.

吕和发, 蒋璐, 王同军, 等. 公示语汉英翻译错误分析与规范[M]. 北京: 国防工业出版社, 2011.

吕和发, 蒋璐. 景点解说翻译的跨文化诠释[M]. 北京: 中国对外翻译出版有限公司, 2013.

吕和发, 任林静, 等. 全球化商务翻译[M]. 北京: 外文出版社, 2011.

吕和发. 公示语的汉英翻译[J]. 中国科技翻译, 2004（01）: 38—40, 64.

马会娟. 商务英语翻译教程[M]. 北京: 中国商务出版社, 2004.

毛慧洁. 目的论指导下的商务合同英汉翻译[J]. 开封教育学院学报, 2018（7）: 82—84.

莫莉莉. 营销英语的词汇特征及其汉译技巧[J]. 上海翻译, 2006（01）: 35—37.

穆雷. 英汉翻译基础教程[M]. 北京: 高等教育出版社, 2008.

纽马克 P. 翻译问题探讨[M]. 上海: 上海外语教育出版社, 2001.

诺德 C. 目的性行为: 析功能翻译理论[M]. 上海: 上海外语教育出版社, 2001.

欧阳利锋. 中医药说明书的英译[J]. 中国科技翻译, 2002（02）: 17—20.

皮德敏. 公示语及其汉英翻译原则研究[J]. 外语学刊, 2010（02）: 131—134.

邱贵溪. 论法律文件翻译的若干原则 [J]. 中国科技翻译, 2000 (02): 14—17.

桑龙扬, 吴国霞, 肖胜文, 等. 旅游景区公示语的类型及翻译探讨 [J]. 九江学院学报（哲学社会科学版）, 2010 (04): 90—93.

桑龙扬, 赵联斌. 跨文化旅游营销翻译 [M]. 南昌: 江西人民出版社, 2017.

宋天锡. 翻译新概念 英汉互译实用教程 [M]. 北京: 国防工业出版, 2009.

汪玉兰. 金融英语翻译方法和技巧 [J]. 金融与经济, 2005 (05): 74—76.

王颖, 吕和发. 公示语汉英翻译 [M]. 北京: 中国对外翻译出版公司, 2007.

王玉娥. 从目的论的角度分析故宫博物院内景点介绍牌的英译 [D]. 北京: 北京外国语大学, 2018.

翁凤翔. 国际营销英语 [M]. 上海: 上海交通大学出版社, 2016.

翁凤翔. 实用翻译 [M]. 杭州: 浙江大学出版社, 2002.

夏康明, 范先明. 旅游文化汉英翻译概论: 基于功能目的论视角下的跨文化旅游翻译研究 [M]. 北京: 中国社会科学出版社, 2013.

肖娴. 市场营销英语的词汇特点与翻译 [J]. 中国商贸, 2013 (30): 116—117.

徐珺. 国际贸易翻译实务 [M]. 北京: 清华大学出版社, 2018.

杨芳. 浅谈商务合同英语翻译的准确性 [J]. 零陵学院学报, 2004 (03): 84—87.

杨柳. 物流英语的词汇特点及其翻译技巧 [J]. 黑河学刊, 2013 (11): 115—116.

易露霞, 方玲玲, 陈原. 国际贸易实务双语教程 [M]. 3 版. 北京: 清华大学出版社, 2011.

岳峰, 刘茵. 商务英语笔译 [M]. 厦门: 厦门大学出版社, 2014.

张法连. 法律英语翻译教程 [M]. 北京: 北京大学出版社, 2016.

张卉婷, 江秀丽. 金融英语的语言特征及其翻译 [J]. 宿州教育学院学报, 2016 (05): 35—36, 48.

张健. 外宣翻译导论 [M]. 北京: 国防工业出版社, 2013.

张琳琳. 市场营销英语的语体特点及翻译方法 [J]. 天津外国语学院学报, 2010 (03): 55—58, 64.

张顺生. 英汉互译的三种基本方法 [J]. 中国翻译, 2015 (01): 92—94.

中国政法大学法律英语教学与测试研究中心. 法律英语翻译教程 [M]. 3 版. 北京: 中国法制出版社, 2013.

邹春荣, 杨晓斌. 英文广告汉译策略初探 [J]. 南昌大学学报（人文社会科学版）, 2009 (02): 157—160.

邹力. 商务英语翻译教程（笔译）[M]. 3 版. 北京: 中国水利水电出版社, 2013.